MIDRASH RABBAH

RUTH

MIDRASH

TRANSLATED INTO ENGLISH

WITH NOTES, GLOSSARY AND INDICES

UNDER THE EDITORSHIP OF

RABBI DR. H. FREEDMAN, B.A., PH.D.

AND

MAURICE SIMON, M.A.

RABBAH

RUTH

TRANSLATED BY

RABBI DR. L. RABINOWITZ, M.A., PH.D.

THE SONCINO PRESS
LONDON • NEW YORK

THIRD EDITION 1983

ISBN: 0-900689-38-2

MANUFACTURED IN THE UNITED STATES OF AMERICA
PRINTED BY NOBLE OFFSET PRINTERS, INC.

CONTENTS

Introduction	*page* vii
Proem	1
Chapter I	16
Chapter II	23
Chapter III	41
Chapter IV	49
Chapter V	58
Chapter VI	73
Chapter VII	82
Chapter VIII	92

INTRODUCTION

Ruth Rabbah, like Song of Songs Rabbah and Ecclesiastes Rabbah, occupies an intermediate position between the older Midrashim such as Genesis Rabbah, Leviticus Rabbah, and Ekah (Lamentations) Rabbati, from which much of its material is taken, and the later Midrashim such as Exodus Rabbah and Deuteronomy Rabbah, of which it is one of the sources.

As in Ekah Rabbati, the actual Midrashic commentary is preceded by a long Introduction (*Petiḥta*) consisting of a number of unconnected proems. Thereafter follows the commentary proper, which is divided into eight chapters of uneven length, the first and the last covering the first and the last two verses of the text respectively, the others being as follows: I, 3–I, 17, I, 18–I, 21, I, 22–II, 9, II, 10–III, 7, III, 8–III, 13, and III, 14–IV, 15.

The commentary covers the whole of the Biblical text, interpreting it verse by verse, with the sole exception of verses 16 and 17 of Chapter IV, and although the exposition is mostly homiletical, there are a number of passages of purely literal exegetical value.

One of the most interesting and original features of this Midrash is its portrayal of the characters of Elimelech, Ruth, and Boaz. The clue to the apparently unmerited misfortunes and calamities which dogged the footsteps of Elimelech is found in his character. The famine, with the mention of which the book opens, was not a devastating one, but merely a scarcity which caused a rise in the price of commodities, and hardship to the poor. Elimelech was not one of these. On the contrary, he was one of the leading men of his generation (I, 4, p. 21), an aspirant to the throne of Israel (II, 5, p. 29), and his departure from Bethlehem was not on account of lack of means of subsistence, but a reprehensible flight from his responsibilities towards the poor who looked to him to provide for them in their distress (I, 4, p. 20). The punishment which came upon him was for this reason fully merited.

The character of Ruth is treated, on the whole, generously

and sympathetically. She is modest and of exemplary manners (IV, 9, p. 55), though in one acute and ingenious passage it is hinted that she had not entirely rid herself of the unchaste thoughts which characterised the heathens (V, 11, p. 69), and the story of her conversion is told in a vivid and dramatic manner.

Boaz is throughout treated on heroic lines as a pattern of virtue and uprightness, a moral giant among men (IV, 3, p. 50), proof against every temptation (VI, 4, p. 81).

There are in the Midrash a few reflections of conditions contemporary with the time in which it was written, such as the warning of Naomi to Ruth, 'It is not the custom for Jewish maidens to frequent theatres and circuses' (II, 22, p. 40), but in general it makes a serious attempt correctly to estimate the customs and conditions of the time in which the incidents of Ruth took place, the period of the Judges.

Of more than ordinary interest is the story of the apostasy of the arch-apostate of Talmudic history, Elisha b. Abuyah (VI, 4, p. 76 *et seq.*). The account given here differs in many respects from that given in T. B. Ḥagigah, 15*a*, the most important being the reason adduced for his apostasy. It is here given by Elisha b. Abuyah himself.

Interesting, too, is the passage on the propriety of kissing. According to the anonymous authority quoted in the Midrash, it is permitted on three occasions only, on conferment of high office, at meetings and at partings, and to those three R. Tanḥuma adds the kissing of relatives. Under all other circumstances it is regarded as indecent (II, 21, p. 39).

Owing to the intermediate position which Ruth Rabbah occupies in the literary history and development of the Midrash, it has perhaps more parallel passages in the other Midrashim than have the other books, and it affords valuable material for the study of *variae lectiones*.

L. RABINOWITZ.

RUTH

Proem

I. AND IT CAME TO PASS, IN THE DAYS THAT THE JUDGES JUDGED (I, I). R. Joḥanan introduced his exposition with the verse *Hear, O My people, and I will speak; O Israel, and I will testify against thee* (Ps. L, 7). R. Joḥanan said: Evidence is given only in the hearing [of the defendant].[1] R. Judan b. R. Simon said: In the past, Israel had a name like all the nations, [for instance] *And Sabta, and Raamah, and Sabteca* (Gen. X, 7); henceforth they are called solely '*My people*',[2] thus: '*Hear*, O My people, *and I will speak*': Whence have ye merited to be called '*My people*'? From the time of '*and I will speak*',[3] from that which ye uttered before Me at Sinai and said, *All that the Lord hath spoken will we do, and hearken* (Ex. XXIV, 7).[4]

R. Joḥanan said '*Hear, O My people*', to that [which was said] in the past; '*and I will speak*'[5] in the future; '*Hear, O My people*' in this world; '*and I will speak*' in the World to Come,[6] in order that I may have a retort to the princes of the nations of the world,[7] who are destined to act as their prosecutors before Me, and say 'Lord of the Universe, they have served idols and we have served idols; they have been guilty of immorality and we have been guilty of immorality; they have shed blood and we have

[1] Since God does not speak unless His people hears.
[2] 'E.J. (with a slightly different reading) explains: originally they were called 'Israel' after their ancestor, just as Sabta, etc., were called so after theirs, but henceforth (i.e. since they accepted the Torah) they would simply be called God's people; v. Gen. R. LXIII, 7, and Ex. R. XLVII, 3, and notes *ad loc.* for other meanings.
[3] I.e. when I came to speak to you at Sinai.
[4] This translation is preferable to the usual *and obey*, since it brings out the merit which the Rabbis saw in this verse, that Israel promised to *do* before they *heard*.
[5] If Israel keeps the Torah, God will yet again speak to them.
[6] By keeping the Torah, they will merit the world to come.
[7] Every nation, and even individuals, were credited with having a special genius, called here 'prince', watching over their interests.

shed blood.[1] Why do they go into the Garden of Eden while we descend to Gehenna?' In that moment the defender of Israel[2] keeps silence.[3] That is the meaning of the verse *And at that time shall Michael stand up* (Dan. XII, 1). Do they then as a rule sit in Heaven? Did not R. Ḥanina say, there is no sitting in Heaven, as it is written *I came near unto one of* ḳa'amaya (*ib.* VII, 16), the meaning of this word '*ḳa'amaya*' being *that stood by*, as it is written, *Above him stood the seraphim* (Isa. VI, 2), and it is also written *And all the host of heaven standing on His right hand and on His left* (II Chron. XVIII, 18)? And yet the verse says '*shall* [*Michael*] *stand up*'! What then is the meaning here of '*stand up*'? 'Stand silent,' as it is said, *And shall I wait because they speak not, because they stand still, and answer no more?* (Job XXXII, 16). And the Holy One, blessed be He, says to him: 'Dost thou stand silent and hast no defence to offer for My people? By thy life, I will speak righteousness[4] and save My people!' With what righteousness? R. Eleazar and R. Joḥanan:—one says: The righteousness which ye wrought for My word in that ye accepted My Torah, for had ye not accepted My Torah, I should have caused the world to revert to void and desolation.[5] For R. Huna said in the name of R. Aḥa: *When the earth and all the inhabitants thereof are dissolved* (Ps. LXXV, 4) means that the world would long have gone into dissolution had not Israel stood before Mount Sinai. Who then set the world firmly upon its foundation? *I myself establish the pillars of it* (*ib.*). By the merit of '*I*'[6]: I have established its pillars for ever. The other Rabbi says: By the righteousness which ye wrought unto yourselves in that ye accepted my Torah; for were it not for this, I should have caused thee to disappear from the nations.[7]

[1] Idolatry, immorality, and shedding of blood are the cardinal sins of Judaism. [2] The angel Michael. [3] He has no answer to this charge.
[4] Righteousness (Heb. *ẓedaḳah*) often has the sense of 'grace', 'action of charity and love'.
[5] The world without the Torah, God's moral law, is morally void and desolate.
[6] The first word of the Ten Commandments—i.e. because Israel accepted the 'I'. [7] Only the Torah preserves Israel's identity.

God, thy God, am I.[1] R. Joḥanan said: It means, Let it suffice thee that I am thy patron.[2] Resh Laḳish says: It means even although I am thy patron, what does patronage help in the day of judgment?

R. Simeon b. Yoḥai taught: I am God to all the inhabitants of the world, but I have associated My name only with my people Israel. I am not called the God of the nations, only the God of Israel. '*God, thy God, am I.*' R. Judan interpreted this verse to apply to Moses. The Holy One, blessed be He, said, 'Even although I called thee a god to Pharaoh,[3] *I am thy God*, I am over thee.' R. Abba b. Judan interpreted the verse to apply to Israel. Even although I called ye godlike beings, as it is said, '*I said: Ye are godlike beings* (Ps. LXXXII, 6), yet '*I am thy God*': know nevertheless that I am over you. The Rabbis interpreted the verse to refer to the judges. Even although I called ye gods, as it is said *Thou shalt not revile judges*[4] (Ex. XXII, 27), know that I am over you. And He spoke to Israel again and said: 'I have imparted of my glory to the judges and called them gods, and they contemn them. Woe unto the generation that judges its judges!'[5]

II. AND IT CAME TO PASS, IN THE DAYS THAT THE JUDGES JUDGED: *Slothfulness casteth into a deep sleep* (Prov. XIX, 15). [Israel was cast into a deep sleep] in that they were negligent in paying the appropriate honours[6] to Joshua after his death. That is the meaning of the verse *And they buried him in the border of his inheritance . . . on the north of the mountain of Gaash* (Josh. XXIV, 30). R. Berekiah said: We have examined the whole of Scripture and we have not found mention of a place called Gaash. What then is the meaning of '*the mountain of Gaash*'? That Israel were too much preoccupied (*nith-gaashu*)[7] to pay

---

[1] A continuation of Ps. L, 7. [2] Your belief in Me and observance of My laws will suffice to protect you (Y.A.). 'E.J. (on basis of Yalḳ.) emends the text to 'I am thy judge, I am thy patron', for *Elohim*, 'God,' always refers to God's attribute of justice. [3] Ex. VII, I. [4] The word *Elohim* (God) is used for judges. [5] Midrashic interpretation of Ruth I, I. [6] Lit. 'doing kindness'. All services done for the dead are included in this term. [7] The root is *ga'ash*.

proper honour to Joshua after his death. The land of Israel was divided up at that time, and they became unduly absorbed in the division. Israel were all occupied with their tasks. One was occupied with his field, the other with his vineyard, yet another with his olive trees, and a fourth with quarrying stones, thus exemplifying the words, *And the idle soul shall suffer hunger* (Prov. *loc. cit.*).[1] They therefore neglected to show honour to Joshua after his death, and the Holy One, blessed be He, sought to bring an earthquake upon the inhabitants of the world, as it is said, *Then the earth did shake* (wa-tig'ash) *and quake* (Ps. XVIII, 8).[2] '*And the idle soul shall suffer hunger.*' In that there were among them those who deceived[3] God by idolatry; he therefore starved them of the Holy Spirit, as it is written, *And the word of the Lord was precious in those days* (I Sam. III, I).

Another interpretation of '*Slothfulness casteth into a deep sleep*' is that Israel were neglectful in doing repentance during the days of Elijah, and 'a deep sleep was cast', i.e. prophecy increased. Increased? But the verse says '*casteth*'.[4] It is as one says, 'the market for fruit has fallen.'[5] R. Simon says: It is as if a man were to say to his fellow, 'Here is the bag, and here the money, and here the measure. Arise and eat.'[6] For R. Derusa said: Sixty myriads of prophets arose in Israel during the days of Elijah. R. Jacob said: One hundred and twenty myriads. R. Johanan said: Between Gabbath and Antipatris[7] there were sixty myriads of townships and none were more corrupt than Jericho and Beth-el, Jericho because Joshua cursed it,[8] and Beth-el

[1] Hence their preoccupation—to avoid hunger (M.K.). Mah. and Rad. omit this altogether, as it is out of place.

[2] Thus '*the mountain of Gaash*' is given a double meaning: (i) where the Israelites were too preoccupied; and (ii) where God wished to make the earth tremble.

[3] The word רמיה, translated '*idle*', also means deceitful.

[4] Lit. 'causes to fall', which implies deprivation of prophecy.

[5] I.e. owing to the abundance of fruit.

[6] There was such abundance.

[7] The Talmudic equivalent to *From Dan to Beersheba*, Gabbath (The Biblical Gibbethan) being the most northerly town and Antipatris (founded by Herod) the most southerly.

[8] Josh. VI, 26.

because the Golden Calf of Jeroboam was set up there,[1] and yet it is written, *And the sons of the prophets who were at* Beth-el *came forth to Elishah* (II Kings II, 3).[2] The verse says '*prophets*', which signifies a minimum of two.[3] For what reasons were not their prophecies made public? Because they had no *permanent* value for [future] generations. Deduce from this that a prophecy of which there is no need for [future] generations is not published. But in the time to come the Holy One, blessed be He, will come and bring them with Him and their prophecies will be published. That is the meaning of, *And the Lord my God shall come, and all the holy ones with Thee* (Zech. XIV, 5).

'*And the idle soul shall suffer hunger.*' They deceived God in that some of them worshipped idols, and others worshipped the Holy One, blessed be He. That is the meaning of what Elijah said to them, *How long halt ye between two opinions* (I Kings XVIII, 21). '*Shall suffer hunger*,' in that the Lord brought a famine in the days of Elijah, as it is said *As the Lord of hosts liveth, before whom I stand*, etc. (*ib.* 15).[4] Another interpretation of '*slothfulness casteth into a deep sleep*', is that, because Israel was neglectful in doing repentance in the days of the Judges, they were cast into a deep sleep. '*And the idle soul shall suffer hunger*'; because they sought to deceive the Holy One, blessed be He, some serving idols and others serving God, the Holy One, blessed be He, caused them to suffer hunger in the famine of the days of the Judges.

III. AND IT CAME TO PASS, IN THE DAYS WHEN THE JUDGES JUDGED, THAT THERE WAS A FAMINE. *The way of man is froward and strange* (Prov. XXI, 8). This refers to Esau[5] who is constantly planning[6] evil

[1] I Kings XII, 29. [2] Rash. adds: and also, *And the sons of the prophets that were at* Jericho *came near to Elisha* (*ib.* 5).
[3] If in the most corrupt towns there was a minimum of two prophets, the sixty myriad townships had a minimum of 120 myriads of prophets.
[4] It is preferable to read I Kings XVII, 1: *As the Lord, the God of Israel, liveth, before whom I stand, there shall not be rain nor dew these years* ('E.J.)—hence a famine. [5] The Roman nation. [6] Lit. 'turns himself about'—מתהפך, of the same root as the word translated '*froward*'.

decrees wherewith to assail Israel. Thus they accuse them: 'Ye have stolen'; [and they answer] 'We have not stolen'; 'ye have been guilty of murder?' [and they answer] 'We have not been guilty of murder'. 'You have not stolen? Who stole with you?' 'You have not been guilty of murder? Who murdered with you?'[1] He thereupon fines them on false charges [saying], bring your *annonae*, bring your poll-tax, bring your state-tax.[2]

'*A man*' refers to the wicked Esau, as it is said, *And Esau was a man, a cunning hunter* (Gen. XXV, 27), '*And strange,*' because he estranged himself from circumcision and from the commandments of the Torah. [*But as for the pure, his work is right.*][3] '*The pure*' refers to the Holy One, blessed be He, who deals with him uprightly and gives him his reward in this world, as a labourer who does work for his employer faithfully.[4] Another interpretation of, '*The way of man is froward and strange.*' This refers to the nations of the world who constantly scheme evil decrees wherewith to come against Israel. [They are called] '*a man*', since they are descended from Noah who is called '*a man*'[5]; '*and strange,*' for they serve strange gods. '*But as for the pure, his work is right,*' refers to the Holy One, blessed be He, who deals with them with uprightness.

R. Aḥa said: '*The way . . . is froward*' refers to Israel, as it is said, *For they are a very froward generation* (Deut. XXXII, 20). '*A man,*' [as it is said] *Now the men*[6] *of Israel had sworn* (Judg. XXI, 1), '*And strange,*' in that they made themselves as strangers to the Holy One, blessed be He, as it is said, *They have dealt treacherously against the Lord, for they have begotten strange children* (Hos. V, 7). '*But as for the pure*, etc.,' refers to the Holy One, blessed be He, who deals with them with uprightness in this world and yet gives them their full reward in the future, like a

[1] They ignore the denials of Israel and proceed to question as though the charges were proved; cf. Gen. R. LXIII, 10.

[2] Various kinds of taxes are meant. Probably taxes on cattle and crops and land, as well as the poll-tax mentioned.

[3] A continuation of Prov. XXI, 8.

[4] Esau receives his reward in this world, Israel in the next.

[5] Gen. VI, 9. [6] Lit. 'man'.

craftsman[1] who works faithfully for his employer. At that moment the Holy One, blessed be He, says, 'My children are rebellious; yet to destroy them is impossible, to take them back to Egypt is impossible, change them for another people I cannot; what then shall I do to them? I will chastise them with suffering and try[2] them with famine in the days when the judges judge.' That is the meaning of the verse, AND IT CAME TO PASS IN THE DAYS WHEN THE JUDGES JUDGED THAT THERE WAS A FAMINE IN THE LAND.

IV. R. Judah b. R. Simon introduced his exposition with the verse *And he said: I will hide My face from them* (Deut. XXXII, 20). Israel could be compared with a king's son who goes into the market place, and smites people, but he himself is not smitten.[3] He insults, but is not insulted, and he goes up to his father arrogantly. His father says to him, 'What do you think? That you are respected on account of yourself? It is only on account of the respect given to me that you are respected.' What did his father do? He renounced him, with the result that no one took any notice of him. So when Israel went out of Egypt, their terror fell upon all the nations, as it is said, *The people have heard, they tremble; pangs have taken hold of the inhabitants of Philistia. Then were the chiefs of Edom affrighted; the mighty men of Moab, trembling hath taken hold of them. All the inhabitants of Canaan are melted away. Terror and dread falleth upon them* (Ex. XV, 14–16). But when they were guilty of transgressions and evil deeds, the Holy One, blessed be He, said, 'What do you think? That you are respected on account of yourselves? Indeed ye are respected only on account of the respect which is due to Me.' What did the Holy One, blessed be He, do? He turned away from them a little, and the Amalekites came and attacked Israel, as it is said, *Then came Amalek, and fought with Israel in Rephidim* (Ex. XVII, 8). And then the Canaanites came and fought with Israel, as it is said, *And the Canaanite*

[1] A skilled labourer, or a professional man, of a higher rank than the labourer. [2] In the sense of purify, purge. [3] Because of his position.

. . . *heard*, etc. (Num. XXI, 1). The Holy One, blessed be He, said, 'Ye have no genuine faith. Ye have no faith in your own words.[1] Ye are froward, as it is said, *For they are a very froward generation, children in whom is no faithfulness*—emun (Deut. XXXII, 20). This is written defectively as *amen*.[2] When the prophets blessed them, not one of them opened his lips to utter *amen* until Jeremiah uttered it, as it is said, *Then answered I and said: Amen, O Lord* (Jer. XI, 5).[3] In that moment the Holy One, blessed be He, said, 'Ye are froward, ye are troublesome, ye are rebellious. Yet to destroy them is impossible, to take them back to Egypt is impossible, to change them for another nation is impossible, etc.'[4]

V. R. Nehemiah introduced his exposition with the verse, *O Israel, thy prophets have been like foxes in ruins* (Ezek. XIII, 4). Just as the fox looks about in the ruins to see where it can escape if it sees men coming, so were thy prophets in the ruins.[5] *Ye have not gone up in the breaches* (*ib.*) like Moses. To whom can Moses be compared? To a faithful shepherd whose fence fell down in the twilight. He arose and repaired it from three sides, but a breach remained on the fourth side, and having no time to erect the fence, he stood in the breach himself. A lion came, he boldly withstood it; a wolf came and still he stood against it. But ye! Ye did not stand in the breach as Moses did. Had ye stood in the breach like Moses, ye would have been able to stand in the battle in the day of God's anger.[6]

VI. AND THE NAME OF THE MAN WAS ELIMELECH (I, 2). Because trouble has come to thee, thou hast forsaken them?[7] AND A CERTAIN MAN OF BETHLEHEM IN JUDAH WENT (I, 1). That is the meaning of the verse

[1] Radal translates: You do not prove your own words true, viz. when you promised to fulfil God's commands. [2] אֵמֻן, which differently vocalised reads אָמֵן, *amen*. [3] '*Amen*' is a declaration of belief and allegiance.
[4] Concluding as the end of the previous paragraph.
[5] Hiding and skulking, instead of going about to save Israel (Mah.).
[6] V. end of the verse quoted. [7] The Midrash regards Elimelech's departure from his land as a gross breach of faith. V. *infra*.

Whose leaders are borne with.[1] *There is no breach and no going forth* (Ps. CXLIV, 14). R. Joḥanan said: It is not written 'who bear', but '*who are borne*'. When the young bear with the old,[2] *there is no breach*, i.e. there is no breaking out of plague, as it is said, *And the plague broke in upon them* (Ps. CVI, 29). '*And no going forth*,' there is no going forth of plague, as it is said, *And there came forth fire from before the Lord* (Lev. X, 2). *And no outcry*, there is no outcry from the plague, as it is said, *And all Israel that were around about them fled at the cry* of them (Num. XVI, 34).

Resh Lakish transposes the verse.[3] When the great bear with the small, '*there is no breach*' of exile, as it is written, *And ye shall go out at the breaches* (Amos IV, 3), '*and there is no going forth*' into exile, as it is written, *Cast them out of My sight and let them go forth* (Jer. XV, 1), '*and there is no outcry*' of exile, as it is written, *Behold the voice of the cry of the daughter of my people* (*ib.* VIII, 19), and it is written, *And the cry*[4] *of Jerusalem went up*. R. Lulianus[5] said: When the small hearken to the great, but the great do not bear the burden of the small upon them, then the verse applies, *And the Lord will enter into judgment* (Isa. III, 14). AND THE NAME OF THE MAN WAS ELIMELECH. When trouble came, thou hast departed and left them. [This is the meaning of the verse], AND A CERTAIN MAN OF BETHLEHEM IN JUDAH WENT.

VII. R. Tanḥuma in the name of R. Ḥiyya Rabbah and R. Berekiah in the name of R. Eliezer said: The following exposition has been transmitted to us from the Exile[6]; wherever it is said *wayyehi* (and it came to pass), it denotes trouble.[7] R. Ḥiyya Rabbah said: Wherever it is said '*and it came to pass*', it may denote either trouble or joy; if trouble, unprecedented trouble, if joy, unprecedented

[1] For this translation of אלוף, cf. Gen. XXXVI, 15 *passim*. E.V. '*Whose oxen are well laden*'. [2] Accepting their orders and guidance.
[3] As though it read: 'Our leaders bear' (i.e. reading מְסַבְּלִים instead of מְסֻבָּלִים, which only requires a change of vocalisation.—Mah. and Y.'A.).
[4] The same word is used here as in the text that is being discussed (*ẓewaḥah*). [5] Probably a corruption of Julianus. [6] The Babylonian exile.
[7] By a play on words, *wayyehi* is read *way yehi*: there was (will be) woe.

joy. R. Samuel said: There are five verses [beginning *'and it came to pass'*] *in the days of* [which refer to trouble].[1] (i) *And it came to pass in the days of Amraphel* (Gen. XIV, 1). What trouble was there in that case? *That they made war* (*ib.*). A parable. A king's friend dwelt in a certain region, and for his sake the king was attached to that region. On a certain occasion barbarians came and attacked him, whereupon [the inhabitants] said, 'Woe unto us, that the king is not attached to us as he used to be.' So in this case. The whole world was created only for the merit of our father Abraham; for so it says, *And they turned back, and came to En-mishpat*[2]*—the same is Kadesh* (*ib.* 7),[3] on which R. Aḥa said: They came to attack the eyeball of the world[4]; that eye which brought the Attribute of Justice to the world, ye wish to blind? *'The same is Kadesh.'* R. Aḥa said: *'He is Kadesh,'*[5] meaning, that is our father Abraham who sanctified His Name in the fiery furnace.[6] And when those kings came and attacked him, all cried out, Woe! That is the meaning of *'and it came to pass in the days of Amraphel'*. (ii) *And it came to pass in the days of Ahaz* (Isa. VII, 1). What trouble was there in that case? *Syria from before and Philistia from behind.* A parable. There was a prince whose tutor wished to slay him. He said: 'If I kill him myself, I will forfeit my life. I will therefore deprive him of his wet-nurse, and he will die of himself.' So did Ahaz say: 'If there are no kids, there can be no goats. If there are no goats, there is no flock. If there is no flock, there is no shepherd!' So did Ahaz calculate: 'If there are no children, there will be no adults. If there are no adults, there are no disciples. If there are no disciples, there are no sages, if there are no sages, there will be no synagogues or schools, and if there are no synagogues or schools, the Holy One, blessed be He, so to speak,[7] cannot make His Spirit rest upon the world.

[1] R. Samuel says that only where the verse begins with both words ויהי בימי *and it came to pass in the days of*.
[2] Lit. 'the eye of judgment'. [3] Lit. 'sanctity'. [4] Abraham.
[5] The word for 'the same', היא, is written הוא (*hu*) = he. 'E.J. emends in this sense, reading: the word '*hu*' (he) is written.
[6] V. Gen. R. § 38 end. [7] כביכול 'as it were', 'so to speak', always added when an allegorical or anthropomorphic expression is applied to God.

I will therefore seize the synagogues and schools'; and of him Scripture says, *Shut up the testimony*,[1] *seal the instruction among My disciples* (Isa. VIII, 16). R. Ḥanina said: Why was he called Ahaz? Because he seized (*aḥaz*) the synagogues and schools. R. Jacob said in the name of R. Abin: Isaiah said, *And I will wait for the Lord, that hideth His face from the house of Jacob* (*ib.* 17). There is no hour as dark as that hour of which it is said, *And I will surely hide My face in that day* (Deut. XXXI, 18). And yet, from that hour *I will look for Him* (Isa. *loc. cit.*) who said, *For it shall not be forgotten out of the mouths of their seed* (Deut. *ib.* 21). How did it avail him?[2] [It is written] *Behold, I and the children whom the Lord hath given me* (Isa. VIII, 18). Were they then his children? They were his disciples! But it teaches that they were dear to him as his children. And when Ahaz seized the synagogues and schools, they began to cry out, 'Woe!' That is the meaning of '*And it came to pass in the days of Ahaz*'.

(iii) *And it came to pass in the days of Jehoiakim* (Jer. I, 3). What trouble was there in that case? *I beheld the earth, and, lo, it was waste and void; and the heavens, and they had no light* (*ib.* IV, 23). A parable. A king sent a proclamation to his country. What did the inhabitants of the country do with it? They took it, tore it up, and burnt it. They then said, 'Woe unto us when the king hears of this!' Thus it is written, *And it came to pass, when Jehudi had read three or four columns* (Jer. XXXVI, 23). It means three or four verses.[3] When he came to the fifth verse, *Her adversaries are become the head* (Lam. I, 5), he[4] immediately *Cut it with a penknife and cast it into the fire that was in the brazier, until all the roll was consumed in the fire that was in the brazier* (Jer. *loc. cit.*). When they saw this, they began to cry out, 'Woe!' That is the meaning of, '*And it came to pass in the days of Jehoiakim.*' (iv) *And it came to pass in the days of Ahasuerus.*[5] What was the trouble in that case? [The

[1] I.e. make it inaccessible, so that 'instruction' is then sealed.
[2] 'E.J. understands this as part of what Isaiah said: What did it avail Ahaz to close the synagogues and schools in face of God's promise?
[3] Of the book of Lamentations. [4] The king. [5] Est. I, I.

decree] *To slay, and to cause to perish, all the Jews* (Est. III, 13). A parable. A king had a vineyard, and three enemies came and attacked it. One proceeded to cut down the bunches of grapes, the second to lop off the clusters, and the third sought to uproot the vines themselves. So Pharaoh the wicked began to cut off the children,[1] as it is said, *Every son that is born, ye shall cast into the river* (Ex. I, 22). Nebuchadnezzar proceeded to thin the clusters,[2] as it is said, *And the craftsmen and the smiths, a thousand* (II Kings, XXIV, 16). R. Berekiah said in the name of R. Judah: It means a thousand craftsmen and a thousand smiths. R. Joḥanan said: A thousand in all. R. Samuel said: It refers to the men of the council. R. Jose b. R. Simon said: It refers to the scholars. Haman the wicked, however, sought to tear out the very root, as they say, to 'buy the hen with all the eggs',[3] [as it is written,] '*To destroy, to slay and to cause to perish*': and when they saw this, they began to cry out 'Woe!' That is the meaning of, '*And it came to pass in the days of Ahasuerus.*'

(v) AND IT CAME TO PASS IN THE DAYS WHEN THE JUDGES JUDGED. What was the trouble in this case? THAT THERE WAS A FAMINE IN THE LAND. A parable. A province owed taxes to the king. What did the king do? He sent a tax-collector to collect them. What did the people of the region do? They seized him, assaulted him, and made him pay taxes,[4] saying, 'We have done to him what he sought to do to us.' So in the days when the judges judged, when a man had been guilty of idolatry and the judge wished to pass judgment on him, he came and flogged the judge, saying, 'I have done to him what he wanted to do to me.' Woe unto the generation whose judges are judged! That is the meaning of the verse AND IT CAME TO PASS IN THE DAYS OF THE JUDGING OF THE JUDGES.[5]

[1] The word עוללות means either 'bunches' or 'children'.
[2] Metaphorical for scholars. It was particularly applied to the scholars of the early Maccabean period; v. Soṭ. 47*a*, Tem. 15*b*. [3] A proverb meaning 'lock, stock, and barrel'. [4] Yal. reads: They insulted him.
[5] This alternative translation brings out the force of the homily.

Simeon b. Abba said in the name of R. Joḥanan: Wherever the word *'and it came to pass'* occurs, it signifies the occurrence of either trouble or joy. If of trouble, of unprecedented trouble; if of joy, of unprecedented joy. R. Samuel b. Naḥmani came and made a distinction. Wherever *'and it came to pass'* is found, it refers to trouble; where *'and it shall be'* it refers to joyous occasions.

But it is written *And God said: Let there be light?*[1] He answered: This also is not the light of joy, in that the world was not vouchsafed to have the use of that light, for in the light which was created on the first day, one could see from one end of the world to the other. But when [God] saw that wicked people were destined to arise, such as the generation of Enosh[2] and the generation of the Flood, and the generation of the Division,[3] and the men of Sodom, he took it away. That is the meaning of the verse, *But from the wicked, their light is withholden* (Job. XXXVIII, 15), and He hid it away for the righteous in the time to come, as it is said, *Light is sown for the righteous* (Ps. XCVII, 11).

They raised an objection to him: But it is written, *And there was*[4] *evening, and there was morning, one day?* (Gen. I, 5). He answered them: That also was no occasion for joy, for the heavens are destined to be consumed, as it is said, *For the heavens shall vanish away like smoke* (Isa. LI, 6).[5]

They raised another objection to him. But it is written, *And there was evening and there was morning, a second day* (Gen. I, 8). [And so], the third day, the fourth day, the fifth day, and the sixth day? He answered them: That also was not an occasion for joy, for everything that was created during the six days still needs further preparation[6]; for instance, mustard needs sweetening, lupines have to be sweetened, and wheat to be milled. But it is written, *And*

[1] יהי *'Let there be'* is the word ויהי *'and it came to pass'* without its prefix.
[2] Gen. IV, 26, referring to the generation of Enosh, is translated 'then profanation of God's name began'.
[3] Gen. X, 25, is translated disparagingly. [4] ויהי.
[5] It may be observed that the Midrash does not regard anything as a joyous occasion which was not permanent or which was destined to come to an end, no matter at how remote a period.
[6] I.e. man has to toil before he can enjoy the fruits of creation.

the Lord was (wayyehi) *with Joseph?* (Gen. XXXIX, 21). He answered: That also was no occasion for joy, as it is written, *That they should put me into the dungeon* (*ib.* XL, 15).[1]

But it is written, *And it came to pass on the day that Moses had made an end* [*of setting up the tabernacle*] (Num. VII, 1). He answered them: That also was no occasion for joy, for on the day when the Temple was built it [the Tabernacle] was hidden,[2] as it is said, *And Moses was not able to enter into the tent of meeting* (Ex. XL, 35).[3]

But it is written, *And it came to pass, when Joshua was* [*by Jericho*]? (Josh. V, 13).[4] He answered them: This also was no occasion for joy, for on that occasion Joshua rent his garments [in anguish], as it is said, *And Joshua rent his clothes* (Josh. VII, 6). But it is written, *And it came to pass on the eighth day?* (Lev. IX, 1).[5] He answered them: That also was no occasion for joy, for on that day Nadab and Abihu died. But it is written, *And it came to pass, when the king dwelt in his house* (II Sam. VII, 1). He answered them: That also was no occasion for joy, for on it Nathan the prophet came to him and said, *Nevertheless, thou shalt not build the house* (I Kings VIII, 19).

They[6] said to him: We have quoted all our verses[7]; say now yours.[8] He quoted to them, *And it shall come to pass in that day, that the mountains shall drop down sweet wine* (Joel IV, 18). *And it shall come to pass in that day, that living waters shall go out from Jerusalem* (Zech. XIV, 8). *And it*

[1] The very favour that God showed him led indirectly to the false accusation by Potiphar's wife, as a result of which he was thrown into prison ('E.J.).

[2] Emended text (on the basis of Gen. R. XLII, 3 *et passim*). This implies that the Tabernacle was in existence (though probably not in an erected form) until the Temple was built.

[3] This verse is irrelevant to the preceding note. It is probably quoted loosely to intimate that there came a time when it could no longer be entered.

[4] That was obviously no occasion for joy, and no objection can be raised. Rash. substitutes as in Gen. R. *loc. cit.*: *And the Lord was* (wayyehi) *with Joshua* (Josh. VI, 27).

[5] When Aaron and his sons were invested.

[6] The objectors to R. Samuel b. Naḥmani.

[7] To disprove your statement.

[8] To prove that והיה *'and it shall come to pass'* refers to joy.

shall come to pass in that day, that the Lord will set His hand again the second time (Isa. XI, 11). *And it shall come to pass in that day, that a man shall rear*, etc. (*ib.* VII, 21). *And it shall come to pass in that day, that a great horn shall be blown* (*ib.* XXVII, 13). *And it shall come to pass, that he that is left in Zion, and he that remaineth in Jerusalem* (*ib.* IV, 3).

They raised an objection to him. But it is written, *And it came to pass* (vehaya), *when Jerusalem was taken?* (Jer. XXXVIII, 28). He answered them: That also was an occasion not of trouble but of joy, for on that day they received full quittance for all their iniquities, on the day that the Temple was destroyed.[1]

[1] The destruction of the Temple was more than ample expiation for all their transgressions.

Chapter I

1. And it came to pass, in the days of the judging of the judges.[1] Woe unto that generation which judges its judges, and woe unto the generation whose judges are in need of being judged! As it is said, *And yet they hearkened not unto their judges* (Judg. II, 17). Who were [the judges referred to?] Rab said: They were Barak and Deborah; R. Joshua b. Levi said: They were Shamgar and Ehud; R. Huna said: They were Deborah, Barak, and Jael.[2] The word '*judge*' implies one, '*judges*' implies two, 'the *judges*' three.

2. Rabbi [Judah Ha-nasi] asked R. Bezalel: What is the meaning of the verse, *For their mother hath played the harlot* (Hos. II, 7)? Is it conceivable that our matriarch Sarah was a harlot? He answered: God forbid! But [the meaning is], when are the words of the Torah despised by the common people? When those who are versed in the Torah themselves despise it.[3] R. Jacob b. Abdimi came and made an exposition of it. When are the words of the Torah regarded as harlots by the ignorant? When its own possessors despise it. R. Joḥanan deduced it from the following verse: *The poor man's wisdom is despised* (Eccl. IX, 16). Was then the wisdom of R. Akiba, who was a poor man,[4] despised? What then is the meaning of '*a poor man*'? One who is despised on account of his own words. For instance, a sage sits and expounds, *Thou shalt not wrest judgment* (Deut. XVI, 19), and yet he wrests judgment; *Thou shalt not respect persons* (*ib.*), and yet he is a respecter of persons. *Neither shalt thou take a gift*, and he accepts bribes; *Ye shall not afflict any widow, or fatherless child* (Ex. XXII, 21), and he does afflict them. Samson followed the desire of his eyes, as it is said, *Get her for me; for she pleaseth me well* (Judg. XIV, 3). Gideon worshipped idols,

[1] V. *supra, Proem*, VII, p. 12.
[2] Jael is thus counted as a judge.
[3] The Torah is regarded as the 'mother' of its disciples.
[4] V. Ned. 50*a*.

as it is said, *And Gideon made an ephod thereof* (*ib.* VIII, 27). There is no greater '*poor man*' than this. Woe unto the judge who respects persons in judgment! R. Ḥiyya taught: *Ye shall do no unrighteousness in judgment* (Lev. XIX, 15). This teaches that the judge who perverts justice is called by five names, unrighteous, hated, repulsive, accursed, and an abomination.[1] And the Holy One, blessed be He, also calls him five [names], viz. evil, despiser, a breaker of the covenant, an incenser, and a rebel against God.[2] And he is the cause of five evils to the world, in that he pollutes the land, profanes the name of God, causes the *Shechinah*[3] to depart, makes Israel fall by the sword, and is the cause of their exile from their land. Woe unto the generation which is corrupt in this respect!

R. Ḥiyya taught: *Ye shall do no unrighteousness in judgment* (*ib.* 35), that is, in law.[4] But if it refers to law, this has already been mentioned.[5] If so, why is it stated: *in judgment*, *in meteyard* (*ib.*)?[6] To teach that a man who measures is called a judge, and if he falsifies [his measures], he is called by these five names and is the cause of these five evils. Woe unto the generation which has false measures; for R. Banya said in the name of R. Huna: If thou hast seen a generation whose measures are false, the government comes and launches an attack against that generation. Whence do we know? [Since it is written], *A false balance is an abomination to the Lord*, which is followed by, *When presumption cometh, then cometh shame* (Prov. XI, 1 f.).[7]

R. Berekiah said in the name of R. Abba: It is written, *Shall I be pure with wicked balances* (Micah VI, 11)? Is it

[1] Rashi on Lev. XIX, 16, explains that all these terms are found to be synonymous and interchangeable.

[2] This portion does not appear in the original passage, Sifra XIX, 4. The Scriptural verses are worked out at great length by Y.'A.; cf. Sifre, §§ 226 and 295.

[3] The Divine Presence.

[4] In adjudicating in a lawsuit, which is the ordinary meaning of 'judgment' (*mishpaṭ*).

[5] In v. 15.

[6] Scripture should simply state: . . . 'unrighteousness in meteyard', etc., and omit '*in judgment*'.

[7] The '*presumption*' of a '*false balance*' mentioned in the previous verse, and '*the shame*' sustained by suffering defeat from the enemy's attack.

possible for a generation whose measures are false to be meritorious?[1] No! [For the verse continues] *And with a bag of deceitful weights.*[2]

R. Levi said: Moses also hinted at this fact to Israel in the Torah. [It is written] *Thou shalt not have in thy bag diverse weights . . . thou shalt not have in thy house diverse measures* (Deut. XXV, 13f.). But if you do, the result will be that the government will come and attack you, as it is written, *For all that do such things, even all that do unrighteously, are an abomination unto the Lord thy God,* and there immediately follows *Remember what Amalek did unto thee by the way as ye came forth out of Egypt* (*ib.* 16 f.).[3]

3. Rabba said: Blessings bless those who deserve them, and curses curse those who deserve them.[4] Blessings bless those who deserve them, since it is written, *A perfect and just weight there shall be;* and if thou hast acted so, *there shall be to thee* [i.e. *thou shalt have*][5]; curses curse those who deserve them, as it is written, *Thou shalt not have in thy bag diverse weights.* But if thou hast acted so, the Holy One, blessed be He, says: 'Thou hast sought to make both large and small. By thy life! That wicked man will not manage to have even small,' as it is written, '*Thou shalt not have in thy bag.*' Similarly [with the verse] *Ye shall not make with Me—gods of silver, or gods of gold* (Ex. XX, 20). The Holy One, blessed be He, said: 'Thou hast sought to make with Me gods of silver and gods of gold. By thy life! That wicked man will not even manage to have gods of wood,' as it goes on, *Ye shall not make* [*aught*] *unto you!*

[1] The root זכה 'to be pure' also means 'to have merits'.
[2] His possessions (in the bag) are illusory (*deceitful*).
[3] Amalek attacked Israel, and the verse hints that false weights are always followed by such.
[4] The expression is somewhat unusual. Mah. explains: good deeds, which merit a blessing, are expressed in a form which in itself implies a blessing. Y.T. explains: good deeds are called blessings, while evil deeds are called curses. Thus good deeds bless and evil deeds curse their doers.
[5] יהיה לך (E.V. '*thou shalt have*') is lit. *there shall be to thee*, and יהיה '*there shall be*' is read twice, once with what precedes and once with what follows. Similarly with the second half: *thou shalt not have.*

4. THAT THERE WAS A FAMINE IN THE LAND. Ten famines have come upon the world. One in the days of Adam, one in the days of Lamech, one in the days of Abraham, one in the days of Isaac, one in the days of Jacob, one in the days of Elijah, one in the days of Elisha, one in the days of David, one in the days when the judges judged, and one which is destined still to come upon the world.[1]

One in the days of Adam, as it is said, *Cursed is the ground for thy sake* (Gen. III, 17); one in the days of Lamech, as it is said, *From the ground which the Lord hath cursed* (*ib.* V, 29); one in the days of Abraham, as it is said, *And there was a famine in the land; and Abram went down into Egypt* (*ib.* XII, 10); one in the days of Isaac, as it is said, *And there was a famine in the land, beside the first famine* (*ib.* XXVI, 1); one in the days of Jacob, as it is said, *For these two years hath the famine been in the land* (*ib.* XLV, 6); one in the days of Elijah, as it is said, *There shall not be dew nor rain these years* (I Kings XVII, 1); one in the days of Elisha, as it is said, *And there was a great famine in Samaria* (II Kings VI, 25); one in the days of David, as it is said, *And there was a famine in the days of David three years* (II Sam. XXI, 1); one in the days of the judges, as it is said, THERE WAS A FAMINE IN THE LAND; and one which is destined to come to the world, as it is said, *That I will send a famine in the land, not a famine of bread, nor a thirst for water, but of hearing the words of the Lord* (Amos VIII, 11).

R. Huna said in the name of Samuel: The real famine ought to have come in the days of Saul, and not in the days of David, but since Saul was but the stump of a sycamore-tree[2] and would have been unable to withstand it, the Holy One, blessed be He, deferred it and brought it in the time of David who, since he was a scion of an olive-tree,[3] was able to withstand it. As the proverb expresses it, 'Shela hath sinned, but John must pay.' So all these [famines] did not come upon feeble people, but upon strong ones, who could

[1] Or: travels about and visits the world. V. Gen. R. XXV, 3.
[2] I.e. of small merit. [3] I.e. rich in merit.

withstand them. R. Ḥiyya Rabbah said in the name of R. Simeon b. Eleazar: It is as if a dealer in glassware has in his hand a basket of cut glass, and, wanting to hang the basket up, he brings a peg and hammers it into the wall, upon which he suspends the basket[1]; so all these famines came, not upon [spiritually] enfeebled men, but upon mighty men.[2] R. Berekiah applied to them the verse, *He giveth power to the faint* (Isa. XL, 29). R. Berekiah said in the name of R. Ḥelbo: Two [famines] came in the days of Adam.[3] R. Huna said in the name of R. Aḥa: One in the days of Abraham, and one in the days of Lamech.

The famine which came in the days of Elijah was a famine of dearth, a year of produce followed by a year of no produce, but the famine which came in the days of Elisha was a famine due to war,[4] as it is said, *Until an ass's head was sold for fourscore pieces of silver* (II Kings VI, 25).

Of the famine which came in the days when the judges judged, however, R. Huna said in the name of R. Dosa that instead of the normal produce of forty-two *se'ahs*, there were only forty-one.[5] But we have learnt[6]: A man should not leave Palestine unless two *se'ahs* [of wheat] cost a shekel? And Rabban Simeon b. Gamaliel said: When is this? When even then it is difficult to obtain, but if it is possible to obtain even one *se'ah* for a shekel, a Jew should not leave Palestine? But it has been taught: In time of pestilence and in time of war, gather in thy feet,[7] and in time of famine, spread out thy feet.[8] Why then was Elimelech punished? Because he struck despair into the hearts of Israel. He was like a prominent man who dwelt in a certain country, and the people of that country depended upon him and said that if a dearth should come

[1] The text is probably defective; v. Gen. R. *loc. cit.*
[2] By whose merits the famine ultimately came to an end.
[3] This should be emended to Abraham, as in Gen R. XXV, 3.
[4] Or: one of consternation.
[5] I.e. a not very serious scarcity.—This would hardly be called a famine at all. Th. on Gen. R. *loc. cit.* emends: From the price of two *se'ahs* (wheat per *sela'*) is advanced to one *se'ah* (per *sela'*); v. note *ad loc.*
[6] Cf. B.B. 91*b*. [7] I.e. remain at home. [8] I.e. go abroad.

he could supply the whole country with food for ten years. When a dearth came, however, his maidservant went out and stood in the market place with her basket in her hand. And the people of the country said, 'This is the man upon whom we depended that if a dearth should come he would supply our wants for ten years, and here his maidservant stands in the market-place with her basket in her hand!' So with Elimelech! He was one of the notables of his place and one of the leaders of his generation.[1] But when the famine came he said, 'Now all Israel will come knocking at my door [for help,] each one with his basket.' He therefore arose and fled from them. This is the meaning of the verse AND A CERTAIN MAN OF BETH-LEHEM IN JUDAH WENT.[2]

5. AND A CERTAIN MAN . . . WENT—like a mere stump![3] See now how the Holy One, blessed be He, favours the entry into Eretz Israel over the departure therefrom! In the former case it is written, *Their horses . . . their mules . . . their camels*, etc. (Ezra II, 66),[4] but in this case it is written AND A CERTAIN MAN WENT—like a mere stump. The reason is that in the latter case, since they were leaving the country for another land, Scripture makes no mention of their property, [but states simply] AND A CERTAIN MAN WENT—as though empty-handed.

TO SOJOURN IN THE FIELDS OF MOAB (I, 1). R. Levi said: Whenever the word 'field' occurs, it refers to the city; the word 'city' refers to the province. Where 'province' occurs, it refers to the whole administrative district. The word 'field' refers to the city, [as it is said] *Get thee to Anathoth, unto thine own fields* (I Kings II, 26).[5] 'City' means 'province', [as in the verse] *Go through the midst of the city, through the midst of Jerusalem* (Ezek. IX, 4).

[1] According to Büchler, '*The Political and the Social Leaders of Sepphoris*,' Chap. I, these are titles conferred upon political leaders of the Community.
[2] Radal suggests that the Midrash makes a play on the name: A certain man went so as not to give from his house (*beth*) bread (*lehem*) to Judah.
[3] To which nothing is attached—surely he did not go empty-handed! Why then is nothing said about what he took with him?
[4] Of the return from Babylon.
[5] Anathoth was a city, v. Jer. I, 1.

'Province' means administrative district, [as in the verse] *Over a hundred and seven and twenty provinces* (Est. I, I).

HE AND HIS WIFE AND HIS TWO SONS. He was the prime mover, and his wife secondary to him, and his two sons secondary to both of them.[1]

[1] This is deduced from the order in which the words occur, first '*he*', then '*his wife*', then '*his two sons*'.

CHAPTER II

1. R. Simon said in the name of R. Joshua b. Levi, and R. Ḥama, the father of R. Hosea, in the name of Rabbi: The book of Chronicles was given only for purposes of [midrashic] interpretation.[1] [For instance] that which is written, *The sons of Shelah, the son of Judah: Er the father of Lecah, and Ladah the father of Mareshah, and the families of the house of them that wrought fine linen, of the house of Ashbea; and Jokim, and the men of Cozeba, and Joash, and Saraph, who had dominion in Moab, and Jashubi-lehem. And the records are ancient. These were the potters, and those that dwelt among plantations and hedges; there they dwelt, occupied in the king's work* (I Chron. IV, 21–3).[2] '*The father of Lecah*' means the Ab Beth Din[3] of Lecah; '*the father of Mareshah*' means the Ab Beth Din of Mareshah.[4] '*And the families of the house of them that wrought fine linen,*' refers to Rahab the harlot who concealed the spies in flax,[5] as it is said, *And she hid them with the stalks of flax* (Josh. II, 6). R. Judah b. Simon said: Her occupation was with perfumes.[6] '*Of the house of Ashbea,*' since the spies swore[7] to her, as it is said, *Now therefore, I pray you, swear unto me by the Lord* (Josh. II, 12). '*And Jokim,*' since they kept[8] their oath, as it is said, *And the young men the spies went in, and brought out Rahab*, etc. (Josh. VI, 23). And what is the meaning of the words, *And all her families*[9] *also they brought out* (*ib.*)? R. Simeon b. Yoḥai taught: That even if her family consisted of two hundred individuals, and they

[1] Chronicles, especially the genealogical lists at the beginning, are not to be understood literally, but allegorically.

[2] The whole passage is quoted in sequence, since it is the basis of the following interpretations. In the text, every verse is followed by its interpretation. [3] The chief of the Court.

[4] Mareshah is mentioned as a town in Micah I, 15. Thus it is assumed that Lecah is also a town. [5] Lit. 'linen'.

[6] An alternative and preferable reading is 'inn-keeping', the word *Ashbea* being connected with שבע 'plenty'. 'E.J. suggests simply: her occupation was with fine linen.

[7] *Nishbe'u*, connected by a play on words with *Ashbea*.

[8] *Ḳiyemu*, of the same root as *Jakim*. [9] Lit. translation. E.V. '*kindred*'.

attached themselves to two hundred other families, all were delivered by her merit, since it does not say 'all her family', but '*all her families*'. '*And the men of Cozeba,*' since she deceived (*kozebah*) the king of Jericho, as it is said, *Yea, the men came unto me* (Josh. II, 4). '*And Joash,*' since she despaired (*nith-ya'ashah*) of her life: '*And Saraph,*' in that she was prepared to be burnt (*saraph*) to death. '*Who had dominion in Moab,*' for she came and attached herself to Israel, and her deeds went up to her Father in Heaven.[1] '*And Jashubi-lehem,*' in that she clove to Israel who accepted the Torah in which it is written, *Fight* (lahmu) *against them that fight against me*—lahami (Ps. XXXV, 1). '*And the records are ancient*': R. Aibo and R. Judah b. Simon said: The meaning of these words is cryptic here, but they are explained elsewhere.[2] '*These were the potters.*' These were the spies, as it is said, *And Joshua the son of Nun sent out of Shittim two spies secretly* (ḥeresh), *saying* (Josh. II, 1). R. Judah and R. Nehemiah: One said they had carpenters' tools in their hands, [since it says] '*spies, saying: "[we are] carpenters"*' (ḥarash). R. Nehemiah said: They had earthenware vessels in their hands, pretending to be potters, [since it says], '*saying, "we are potters"* (ḥeres).' R. Simeon b. Yoḥai taught: The word '*ḥeresh*'[3] is to be taken literally. Joshua said to them, 'Make yourselves as mutes and you will discover their secrets.' R. Simeon b. Eleazar said: By pretending to be mutes, you will find out all about their affairs.

'*And those that dwelt among plantations,*' means that they were experts with plants, as it is said, *And they cut down from thence a branch* (Num. XIII, 23).[4] '*And hedges,*' since she hid them behind a hedge and said to them, *Go up into the mountain* (*ib.* 17). Some say that the meaning is that

[1] *Ba'alu bemo'ab* is read *ba'u we-'alu le'ab*: 'They came and went up to the Father' [in Heaven].

[2] As follows.

[3] The word is חֶרֶשׁ translated '*secretly*'; it is interpreted by R. Judah as חָרָשׁ 'artisan' or 'carpenter', by R. Nehemiah as חֶרֶשׂ 'a potter', and by R. Simeon b. Yoḥai as חֵרֵשׁ 'dumb'.

[4] This verse refers to the spies whom Moses sent. Tradition states that Caleb was a member of both expeditions.

the Divine Spirit rested upon her,[1] before Israel entered the land. For how did she know that [the pursuers] would return in three days?[2] Hence [we must say that] the Divine Spirit [of prophecy] rested upon her.

There they dwelt, 'occupied in the king's work.' It was on the strength of this verse that they said: Ten priests who were also prophets descended from Rahab the harlot,[3] [viz.] Jeremiah, Hilkiah, Seraiah, Mahasyah, Hanameel, Shallum, Baruch, Neriah, Ezekiel, and Buzzi; while some add that Huldah the prophetess was also a descendant of Rahab the harlot.

2. R. Samuel b. Naḥmani interpreted this passage to refer to David: '*The sons of Shelah the son of Judah: Er the father of Lecah,*' i.e. the Ab Beth Din of Lecah; '*And Ladah the father of Mareshah,*' i.e. the Ab Beth Din of Mareshah. '*And the families of the house of them that wrought fine linen,*' refers to David who busied himself with the curtain [of the Ark].[4] That is the meaning of the verse, *And Elhanan the son of Jaare-oregim the Bethlehemite slew Goliath* (II Sam. XXI, 19). [He was called] Elhanan since the Holy One, blessed be He, was gracious (*el ḥanan*) to him. '*The son of Jaare,*' the son who grew up in the forest (*ja'ar*). '*Oregim,*' since he wove (*oreg*) the curtain. Another interpretation of '*oregim*' is that they brought him the law, and he wove it.[5] Another interpretation is that it refers to the Sanhedrin who wove with him the words of the Torah. '*Of the house of Ashbea,*' since the Holy One, blessed be He, swore to him, as it is said, *I have made a covenant with My chosen* (Ps. LXXXIX, 4). '*And Jakim,*' since he kept that oath, as it is said, *The Lord swore unto David in truth; He will not turn back from it* (*ib.* CXXXII, 11).

[1] M.K.: *Gedarah* 'a fence' is connected with 'the father of Gedor', i.e. Moses in I Chron. IV, 18; v. Lev. R. I, 3. Rash. quotes Ezek. XIII, 5, where the prophets are criticised for not fencing the house of Israel, whence we learn that 'fence' is metaphorical for the work of prophets. [2] *Ib.* [3] By interpreting 'king' as referring to God, and 'his word' the work of morally elevating the people; also, the work in the Temple. It is priests and prophets that engage in this (Mah. and 'E.J.). [4] Cf. II Sam. VI. [5] Expounded clearly.

'And the men of Cozeba.' R. 'Azariah and R. Jonathan and R. Isaac b. Meryon (some say R. Jose b. Ḥanina) said: The main part of the Sanhedrin[1] came from the tribe of Judah. What is the proof? The verse, *His eyes shall be red with wine, and his teeth white with milk* (Gen. XLIX, 12). [This refers to the Sanhedrin who] arranged the *halachah* with their teeth, and caused it to emerge pure as milk.[2] *'And Joash,'* in that he despaired of life, [as it is said] *Let Thy hand, I pray thee, O Lord, be against me* (I Chron. XXI, 17). *'And Saraph,'* since he made mention of the deeds of those that were willing to be burnt[3] [saying], *O Lord, the God of Abraham, of Isaac, and of Israel, our fathers* (I Chron. XXIX, 18). *'Who had dominion in Moab,'* in that he was descended from Ruth the Moabitess. *'And Jashubi-lehem,'* since he came from Beth-lehem in Judah. *'And the records are ancient.'* R. Aibo said: This refers to David and Solomon who combined before the Holy One, blessed be He,[4] in the building of the Temple. R. Judah b. Simon said: It refers to Benaiah the son of Jehoiada who devoted his efforts with King Solomon to the erection of the Temple.[5] R. Judah said: It refers to Jehoiada the High Priest who was engaged with Joash in the repair of the Temple.[6] R. Nehemiah said: It refers to Jeremiah and Ezekiel who prayed before the Holy One, blessed be He, not to destroy the Temple.

'These were the potters'[7] refers to Ruth and Boaz.[8] *'And those that dwelt among plantations'* refers to Solomon who was like a plant[9] in his kingship. *'And hedges'*: these are the Sanhedrin who with him made a hedge[10] round the words of the Torah. *'There they dwelt, occupied in the king's*

[1] It is very difficult to explain how *'Cozeba'* refers to the Sanhedrin. M.K. suggests that its numerical equivalent is 36, the majority of the Sanhedrin of 71. Another suggestion is that it means 'deceit' since the Rabbis could find a plausible argument for proving that that which is unclean should be clean. [2] They 'chewed' it.

[3] Abraham, Isaac, and Jacob. Abraham according to the Midrash had to pass through a fiery furnace, Isaac was bound on the altar, while Jacob risked his life for God. [4] The Ancient of days, Dan. VII, 22.

[5] I Chron. XXVII, 5; I Kings I, 44. He remained faithful to Solomon.

[6] II Kings XII. [7] Or 'formers', 'creators'. [8] Who were the 'creators' (progenitors) of David. [9] Continually growing. [10] Cf. Aboth I, I.

work.' On the strength of this verse they said that Ruth the Moabitess did not die until she saw her descendant Solomon sitting and judging the case of the harlots.[1] That is the meaning of the verse, *And caused a throne to be set for the king's mother*, i.e. Bath Sheba, *And she sat at his right hand* (I Kings II, 19), referring to Ruth the Moabitess.

3. R. Menaḥem b. Abin interpreted the verse to refer to Moses. '*And Jokim*,' in reference to *Rise up*, (kumah) *O Lord, and let Thine enemies be scattered* (Num. X, 35). '*And the men of Cozeba*,' since he made the word of the Holy One, blessed be He, to appear like a lie,[2] as it is said, *Lord, why doth Thy wrath wax hot against Thy people?* (Ex. XXXII, 11). '*Joash*,' in that he despaired of his life, as it is said, *And if not, blot me, I pray Thee, out of thy book which Thou hast written* (*ib.* 32). '*And Saraph*,' since he made mention of the deeds of those that were willing to be burnt, as it is said, *Remember Abraham, Isaac, and Israel thy servants* (*ib.* 13). '*Who had dominion in Moab*,' in that his worthy deeds came and ascended before His Father in heaven. '*And Jashubi-lehem*,' since he ascended on high and captured (*shabah*) the Torah, as it is said, *Thou hast ascended on high, Thou hast led captivity captive* (Ps. LXVIII, 19). '*And the records are ancient* (attiḳim).' R. Aibu and R. Judah b. Simon. R. Aibu said: Even the things of which they [the Israelites] had been deprived (*nith-ateḳu*)[3] he restored to them, as it is said, *Hew thee two tables of stone* (Ex. XXXIV, 1). These words were said of Him who moves (*ma'atiḳ*) the world, as it is said, *And he removed* (wayya'ateḳ) *from thence* (Gen. XII, 8).[4] R. Judah b. Simon

[1] I Kings III, 16–28. The word ישב 'to dwell', or 'to sit', refers specifically to 'sitting as a judge', cf. Gen. R. L, 3.

[2] *Cazab.* In that he persuaded God to repent.

[3] Deriving *attiḳim* from *ha'ateḳ*, to draw away from, hence to deprive. The next comment derives it in the same way, giving *ha'ateḳ* the secondary meaning of to move (trans.)—Israel had been deprived of the Tables of Stone, since Moses had broken them, and he prevailed upon God to restore them. (The translation is based on the Warsaw ed. [likewise Yalḳuṭ] which reads שנתעתקו, not שנתעסקו as in Vilna ed.)

[4] The passage 'These words . . . *from thence*' has been transposed, and fits in better before '*And the records are ancient*' (Mah.).

said: These words are cryptic here, but explained elsewhere,[1] as it is said, *And the Lord said unto Moses: Write thou these words, for after the tenor of these words*, etc. (Ex. XXXIV, 27).

'*These are the potters*,' or 'formers' as in the verse, *And the Lord formed* (wayyiẓer) *man* (Gen. II, 7).[2] Another interpretation is, '*These are the formers*,' these are the souls of the righteous with whom the Holy One, blessed be He, decided to create the world. '*And those that dwelt among plants*,' with reference to, *And the Lord God planted a garden* (Gen. II, 8). '*And hedges*,' with reference to that which is said, *Who have placed the sand for the bound of the sea* (Jer. V, 22).[3] '*There they dwelt, occupied in the king's work*.' With the Almighty King of kings, the Holy One, blessed be He, dwelt the souls of the righteous with whom He decided to create the world.

4. Another interpretation is that '*Jokim*' refers to Elimelech. '*And the men of Cozeba*' are his sons, who were lost (*me-kuzabim*).[4] '*Joash*' in that they despaired of the land of Israel, '*And Saraph*' in that they burned (*saraf*) the Torah. R. Menaḥema said in the name of R. Aḥa: Did they then burn it? In fact this is meant to teach that he who annuls one word of the Torah is regarded as though he had burnt it. '*Who had dominion in Moab*': since they married[5] Moabitish women and left Israel and settled in[6] the fields of Moab. '*And Jashubi-lehem*'[7] refers to Naomi, as it is said, *So Naomi returned, and Ruth the Moabitess, her daughter-in-law, with her, who returned out of the field of Moab—and they came to Beth-lehem* (Ruth I, 22). '*And the records are ancient*.' Each one of these points has already been fully explained separately.[8]

[1] They are elucidated by a comparison with the following verse that he quotes.—Cur. edd. reads: 'He restored them to him,' but M.K. deletes it. [2] This interpretation makes the passage refer to creation. [3] A hedge likewise confines an area. [4] Cf. Isa. LVIII, 11—i.e. they died. [5] בעלו, besides meaning '*they had dominion*', can be translated 'they married'. [6] Lit. 'became attached to'. [7] Lit. 'returned to Lehem'. [8] In the Book of Ruth. *Attiḳim* (E.V. 'ancient') is now derived from *ha'ateḳ*, 'to translate,' 'quote,' 'record.'

5. AND THE NAME OF THE MAN WAS ELIMELECH (I, 2). R. Meir was wont to interpret names and R. Joshua b. Ḳarḥah was wont to interpret names. AND THE NAME OF THE MAN WAS ELIMELECH, since he used to say, 'To me shall the kingdom come.'[1] AND THE NAME OF HIS WIFE WAS NAOMI, for her actions were pleasant and sweet.[2] AND THE NAME OF HIS TWO SONS MAHLON AND CHILION, MAHLON, in that they were blotted out (*nimḥu*) from the world, and CHILION, in that they perished (*kalu*) from the world. EPHRATHITES. R. Joshua b. Levi [interpreted it to mean] courtiers; and Rabbi b. R. Nehemiah said: Aristocrats. Another interpretation of EPHRATHITES is, R. Phinehas said, [possessing] all that crown with which Ephraim was crowned by our patriarch Jacob at the time of his departure from the world. He said to him: 'Ephraim, leader of the tribe, leader of the college, all that is exalted and praiseworthy in my children shall be called by thy name.'[3] For example, *The son of Tohu, the son of Zuph, an Ephraimite* (I Sam. I, 1), *And Jeroboam the son of Nebat, an Ephraimite* (I Kings XI, 26). *Now David was the son of an Ephrathite* (I Sam. XVII, 12). So MAHLON AND CHILION, EPHRATHITES.

6. AND THEY CAME INTO THE FIELD OF MOAB AND CONTINUED THERE (I, 2). At first they came to the cities, but they found the inhabitants steeped in transgression. They then went to the large cities and found a dearth of water. They thereupon returned to the cities,[4] AND THEY CAME TO THE FIELDS OF MOAB AND CONTINUED THERE.[5]

[1] *Eli-Melech*, 'to me, the king.' [2] Naomi means sweet. Cf. Ruth I, 20.
[3] The word אפרתי, sometimes translated 'Ephraimite' and sometimes Ephrathite', is regarded by R. Phinehas as a title of honour.
[4] As a rule, the larger the city the more iniquitous it is. Radal therefore reverses the text: they came to the cities, where they found a scarcity of water: they went on to the large cities, but found them steeped in sin, etc. The other commentaries do not support this emendation.
[5] The Midrash apparently translates: . . . AND THEY HAD (already) BEEN THERE—hence this comment: they had been there, gone away, and returned.

7. AND ELIMELECH, NAOMI'S HUSBAND, DIED (I, 3). It has been taught[1]: All must die, and death must come to all. Happy then that men who departs this world with a good name! The death of a man is felt by none but his wife, as it is said, AND ELIMELECH, NAOMI'S HUSBAND, DIED. The death of a woman is felt by none but her husband, as it is said, *And as for me, when I came from Paddan, Rachel died unto me* (Gen. XLVIII, 7). R. Joḥanan said: [The meaning is] the death of Rachel is [heavy] upon me. Our Patriarch Jacob said, 'The death of Rachel is more grievous to me than all the calamities which have befallen me.'

8. R. Joḥanan said on behalf of R. Simeon: The Holy One, blessed be He, brings into the world numbers of associations[2] and numbers of brotherhoods. If one of the association die, let the whole association become apprehensive, since R. Samuel b. Abba said in the name of R. Joḥanan: There are [predetermined] periods of office, and one does not overlap that of the other even a hairsbreadth. R. Jose b. Ḥalafta said: Never during my life did I call my wife 'my wife' or my home 'my home', but I called my wife 'my home' and my home 'my wife'. Nor did I call my ox 'my ox' or my fields 'my fields', but I called my ox 'my fields' and my fields 'my ox'.[3]

AND SHE WAS LEFT, AND HER TWO SONS (*ib.*). R. Ḥanina, the son of R. Abbahu, said: She became like the remnants of the meal-offerings.[4]

9. AND THEY TOOK THEM WIVES OF THE DAUGHTERS OF MOAB (I, 4). It was taught in the name of R. Meir: They neither proselytised them, nor gave them ritual immersion,[5] nor had the new law, *Ammonite*, but not Ammonitess, *Moabite*, but not

[1] Cf. Ber. 17*a*.
[2] Of coevals. Those born under the same planetary influence (M.K.).
[3] The idea is that the interchangeability of terms shows their close association. 'The wife is the spirit of the home'; the field is useless without the ox. [4] Of little importance, now her husband was dead.
[5] An essential prerequisite of conversion to Judaism.

Moabitess,[1] been propounded, that they should escape punishment on its account. THE NAME OF THE ONE WAS ORPAH, because she turned her back (*'oref*) on her mother-in-law.[2] AND THE NAME OF THE OTHER, RUTH, because she considered well[3] (*ra'athah*) the words of her mother-in-law.

R. Bibi said in the name of R. Reuben: Ruth and Orpah were the daughters of Eglon,[4] as it is said, *I have a secret errand unto thee, O King. And he said: Keep silence*, etc. (Judg. III, 19), and it is written, *And Ehud came unto him . . . and Ehud said: I have a message from God unto thee. And he arose out of his seat* (*ib.* 20). The Holy One, blessed be He, said to him: 'Thou didst arise from thy throne in honour of Me. By thy life, I shall raise up from thee a descendant sitting upon the throne of the Lord.'[5]

AND THEY DWELT THERE ABOUT TEN YEARS (I, 4). [The force of the *kaph* prefixed to the word 'ten', as in] 'about thirty', 'about forty', is, 'either less or more.'[6]

10. AND MAHLON AND CHILION DIED, BOTH OF THEM (I, 5). R. Hunia and R. Joshua b. Abin, and R. Zabda the son-in-law of R. Levi said: The Merciful One never exacts retribution of man's life to begin with.[7] Whence is this taught? From Job, as it is said, *There came a messenger unto Job, and said: The oxen were plowing*, etc. (Job I, 14). R. Ḥama b. R. Ḥanina said: The Holy One, blessed be He, gave him[8] a foretaste of the World to

[1] The justification of marrying a Moabitess is to be found in the interpretation of Deut. XXIII, 4, to refer only to males. This *new law* had not yet been propounded. V. *infra*.

[2] She left Naomi at her bidding. Orpah is thus derived from *'oref*, the nape of the neck. [3] Lit. 'saw', connecting רות with ראתה.

[4] King of Moab. Judg. III, 12. [5] Viz. David, Ruth's descendant.

[6] We have here a grammatical explanation of the prefix *kaph*.

[7] First God punishes a man by depriving him of his property and only after that does He smite him in his person.

[8] Emended text as in Lev. R. XVII, 4 ('E.J.). God had given Job a foretaste of the Messianic era (with which 'the world to come' must here be identified) in that '*the oxen were plowing, and the asses feeding* immediately after them'—immediately they were finished ploughing the grass was already fit for grazing. (Presumably the Midrashic translation of the verse, and it then accords with the verse from Amos that follows.)

Come, [as it is said], *The plowman shall overtake the reaper* (Amos IX, 13).[1]

And the Sabeans made a raid, and took them away (Job *ib.* 15). R. Abba b. Kahana said: They sallied forth from K'far Kiryanos and traversed the whole of Abilena as far as the tower of [the mountain of] Zeboim, and there they died.[2]

And I only am escaped alone to tell thee (*ib.*). R. Ḥanina said: The word *ak* (only) intimates a limitation; he also was smitten and wounded.[3] R. Judah said: *Alone. While he was yet speaking*[4]: he also, having told the news, immediately expired. *While he was yet speaking, there came also another, and said: The Chaldeans set themselves in three bands* (*ib.* 17). R. Samuel b. Naḥman said: As soon as Job heard this, he began to array his troops for war, saying, 'How many armies can I mobilise, how many troops can I assemble. And this against the most despised nation in the world, as it is said, *Behold, the land of the Chaldeans—this is the people that was not* (Isa. XXIII, 13). [Meaning], would that it did not exist![5]—[this nation] comes to cast its terror upon me!' But when he [the messenger] told him, *A fire of God fell from Heaven* (Job I, 16), he said, 'It comes from heaven, what am I able to do?' [as it is said] *So that I kept silence, and went not out of the door* (*ib.* XXXI, 34). Immediately he took a shard with which to scrape himself.[6]

In the case of Egypt, too, it was so. [First of all] *He smote their vines also, and their fig-trees* (Ps. CV, 33). After this, *He gave over their cattle also to the hail* (*ib.* LXXVIII, 48), and only then [do we read], *And smote all the firstborn in Egypt* (*ib.* 51).[7]

[1] Referring to the Messianic time.
[2] K'far Kiryanos appears to be in Media. (V. Est. R. VI, 10.) Abilena is in Perea (Graetz. *Hist.* II, p. 257) and Zeboim in Palestine. The Midrash seems therefore to mean 'a very long distance'.
[3] Even I am not left whole.
[4] By combining the last word of Job I, 15, with the first of v. 16, we get the suggestion that he lived only long enough to speak.
[5] As though God regretted having created them (M.K. and 'E.J.)
[6] I.e. only after the loss of his wealth was he bodily smitten (Mah.).
[7] V. text in Lev. R. XVII, 4, which is preferable.

And even in the case of the plague-spots it is so. First they come upon a man's house. If he repents of his evil, it is well, but if not, the house must have the stones removed, as it is said, *Then the priest shall command that they take out the stones* (Lev. XIV, 40). If he repents, it is well; if not, the house must needs be demolished.[1] If he repents, it is well; if not, the plague comes upon his garments[2] and they must be cleansed (*ib.* XIII, 54). If he repents, it is well; if not, they must be rent, as it is said, *Then he shall rend it out of the garment* (*ib.* 56). If he repents, it is well; if not they must be burnt, as it is said, *And he shall burn the garment* (*ib.* 52). Then only do they come upon his body. If he repents, it is well; if not, he has to leave [the camp for seven days] and return.[3] If he repents, it is well; if not, *He shall dwell alone; without the camp shall his dwelling be* (*ib.* 46).

And so it was with Mahlon and Chilion also. First of all their horses, their asses, and their camels died, then Elimelech, and lastly the two sons. AND THE WOMAN WAS LEFT. R. Ḥanina said: She was left as the remnants of the remnants [of the meal-offering].[4]

11. THEN SHE AROSE WITH HER DAUGHTERS-IN-LAW, THAT SHE MIGHT RETURN FROM THE FIELD OF MOAB; FOR SHE HAD HEARD IN THE FIELD OF MOAB HOW THAT THE LORD HAD REMEMBERED HIS PEOPLE (I, 6). She heard from pedlars making their rounds from city to city. And what was it she heard? HOW THAT THE LORD HAD REMEMBERED HIS PEOPLE IN GIVING THEM BREAD. One verse says, *For the Lord will not cast off His people, neither will He forsake His inheritance* (Ps. XCIV, 14), whereas another verse says, *For the Lord will not forsake His people for His*

[1] *Ib.* 45. [2] Although in the Bible, the chapter of the garments precedes that of the house, and that of the body comes first of all.

[3] I.e. he must go without the camp, where he is shut up for seven days, and then return for re-examination; v. Lev. XIII, 4 ff.

[4] Which are of no value whatsoever—After her husband's death, she was yet of some little importance; with her sons' death that, too, went (Mah.).

great Name's sake (I Sam. XII, 22). R. Samuel b. Naḥmani said: Sometimes He does it for the sake of His people and His inheritance, and sometimes He does it for the sake of His Great Name. R. Ibbi said: When Israel merits it, [He does it] for the sake of His people and His inheritance, but when Israel does not merit it, for the sake of His Great Name. The Rabbis say: In the land of Israel [He does it] for the sake of His people and His inheritance; in the Diaspora, for the sake of His Great Name, as it is said, *For Mine own sake, for Mine own sake, will I do it* (Isa. XLVIII, 11).

12. AND SHE WENT FORTH OUT OF THE PLACE WHERE SHE WAS (I, 7). AND SHE WENT FORTH. Was she then the only one that went forth from the place? Did not many camel-drivers and how many ass-drivers also go forth? And yet it says only AND SHE WENT FORTH? R. 'Azariah in the name of R. Judah b. R. Simon explained: The great man of a city is its shining light, its distinction, its glory, and its praise. When he departs, its brilliance, its distinction, its glory, and its praise depart with him.[1] And so you find with our father Jacob when he departed from Beer-sheba.[2] Was he then the only one who departed therefrom? Did not ever so many camel-drivers and how many ass-drivers go forth thence? And yet it says, *And he went forth* (Gen. XXVIII, 10). But when a righteous man is in a city, he is its shining light, its majesty, its glory. When he departs, its brilliance, its majesty, and its glory depart with him.

[This explanation is] justified in the former case since there was no other righteous person but her. But in this case, did not Isaac remain there? The fact is, said R. 'Azariah in the name of R. 'Azariah b. R. Simon, that the merit of one righteous man cannot be compared to the merit of two righteous men. AND THEY WENT ON THE WAY TO RETURN UNTO THE LAND OF JUDAH (I, 7). Rab Judah said in the name of R. Joḥanan: They

[1] Thus her departure was particularly noticeable. [2] Gen. XXVIII, 10.

transgressed the letter of the Law and journeyed on the Festival.[1] Another interpretation of AND THEY WENT ON THE WAY is that the way was hard for them because they went unshod. AND THEY WENT, discussing the laws of proselytes.[2]

13. AND NAOMI SAID UNTO HER TWO DAUGHTERS-IN-LAW: GO, RETURN EACH OF YOU TO HER MOTHER'S HOUSE (I, 8)—i.e. to her people's[3] house. The mother of Abnimos[4] of Gadara[5] died, and R. Meir went up to condole with him[6] and he found them sitting in mourning. Some time later his father died, and R. Meir again went up to condole with him, and found them engaged in their normal occupations. He said to him: 'It appears to me that your mother was more dear to you than your father!' He answered him: 'Is it not then written, TO HER MOTHER'S HOUSE, but not "to her father's house"?' R. Meir answered him: 'Thou hast spoken well, for a heathen indeed has no father.'[7]

14. THE LORD DEAL KINDLY WITH YOU (*ib.*). R. Ḥanina b. Adda said: The *ketib*[8] is *ya'aseh.*[9] He certainly will deal kindly with you. AS YE HAVE DEALT WITH THE DEAD, in that ye busied yourselves with their shrouds; AND WITH ME, in that they renounced their marriage settlement. R. Ze'ira said: This scroll [of Ruth] tells us nothing either of cleanliness or of uncleanliness, either of prohibition or permission. For what purpose then was it written? To teach how great is the reward of those who do deeds of kindness.

[1] It is not clear on what this is based. Mah. suggests that ON THE WAY is superfluous, and therefore he deduces that it was only that road—to Eretz Israel—that they would have travelled at such a time, since it was a festival. [2] The *halachah*, 'procedure' or 'going', of the same root as ותלכנה 'And they went'. [3] אמה '*her mother*' is translated as אומתה 'her people'. [4] Probably identical with Oeonamus, a famous heathen philosopher and friend of R. Meir. [5] A Hellenistic city often identified with Gadara, the capital of Peraea; v. *J.E.* art. 'Gadara'. [6] Lit. 'to show his face to him'. [7] In Jewish law, the child of a non-Jewish marriage has only mother-right. [8] The traditional spelling, as opposed to *k'ri*, the reading. [9] The Midrash rightly distinguishes the optative יעש 'may he do' from the future יעשה 'he *will* do'.

15. THE LORD GRANT YOU (I, 9). R. Jose said: All the boons and all the consolations which the Holy One, blessed be He, is destined to bestow on Solomon, as it is written, *And God gave Solomon wisdom and understanding* (I Kings V, 9), shall come from you. THAT YE MAY FIND REST (I, 9). The *ketib* is *u'mzen*.[1] One of you will find rest, not both. EACH OF YOU IN THE HOUSE OF HER HUSBAND (*ib.*). From this we see that a woman has no contentment except in her husband's house. THEN SHE KISSED THEM, AND THEY LIFTED UP THEIR VOICE AND WEPT. AND THEY SAID TO HER . . . AND NAOMI SAID: TURN BACK, MY DAUGHTERS, WHY WILL YE GO WITH ME? HAVE I YET SONS IN MY WOMB, THAT THEY MAY BE YOUR HUSBANDS (I, 9–11)? Can then a man marry the widow of his brother [who became widowed] before he was born?[2]

16. TURN BACK, MY DAUGHTERS, GO YOUR WAY (I, 12). R. Samuel b. Naḥmani said in the name of R. Judah b. Ḥanina: Three times is it written here '*turn back*', corresponding to the three times that a would-be proselyte is repulsed[3]; but if he persists after that, he is accepted. R. Isaac said: [It is written,] *The stranger*[4] *did not lodge in the street* (Job XXXI, 32): A man should rebuff with his left hand, but bring near with the right. FOR I AM TOO OLD TO HAVE A HUSBAND, etc. SHOULD I EVEN HAVE A HUSBAND TO-NIGHT (I, 12). R. Joḥanan said: The Torah teaches us a lesson of decency, that intercourse should take place not by day but by night. That is the meaning of what is written, *In the evening she went in, and on the morrow she returned* (Est. II, 14). While

[1] Suggesting a singular.

[2] Had Naomi been pregnant, the law of levirate marriage (Deut. XXV, 5 f.) would apply, since the unborn child is regarded as 'in the world'. But since she was not so, any child which she might have later would not be bound by this law, since it would be only a half-brother on the mother's side.

[3] A would-be proselyte is not accepted with open arms, but first repulsed, being warned of the difficulties of Judaism, to make sure of the sincerity of his convictions.

[4] In Rabbinical Hebrew, גר 'stranger' means 'proselyte'.

it is written here SHOULD I EVEN HAVE A HUSBAND TO-NIGHT.

17. SHOULD I EVEN HAVE A HUSBAND AND ALSO BEAR SONS (I, 12). Thus if I had had a husband this night, I might have borne sons; but even in this case, WOULD YE TARRY FOR THEM TILL THEY WERE GROWN (I, 13)? Can ye then sit and wait until they are grown? WOULD YE SHUT YOURSELVES OFF FOR THEM AND HAVE NO HUSBANDS (*ib.*)? You might remain *agunahs*[1] without ever marrying. NAY, MY DAUGHTERS (*ib.*): [translate] woe is me,[2] my daughters, FOR IT GRIEVETH ME MUCH FOR YOUR SAKES, meaning on account of you,[3] FOR THE HAND OF THE LORD IS GONE FORTH AGAINST ME: against me, against my sons, and against my husband.

18. R. Ḥanina, the son of R. Abbahu, interpreted this verse[4] to refer to Moses. Moses said to the Holy One, blessed be He: 'Lord of the Universe! With the word *hen* (behold) I uttered thy praise, as it is said, *Behold, unto the Lord thy God belongeth the heaven, and the heaven of heavens* (Deut. X, 14), and I did hope that thou wouldest give me preferment,[5] but alas! With *hen* Thou hast wearied me.[6] Thou hast wearied me with the Angel of Death, Thou hast abandoned the *hen* in my favour,[7] and said unto me, *Hen!* (behold) *Thy days approach that thou must die*' (Deut. XXXI, 14). And he then turns to Israel and says, 'NAY, MY DAUGHTERS: Woe unto me! my children, FOR IT GRIEVETH ME MUCH FOR YOUR SAKES. It is on account of you that THE HAND OF THE LORD

[1] Deserted wives, grass widows. [2] אַל 'No!' is translated as אללי 'Woe is me'. [3] This adds nothing to E.V., but really confirms it, for the Heb. could be translated: For it is more bitter for me than for you ('E.J.).
[4] Ruth I, 13. 'For then' ought to be הלכם in the masculine Since it is in the feminine, הלהן, it is taken as the word הן 'behold' prefixes.
[5] Thus הלהן תשברנה is translated: didst thou hope in the *hen* ('Behold'), i.e. did you think that you would be given preferment because you said 'Behold, etc.'? [6] תעגנה is regarded as derived from יגע 'to weary'.
[7] Or: Thou hast left me with *hen*, saying to me, *Hen* ('behold').

IS GONE FORTH AGAINST ME: against me and against my brother.'

19. R. Levi said: Wherever the '*hand*' of the Lord is mentioned, it refers to the pestilence, and the *locus classicus* is the verse, *Behold, the hand of the Lord is upon thy cattle* (Ex. IX, 3). Bar Kappara said: They asked for the '*hand*',[1] and the '*hand*' smote them with pestilence. R. Simon said: The pestilence smote those that went out, but not those who remained [at home].[2] The disciples of R. Nehemiah deduced this fact from the verse, *Whithersoever* they went out, *the hand of the Lord was against them for evil* (Judg. II, 15). The pestilence smote those that '*went out*', but not those who remained. R. Reuben said: Even their children were anxious for [their death] and said, 'When will they die, that we may enter the land!'

20. AND THEY LIFTED UP (WATTISENAH) THEIR VOICES AND WEPT (I, 14). There is an *alef* missing [from WATTISENAH] teaching that they went on their way weeping, with diminishing strength.[3] R. Berekiah said in the name of R. Isaac: Forty paces did Orpah go with her mother-in-law, and [for this reason retribution] was suspended for her descendant[4] for forty days, as it is said, *And the Philistine drew near morning and evening, and presented himself forty days* (I Sam. XVII, 16). R. Judah said in the name of R. Isaac: Four miles did Orpah proceed with her mother-in-law, and as a reward four mighty men descended from her, as it is said, *These four were born to the giant* (II Sam. XXI, 22).[5] R. Isaac said: The whole of

[1] They said *Would that we had died by the* hand *of the Lord* (Ex. XVI, 3).
[2] The allusion is not at all clear. 'E.J. explains: only those who had gone forth as spies were smitten with pestilence (v. Num. XIV, 37), but the rest (i.e. the whole nation) who had remained at home, though they all died in the wilderness in the course of the forty years' wandering, died natural deaths. Y.T. refers this to the period under discussion: only those who left Eretz Israel on account of the famine were smitten like Elimelech and his sons, but not those who remained in Eretz Israel. M.K. and Mah. explain it quite differently.
[3] The word ותשנה '*and they lifted up*' is connected with תשש 'to be weak'.
[4] Goliath. [5] הרפה (*harapah*), 'the giant,' is explained as ערפה *Orpah*.

that night when Orpah separated from her mother, a hundred heathens raped her. That is the meaning of the verse, *And as he talked with them, behold, there came up the champion . . . out of the ranks of the Philistines* (I Sam. XVII, 23). The *ketib* is *mimma'arwoth*,[1] referring to the hundred men[2] who violated her that night. R. Tanḥuma said: And one dog also, as it is written, *And the Philistine said unto David: am I a dog* (I Sam. XVII, 43).

21. AND ORPAH KISSED HER MOTHER-IN-LAW (I, 14). All kissing is folly except on three occasions, the kiss of high office, the kiss of meeting after separation, and the kiss of parting. Of high office, as it is written, *Then Samuel took the vial of oil, and poured it upon his head, and kissed him* (I Sam. X, I). Of meeting, as it is written, *And he met him in the mountain of God and kissed him* (Ex. IV, 27); of parting, as it is written, AND ORPAH KISSED HER MOTHER-IN-LAW. R. Tanḥuma added: Also the kiss of kinship, as it is said, *And Jacob kissed Rachel* (Gen. XXIX, 11): Why? Because she was his relation. AND SHE SAID: BEHOLD, THY SISTER-IN-LAW IS GONE BACK, etc. (I, 15). Once she returned UNTO HER PEOPLE (*ib.*), she returned UNTO HER GOD (*ib.*).

22. AND RUTH SAID: ENTREAT ME NOT TO LEAVE THEE, AND TO RETURN FROM FOLLOWING AFTER THEE (I, 16). What is the meaning of ENTREAT ME NOT? She said to her, 'Do not sin against me; do not turn your misfortunes[3] away from me.' TO LEAVE THEE AND TO RETURN FROM FOLLOWING AFTER THEE. I am fully resolved to become converted under any circumstances, but it is better that it should be at your hands than at those of another. When Naomi heard this, she began to unfold to her the laws of conversion, saying: 'My daughter, it is not the custom of daughters of Israel

[1] The *ketib* of מערכות 'ranks' is מערות, suggesting sexual relationship.
[2] Lit. 'foreskins'. [3] The root פגל to entreat, also means a 'misfortune', 'a plague'. Y.'A.: do not seek to turn me away by reciting your misfortunes to me. M.K. and 'E.J.: do not court misfortune through me—by repulsing me.

to frequent Gentile theatres and circuses,'[1] to which she replied, 'WHITHER THOU GOEST, I WILL GO' (*ib.*). She continued: 'My daughter, it is not the custom of daughters of Israel to dwell in a house which has no *mezuzah*,'[2] to which she responded, 'AND WHERE THOU LODGEST, I WILL LODGE' (*ib.*). THY PEOPLE SHALL BE MY PEOPLE (*ib.*) refers to the penalties and admonitions [of the Torah], AND THY GOD MY GOD (*ib.*) to the other commandments of the Bible.

23. Another interpretation: WHITHER THOU GOEST I WILL GO: to the tent of testimony, to Gilgal, Shiloh, Nob, Gibeon, and the Permanent Temple.[3] AND WHERE THOU LODGEST I SHALL LODGE: I shall lodge overnight with the sacrifices.[4] THY PEOPLE SHALL BE MY PEOPLE, in that I will destroy all idolatry within me, and then THY GOD SHALL BE MY GOD, to pay me the reward of my labour.

24. WHERE THOU DIEST WILL I DIE (I, 17) refers to the four forms of capital punishment inflicted by the Court, viz. stoning, burning, beheading, and strangulation.[5] AND THERE WILL I BE BURIED; these are the two graves prepared by the Beth din, one for those who have suffered stoning and burning, the other for those decapitated and strangled. THE LORD DO SO TO ME AND MORE ALSO. Naomi said to her: 'My daughter, whatever good deeds and righteous actions you are able to acquire, acquire in this world, for in the World to Come, DEATH SHALL PART THEE AND ME.'

[1] Theatres and circuses had a well-deserved reputation for lewdness.
[2] The scroll attached to the doorpost in obedience to Deut. VI, 9.
[3] The different places where the Sanctuary was, until the Temple was erected permanently in Jerusalem—the first two mentioned are an anachronism, since they were no longer in existence by this time (Radal).
[4] Deut. XVI, 7, was interpreted to mean that one had to lodge overnight in Jerusalem on the first night of the Festivals, after the Festal sacrifice had been offered.
[5] Probably translating: By whatever mode thou diest, etc.—i.e. I am prepared to face death for capital offences.

Chapter III

1. This[1] is the meaning of the Scriptural verse, *The small and great are there alike; and the servant is free from his master* (Job III, 19). R. Simon said: This is one of four similar Scriptural verses.[2] '*The small and great are there alike.*' In this world he who is small can become great and he who is great can be rendered small, but in the world to come he who is small cannot become great nor he who is great small. '*And the servant is free from his master,*' he who performs the will of his creator (*yoẓer*) angers his evil inclination (*yeẓer*),[3] but once he is dead he emerges into freedom, as it is said, '*And the servant is free from his master.*'

R. Measha, the grandson of R. Joshua, was unconscious for three days on his sick bed. After the three days he regained consciousness. His father said to him, 'Where were you?' He answered, 'I was in a mixed world.' He said to him, 'And what did you see there?' To which he replied, 'I saw there in disgrace many men who are held here in honour.'[4] When R. Joḥanan and Resh Laḳish heard of this, they went up to visit him and the father said to them, 'Did you hear what this youth said?' They said, 'What?' And he related to them the incident. Resh Laḳish commented: Is there not an explicit Scriptural verse to this effect? *Thus saith the Lord God: the mitre shall be removed, and the crown taken off; this shall be no more the same: that which is low shall be exalted, and that which is high abased* (Ezek. XXI, 31). R. Joḥanan said: Had I come up only to hear this exposition I should have been content.

R. Huna the Exilarch inquired of R. Ḥasdai: What is the meaning of the verse, '*The mitre shall be removed and the crown taken off?*' He answered: The mitre shall be removed from our Rabbis and the crown taken off from the Gentile

[1] The idea that after death it is too late to repent.
[2] With the same lesson. The Midrash gives them all.
[3] I.e. man has two masters with conflicting claims, his creator (*yoẓer*) and his evil inclination (*yeẓer*). [4] Cf. a similar story in Pes. 50*a*.

nations.[1] He said to him: Thy name is *Ḥesed* (loving-kindness) and what thou sayest[2] is *ḥesed* (full of grace).

2. It is written, *For to him that is joined to all living there is hope; for a living dog is better than a dead lion* (Eccl. IX, 4). We have learnt elsewhere[3]: If one sees idolatry, what [benediction] should he recite? 'Blessed be He Who is long-suffering to those who transgress His will.' [If he sees] a place whence idolatry has been uprooted, what [benediction] should he recite? 'Blessed be He Who hath uprooted idolatry from our land; and may it thus be Thy Will, O Lord our God, to uproot it from all places and turn the heart of those who worship it to serve Thee with a perfect heart!' But does he not thereby pray for the wicked?[4] Said R. Joḥanan: the *k'tib* is *yebuḥar* (he shall be chosen)[5]; even for those who laid hands upon the Temple there is hope [if they repent].[6] To resurrect them is impossible, since they laid their hands on the Temple, to destroy them is also impossible, since they have already repented; hence to them refers the verse, *They shall sleep a perpetual sleep, and not wake* (Jer. LI, 39).[7]

It has been taught[8]: The children[9] of Gentiles and the armies of Nebuchadnezzar shall neither be resurrected nor punished, and to them refers the verse, '*They shall sleep a perpetual sleep, and not wake.*'

'*For a living dog is better than a dead lion.*' In this world, he who is a dog can become a lion, and he who is a lion can become a dog, but in the world to come, neither can the lion become a dog nor the dog a lion.

Hadrian (may his bones crumble!)[10] questioned R. Joshua

[1] Cf. Giṭ. 7*a*. [2] Emended text (Rashash). [3] Ber. 59*a*. Cf. Eccl. R. IX, 4, § 2. [4] By praying for their conversion, their being 'joined' to Israel, he prays for them without praying for idolaters.

[5] The *k'ri* (Massoretic reading) is יחובר 'joined', but the *k'tib* (spelling) is יבוחר 'chosen'.

[6] Thus their repentance is accepted; hence one may certainly pray for it. The translation follows Y.'A. and 'E.J.

[7] I.e. they shall not be resurrected, but on the other hand, neither shall they awake to punishment (Mah.). [8] Jer. Sheb. IV. [9] Minors.

[10] An imprecation used whenever the name of Hadrian, the destroyer of the Jews in the Bar-Kochba War (132–135 C.E.), is mentioned.

b. Ḥananiah. He said to him, 'Am I not better than your Master Moses?' He said to him, 'Why?' He answered, 'Because I am alive and he is dead, and it is written, "*A living dog is better than a dead lion.*"' He retorted, 'Can you make a decree that no one shall kindle fire for three days?' He answered, 'Yes!' In the evening they both ascended to the roof of the palace, and saw smoke ascending from afar, and he said, 'What is this?' To which he answered, 'One of my nobles is ill, and the physician has been to visit him and has told him that he will not be cured until he drinks warm water.' He retorted, 'Plague on him![1] While you are still alive your decree is nullified, whereas from the time that our master Moses decreed upon us, *Ye shall burn no fire in your dwelling place on the Sabbath Day* (Ex. XXXV, 3), no Jew has ever kindled fire on the Sabbath, and the decree is not yet nullified to the present day, and still you say that you are better than he!'

Lord, make me to know mine end, and the measure of my days what it is (Ps. XXXIX, 5).

David said to the Holy One, blessed be He, 'Lord of the World, Let me know when I am destined to die.' He answered, 'It is a secret which is not revealed to man, and it cannot be revealed to you.' '*And the measure of my days what it is?*' He answered, 'Seventy years.' '*Let me know how short-lived I am* (*ib.*). Let me know on what day I am destined to die.' He answered, 'On the Sabbath.' He said, 'Take off one day!'[2] He answered 'No!' 'Why?' asked David. He replied, 'The one prayer which you stand and pray before me is more precious in my sight than the thousand burnt-offerings which Solomon your son is destined to offer up before me, as it is said, *A thousand burnt-offerings did Solomon offer upon that altar*' (I Kings III, 4). He said, 'Then add one day!' He answered, 'No! Why?' He answered, 'Your son's term of office presses.' As R. Simeon b. Abba said in the name of R. Joḥanan:

[1] Lit. 'may he give up the ghost'.
[2] In order that he should not die on the Sabbath, since the body may not be moved, etc., until the conclusion of the Sabbath.

The terms of office are predestined and one does not overlap the other to the extent of a hair's breadth.[1]

And David died on a Pentecost which coincided with the Sabbath and the Sanhedrin went up to present themselves to Solomon. He said to them, 'Move him from place to place.' They said to him, 'But does not a Mishnah state that a corpse may be anointed and washed as long as the limbs are not moved?'[2] He said to them, 'The dogs of my father's house are hungry.'[3] They answered him, 'Does not a Mishnah[4] state that pumpkins may be cut [on the Sabbath] for an animal, and a carcase for dogs?' What did he do? He took a curtain and spread it over [the body] that the sun should not beat down upon it, while others explain that he summoned eagles[5] who spread their wings over him that the sun should not beat down upon him.

3. It is said, *That which is crooked cannot be made straight; and that which is wanting cannot be numbered* (Eccl. I, 15). In this world, he who is crooked can be made straight, and he who is straight can become crooked, but in the hereafter he who is crooked cannot be made straight, nor he who is straight crooked. '*And that which is wanting cannot be numbered.*'[6] Consider two wicked men who associated with one another in this world. One of them repented of his evil deeds before his death while the other did not, with the result that the former stands in the company of the righteous while his fellow stands in the company of the wicked. And beholding him he says, 'Woe is me, is there then favour shown here? We both of us committed robberies, we both of us committed murders together, yet he stands in the company of the righteous and I in the company of the wicked!' And they [the angels] reply to him and say, 'You fool! You were despicable after

[1] V. *supra*. [2] Mish. Shab. XXIII, 5. [3] And how are they to be fed? The underlying idea seems to be that even the wisest of men must learn the law. [4] Mishnah. Shab. XXIV, 4. [5] On the basis of I Kings V, 13, Solomon is said to have had complete control over nature.
[6] This is either understood in the sense that the wicked cannot make up for his shortcomings in the hereafter; or as Y.'A. maintains: the wicked cannot be numbered there together with the righteous or penitent.

your death and lay for three days, and did not they drag you to your grave with ropes? *The maggot is spread under thee, and the worms cover thee* (Isa. XIV, 11). And your associate understood and repented of his evil ways, and you, you also had the opportunity of repenting and you did not take it.'

He thereupon says to them, 'Permit me to go and repent!' And they answer him and say, 'You fool! Do you know that this world is like the Sabbath and the world whence you have come is like the eve of the Sabbath? If a man does not prepare his meal on the eve of the Sabbath, what shall he eat on the Sabbath? And do you not know also that the world is like the sea, and the world whence you have come is like the dry land? If a man does not prepare his food on the dry land, what shall he eat at sea? And do you not know also that this world is like the wilderness and the world whence you have come like cultivated land? If a man does not prepare his food on cultivated land, what shall he eat in the wilderness?' What does he do? He folds his hands and eats his flesh [in anguish], as it is said, *The fool foldeth his hands together, and eateth his own flesh* (Eccl. IV, 5), and he says, 'Permit me to look upon my associate in his glory,' and they answer him, 'You fool! We have been commanded by the Almighty that the wicked shall not stand by the side of the righteous, nor the righteous by the side of the wicked; neither impure with pure nor pure with impure.' To what does this commandment refer? To this gate, as it is said, *This is the gate of the Lord; the righteous shall enter into it* (Ps. CXVIII, 20).

4. Once R. Ḥiyya Rabbah and R. Simeon b. Ḥalafta were sitting studying the law in the Great College of Tiberias on the eve of Passover (some say on the eve of the Great Fast), and they heard the sound of people murmuring. Said one[1] to the other, 'What are these people doing?' He answered: 'He who has [money] is purchasing [his needs for the Festival] and he who has

[1] R. Simeon b. Ḥalafta, who was very poor, to R. Ḥiyya.

not is going to his employer that he may give it to him.' He said: 'If so, I will also go to my Master that he should give me.' He went out and prayed in the Ilsis[1] of Tiberias, and he beheld a hand holding out to him a pearl. He went and took it to our teacher[2] who said to him: 'Whence have you this? It is priceless. Take these three *dinars* and go and make preparations in honour of the day, and after the Festival we shall advertise it, and whatever price we obtain for it, you shall have.' He took the three *dinars* and went and made his purchases and went home. Said his wife to him: 'Simeon! Have you turned thief? All your possessions do not amount to a hundred *manehs*,[3] and whence then have you all these purchases?' He immediately related to her the incident, whereupon she said: 'Do you then desire that your canopy[4] should contain one pearl less than that of your fellow in the World to Come?' He said to her: 'What then is to be done?' She said to him, 'Go and return your purchases to their owners and the *dinars* to their owner and the pearl to its owner.' When our teacher heard of it, he was grieved, and he sent and brought her to him, and said to her, 'How much anguish have you caused this righteous man?' She retorted, 'Do you then desire that his canopy should have one pearl less than yours in the world to come?' He said to her, 'And even if it does lack it, cannot we make it up?' She answered him, 'Rabbi, in this world we are vouchsafed to see thy face, but [in the World to Come] did not Resh Laḳish[5] say: Every righteous man has his own chamber?'[6] And he admitted that she was right. And not only so, but it is the custom of celestial beings to give but not to take back. [Nevertheless, the pearl was returned] and this latter miracle was greater than the former. When [R. Simeon]

[1] The famous grotto of Tiberias. V. Jos. B.J. II, 20, 6.
[2] A title of honour often given, as here, to R. Judah ha-Nasi.
[3] This as a matter of fact was a very large sum and its possessor would have been a rich man. Either she spoke sarcastically or the text needs emendation.
[4] Under which the righteous will sit in the World to Come.
[5] Resh Laḳish lived a generation later. His statement expresses her thought. [6] Ex. R. LII, 3.

took it his hand was below and when he gave it back his hand was above, as a man who lends to his fellow.[1]

5. AND WHEN SHE SAW THAT SHE WAS STEADFASTLY MINDED TO GO WITH HER (I, 18). R. Judah b. Simon commented: Come and see how precious in the eyes of the Omnipresent are converts. Once she decided to become converted, Scripture ranks her equally with Naomi.[2]

6. SO THEY TWO WENT (I, 19). R. Samuel b. Simon said: That day was the day of the reaping of the *Omer*,[3] as we have learnt elsewhere[4]: All the towns near by assembled together that it might be reaped with great ceremony. Others say that on that day Ibzan[5] married his daughter. R. Tanḥuma in the name of R. 'Azariah and R. Menaḥema in the name of R. Joshua b. Abin said: It is written, *O Lord God of Hosts, who is a mighty one, like unto Thee, O Lord* (Ps. LXXXIX, 9), who brings things about in their due season. The wife of Boaz died on that day, and all Israel assembled to pay their respects, and just then Ruth entered with Naomi. Thus one was taken out when the other entered and ALL THE CITY WAS ASTIR CONCERNING THEM, AND THE WOMEN SAID: IS THIS NAOMI? (I, 19). Is this the one whose actions were fitting and pleasant (*ne'imim*)? In the past she used to go in a litter, and now she walks barefoot, and you say, IS THIS NAOMI? In the past she wore a cloak of fine wool, and now she is clothed in rags, and you say, IS THIS NAOMI? Before her countenance was ruddy from abundance of food and drink, and now it is sickly from hunger, and yet you say, IS THIS NAOMI? And she said to them, CALL ME NOT NAOMI, CALL ME MARAH. Bar Ḳappara said: Her case was like that of an

[1] When R. Simeon took the pearl, it was as one receiving a gift, but when he returned it it was as one giving a gift, in that the hand which received it was below his. [2] 'To go *with her*.'
[3] The measure of barley which was offered on the second day of Passover.
[4] Men. 65*a*.
[5] The Judge of Bethlehem. Judg. XII, 8 and 9. He had 30 daughters. V. *infra*.

ordinary ox which its owner puts up for sale in the market-place, saying, 'It is excellent for ploughing, and drives straight furrows.' 'But,' say the bystanders, 'if it is good for ploughing, what is the meaning of those weals on its back?'[1] So said Naomi, WHY CALL YE ME NAOMI (PLEASANT),[2] SEEING THE LORD HATH TESTIFIED AGAINST ME, AND THE ALMIGHTY HATH AFFLICTED ME (I, 21).

7. I WENT OUT FULL AND THE LORD HATH BROUGHT ME BACK EMPTY (*ib.*). I went out full with sons and daughters. Another interpretation of I WENT OUT FULL, is, I was pregnant. WHY CALL YE ME NAOMI, SEEING THE LORD HATH AFFLICTED ('ANAH) ME, AND THE ALMIGHTY HATH DONE EVIL TO ME. God has afflicted me with His Attribute of Justice, as in the verse, *If thou afflict* ('aneh) *him in any wise* (Ex. XXII, 22). Another interpretation of *'anah* is 'testified' against me, as in the verse, *He hath testified* ('anah) *falsely against his brother* (Deut. XIX, 18). Another interpretation: All His concern[3] was with me,[4] for in this world THE LORD HATH AFFLICTED ME, but of the Messianic future it is written, *Yea, I will rejoice over them to do them good* (Jer. XXXII, 41).[5]

[1] A ploughing ox is the best kind. If it was for ploughing why did it have to be cruelly chastised? Obviously it is a sorry animal.

[2] 'E.J.: why (do I tell you to call me Marah instead of Naomi)? Because THE LORD, etc. According to this, the reference is to v. 20, which keeps the order of Scripture.

[3] Three different interpretations are given of the word ענה: (*a*) 'to testify', (*b*) 'to afflict', (*c*) from ענין 'concern'.

[4] I have been afflicted more than others (or, more than my husbands and sons, who are now at rest—Y.'A.).

[5] This is really irrelevant, but added in order to end on a cheerful note (commentaries).

Chapter IV

1. This is the meaning of the verse, *And Shaharaim begot children in the field of Moab, after he had sent them away, to wit, Hushim and Baara his wives; he begat of Hodesh his wife* (I Chron. VIII, 8 f.).[1] Elijah[2] (of blessed memory) inquired of R. Nehorai: What is the meaning of the verse, '*And Shaharaim begat children in the field of Moab*'? He answered him: It means that a great man[3] begat children in the field of Moab. '*After he had sent them away*' means that they came of the tribe of Benjamin, as it is written, *And the tribes of Israel sent men through all the tribe of Benjamin, saying* (Judg. XX, 12).[4]

Another interpretation is that *Shaharaim* is Boaz; and why is he called *Shaharaim?* Because he was free (*m'shuḥrar*) from iniquity. '*Begot children in the field of Moab*,' in that he had children with Ruth the Moabitess. '*After he had sent them away*' means that he was of the tribe of Judah, as it is said, *And he* sent *Judah before him unto Joseph* (Gen. XLVI, 28).[5] '*Hushim and Baara his wives.*' Can then a man beget his wives as children?[6] It means that he was swift (*ḥash*) as a leopard[7] and explained (*bi'er*) the law: 'Ammonite but not Ammonitess, Moabite but not Moabitess.'[8]

'*He begat of Hodesh his wife.*' It ought to say 'he begat of Baara his wife'? It means that in his day the new (*hodosh*) law was enacted: 'Ammonite and not Ammonitess, Moabite and not Moabitess.'

One verse says, *Ithra the Jesraelite* (II Sam. XVII, 25),

[1] As at the beginning of Ch. III, the whole passage is given here.
[2] Elijah did not die, but was taken to Heaven in a whirlwind (II Kings II) and Jewish tradition represents him as appearing in every generation.
[3] Shaharaim is connected here with *shaḥwawr*, a captain (M.K.).
[4] Translating: begot children . . . of those to whom man had been sent (i.e. of the tribe of Benjamin). [5] Cf. preceding note.
[6] The verse reads '*He begat children . . . to wit, Hushim and Baara his wives*'. [7] This should probably read 'eagle' or vulture, as in Hab. I, 8 (Radal and Mah.).
[8] V. Deut. XXIII, 4. Only by his showing that the males alone are excluded but not the females could Boaz marry Ruth.

while another verse says, *Jether the Ishmaelite* (1 Chron. II, 17).[1] R. Joshua b. Levi said: '*Ithra the Israelite*' is the same as '*Jether the Ishmaelite*'. R. Samuel b. Naḥman and the Rabbis [give different explanations]. R. Samuel says: He was an Ishmaelite and yet you call him Israelite? Indeed he was an Ishmaelite, but he entered the house of study and found there Jesse expounding the verse, *Look unto Me, and be ye saved, all the ends of the earth* (Isa. XLV, 22), and he became converted and he [Jesse] gave him his daughter to wife. The Rabbis say he was an Israelite, and yet you call him an Ishmaelite? Indeed he was an Israelite, but he girded on his sword like an Ishmaelite and he stuck it in the middle of the house of study and exclaimed, 'Either I will slay or be slain, until I establish this law publicly so that whoever annuls it I will behead him with this sword.' [Which law?] 'Ammonite but not Ammonitess, Moabite but not Moabitess.'

2. SO NAOMI RETURNED, AND RUTH THE MOABITESS HER DAUGHTER-IN-LAW WITH HER, WHO RETURNED OUT OF THE FIELD OF MOAB (I, 22). [People pointed to her saying] 'This is the one who returned from the field of Moab!'

AND THEY CAME TO BETHLEHEM IN THE BEGINNING OF THE BARLEY-HARVEST (*ib.*). R. Samuel b. Naḥman said: Wherever the words *barley-harvest* occur in Scripture, they refer to the harvest of the *Omer*. Wherever the words *wheat-harvest* occur, it refers to the Two Loaves.[2] If it states simply *harvest* it may be applied to both.

3. AND NAOMI HAD A *MODA* OF HER HUSBAND'S, A MIGHTY MAN OF VALOUR (II, 1). The word '*moda*' means kinsman.[3] R. Abbahu said: If a giant marries a giantess, what do they produce? Mighty men. Boaz married Ruth. Whom did they produce? David, of whom it is said, *Skilful in playing, and a mighty man of valour*,

[1] Both as the father of Amasa; cf. Yeb. 77*a*. [2] Lev. XXIII, 17. The Two Loaves of Shewbread were of wheat. [3] As E.V.

and a man of war, and prudent in affairs, and a comely person and the Lord is with him (I Sam. XVI, 18). '*Skilful in playing*' refers to his knowledge of Scripture. '*A mighty man of valour,*' in the Mishnah; '*And a man of war,*' who knows how to give and take in the contests of the Torah; '*And prudent in affairs,*' in good deeds; '*And a comely person*' in Talmud.

Another interpretation of '*Prudent in affairs*' is that he could deduce one matter from another. '*And a comely* (to'ar) *person*' in that he was well enlightened (*me'ir*) in *halachah*. '*And the Lord is with him.*' The law followed his decisions.

OF THE FAMILY OF ELIMELECH, AND HIS NAME WAS BOAZ (II, 1). In the case of wicked men,[1] the name precedes the word '*his name*', e.g. *Goliath was his name* (I Sam. XVII, 4), *Nabal was his name* (*ib.* XXV, 3), *Sheba, the son of Bichri, was his name* (II Sam. XX, 1). But in the case of the righteous, the word '*his name*' precedes the name, e.g. *And his name was Kish* (I Sam. IX, 1). *And his name was Saul* (*ib.* 2). *And his name was Jesse* (*ib.* XVII, 12). *And his name was Mordecai* (Est. II, 5). *And his name was Elkanah* (I Sam. I, 1). AND HIS NAME WAS BOAZ. [Why is this?] Because they are like their Creator, as it is said: *But by My name 'The Lord'*[2] *I made Me not known to them* (Ex. VI, 3). They objected: But it is written, *And his name was Laban* (Gen. XXIV, 29)? R. Isaac answered: This is an exception.[3] R. Berekiah said: It means refined in wickedness.[4] But it is also written, *The name of his firstborn was Joel; and the name of his second, Abijah* (I Sam. VIII, 2)?[5] The Rabbis say: The meaning is, just as one was wicked, so was the other. R. Judah b. R. Simon says: They changed their evil ways and were vouchsafed the Holy Spirit [of Prophecy], as it is said,

[1] Cf. Num. R. x, 5.
[2] The original has the Tetragrammaton.
[3] So Levi. Jast. translates differently.
[4] I.e. Laban was not actually his name but rather an epithet denoting that he was clever or refined (Y.'A., 'E.J., Jast.).
[5] Though in fact they were wicked.

The word of the Lord that came to Joel the son of Pethuel (Joel I, I).[1]

4. AND RUTH THE MOABITESS SAID UNTO NAOMI: LET ME NOW GO TO THE FIELD, AND GLEAN AMONG THE EARS OF CORN AFTER HIM IN WHOSE SIGHT I SHALL FIND FAVOUR. AND SHE SAID UNTO HER: GO, MY DAUGHTER (II, 2). R. Jannai said: She was forty years of age and yet you call her daughter? The answer is that she looked like a girl of fourteen.[2]

AND SHE WENT AND CAME (II, 3). She had not yet gone, yet you say, AND CAME?[3] R. Judah b. R. Simon answered: She began to mark out the ways.

AND HER HAP WAS (II, 3). R. Joḥanan said: Whoever saw her was sexually excited.[4] THE PORTION OF THE FIELD BELONGING UNTO BOAZ WHO WAS OF THE FAMILY OF ELIMELECH (*ib.*). I.e. it was given to her from what was due to be her portion [i.e. heritage].[5]

5. AND BEHOLD BOAZ CAME FROM BETHLEHEM (II, 4). R. Tanḥuma said on behalf of the Rabbis: Three things did the earthly Beth din decree, and the heavenly Beth din intimated its approval. These are, to greet by the name of God, the [reciting of the] scroll of Esther, and tithes. Whence do we know about greeting by the

[1] *Pethuel*, 'he who entreated God,' is regarded as a pseudonym of Samuel. 'E.J. interprets the passage thus: But it is written, *The name . . . Abijah*, whereon the Rabbis said: just as the one was wicked so was the other? R. Judah b. R. Simon *answered:* They changed, etc.; and the verse was written after their reformation.—This on the whole is preferable, but it probably necessitates some slight emendation of the text.

[2] Emended text (Radal). Cur. edd.: 'She was forty years of age, and one is called daughter only when one is forty years of age.'—It must be assumed that they had a tradition as to her age (Y.'A.).

[3] M.K., 'E.J. The point of the difficulty is not quite clear. Y.'A. explains that the Midrash now assumes that AND CAME means to her mother-in-law, for otherwise it should state, and came to the field and gleaned; hence the difficulty, now say: she went to the field, came (to her mother-in-law), and gleaned (in the field)? R. Judah then answers that the text means that she went backwards and forward until she knew the road to the field.

[4] The word מקרה 'a happening' is connected by R. Joḥanan with קרי 'semen'. [5] Comment based on the word PORTION in the text.

name of God? As it is said, *That think to cause My people to forget My name* (Jer. XXIII, 27). When did they so think? In the days of Athaliah. The Rabbis say: In the days of Hananiah, Mishael, and Azariah. R. Ḥananiah in the name of R. Judah b. R. Simon said: In the days of Mordecai and Esther. And Boaz and his court arose and instituted that greeting should be by the name of God, as it is said, AND BEHOLD, BOAZ CAME FROM BETHLEHEM, AND SAID UNTO THE REAPERS: THE LORD BE WITH YOU.[1] And so the Angel said to Gideon, *The Lord is with thee, thou mighty man of valour* (Judg. VI, 12).

Whence do we know about the scroll of Esther? R. Jeremiah in the name of R. Samuel b. Isaac answered: What did Mordecai and Esther do? They wrote letters which they sent to all the exiles, saying, 'Do you undertake to celebrate these two days in the future.'[2] They replied and said, 'Were not the troubles of Haman enough, that you place upon us the burden of celebrating those two days?'[3] And they answered: 'If it is because of that that you fear to do so, is it not already recorded in the annals, as it is said, *Are they not written in the book of the Chronicles'* (Est. X, 2). What did they do? They wrote a second letter and sent them *This second letter of Purim* (*ib.* IX, 29).

R. Ḥelbo said in the name of R. Samuel b. Naḥman: Eighty-five elders, and among them some thirty prophets were troubled by the verse These *are the commandments which the Lord commanded Moses* (Lev. XXVII, 34), '*these*,' indicating that nothing can be added to them and nothing taken from them, nor is any prophet permitted to make a new law henceforth, and yet Mordecai and Esther request us to promulgate a new law. Until the Holy One, blessed be He, enlightened them and they found it intimated in

[1] Boaz, of course, was very much earlier than Athaliah. The Midrash means that Boaz was originally responsible for this law of greeting in God's name; it was annulled (or became obsolete) in the days of Athaliah, and was then reintroduced (Radal). [2] Est. IX.

[3] The commemoration of Haman's defeat might evoke the hostility of other peoples (M.K. and Mah.).

the Pentateuch, the Prophets, and the Hagiographa. In the Pentateuch, as it is written, *Write this for a memorial in the book* (Ex. XVII, 14)[1]; in the Prophets, as it is written, *Then they that feared the Lord spoke one with another; and the Lord hearkened, and heard, and a book of remembrance was written before Him* (Mal. III, 16). In the Hagiographa, as it is written, '*Are they not written in the book of the Chronicles*' (Est. X, 2). Rab, R. Ḥanina, R. Jonathan, and Bar Ḳappara all said: This scroll was not composed by the Court of that time, but was said upon Mt. Sinai, [and the reason that it is written here is that] there is no chronological order in the Torah.

And whence do we know that the Holy One, blessed be He, intimated his agreement with them? Rab answered: The *ketib*[2] is not *kiblu* (they took upon themselves) but *ḳibel* (*he* took upon himself). Who? The Master of the Jewish people.

Whence do we know about tithes? Since R. Berekiah said in the name of R. Crespia: The children of Israel were exiled on account of the transgression of the laws of *terumoth* and tithes. Simeon b. Abba said in the name of R. Joḥanan: Once they were exiled they were automatically exempt from this duty, but they themselves accepted liability for it. How did the men of the Great Synagogue[3] act? They wrote a document and spread it out in the Courtyard of the Temple, and in the morning they found a seal appended. That is the meaning of the verse, *And yet for all this we make a sure covenant and write upon what is sealed* (Neh. X, 1).[4] One verse says, *'al haḥatum* (upon what is sealed) and the other[5] *'al haḥatumin* (upon what are sealed). How can this be explained? *'Al haḥatum* refers to the earthly court; *'al haḥatumin* to the additional seal of the heavenly court.

Some add [to the three things mentioned] also the

[1] Haman was regarded as a descendant of Amalek, and his attempt to destroy the Jews as one more incident in the age-long struggle between Israel and Amalek. [2] The Massoretic spelling of Est. IX, 27.
[3] The authoritative council of the Jews from Ezra to Simeon the Just, *c.* 300 B.C.E. [4] E.V. '*set their seal unto it*'. [5] Neh. X, 2.

prohibition against using the spoil of Jericho. For so said the Holy One, blessed be He, to Joshua, *Israel hath sinned* (Josh. VII, 11). But was it not Joshua who made the decree? It therefore teaches that the Holy One, blessed be He, intimated his agreement with it.

6.[1] THEN BOAZ SAID TO HIS SERVANT THAT WAS SET OVER THE REAPERS (II, 5). Over how many was he appointed? R. Eliezer, the son of Miriam, said: He was set over forty-two, as we see from the verse, *And Solomon numbered all the strangers that were in the land of Israel . . . and he set three score and ten thousand of them to bear burdens, and fourscore thousands to be hewers in the mountains, and three thousand and six hundred overseers to set the people at work* (II Chron. II, 16 f.).[2] One who adopts this plan is able to go on, and knows what he is about. WHOSE DAMSEL IS THIS? Did he then not recognise her? The meaning is that when he saw how attractive she was, and how modest her attitude, he began to inquire concerning her. All the other women bend down to gather the ears of corn, but she sits and gathers; all the other women hitch up their skirts, and she keeps hers down; all the other women jest with the reapers, while she is reserved; all the other women gather from between the sheaves, while she gathers from that which is already abandoned.

In the same way one must understand the verse, *And when Saul saw David go forth against the Philistine, he said unto Abner, . . . Whose son is this youth?* (I Sam. XVII, 55). Did he then not recognise him? But yesterday he sent to Jesse saying, *Let David, I pray thee, stand before me; for he hath found favour in my sight* (*ib.* XVI, 22), and now he inquires concerning him? The meaning is that when Saul saw the head of the Philistine (Goliath) he began to ask concerning David, 'Is he a descendant of Perez, a king?[3]

[1] Printed edd. wrongly number this and the following sections, 9, 10, 11, and 12.
[2] I.e. 3,600 overseers for 150,000 people (actually 153,600), an average of one overseer for 42.
[3] Perez and Zarah, the sons of Judah (Gen. XXXVII, 29–30). The former means a 'breach' and thus refers to a king who makes breaches in the enemy walls. Cf. 'A.Z. 76*b*.

Is he a descendant of Zarah, a judge?' And Doeg, the Edomite, was there, at that time, and he said to him, 'Even if he is a descendant of Perez, is he not of impure descent? Is he not a descendant of Ruth, the Moabitess?' But Abner said to him, 'But has not the new law been made, "Ammonite but not Ammonitess, Moabite but not Moabitess"?' He answered him, 'But if so, let us also say Edomite but not Edomitess, Egyptian but not Egyptian women?[1] Why were the men spurned, was it not *Because they met you not with bread and with water?* (Deut. XXIII, 5). The women ought also to have met the women?' And for the moment Abner forgot the law. Said Saul to him, 'Go and inquire concerning that law which you have forgotten from Samuel and his Court.' When he came to Samuel and his Court, he said to him: 'Whence have you this? Not from Doeg? Doeg is a heretic and will not depart from this world in peace, and yet I cannot let you leave without an answer.'[2] *All glorious is the king's daughter within the palace* (Ps. XLV, 14).[3] It is not for a woman to go out and bring food, but only for a man. *And because they hired against thee Balaam* (Deut. XXIII, 5). A man hires, but not a woman. AND THE SERVANT THAT WAS SET OVER THE REAPERS ANSWERED AND SAID: IT IS A MOABITISH DAMSEL (II, 6), and yet you say that her conduct is praiseworthy and modest? Her mother-in-law had instructed her well.

7. AND SHE SAID: LET ME GLEAN, I PRAY YOU, AND GATHER AFTER THE REAPERS, etc. (II, 7). She gathered but a small quantity for her who was in the house [Naomi], since she was waiting for it.[4]

THEN SAID BOAZ TO RUTH: HEAREST THOU NOT

[1] Deut. XXIII, 8. The law of Ammon and Moab applies only to the males; of Edom and Egypt to males and females.

[2] Although one should not answer a heretic.

[3] I.e. a woman should remain indoors.

[4] The translation probably gives the general sense (though M.K. and Y.'A. suggest other renderings), but the language of the original is somewhat obscure.

MY DAUGHTER? GO NOT TO GLEAN IN ANOTHER FIELD (II, 8), as in the verse, *Thou shalt have no other gods before Me* (Ex. XX, 3).[1] NEITHER PASS FROM HENCE, compare This *is my God, and I will glorify Him* (Ex. XV, 2). BUT ABIDE HERE FAST BY MY MAIDENS, this refers to the righteous who are called maidens, as it is said, *Wilt thou play with him as with a bird, or wilt thou bind him for thy maidens?* (Job XL, 29).

8. LET THINE EYES BE ON THE FIELD THAT THEY DO REAP, AND GO THOU AFTER THEM. HAVE I NOT CHARGED THE YOUNG MEN THAT THEY SHALL NOT TOUCH THEE? AND WHEN THOU ART ATHIRST, GO UNTO THE VESSELS, AND DRINK OF THAT WHICH THE YOUNG MEN HAVE DRAWN (II, 9). THINE EYES refers to the Sanhedrin. There are two hundred and forty-eight limbs in the human body, and they follow only the eyes. This is the meaning of the verse, LET THINE EYES BE ON THE FIELD, etc., AND GO THOU AFTER THEM. THAT THEY SHALL NOT TOUCH THEE, i.e. that they will not discourage you [from becoming a Jewess]. AND WHEN THOU ART ATHIRST, GO UNTO THE VESSELS, these are the righteous who are called vessels, as in the verse, *How are the mighty fallen and the vessels*[2] *of war perished* (II Sam. I, 27).

AND DRINK OF THAT WHICH THE YOUNG MEN HAVE DRAWN refers to the Festival of Water-Drawing.[3] And why is it called 'Drawing'? For from there they drew the inspiration of the Holy Spirit, as it is said, *Therefore with joy shall ye draw water out of the wells of salvation* (Isa. XII, 3).

[1] The verse is homiletically applied to gleaning in other spiritual fields, etc.
[2] כלי translated in E.V. as '*weapons*'. [3] See Mishnah Suk. V, I.

Chapter V

1. *He was with David at Pas-dammim, and there the Philistines were gathered together to battle, where there was a plot of ground full of barley . . . But they . . . defended it* (1 Chron. XI, 13 f.). R. Joḥanan said: '*Pas-dammim*' means 'the red field'. R. Samuel b. Naḥmani said: '*Pas-dammim*' means that there bloodshed[1] ceased (*pasaḵ*).

'*And there the Philistines were gathered together to battle, where there was a plot of ground full of barley.*' One verse says barley, whereas a parallel passage says lentils?[2] R. Jacob explained: It was barley, but the kernels were like lentils. R. Levi explained: The Philistines came tall like barley and departed lowly like lentils. '*But they stood in the midst of the plot, and* [they] *defended it,*' whereas the parallel passage[3] has *and he defended it.* This teaches that they returned it to its original owner[4] in whose eyes it was as precious as a field full of saffron.[5]

R. Samuel b. Naḥman said: The incident occurred in one year[6] but concerned two fields. He[7] knew for certain that it was permitted to destroy the field[8] and pay compensation. What then was the question? Whether it was permitted to destroy it without paying compensation, and if so which one was it to be, that of barley or that of lentils. Lentils are human food and barley fodder for animals. On the other hand, lentils are not used for bringing the '*Omer,*[9] whereas barley is. *Ḥallah* is not separated from lentils,[10] but it is from barley.

The Rabbis, however, say that the passages concern

---

[1] R. Joḥanan connects *dammim* with *adom* 'red', R. Samuel with *dam* 'blood'.   [2] II Sam. XXIII, 11.   [3] II Sam. *loc. cit.*, v. 12.
[4] ויצילוה '*and they defended it*', more properly means 'and they rescued it', by returning it to its owner; but subsequently it was defended against the Philistines by one person, viz. Shammah the son of Age the Aarite—*ib.* v. 11 (Y.'A. and 'E.J.).
[5] A precious commodity.   [6] I.e. both refer to one incident.
[7] Sc. David.   [8] In order to make a road.
[9] The measure of barley brought on the second day of Passover.
[10] Since it cannot form a dough (Num. XV, 20)—The last two facts give a certain superiority to barley.

one and the same field, but refer to different years. Let them then decide in the second year in accordance with their decision in the first? The answer is that we do not base decisions of law on actual happenings.

And David longed, and said: Oh that one would give me water[1] *to drink of the well of Bethlehem* (II Sam. XXIII, 15). R. Ḥiyya said: He was in need of a legal decision. *And the three mighty men broke through.*[2] Why three? Because a law cannot be decided except by three, *And they drew water out of the well of Bethlehem, that was by the gate, and took it, and brought it to David; but he would not drink thereof* (*ib.* 16); i.e. he was unwilling that the law should be established in their name, so he made it an anonymous decision for future generations that a king may make a breach in order to make a highway, and none may object.

Bar Ḳappara said: It was the Festival of Tabernacles, and it was the time of the water oblation, and it was during the time that the High Places were permitted.[3] '*And the three mighty men broke through.*' Why three? One to slay the enemy, one to remove the slain, and the third to bring the jug in purity. R. Hunya in the name of R. Joseph said: He had need of [information on] the laws concerning a captive maiden.[4] R. Simeon b. Rabbi said: He sought to build the Temple.[5]

2. THEN SHE FELL ON HER FACE AND BOWED DOWN TO THE GROUND, AND SAID: WHY HAVE I FOUND FAVOUR IN THY SIGHT THAT THOU TAKEST COGNISANCE OF ME (II, 10). This teaches that she prophesied that he would make her his wife.[6]

[1] *Water* refers to the Torah. [2] And gave a decision.
[3] Since the verse continues *And he poured it out before the Lord*. The High Places were permitted after the destruction of Shiloh and before the building of the Temple. The water was required for the oblation.
[4] V. Deut. XXI, 10–14. The Hebrew word translated *longed* in the present passage from Samuel is usually applied to sexual desire.
[5] I.e. it refers to David's well-known longing to build the Temple. All these interpretations understand David's desire for water to be meant symbolically.
[6] *To take cognisance* is understood as 'to know one's wife', carnally; cf. Gen. IV, 1 for a similar use of *knew*.

3. AND BOAZ ANSWERED AND SAID: IT HATH BEEN FULLY TOLD ME (II, 11). Why is the verb repeated?[1] It hath been told me in the house, and it hath been told me in the field, ALL THAT THOU HAST DONE UNTO THY MOTHER-IN-LAW SINCE THE DEATH OF THY HUSBAND, and certainly during his lifetime,[2] AND HOW THOU HAST LEFT THY FATHER AND MOTHER AND THE LAND OF THY NATIVITY—this means, 'thy country'; AND[3] THOU HAST LEFT THY FATHER AND THY MOTHER—i.e. thy idolatry, as it is said, *Who say to a stock: Thou art my father, and to a stone: Thou hast brought us forth* (Jer. II, 27). AND THE LAND OF THY NATIVITY refers to her surroundings, AND ART COME UNTO A PEOPLE THAT THOU KNEWEST NOT HERETOFORE, for had you come heretofore, you would not have been [accepted].[4]

4. THE LORD RECOMPENSE THY WORK, AND BE THY REWARD COMPLETE FROM THE LORD (II, 12). R. Ḥasa said: Solomon shall be thy reward.[5] UNDER WHOSE WINGS THOU ART COME TO TAKE REFUGE. R. Abin said: We gather from Scripture that there are wings to the earth, as it is said, *From the uttermost parts* (lit. 'wings') *of the earth we heard songs* (Isa. XXIV, 16); wings to the sun, as it is said, *But unto you that fear My name shall the sun of righteousness arise with healing in its wings* (Mal. III, 20); wings to the Ḥayyoth, as it is said, *Also the noise of the wings of the Ḥayyoth* (Ezek. III, 13); wings to the cherubim, as it is said, *For the cherubim spread forth their wings* (I Kings VIII, 7); wings to the seraphim, as it is said, *Above Him stood the seraphim; each one had six wings* (Isa. VI, 2). Come and consider how great is the power of the righteous, and how great is the power of

[1] The words הגד הגד *'it hath been fully told'*.
[2] This emendation of the text is suggested by I. Ashkenazi.
[3] According to 'E.J. AND should be preceded by 'Another interpretation'.
[4] Since the new law of 'Moabite and not Moabitess' had not yet been enacted. 'E.J. adds this in the text.
[5] This depends on the connection between שלמה *'complete'* and שלמה Solomon; missing from printed text but added by Z. Einhorn, as in Yalḳ.

righteousness,[1] and how great the power of those who do kindly deeds, for they shelter neither in the shadow of the morning, nor in the shadow of the wings of the earth, nor in the shadow of the sun, nor in the shadow of the wings of the Ḥayyoth, or the cherubim or the seraphim, but under whose wings do they shelter? Under the shadow of Him at whose word the world was created, as it is said, *How precious is Thy lovingkindness, O God, and the children of men take refuge in the shadow of Thy wings* (Ps. XXXVI, 8).

5. THEN SHE SAID: LET ME FIND FAVOUR IN THY SIGHT, MY LORD . . . THOUGH I BE NOT AS ONE OF THY HANDMAIDENS (II, 13). He said unto her, 'Heaven forfend! Thou art not as one of the handmaidens (*amahoth*) but as one of the matriarchs (*imahoth*).' Similarly to be explained is the verse, *And Nobah went and took Kenath, and the villages thereof, and called it Nobah* (Num. XXXII, 42), teaching that it did not retain this name. And similarly the verse, *And he said unto me: To build her a house in the land of Shinar* (Zech. V, 11), teaching that there is no salvation for falsehood.[2]

6. AND BOAZ SAID UNTO HER AT MEAL TIME: COME HITHER, AND EAT OF THE BREAD, AND DIP THY MORSEL IN THE VINEGAR. AND SHE SAT BESIDE THE REAPERS; AND THEY REACHED HER PARCHED CORN, AND SHE DID EAT AND WAS SATISFIED AND LEFT THEREOF (II, 14). R. Jonathan interpreted this verse in six ways. The first refers it to David. COME HITHER means, approach to royal state, as in the verse, *That Thou hast brought me hither* (II Sam. VII, 18). AND EAT OF THE BREAD refers to the bread of royalty. AND DIP THY BREAD IN THE VINEGAR refers to his sufferings, as it is said, *O Lord, rebuke me not in Thine anger* (Ps. VI, 2). AND SHE SAT BESIDE THE

[1] Or, charity. The same word (צְדָקָה) expresses both in Hebrew.

[2] In all the three verses quoted here, there is a Massoretic peculiarity in the word לה 'to her', in that it is written without the *mappiḳ* and is therefore regarded as including the negative לא 'no'. Thus Boaz said, 'Thou art *not* a maidservant'; Kenath was *not* called permanently by the name of Nobah, and the house of falsehood will *not* stand for ever.

REAPERS, in that the throne was taken from him for a time,[1] as R. Huna said: All these six months that David was in flight from Absalom are not included in his reign[2] and he atoned for his sins with a she-goat, like a commoner.[3] AND THEY REACHED HER PARCHED CORN: [this intimates] that he was restored to the throne, as it is said, *Now know I that the Lord saveth His anointed* (Ps. XX, 7). AND SHE DID EAT, AND WAS SATISFIED, AND LEFT THEREOF: this indicates that he would eat in this world, and in the Messianic age, and in the World to Come.[4]

The second interpretation of COME HITHER, etc., refers it to Solomon. COME HITHER; approach to royal state; AND EAT OF THE BREAD refers to the bread of royalty, as it is said, *And Solomon's provision*[5] *for one day was thirty measures of fine flour, and three score measures of meal* (I Kings V, 2). AND DIP THY MORSEL IN THE VINEGAR refers to the stain on his character. AND SHE SAT BESIDE THE REAPERS, in that the throne was taken from him for a time, as R. Yoḥai b. Ḥanina said: An angel descended in the likeness of Solomon and sat upon his throne, while he went from door to door throughout Israel saying, *I, Koheleth, have been king over Israel in Jerusalem* (Eccl. I, 12). What did one of the housewives do? She gave him a plate of pounded beans, and struck him upon the head, saying, 'Does not Solomon sit upon his throne? And yet you say "I am Solomon king of Israel".' AND THEY REACHED HER PARCHED CORN; this indicates that he was restored to the throne. AND SHE DID EAT AND WAS SATISFIED AND LEFT THEREOF; he would eat in this world, and in the Messianic age, and in the World to Come.

[1] During the rebellion of Absalom. This is a play on *mizzad* (BESIDE), which is connected with *nozad*, to destroy or take away (Rash. and Y.'A.).
[2] According to II Sam. V, 4, and I Kings II, 11, David reigned for forty years; according to II Sam. V, 5, it was forty years and six months, which latter are not included.
[3] A king atoned with a he-goat, a commoner with a she-goat (Lev. IV, 23).
[4] 'E.J. reads: DID EAT in this world; will be SATISFIED in the Messianic age; AND WILL LEAVE THEREOF (understanding it now in the future tense) in the World to Come. [5] Lit. 'bread'.

The third interpretation of COME HITHER refers it to Hezekiah; COME HITHER, approach to royal state. AND EAT OF THE BREAD, the bread of royalty. AND DIP THY MORSEL IN THE VINEGAR refers to his sufferings [in illness], as it is said, *And Isaiah said: Let them take a cake of figs*, etc. (Isa. XXXVIII, 21).[1] AND SHE SAT BESIDE THE REAPERS, in that the throne was taken from him for a time, as it is said, *Thus saith Hezekiah: This day is a day of trouble and rebuke* (Isa. XXXVII, 3). AND THEY REACHED HER PARCHED CORN indicates that he was restored to the throne, as it is said, *So that he was exalted in the sight of all nations from thenceforth* (II Chron. XXXII, 23). AND SHE DID EAT AND WAS SATISFIED AND LEFT THEREOF; he would eat in this world, and in the Messianic age, and in the World to Come. The fourth interpretation of COME HITHER, etc., makes it refer to Manasseh. COME HITHER; approach to the royal state. AND EAT OF THE BREAD refers to the bread of royalty. AND DIP THY MORSEL IN THE VINEGAR, because his actions were sour as vinegar[2] on account of his evil deeds. AND SHE SAT BESIDE THE REAPERS, in that he was deprived of his throne for a time, as it is said, *And the Lord spoke unto Manasseh, and to his people; but they gave no heed. Wherefore the Lord brought them the captains of the host of the king of Assyria, who took Manasseh with hooks* (II Chron. XXXIII, 10 f.). R. Abba b. Kahana said: It means, with manacles. R. Levi b. Ḥayyatha said: They made a mule of bronze and seated him on it and kindled a fire underneath it, and he cried out, 'O idol so-and-so, O idol so-and-so, save me!' And when he saw that it was of no avail, he said, 'I recollect that my father used to read before me the verse, *In thy distress, when all these things are come upon thee . . . He will not fail thee* (Deut. IV, 30 f.). I will call unto Him; if He answers me, it is well; and if not, then it is all one, and all gods are

[1] This verse treats of his healing; his illness is recorded in v. 1.
[2] Lit. 'his actions stained like vinegar'—perhaps a reference to the corrosive powers of acid, and understood here metaphorically.

the same.' At that moment the ministering angels arose and closed all the windows of heaven and appealed to God: 'Lord of the Universe! Wilt Thou accept in repentance a man who set up an idol in the very Temple?' He answered: 'If I do not accept him in repentance, I close the door in the face of all future penitents.' What did the Holy One, blessed be He, do? He dug an opening for his prayer from under the Throne of Glory, where the angels could not reach. That is the meaning of the verse, *And he prayed unto Him; and He was entreated* (wayye'ather)[1] *of him, and heard his supplication* (II Chron. XXXIII, 13). R. Levi commented: In Arabia for *'athira* they say *ḥathira*. AND THEY REACHED HER PARCHED CORN, i.e. he was restored to the throne, as it is said, *And brought him back to Jerusalem to his kingdom* (*ib.*). How did He bring him back? R. Samuel said in the name of R. Aba: He brought him back with a wind, as we say 'who causeth the wind to blow'.[2] AND SHE DID EAT AND WAS SATISFIED AND LEFT THEREOF: he would eat in this world, and in the Messianic age, and in the World to Come.

The fifth interpretation makes it refer to the Messiah. COME HITHER: approach to royal state. AND EAT OF THE BREAD refers to the bread of royalty; AND DIP THY MORSEL IN THE VINEGAR refers to his sufferings, as it is said, *But he was wounded because of our transgressions* (Isa. LIII, 5). AND SHE SAT BESIDE THE REAPERS, for he will be deprived of his sovereignty for a time, as it is said, *For I will gather all nations against Jerusalem to battle; and the city shall be taken* (Zech. XIV, 2). AND THEY REACHED HER PARCHED CORN, means that he will be restored to his throne, as it is said, *And he shall smite the land with the rod of his mouth* (Isa. XI, 4). R. Berekiah said in the name of R. Levi: The future Redeemer will be like the former Redeemer.[3] Just as the former Redeemer revealed himself and later was hidden from them

[1] From *'athar*, to entreat, which is now connected with *ḥathar* 'to dig', as R. Levi points out.

[2] I.e. the same root שוב is applied to the blowing of the wind. Cf. Ps. CXLVII, 18.

[3] Moses.

(and how long was he hidden? Three months, as it is said, *And they met Moses and Aaron* (Ex. V, 20)[1]), so the future Redeemer will be revealed to them, and then be hidden from them. And how long will he be hidden? R. Tanḥuma, in the name of the Rabbis, said: Forty-five days, as it is said, *And from the time that the continual burnt-offering shall be taken away . . . there shall be a thousand two hundred and ninety days. Happy is he that waiteth, and cometh to the thousand three hundred and five and thirty days* (Dan. XII, 11–12).[2] What are these extra days? R. Isaac b. Ḳazarta[3] said on behalf of R. Jonah: These are the forty-five days during which Israel shall pluck salt-wort and eat it, as it is said, *They pluck salt-wort with wormwood* (Job XXX, 4).[4] Where will he lead them? From the land of Israel to the wilderness of Judah, as it is said, *Behold, I will allure her, and bring her into the wilderness* (Hos. II, 16); while some say to the wilderness of Sihon and Og, as it is said, *I will yet again make thee to dwell in tents, as in the days of the appointed season* (*ib.* XII, 10).[5] He who believes in him will live, and he who does not believe will depart to the Gentile nations and they will put him to death.[6] R. Isaac b. Marion said: Finally the Holy One, blessed be He, will reveal Himself to them, and He will rain down manna upon them, *And there is nothing new under the sun* (Eccl. I, 9).[7]

The sixth interpretation makes COME HITHER, etc., refer to Boaz himself.[8] COME HITHER means approach here. AND EAT OF THE BREAD: the bread of the reapers. AND DIP THY MORSEL IN THE VINEGAR, for reapers are wont to dip their bread in vinegar. R. Jonathan said: From this we can infer that dishes prepared with

[1] V. Ex. R. V, 20; the reading there is 'six months'. [2] The difference between the two periods. [3] Probably: the son of a laundress.
[4] This verse is applied to the period immediately preceding the Messianic age, when owing to the great scarcity of food the faithful will eat salt-wort.
[5] It was in the wilderness of Sihon and Og that Balaam blessed the 'tents of Israel' (Num. XXIV, 5)—hence '*tents*' in this verse is understood to refer to that place.
[6] Perhaps meant in a religious sense. There he will die to Judaism.
[7] Whatever is destined to occur in the future Redemption occurred in the first. [8] I.e. the literal meaning.

vinegar are brought into the granaries.[1] AND SHE SAT BESIDE THE REAPERS, actually at their side.[2] AND THEY REACHED HER PARCHED CORN; just a pinch between his two fingers.[3] R. Isaac said: From this we can infer one of two things, that a blessing reposed either in the fingers of that righteous man [Boaz] or in the stomach of that righteous woman[4] [Ruth]; but since it says, AND SHE DID EAT AND WAS SATISFIED AND LEFT THEREOF, it is more probable that the blessing was in the stomach of that righteous woman.

R. Isaac b. Marion said: This verse can teach us that if a man is about to perform a good deed, he should do it with all his heart. For had Reuben known that Scripture would record of him, *And Reuben heard it, and delivered him out of their hand* (Gen. XXXVII, 21), he would have borne Joseph on his shoulder to his father; and had Aaron known that Scripture would record of him, *And also, behold, he cometh forth to meet thee* (Ex. IV, 14), he would have gone forth to meet him with timbrels and dances. And had Boaz known that Scripture would record of him, AND HE REACHED HER PARCHED CORN, AND SHE DID EAT AND WAS SATISFIED AND LEFT THEREOF, he would have fed her with fatted calves. R. Cohen and R. Joshua of Siknin said in the name of R. Levi: In the past when a man performed a good deed, the prophet placed it on record; but nowadays when a man performs a good deed, who records it? Elijah records it and the Messiah and the Holy One, blessed be He, subscribe their seal to it. This is the meaning of the verse, *Then they that feared the Lord spoke with one another; and the Lord hearkened, and heard, and a book of remembrance was written before Him* (Mal. III, 16).

7. AND WHEN SHE WAS RISEN UP TO GLEAN, BOAZ COMMANDED HIS YOUNG MEN, SAYING . . . AND ALSO PULL OUT SOME FOR HER OF PURPOSE

[1] I.e. are liable to tithes. [2] A sign of her modesty. Not among them, but at their side. [3] The word קלי 'parched corn' is connected with קליל 'a little'. [4] Since such a small portion satisfied her.

FROM THE BUNDLES (II, 15–16). R. Joḥanan used to scatter coins about in order that R. Simeon b. Abba might acquire them, and R. Judah used to leave lentils about in order that R. Simeon b. Ḥalafta might acquire them.[1]

8. SO SHE GLEANED IN THE FIELD UNTIL EVEN ... AND IT WAS ABOUT AN EPHAH (*ib.* 17). How much is an *ephah?* R. Joḥanan said: Three *se'ahs*, as we have learnt[2]: the *ephah* is three *se'ahs*. AND SHE TOOK IT UP AND WENT INTO THE CITY.[3]

9. AND HER MOTHER-IN-LAW SAID UNTO HER: WHERE HAST THOU GLEANED TO-DAY? (*ib.* 19). It was taught in the name of R. Joshua: More than the householder does for the poor man does the poor man do for the householder, for Ruth said to Naomi: THE MAN'S NAME FOR WHOM[4] I WROUGHT TO-DAY. She did not say, 'who wrought for me,' but FOR WHOM I WROUGHT. I wrought him many benefits in return for the one morsel of food which he gave me. R. Jose said[5]: *ya'an ubeya'an*[6]; the word *ya'an* (because) has the same letters as *'ani* (a poor man).[7] R. Shiloh of Noveh[8] said: Your wealth depends upon the poor man.[9] R. Naḥman said: It is written, *Because that* (bigelal) *for this thing the Lord thy God will bless thee in all thy work:* (Deut. XV, 10) it [poverty] is a wheel (*galgal*) which comes round to all in the world, like the wheel of a pump[10] which empties that which is full and fills that which is empty. Bar Ḳappara

[1] R. Simeon b. Abba and R. Simeon b. Ḥalafta were extremely poor, and in this way they were able to help them, as Boaz did Ruth—their pride would not have permitted them to accept charity.

[2] Mishnah, Men. VII, 1.

[3] This quotation is apparently pointless, not being followed by any comment. 'E.J. explains that R. Joḥanan means that though three *se'ahs* is normally too much for one person to carry, she did so, thus proving that she was very strong.

[4] The literal translation is '*with whom*'.

[5] Cf. Lev. R. XXXIV, 9, in the name of R. Cohen.

[6] *Because, even because*, Lev. XXVI, 43.

[7] The word יען can be transposed to עני 'a poor man', i.e. all the calamities in this chapter come as a result of neglect of the poor.

[8] A town in Galilee, east of Gadara. V. Neub. *Geog.*, p. 245.

[9] If you give charity, you will retain your wealth.

[10] Made of a revolving wheel with buckets attached which alternately fill and empty.

said: There is no man who does not come to this state [poverty], and if he does not his son does, and if not his son, his grandson.

It was taught: R. Eliezer b. Jacob said: The vengeance taken of the idolatrous nations will be on account of Israel, while the vengeance taken of Israel will be on account of their poor. The vengeance taken of the idolatrous nations will be on account of Israel, as it is said, *And I will lay My vengeance upon Edom by the hand of My people Israel* (Ezek. XXV, 14); the vengeance taken of Israel will be on account of their poor, as it is said, *And he cry unto the Lord against thee, and it be sin in thee* (Deut. XV, 9).

R. Abun said: The poor man stands at your door, and the Holy One, blessed be He, stands at his right hand. If you give unto him, He who stands at his right hand will bless you, but if not, He will exact punishment from you, as it is said, *Because He standeth at the right hand of the needy* (Ps. CIX, 31).

R. Abbahu said: We should be grateful even to the impostors among them. It has been stated: R. Joḥanan and Resh Laḳish went down to bathe in the public baths of Tiberias, and a poor man accosted them. He said to them, 'Give me something.' They answered, 'When we come out we will give it.' When they came out they found him dead. They said: 'Since we did not assist him during his life, let us attend to him after his death.' When they arose from washing his body, they found a purse of *dinars* by him, and they said: 'It is well.' Whereupon R. Abbahu said: 'We should be grateful even to the impostors among them, for were it not for the impostors among them, were a man to see a beggar begging alms and refuse him, he would be punished with death immediately.'

10. AND NAOMI SAID UNTO HER DAUGHTER-IN-LAW: BLESSED BE HE OF THE LORD, WHO HATH NOT LEFT OFF HIS KINDNESS TO THE LIVING (II, 20), for he has fed and sustained the living, AND TO THE DEAD, in that he occupied himself with their

shrouds.[1] AND NAOMI SAID UNTO HER: THE MAN IS NIGH OF KIN UNTO US, ONE OF OUR NEAR KINSMEN (*ib.*). R. Samuel B. Naḥman said: Boaz was one of the notables of his generation, and yet the woman made him her relative,[2] as it is said, THE MAN IS NIGH OF KIN UNTO US.

11. AND RUTH THE MOABITESS SAID: YEA, HE SAID UNTO ME: THOU SHALT KEEP FAST BY MY YOUNG MEN (II, 21). R. Ḥanin b. Levi said: In truth she was a Moabitess,[3] for Boaz said to her, *Abide here fast by my maidens* (II, 8), while she said, BY MY YOUNG MEN.

SO SHE KEPT FAST BY THE MAIDENS OF BOAZ TO GLEAN UNTO THE END OF BARLEY HARVEST AND OF WHEAT HARVEST (*ib.* 23). R. Samuel b. Naḥman said: From the beginning of the barley harvest until the end of the wheat harvest is three months. AND SHE DWELT WITH HER MOTHER-IN-LAW. AND NAOMI HER MOTHER-IN-LAW SAID UNTO HER: MY DAUGHTER, SHALL I NOT SEEK REST FOR THEE . . . AND NOW IS THERE NOT BOAZ OUR KINSMAN (II, 23–III, 2).[4]

12. WASH THYSELF THEREFORE, AND ANOINT THEE (*ib.* 3). WASH THYSELF clean of thine idolatry. AND ANOINT THEE refers to good deeds and righteous conduct. AND PUT THY RAIMENT UPON THEE. Was she then naked? It must refer to Sabbath garments. It was from this verse that R. Ḥanina said: A man should have two sets of garments, one for weekdays and one for

[1] The Midrash suggests that Boaz paid for the shrouds of Mahlon and Chilion. Cf. Midrash to I, 8 (*supra*, II, 14).
[2] I.e. she did not say 'we are related to him', but 'he is related to us'. The reading of the Yalkuṭ suggests that she did this because she was conscious that she had conferred a favour upon him by accepting his charity, as stated above (Y.'A.).
[3] She still harboured impure thoughts.
[4] Cf. *supra*, II, 8. M.K. suggests that Boaz had to wait three months before he could marry her (thus coupling this with R. Samuel b. Naḥman's remark), so as to be sure that she was not pregnant by her former husband. (Assuming that they left Moab immediately after his death.)

Sabbath. And so did R. Simlai expound publicly, whereupon the scholars wept and said: As our raiment on weekdays, so is our raiment on the Sabbath. He said to them: It is nevertheless necessary to change.[1] AND GET THEE DOWN TO THE THRESHING-FLOOR. She said to her, 'My merits will descend with you.'[2] Another interpretation of AND GET THEE DOWN TO THE THRESHING-FLOOR: from this we learn that one should make a threshing-floor in the lowest part of the city. It was stated: R. Simeon b. Ḥalafta purchased a field from R. Ḥiyya. He said to him, 'How much does it produce?' He answered: 'One hundred *kor*.' He sowed it but it produced less than a hundred, and he complained to R. Ḥiyya saying, 'Did not the Master say that it would produce a hundred *kor*, [and it has produced less]?' He answered, 'It is so!' He said to him, 'But it has produced less?' He asked him, 'Where did you set up the threshing-floor?' He answered, 'In the highest point of the city.' R. Ḥiyya retorted: 'Is it not written, AND GET THEE *DOWN* TO THE THRESHING-FLOOR?' All the same, he sifted the chaff and it produced the remainder.

13. AND IT SHALL BE WHEN HE LIETH DOWN, THAT THOU SHALT MARK THE PLACE . . . AND SHE SAID UNTO HER: ALL THAT THOU SAYEST UNTO ME I WILL DO (*ib.* 4 f.). The word *elai* (to me) is a *ḳ'ri*, but not a *ketib*.[3] Ruth said to her, 'But perhaps one of those dogs[4] will come and join me? Nevertheless it is for me to find a way to fulfil your words.'[5]

14. AND SHE WENT DOWN UNTO THE THRESHING-FLOOR (*ib.* 6). It is written concerning Moab: *I know his wrath, saith the Lord; but it is not so; his lies did not so effect it* (Jer. XLVIII, 30).[6] R. Ḥanina b. Papa, R. Simon,

[1] The same garment may be worn differently.
[2] The *ketib* is וירדתי 'and *I* will go down'.
[3] It does not occur in the written text, but is a Massoretic addition.
[4] Fig. 'base fellows'. [5] Without the words '*to me*', it can be understood that Naomi continually urged Ruth against her will; the addition marks Ruth's reluctant agreement. [6] This translation lends itself more to the Midrash.

and the Rabbis explained the verse. R. Ḥanina said: The first impregnation[1] of Moab was not for worthy motives, but for adultery, as it is said, *And Israel abode in Shittim, and the people began to commit harlotry with the daughters of Moab* (Num. XXV, 1); '*His lies shall not so effect it,*' [viz.] for adultery, but for worthy motives instead. Now it does not say, 'and it effected his lies,' but '*they* [sc. his lies] *did not so effect it,*' [viz.] for worthy motives, but for adultery instead, [as it is said,] '*and Israel abode,*' etc. The Rabbis say: The first impregnation was for adultery, but later it was for worthy motives, as it is said, AND SHE WENT DOWN TO THE THRESHING-FLOOR AND DID, etc.[2]

15. AND WHEN BOAZ HAD EATEN AND DRUNK, AND HIS HEART WAS GOOD (III, 7).[3] Why was his heart good? Because he recited the grace after meals.[4] Another interpretation: AND HIS HEART WAS GOOD: he ate different kinds of sweet things after his meal, as they accustom the tongue to the Torah.[5] Another interpretation of AND HIS HEART WAS GOOD: he occupied himself with the words of the Torah, as it is said, *The law of thy mouth is good to me* (Ps. CXIX, 72).[6] Another interpretation: AND HIS HEART WAS GOOD: he sought a wife, as it is said, *Whoso findeth a wife findeth a good thing* (Prov. XVIII, 22). HE WENT TO LIE DOWN AT THE END OF THE HEAP OF CORN. R. Judah Nesiah[7] inquired of R. Phinehas b. Ḥama: Boaz was one of the notables of his generation, and yet it says that HE WENT TO LIE DOWN AT THE END OF THE HEAP OF

[1] The word עברה '*wrath*' is connected with עיבור 'impregnation'.
[2] It is impossible to make sense of this passage as it stands. V. the reading in Gen. R. LI, 10, and notes *ad loc.*
[3] E.V. '*merry*'.
[4] This probably means simply that he was in a satisfied mood, having dined and duly given thanks to God. Maybe the Midrash points out that the passage does not mean that he was merry, as the word is sometimes used (cf. Est. I, 10), but rather that he had recited Grace and been inspired with devoutness (Y.'A.).
[5] Probably, to the study of the Torah, this too being sweet—actual sweetness leading to metaphorical or spiritual sweetness.
[6] E.V. '*Better to me*'. [7] I.e. R. Judah II, ha-Nasi.

CORN: He answered him: That generation was steeped in immorality, and they used to pay harlots from the threshing-floors, as it is said, *Rejoice not, O Israel, unto exaltation, like the peoples . . . Thou hast loved a harlot's hire upon every threshing-floor* (Hos. IX, 1). And righteous men do not act so. Moreover, because the righteous spurn ill-gotten gain, their possessions are precious to them.[1]

[1] He lay there to prevent the corn being used for immoral purposes.

CHAPTER VI

1. *At midnight I will rise to give thanks to Thee because of Thy righteous judgments* (Ps. CXIX, 62). R. Phinehas commented in the name of R. Eliezer b. Jacob: A harp and lyre were suspended over David's head, and when the hour of midnight came he used to rise and play on them. R. Levi said: A harp was suspended, etc.[1] '*Because of Thy righteous judgments*,' the judgments which Thou didst bring upon Pharaoh, as it is said, *And the Lord plagued Pharaoh and his house with great plagues* (Gen. XII, 17),[2] and the righteousness which Thou wroughtest with Abraham and Sarah.[3]

Another interpretation: '*Because of Thy righteous ordinances*,' because of the judgments which Thou didst bring upon the Egyptians and the righteousness which Thou wroughtest with our forefathers in Egypt, for they possessed no virtues or good deeds to justify their redemption, but Thou didst give them two commandments with which they should occupy themselves and be redeemed, and these are the blood of the Paschal lamb and the blood of circumcision. R. Levi said: In that night the two bloods mingled, as it is said, *And when I passed by thee, and saw thee wallowing in thy blood, I said unto thee: In thy blood, live; yea, I said unto thee: In thy blood, live* (Ezek. XVI, 6).[4] Another interpretation: '*Because of Thy righteous ordinances*'; the judgments which Thou didst bring upon the Ammonites and Moabites, and the righteousness which Thou wroughtest for my grandfather and grandmother,[5] for had he hastily cursed her, but once,

[1] V. Lam. R. II, 22, and Ber. 3*b* for the passage in full.
[2] V. Ex. R. XVIII, 2.
[3] The verse is translated 'because of Thy judgments and righteous deeds' which are regarded as two opposing concepts, 'judgments' referring to strict justice, and 'righteous deeds' to charity and lovingkindness (Y.'A.).
[4] According to the Rabbis it was only on that night that they circumcised themselves.
[5] Really 'great-grandfather and great-grandmother', Boaz and Ruth—the speaker is David, who was descended from them.

whence should I have come? But Thou didst inspire him to bless her, as it is said, BLESSED BE THOU OF THE LORD, MY DAUGHTER (III, 10). *The fear of man bringeth a snare; but whoso putteth his trust in the Lord shall be set up on high* (Prov. XXIX, 25). Once when R. Akiba visited Rome, he said to a member of his household, 'Go out and purchase me something from the market-place which is acceptable to all.' He went and brought fowls. He said to him, 'Why have you tarried so long? To catch them?' He answered, 'Yes, because they affright men.'[1] R. Akiba thereupon applied to him the verse, '*The fear of man bringeth a snare.*'[2] [The verse also refers to] the fear which Jacob caused Isaac to fear,[3] as it is written, *And Isaac trembled very exceedingly* (Gen. XXVII, 33), and he might easily have cursed him, but '*Whoso putteth his trust in the Lord shall be set up on high*', and God put it in his heart to bless him, as it is said, *Yea, he shall be blessed* (*ib.*).

[It may also refer to] the fear which Ruth caused Boaz to fear, as it is written, AND IT CAME TO PASS AT MIDNIGHT, THAT THE MAN WAS STARTLED (III, 8), and he might easily have cursed her, but '*Whoso putteth his trust in the Lord shall be set up on high*'. But God put it in his heart to bless her, as it is said, BLESSED BE THOU OF THE LORD, MY DAUGHTER (*ib.* 10).

AND TURNED HIMSELF. She clung to him[4] like ivy, and he began to finger her hair. 'Spirits have no hair,' he thought, so he said, 'WHO ART THOU? (*ib.* 9), a woman or a spirit?' She answered, 'A woman.' 'A maiden or a married woman?' She answered, 'A maiden.' 'Art thou clean or unclean?'[5] She answered, 'Clean.' AND BEHOLD A WOMAN, purest of women, LAY AT HIS FEET (*ib.* 8), as it is said,[6] AND HE SAID: WHO ART

[1] This is the literal translation. Commentaries explain: they run away to places (e.g. among rocks) where men are afraid to follow them.

[2] Probably humorously: because of man's fear (to follow them into dangerous places), they set snares instead. [3] Gen. R. LXVII, 1.

[4] The root לפת means 'to cling', and the word is therefore translated 'and he was clung to'. [5] In a ritual sense.

[6] 'E.J. deletes 'as it is said'.

THOU? AND SHE ANSWERED: I AM RUTH THY HANDMAID.

R. Berekiah said: Cursed be the wicked! Elsewhere[1] it is said, *She caught him by his garment, saying: Lie with me* (Gen. XXXIX, 12), but here, she said, SPREAD THEREFORE THY SKIRT OVER THY HANDMAID.

2. AND HE SAID: BLESSED BE THOU OF THE LORD, MY DAUGHTER. THOU HAST SHOWN MORE KINDNESS IN THE END THAN AT THE BEGINNING (*ib.* 10). R. Joḥanan and Resh Laḳish and the Rabbis commented on this verse. R. Joḥanan said: One should never keep back from going to an elder to be blessed. Boaz was eighty years of age, and had not been vouchsafed children. But when that righteous woman prayed for him, he was immediately vouchsafed, as it is said, *And Naomi said unto her daughter-in-law: Blessed be he of the Lord* (Ruth II, 20). Resh Laḳish said: Ruth was forty years of age and had not yet been vouchsafed children as long as she was married to Mahlon. But as soon as that righteous man prayed for her, she was vouchsafed, as it is said, BLESSED BE THOU OF THE LORD, MY DAUGHTER. The Rabbis, however, say: Both of them were vouchsafed children only as a result of the blessings of righteous people, as it is said, *And all the people that were in the gate, and the elders, said: We are witnesses. The Lord make the woman . . . like Rachel and like Leah* (*ib.* IV, 11).[2]

THOU HAST SHOWN MORE KINDNESS IN THE END THAN AT THE BEGINNING, INASMUCH AS THOU DIDST NOT FOLLOW THE YOUNG MEN, WHETHER RICH OR POOR. R. Samuel b. R. Isaac said: A woman prefers a poor young man to a wealthy old man.

3. AND NOW, MY DAUGHTER, FEAR NOT . . . AND NOW IT IS TRUE THAT I AM A NEAR KINSMAN; HOWBEIT THERE IS A KINSMAN NEARER THAN I (III, 11 f.). The Rabbis and R. Joshua b. Levi commented

[1] In the case of Potiphar's wife.
[2] And through that blessing were children granted to him.

on this. The Rabbis were of the opinion that Tob,[1] Elimelech, and Boaz were brothers, while R. Joshua said that Salmon,[2] Elimelech, and Tob were brothers. It was objected to him: But it is written, *Which was our* brother *Elimelech's* (*ib.* IV, 3)? He answered: A man does not refrain from calling his uncle brother.

4. TARRY THIS NIGHT (III, 13). This night you will spend without a husband, but you will not be without a husband for another night.

AND IT SHALL BE IN THE MORNING, THAT IF HE WILL PERFORM UNTO THEE THE PART OF A KINSMAN, WELL; LET HIM DO THE KINSMAN'S PART; BUT IF HE BE NOT WILLING TO DO THE PART OF A KINSMAN TO THEE, THEN WILL I DO THE PART OF A KINSMAN TO THEE (*ib.* 13).[3]

R. Meir was sitting and expounding the Law in the School of Tiberias, and Elisha his teacher[4] passed by the street on horseback on the Sabbath. They said to R. Meir, 'Look! Elisha your master is passing by in the street.' He went out to him, and Elisha said to him, 'With what were you occupied?' He said to him, 'With the verse, *So the Lord blessed the latter end of Job more than his beginning*' (Job XLII, 12). He said to him, 'And what did you say concerning it?' He answered '"*He blessed him*" means that he doubled his wealth.' Elisha responded: 'Your teacher, Akiba, did not explain thus, but he explained "*And the Lord blessed the latter end of Job more than his beginning*" that he was blessed at the end *because of*[5] the repentance and the good deeds which were to his

[1] V. 13 is translated *If he will perform unto thee the part of a kinsman, well.* The word *tob* 'well' is regarded as the name of a man, the eldest of the three brothers, and thus the nearest kinsman, and the verse is understood as 'If Tob will perform unto thee, etc.'

[2] The father of Boaz (Ruth IV, 21). Thus in his view Elimelech and Tob were his uncles.

[3] The comment on this passage comes at the end of the long story which follows.

[4] Elisha b. Abuya, the famous Rabbi and teacher of Meir, who became an apostate. This story is repeated in Eccl. R. on VII, 8.

[5] R. Akiba translates מראשיתו as '*because of* his beginning'.

credit at the beginning.' He said to him,[1] 'And what else did you expound?' He answered, 'The verse, *Better is the end of a thing than the beginning thereof'* (Eccl. VII, 8). 'And what did you say concerning it?' He answered, 'I said, A man may purchase merchandise in his youth, and lose thereby, and in his old age he makes a profit on it.[2] Another interpretation: "*Better is the end of a thing than the beginning thereof*"; a man may act wickedly in his youth, yet in his old age he may perform good deeds. Another interpretation: "*Better is the end of a thing than the beginning thereof*"; a man may learn Torah in his youth and forget it, but in his old age it returns to him. These are my interpretations of: "*Better is the end of a thing than the beginning thereof.*"' He answered him: 'Akiba, your master, did not expound so, but he explained, *Good is the* end *of a thing, when it is good from its very* commencement.[3] I will give you an example from an incident concerning me personally. My father, Abuyah, was one of the notable men of his generation, and at my circumcision he invited all the notables of Jerusalem, including R. Eliezer and R. Joshua. And when they had eaten and drunk, they sang, some ordinary songs and others alphabetical acrostics.[4] R. Eliezer said to R. Joshua, "They are occupied with their matters[5] while we neglect ours."[6] They began therefore with exposition of the Pentateuch, and from the Pentateuch they went on to the Prophets and from the Prophets to the Hagiographa, and the words of the Pentateuch rejoiced as on the day they were given on Sinai, and fire played round them, for were they not originally given on Sinai in fire, as it is said, *And the mountain burned with fire unto the heart of heaven?* (Deut. IV, 11). [When my father saw this], he said, "Since

[1] Elisha to Meir.
[2] He probably intended to convey some moral teaching with this—Perhaps (as Y.'A. and 'E.J.) that one should never lose hope.
[3] R. Meir with his interpretations wished to persuade Elisha that repentance was effective; Abuyah counters with an exposition that lapses cannot be forgiven.
[4] A favourite form of rhyme, on the model of Psalms CXIX and CXLV.
[5] Profane amusements. [6] Exposition of the Torah.

so great indeed is the power of the Torah, if my son is granted life, I will dedicate him to the Torah." And because his intention was not for the glory of God,[1] my Torah did not remain with me.'

'And what else did you expound?' [continued Elisha. He answered], '*Gold and glass cannot equal it*' (Job XXVIII, 17). He said, 'And what did you say concerning it?' He answered: 'It refers to the words of the Torah which are as difficult to acquire as vessels of gold, and as easily lost as vessels of glass.' He responded: 'Your master Akiba did not expound thus, but he expounded: Just as broken vessels of gold and glass may be repaired, so a scholar who loses his learning may return to it.' At this point, Elisha said to Meir, 'Turn back.' He asked, 'Why?' He answered, 'Up to this point is the Sabbath limit.'[2] He asked, 'Whence do you know?' He answered, 'From the footsteps of my horse which has already traversed two thousand cubits.' Said Meir to him, 'You possess all this wisdom and you will not return?' He responded, 'It is not within my power.' He asked, 'Why?' He answered: 'I was riding on my horse, and was passing by the College on a Day of Atonement which fell on a Sabbath, and I heard a voice break forth and say, "*Return, O backsliding children* (Jer. III, 14). *Return unto Me, and I will return unto you* (Mal. III, 7)—all except Elisha b. Abuyah, who knew My Power, and yet rebelled against Me!"'

How was it that Elisha acted in this manner?[3] They related that once he was sitting and studying in the plain of Gennesaret[4] and he saw a man who ascended to the top of a date-palm and took the dam with the young,[5] and descended safely. At the conclusion of the Sabbath, he saw another man who ascended the tree and took the young, but let the dam go, and when he descended a snake

[1] His intention was that his son should have similar power, which is regarded as an impure motive.
[2] Beyond which one is not permitted to walk on the Sabbath.
[3] Became an apostate.
[4] גינסר, a Hellenisation of Kinnereth on the banks of the sea of Galilee. Cf. Gen. R. XCVIII, 17.
[5] Transgressing the command of Deut. XXII, 6.

stung him and he died. Whereupon he said: It is written, *Thou shalt in any wise let the dam go, but the young thou mayest take unto thyself, that it may be well with thee, and that thou mayest prolong thy days* (Deut. XXII, 7). Where is the goodness, and where the length of days for this man? But he was unaware that R. Akiba had publicly expounded 'That it may be well with thee' in the world which is entirely good, '*And that thou mayest prolong thy days*' in the world of eternity.

Some say that it was when he saw the tongue of R. Judah the Baker[1] in the mouth of a dog. He thereupon said: If this is the reward of the tongue which toiled all its days in the Torah, how much more so the tongue which has not that knowledge and has not toiled! And he said: Since that is so, there is no reward for the righteous, and no resurrection of the dead.

Others say that the reason was that when his mother was pregnant with him she passed by idolatrous temples, and she smelled the dish,[2] and they gave her some of it to eat, and she ate it, and it spread through her like the venom of insects.

After some time Elisha b. Abuyah was taken ill, and they came and told R. Meir, 'Elisha your master is sick.' He went to him and appealed to him, 'Return in penitence.' He said to him, 'Will they accept me after all this?' He responded, 'Is it not written, *Thou turnest man to contrition* (Ps. XC, 3), even when one's life is crushed.'[3] At that, Elisha b. Abuyah burst into tears and died. And R. Meir rejoiced and said, 'It appears that my master passed away in the midst of repentance.' And when they buried him, fire came to consume his grave. They came and told R. Meir, 'The grave of your master is aflame,' and he went and spread his garment over it, and said to him, 'TARRY THIS NIGHT in this world which is all night, AND IT SHALL BE IN THE MORNING, IF THE GOOD

[1] One of the ten martyrs of the Hadrianic persecution.

[2] The reference is to the morbid desire of a pregnant woman to eat what she savours. Cf. Mishnah Yoma, VIII, 4.

[3] דכא means both contrition and crushing (דכדוכה, cf. R.V. '*destruction*').

ONE WILL REDEEM THEE, HE WILL REDEEM THEE.[1] IT SHALL BE IN THE MORNING refers to the world which is all good. IF THE GOOD ONE WILL REDEEM THEE, the GOOD ONE is the Holy One, blessed be He, as it is said, *The Lord is good to all* (Ps. CXLV, 9). BUT IF HE WILL NOT REDEEM THEE, THEN WILL I REDEEM THEE; AS THE LORD LIVETH, LIE HERE TILL THE MORNING,' and the fire subsided. R. Meir's disciples said to him,[2] 'Master, in the World to Come, if they will say to you, "Whom do you desire, your father or your master," what will you answer?' He answered, 'First my father and then my master.' They said to him, 'And will they heed your request?'[3] He answered, 'Is there not a Mishnah to this effect?[4] The case of a scroll may be saved[5] together with the scroll, and the case of phylacteries together with the phylacteries.[6] Elisha will be saved[7] by the merits of his Torah.'

After some time the daughters of Elisha came to beg alms before our Teacher.[8] He quoted, *Let there be none to extend kindness unto him; neither let there be any to be gracious unto his fatherless children* (Ps. CIX, 12), whereupon they[9] said to him, 'Master! Regard not his actions, regard his learning.' At this Rabbi wept, and ordered that they should be given maintenance, and said, 'If one whose Torah was not for the glory of God produced such,[10] how much more so he whose Torah was for the glory of God.'

R. Jose said: Three individuals found their Evil Inclination mastering them, and they fortified themselves against it by taking an oath, namely Joseph, David, and Boaz. Joseph, as it is written, *How then can I do this great*

[1] The Midrash translates Ruth III, 13, in this sense.
[2] When they saw this touching devotion to his master.
[3] To give Elisha a place in Heaven.
[4] Mishnah Shab. XVI, 1. [5] From a fire on the Sabbath.
[6] Although the case is in itself of no religious value, the purpose to which it is put makes it permissible to save it.
[7] From the fires of Gehenna. [8] I.e. R. Judah ha-Nasi.
[9] Either Elisha's daughters, or perhaps R. Judah's disciples.
[10] Either, such disciples, the reference being to R. Meir (Y.'A.); or, such children, Rabbi recognising nobility of character in his daughters (M.K.).

wickedness, and sin against God (Gen. XXXIX, 9). R. Huna said in the name of R. Idi: Is Scripture ever defective?[1] It does not say 'and sin against the Lord' but '*and sin against God*'; he swore to his Evil Inclination and said, 'By God, I will not sin nor do this evil!'[2]

How do we know it of David? Because it is said, *And David said: As the Lord liveth, nay, but the Lord shall smite him* (I Sam. XXVI, 10). To whom did he take this oath? R. Eleazar and R. Samuel b. Naḥman gave different answers. R. Eleazar said: He took an oath to his Evil Inclination; R. Samuel b. Naḥman said: He took an oath to Abishai the son of Zeruiah, saying to him, 'As the Lord liveth, if you touch him, I swear that I will mingle your blood with his.'

How do we know it of Boaz?[3] Because it is said, AS THE LORD LIVETH, LIE DOWN UNTIL THE MORNING. R. Judah and R. Hunya commented on this. R. Judah said: All that night his Evil Inclination contended with him, saying, 'You are unmarried and seek a wife, and she is unmarried and seeks a husband. Arise and have intercourse with her, and make her your wife.' And he took an oath to his Evil Inclination, saying, 'As the Lord liveth, I will not touch her,' and to the woman he said, LIE DOWN UNTIL THE MORNING (III, 13) . . . IF HE WILL PERFORM UNTO THEE THE PART OF A KINSMAN, WELL; LET HIM DO A KINSMAN'S PART (*ib.* 13). R. Hunya said: It is written, *A wise man is strong* (be'oz)*; yea, a man of knowledge increaseth strength* (Prov. XXIV, 5): read not '*be'oz*' (strong), but *Boaz*; '*A wise man is Boaz, and a man of knowledge increaseth strength*,' for he strengthened himself with an oath.

[1] I.e. Scripture is always written so as to convey exactly what it means, though careful examination of its language and phraseology is necessary before this is arrived at.
[2] V. Gen. R. LXXXVII, 5; Lev. R. XXIII, 11, and notes *ad loc.*
[3] The reading here is very faulty and is corrected on the basis of the parallel passage in Lev. R. *loc. cit.*

CHAPTER VII

1. AND SHE LAY AT HIS FEET UNTIL THE MORNING, AND SHE ROSE UP BEFORE ONE COULD DISCERN THE OTHER (III, 14). R. Berekiah said: BEFORE (BE-ṬEREM) is written with an extra *waw*,[1] teaching that she tarried with him for six hours, the numerical equivalent of the letter *waw*.

FOR HE SAID: LET IT NOT BE KNOWN THAT THE WOMAN CAME TO THE THRESHING-FLOOR (*ib.*). To whom did he say this? R. Meir said: To his major-domo. R. Hunya and R. Jeremiah in the name of R. Samuel b. R. Isaac said: All that night Boaz lay stretched out upon his face, and prayed, 'Lord of the Universe, it is revealed and known to Thee that I did not touch her; so may it be Thy will that it be not known that the woman came to the threshing-floor, that the name of Heaven be not profaned through me.'

2. AND HE SAID: BRING THE MANTLE THAT IS UPON THEE (*ib.* 15). BRING (HABI) is written *habah*,[2] teaching that he addressed her in the masculine, that none should notice her. AND HOLD IT, teaches that she girded her loins like a man.[3] AND HE MEASURED SIX MEASURES OF BARLEY, AND LAID IT ON HER. R. Simon said: Bar Ḳappara expounded in Sepphoris[4]: Is it then the custom of a king to betroth a wife with six grains of barley? Or is it the custom of a woman to be betrothed with six *se'ah* of barley?[5] R. Judah

[1] I.e. בטורם instead of בטרם. [2] Masculine instead of הבי feminine. This does not occur in the extant Massorah.

[3] It is not clear how this follows. Perhaps the Midrash holds that the verb *aḥaz* means to seize with strength, hence like a man (Mah.).

[4] Sepphoris. In Upper Galilee. According to the Talmud (Meg. 6*a*), it owes its name to the fact that it is 'perched like a bird' (*ẓippor*) on the top of a mountain'. Seat of Sanhedrin in the time of Rabbi.

[5] The Scriptural text reads literally: And he measured six barleys. Bar Ḳappara holds that he gave her this in order to betroth her, and therefore observes: If it means literally six *grains* of barley, 'surely a king (i.e. Boaz, who was a chief) would not betroth a woman with six grains of barley.' If it means six *measures* (as E.V.), then the ordinary unit of measure was a *se'ah*, but six *se'ah* was a very heavy load.

b. Simon said: The meaning is that as a reward for, AND HE MEASURED SIX BARLEYS AND LAID [THEM] ON HER,[1] he was vouchsafed that there should arise from her six righteous men, each one of them possessing six outstanding virtues, viz. David, Hezekiah, Josiah, Hananiah, Mishael and Azariah,[2] Daniel, and the Messiah. David, as it is said, *Skilful in playing, and a mighty man of valour, and a man of war, and prudent in affairs, and a comely person, and the Lord is with him* (I Sam. XVI, 18); Hezekiah, as it is said, *That the government may be increased, and of peace there be no end, upon the throne of David, and upon his kingdom, to establish it, and to uphold it, through justice and through righteousness* (Isa. IX, 6).[3] *And his name is called Pele-joez-el-gibbor-abi-ad-sar-shalom* (*ib.* 5).[4] Some observe that *l'marbeh* (be increased) is written with a closed *mem.*[5] Josiah, as it is said, *For he shall be as a tree planted by the waters, and that spreadeth out its roots by the river*, etc. (Jer. XVII, 8).[6] Hananiah, Mishael, and Azariah, as it is said, *Youths in whom there was no blemish, but fair to look on, and skilful in all wisdom, and skilful in knowledge, and discerning in thought, and such as had ability* (Dan. I, 4). Daniel, as it is said, *A surpassing spirit, and knowledge, and understanding, interpreting of dreams, and declaring of riddles, and loosing of knots, were found in the same Daniel* (*ib.* V, 12). The Messiah, as it is said, *And the spirit of the Lord shall rest upon him, the spirit of wisdom and understanding*, etc. (Isa. XI, 2).

[1] He answers that in fact it means six barley grains (though he probably gave her more in addition), and these were a hint that she would be blessed by six righteous descendants; Sanh. 93*a*, *b*.

[2] They are regarded as one.

[3] There are six virtues mentioned in this verse, as in the previous verse.

[4] Wonderful, a counsellor, mighty, strong, everlasting Father, Prince of Peace.

[5] The text has 'lacking a *mem*', but it must be corrected as above. It is difficult to see the point of the Midrash. The 'closed' *mem* is that written at the end of a word. The Rabbis maintain that God intended Hezekiah to be the Messiah, but the closed *mem* teaches that he was shut out from that honour because he had not sung God's praises (Sanh. 94*a*).

[6] This is applied to Josiah, since Jeremiah prophesied in his reign and he was the most likely person of whom it might be said ('E.J.).

3. AND HE WENT INTO THE CITY (III, 15). Surely it should have stated that *she* went to the city, yet it says AND HE WENT TO THE CITY? It teaches that he accompanied her lest one of the young men accost her.

4. AND WHEN SHE CAME TO HER MOTHER-IN-LAW, SHE SAID: WHO ART THOU MY DAUGHTER (III, 16). Did she then not recognise her? Yes, but she meant, 'Are you still a virgin or a married woman?' She answered, 'A virgin,' AND SHE TOLD HER ALL THAT THE MAN HAD DONE TO HER (*ib.*).

5. AND SHE SAID: THESE SIX MEASURES OF BARLEY GAVE HE TO ME (III, 17). R. Alexander said: Wherever the children of Israel went, they did not depart therefrom empty-handed. From the spoil of Egypt they did not depart empty-handed, nor did they leave empty-handed the spoil of Sihon and Og, nor did they depart empty-handed from the spoil of the thirty-one kings. The word *reḳam* (empty-handed) occurs in connection with Egypt, as it is said, *And it shall come to pass, that, when ye go, ye shall not go empty-handed*—reḳam (Ex. III, 21). And in connection with the Festival pilgrims, as it is said, *And none shall appear before Me empty-handed*—reḳam (*ib.* XXIII, 15); and in connection with the righteous, as it is said, FOR HE SAID UNTO ME: GO NOT EMPTY-HANDED UNTO THY MOTHER-IN-LAW (III, 17). The word '*reḳam*' which occurs in connection with the righteous is to be compared not to that of Egypt, but to that of the Festival Pilgrims, as we have learnt[1]: The *re'iyyah*-offering must be not less than two pieces of silver in value, and the Festival-offering[2] not less than one *ma'ah* of silver.

6. THEN SAID SHE: SIT STILL MY DAUGHTER . . . FOR THE MAN WILL NOT REST, UNTIL HE

[1] *Mishnah* Ḥag. I, 2. [2] By combining Deut. XVI, 4, and Ex. XXIII, 14, it is deduced that every male Israelite must bring a *re'iyyah* ('seeing'-offering) and a peace-offering. It is a small amount, unlike the 'spoil of Egypt', and it was this that Ruth brought.

HAVE FINISHED THE THING (*ib.* 18). R. Huna said in the name of R. Samuel b. Isaac: The yes of the righteous is yes, and their no, no, as it is said, FOR THE MAN WILL NOT REST UNTIL HE HAVE FINISHED THE THING THIS DAY.

7. NOW BOAZ WENT UP TO THE GATE, AND SAT HIM DOWN THERE; AND, BEHOLD, THE NEAR KINSMAN OF WHOM BOAZ SPOKE CAME BY (IV, 1). Was he then standing waiting behind the gate?[1] R. Samuel b. Naḥman answered: Had he been at the uttermost ends of the earth, the Holy One, blessed be He, would have caused him to fly and would have brought him there in order that that righteous man should not grieve while sitting there. R. Berekiah said: Thus did these great men, R. Eliezer and R. Joshua, expound. R. Eliezer said: Boaz played his part, and Ruth played hers, and Naomi played hers, whereupon the Holy One, blessed be He, said, 'I too must play Mine.' AND HE SAID: HO, *PELONI-ALMONI*![2] TURN ASIDE, SIT DOWN HERE (*ib.*). R. Joshua said: His name was Peloni-Almoni. R. Samuel b. Naḥman said: He was ignorant (*ilem*)[3] of the words of the Torah. He said: 'The former ones[4] died only because they took them[5] to wife; shall I then go and take her? Heaven forfend that I should take her; I will not contaminate my seed,[6] I will not introduce a disqualification into my children.' But he was unaware of the new law already enacted, 'Ammonite but not Ammonitess, Moabite but not Moabitess.'

8. AND HE TOOK TEN MEN OF THE ELDERS OF THE CITY, AND SAID: SIT YE DOWN HERE (*ib.* 2). R. Alexander said: From this we infer that an inferior has no right to take a seat until his superior grants him permission. R. Phinehas said: From this we learn that this

[1] The coincidence is so striking. [2] An anonymous appellation, translated as '*such an one*' (E.V.). [3] Lit. 'dumb'—he had no mouth to interpret the relevant verse (Radal). [4] Mahlon and Chilion. [5] Orpah and Ruth, Moabitish women. [6] Produce half-breeds.

house[1] appoints elders at banquets.[2] R. Eleazar b. R. Jose said: Hence we learn that the blessing of the bridegroom requires a quorum of ten. R. Judan b. Pazzi said: And not only if a bachelor marries a virgin, but even the marriage of a widower to a widow[3] requires a quorum of ten.

9. AND HE SAID UNTO THE NEAR KINSMAN: NAOMI . . . SELLETH THE PARCEL OF LAND, WHICH WAS OUR BROTHER ELIMELECH'S; AND I THOUGHT TO DISCLOSE IT UNTO THEE, SAYING: . . . IF THOU WILT REDEEM IT, REDEEM IT (*ib.* 3 f.)—this he said to the kinsman BUT IF IT WILL NOT BE REDEEMED—this he said to the Beth din.[4] THEN TELL ME THAT I MAY KNOW, that you should not say 'I have a wife and children, but I will take her into my house, on condition that I need not marry her.' When the kinsman heard this, he said, 'Certainly! I WILL REDEEM IT,' whereupon Boaz said, 'Ruth is lost to me.'[5]

10. THEN SAID BOAZ: WHAT DAY THOU BUYEST THE FIELD OF THE HAND OF NAOMI—HAST THOU ALSO BOUGHT OF RUTH THE MOABITESS, THE WIFE OF THE DEAD (*ib.* 5). The *ketib* is *ḳanithi* (*I* have bought). This corroborates the view expressed by R. Samuel b. Naḥman, that he was ignorant of the words of the Torah, saying: 'The former ones died only because they took them to wife, shall I then go and take her? Heaven forfend that I should take her; I will not contaminate my seed, I will not introduce a disqualification into my children.' But he was unaware of the new law which had already been enacted, 'Ammonite but not Ammonitess, Moabite, but not Moabitess.'[6]

11. NOW THIS WAS THE CUSTOM IN FORMER TIME IN ISRAEL CONCERNING REDEEMING AND

[1] Sc. the Sanhedrin (Y.'A., 'E.J., and Jer.). [2] 'E.J.: to be present at banquets, to check unseemly levity. Since presumably it was at the wedding banquet. [3] As Boaz and Ruth.
[4] Since it is in the passive. The Beth din here are the ten elders.
[5] Emendation proposed by Radal.
[6] V. *supra*, 7. He said, according to the *ketib*, 'Shall I then buy?'

CONCERNING EXCHANGING, TO CONFIRM ALL THINGS (*ib.* 7). R. Ḥanina applied this verse to Israel. Just as at first Israel uttered praise for their redemption, as it is said, *This is my God, and I will glorify Him* (Ex. XV, 2), so [did they later praise] for the exchange, as it is said, *Thus they exchanged their glory for the likeness of an ox that eateth grass* (Ps. CVI, 20). There is nothing more repulsive and abominable and uncouth than an ox when it is munching grass. Formerly they used to acquire the title to a purchase by means of a shoe or sandal, as it is said, A MAN DREW OFF HIS SHOE, but later they acquired the title by means of *ḳeẓaẓah*.[1] What is *ḳeẓaẓah?* R. Jose b. Abin answered: If a man sold his field to a Gentile, his relatives used to bring barrels full of parched corn and nuts and break them open in the presence of children, and the children would gather them and proclaim, 'So-and-so is cut off from his inheritance.' If it was returned to him, they used to say, 'So-and-so has returned to his inheritance.' And likewise[2] if a man married a woman who was not fitting for him, his relatives used to bring barrels full of parched corn and nuts and break them open in the presence of children, and the children would gather them and proclaim 'So-and-so is lost to his family.' When he divorced her, they used to say, 'So-and-so has returned to his family.' At a still later period they again acquired a title with a shoe or a sandal, A MAN DREW OFF HIS SHOE AND GAVE IT TO HIS NEIGHBOUR, and at a still later period they acquired title by payment of money, by a deed or by *ḥaẓaḳah*.[3] And all three are referred to in one scriptural verse: *Men shall buy fields for money*—that is purchase by money; *And subscribe the deeds, and seal them* refers to the witnesses to the deed; *and call witnesses* (Jer. XXXII, 44), that is, witnesses to the *ḥaẓaḳah*. R. Jose said in the name of R. Joḥanan: Money cannot be acquired with less than the value of a *peruṭah*,[4] nor can land be acquired with

[1] Lit. 'cutting off'. [2] Keth. 28*b*. [3] A legal term, possession based on undisturbed possession, usually three years, B.B. III, 1, or on some act such as levelling, breaking. [4] The smallest coin of bronze. Money, too, was the object of purchase; v. B.M. 44*a*.

less than the value of a *peruṭah*. The statement of R. Ḥanina contradicts this, since R. Ḥanina said[1]: The *sheḳel* mentioned in the Pentateuch is a *sela'*; in the Prophets it is a *liṭra*, in the Hagiographa it is a *centenarium*.[2] R. Judan b. Pazzi said: With the exception of the *sheḳels* of Ephron,[3] which were *centenaria*.[4] But the two statements cannot be compared,[5] since in this connection it says *keseph* (money, or silver), while R. Ḥanina speaks of *sheḳels*.

But R. Joḥanan's statement does disagree with R. Eliezer, since R. Eliezer used to say that the act of walking through a field establishes the title, as it has been taught[6]: If he walked in the field whether through the length or the breadth thereof, he has acquired as far as he walked—these are the words of R. Eliezer. Sages, however, say: He cannot acquire possession until he has performed a *ḥazaḳah*.[7] But all are in agreement that if a man sells a pathway[8] to his fellow, and he walks in it, he has taken possession.

12. SO THE NEAR KINSMAN SAID UNTO BOAZ: BUY IT FOR THYSELF; AND HE DREW OFF HIS SHOE (IV, 8). Whose shoe? Rab and Levi disagreed. One said the shoe of Boaz, while the other said the shoe of the kinsman. It is more probable that he who says the shoe of Boaz is correct, for it is usual for the purchaser to give the pledge.

There is a similar uncertainty in the verse *And Ahijah laid hold of the new garment* (I Kings XI, 30). Whose garment? Rab and Levi disagreed. One said the garment of Jeroboam, while the other said the garment of Ahijah. R. Samuel b. R. Naḥman said: It is probable that he who

[1] Bek. 50*a*. Gen. R. LVIII, 7. [2] I.e. 100 *sheḳels*—Hence the money (lit. 'silver') referred to in Jeremiah. [3] Gen. XXIII, 16.
[4] The Rabbis regard Ephron as a type of the wicked man who 'says much, but does little'. He spoke as though he were making Abraham a gift of the field, but he exacted an extortionate amount.
[5] That of R. Joḥanan and that of R. Ḥanina.
[6] B.B. 100*a*. [7] I.e. some act like levelling or breaking.
[8] Emended text as in Jer. ('E.J.). Cur. edd. 'field' is obviously an error, since that is precisely the point of controversy.

says the garment of Ahijah is correct, since it is natural for the righteous to rend their garments when there is schism in the kingdom of the House of David.

Similarly the verse, *And as Samuel turned about to go away, he laid hold of the skirt of his robe, and it rent* (I Sam. XV, 27). Whose robe? Rab and Levi disagree; one says the skirt of Saul, while the other says the skirt of Samuel. But reason suggests that he who says the skirt of Samuel is correct, since it is the custom of the righteous to rend their garments when their plans do not turn out well.[1] Similarly with the verse, *Neither did Jeroboam recover strength again in the days of Ahijah; and the Lord smote him and he died* (II Chron. XIII, 20).[2] R. Samuel[3] said: You would think from this verse that it was Jeroboam who was smitten. In fact, it was Ahijah who was smitten. And why was Ahijah smitten? Because he rendered the children of Israel unrecognisable, as it is said, *The show of their countenance doth witness against them* (Isa. III, 9). R. Aḥa said: Because he set guards over them for three days until their appearance changed [and they became unrecognisable], as we have learnt[4]: Testimony[5] may be given only on the face with the nose. R. Joḥanan and Resh Laḳish [gave other reasons]. R. Joḥanan said: Because he publicly gave vent to his suspicions about them, as it is said, *And there are with you the golden calves* (II Chron. XIII, 8). Resh Lakish said: Because he insulted the honour of Ahijah the Shilonite, as it is said, *And there were gathered unto him vain men, base fellows* (*ib.* 7), calling Ahijah the Shilonite a base fellow. The Rabbis say: Because there came idolatry into his power and he did not destroy it. That is the meaning of the verse, *And Ahijah pursued after Jeroboam, and took cities from him, Bethel with the towns thereof* (*ib.* 19), and it is written, *And he*[6] *set the one*[7] *in Beth-el* (I Kings XII, 29). And we may deduce from this an

[1] It was Samuel who anointed Saul. [2] Was Jeroboam or Ahijah smitten? [3] B. Naḥman. V. Lev. R. XXXIII, 5. [4] B.M. 27*b*.
[5] Of the identification of a corpse, to allow the wife to remarry.
[6] Jeroboam.
[7] The Golden Calf. Hence Ahijah captured it, but did not destroy it.

a fortiori argument; if a king who insults a king is smitten, how much more so a commoner who insults a commoner![1]

13. AND ALL THE PEOPLE THAT WERE IN THE GATE, AND THE ELDERS, SAID: WE ARE WITNESSES. THE LORD MAKE THE WOMAN THAT IS COME INTO THY HOUSE LIKE RACHEL AND LIKE LEAH (IV, 11). R. Berekiah[2] said: The majority of those sitting[3] were descendants of Leah, so he mentions Rachel first. R. Abba b. Kahana said: Rachel was the chief wife of Jacob, as it is said, *But Rachel was barren* (Gen. XXIX, 31). [Read not *'akarah'* (barren) but] *'ikarah* (the chief one). R. Simeon b. Yoḥai taught: Since they spake against Rachel,[4] therefore all Jacob's descendants are ascribed to her, as it is written, *Rachel weeping for her children* (Jer. XXXI, 15). And not only to her, but even to her son, as it is said, *It may be that the Lord, the God of hosts, will be gracious unto the remnant of Joseph* (Amos V, 15). And not only to her son, but even to her grandson, as it is said, *Is Ephraim a darling son unto Me? Is he a child that is dandled?* (Jer. XXXI, 20).[5]

14. AND LET THY HOUSE BE AS THE HOUSE OF PEREZ . . . OF THE SEED WHICH THE LORD SHALL GIVE THEE OF THIS WOMAN (IV, 12). They said: 'May all the children which the Holy One, blessed be He, will give you be from this righteous woman.' Similarly, *And Isaac entreated the Lord for*[6] *his wife, because she was barren* (Gen. XXV, 21). What is the meaning of '*opposite his wife*'? It teaches that Isaac prostrated himself in one corner, and Rebekah in the other, and he said, 'Lord of the Universe, may all the children which Thou art destined to grant me be of this righteous woman.' Similarly, *And Eli would bless Elkanah and his wife* (I Sam. II, 20). He

[1] V. Gen. R. LXV, 20, and notes *ad loc.* on the whole passage.
[2] Cf. Gen. R. LXXI, 2. [3] In the presence of Boaz. In order to equalise matters, he mentions Rachel first. [4] Sneered at her because she was barren. [5] Ephraim, the son of Joseph, the son of Rachel, is mentioned as synonymous with Israel. [6] Lit. 'opposite'.

blessed them, saying, 'May all the children which the Holy One, blessed be He, will give you be of this righteous woman.'

SO BOAZ TOOK RUTH, AND SHE BECAME HIS WIFE; AND HE WENT IN UNTO HER, AND THE LORD GAVE HER CONCEPTION (IV, 13). R. Simeon b. Laḳish said: She lacked the main portion of the womb, but the Holy One, blessed be He, shaped a womb for her.[1]

15. AND THE WOMEN SAID UNTO NAOMI: BLESSED BE THE LORD, WHO HATH NOT LEFT THEE THIS THIS DAY WITHOUT A NEAR KINSMAN (*ib.* 14). Just as this day holds dominion in the skies, so shall your seed produce one who shall hold dominion and rule over Israel for ever.[2] R. Ḥunya said: It was as a result of the blessings of those women that the line of David was not cut off entirely in the days of Athaliah.[3] R. Tanḥuma said in the name of R. Samuel: Elsewhere it is written, *That we may preserve seed of our father* (Gen. XIX, 32). It is not written 'son', but '*seed*'; that seed which comes from another place. Who is thus referred to? The Messiah.[4]

16. AND HE SHALL BE UNTO THEE A RESTORER OF LIFE, AND A NOURISHER OF THINE OLD AGE; FOR THY DAUGHTER-IN-LAW, WHO LOVETH THEE, WHO IS BETTER TO THEE THAN SEVEN SONS, HATH BORNE HIM (IV, 15). R. Judah and R. Nehemiah commented on this. R. Judah said: Better than the seven chiefs of fathers' households who are mentioned later, viz. *Ozem the sixth, David the seventh* (I Chron. II, 15).[5] R. Nehemiah said: Better than the seven who are mentioned here, viz. Perez, Hezron, Ram, Amminadab, Nahshon, Salmon, and Boaz (Ruth IV, 18–21).

[1] This is his explanation of the unusual phrase *The Lord gave her conception*. Cf. Gen. R. LXIII, 5, for this and the preceding passages.
[2] The Messiah of the House of David. [3] II Kings XI.
[4] Descendant through Ruth of Moab, of whose incestuous birth the verse speaks. [5] Sons of Jesse.

CHAPTER VIII

1. R. Abba b. Kahana opened [his exposition with the verse], *Tremble, and sin not* (Ps. IV, 5). David said to the Holy One, blessed be He, 'How long will they rage[1] against me and say, "Is he not of tainted descent? Is he not a descendant of Ruth the Moabitess?" *Commune with your own heart upon your bed* (*ib.*). Ye also, are ye not descended from two sisters?[2] Look upon your own genealogy *and be still* (*ib.*). And Tamar who married your ancestor Judah[3]—is it not a tainted descent? She was but a descendant of Shem the son of Noah.[4] Have you then an honourable descent?'

R. Jacob b. Ahijah said: [The meaning of this verse is]: Fight against your [Evil] Inclination and sin not. The Rabbis explain: Anger your Inclination[5] and sin not.

THESE ARE THE GENERATIONS OF PEREZ (IV, 18). R. Abba said: Wherever the word *eleh* (these are) occurs, it invalidates the preceding; *we-eleh* (*and* these are) adds to the preceding.[6]

AND HEZRON BEGOT RAM (IV, 19). But was not Jerahmeel the elder son, as it is written, *The sons also of Hezron, there were born unto him: Jerahmeel, and Ram, and Chelubai* (I Chron. II, 9)? [Jerahmeel is omitted] because he married a Canaanitish woman in order to adorn himself with her, as it is written, *And Jerahmeel had another wife, whose name was Atarah* (I Chron. II, 26).[7]

AND RAM BEGOT AMMINADAB; AND AMMINADAB BEGOT NAHSHON, AND NAHSHON BEGOT SALMON (IV, 19, 20). [Why is he called Salmon?][8] Because up to

[1] רגזו '*tremble*' also means 'rage'. [2] Rachel and Leah.
[3] Presumably he is addressing members of his own tribe of Judah.
[4] The point is obscure. M.K.: This alone was to her credit, but apart from that her union with Judah was a forbidden one. 'E.J.: Since she was of such distinguished descent, her forbidden union with Judah was all the more reprehensible. The Yalḳuṭ on Psalms omits it altogether.
[5] By refusing to do his bidding.
[6] V. Ex. R. XXX, 3, for the whole passage. [7] 'Adornment.'
[8] V. 20 and I Chron. II, 11, call him Salma; v. 21, Salmon.

him they formed ladders (*sulamoth*) of princes, from him onwards they formed ladders of kings.[1]

R. Isaac opened his exposition with the verse *Then said I: Lo, I am come* (Ps. XL, 8). I ought to have sung a song that I have come, since the word *az* (lo!) refers to song, as it is said, *Then* (az) *sang Moses* (Ex. XV, 1). I was included in the verse *An Ammonite and a Moabite shall not come into the assembly of the Lord* (Deut. XXIII, 4), but I have come *with the roll of a book which is prescribed for me* (Ps. *loc. cit.*). '*With the roll*'[2] refers to the verse, *Concerning whom Thou didst command that they should not enter into Thy congregation* (Lam. I, 10). '*In the book*,' as it is said, '*An Ammonite and a Moabite shall not enter into the assembly of the Lord*' (Deut. XXIII, 4). And not only have I been allowed to enter, but in the roll and the book it is written concerning me. '*In the roll*'—Perez, Hezron, Ram, Amminadab, Nahshon, Boaz, Obed, Jesse, David; '*in the book*'; *And the Lord said: Arise, anoint him; for this is he* (I Sam. XVI, 12).

R. Huna said: It is written *For God hath appointed me another seed* (Gen. IV, 25), that is, seed from another place, referring to the Messiah.[3] R. Berekiah and R. Simon said: We may illustrate with a parable of a king who was travelling from one place to another, when a precious pearl fell from his head. So the king and all his retinue stopped there. All the passers-by asked, 'What are the king and his retinue doing here?' They discerned the reason and said, 'A pearl has fallen from his head.' What did he do? He gathered all the soil into heaps and brought brooms. He had one heap swept, but did not find it; a second heap, and he did not find it; but in the third, he found it;[4] and

[1] Salma ends the line of princes, or judges; from Boaz his son begins the line of kings, since it was destined that Boaz and Ruth should be the progenitors of David and his descendants.
[2] '*A roll*' refers to the scrolls of the Hagiographa, particularly the Five Scrolls, Ruth, Esther, Lamentations, Ecclesiastes, and Song of Songs, '*a book*' to the Prophets and Pentateuch.
[3] V. Gen. R. XXIII, 5; LI, 8.
[4] The reading in Gen. R. XXXIX, 10, is preferable: and brought sieves and sifted it. (This requires a very slight emendation, מכברות instead of מכבדות.)

they announced, 'The king has found his pearl!' So the Holy One, blessed be He, said to Abraham, '*Get thee out* (Gen. XII, 1). It was to thee that I looked forward.[1] What need had I to record the genealogy of *Shem, Arpachshad, Shelah, Eber, Peleg, Nahor, and Terah?* (I Chron. I, 24).[2] Only on account of thee, *Abram—the same is Abraham'* (*ib.*); *And foundest his heart faithful before Thee* (Neh. IX, 8). So said the Holy One, blessed be He, to David, 'What need had I to record the genealogy of Perez, Hezron, Ram, Amminadab, Nahshon, Salmon, Boaz, Obed, Jesse? Only on account of thee; *I have found My servant, David.*'

[1] The Heb. literally means *Go* to thee, and the comment is based on this '*to thee*'.
[2] Reu and Serug are included. Cf. Gen. XI.

MIDRASH RABBAH

ECCLESIASTES

MIDRASH

TRANSLATED INTO ENGLISH

WITH NOTES, GLOSSARY AND INDICES

UNDER THE EDITORSHIP OF

RABBI DR. H. FREEDMAN, B.A., PH.D.

AND

MAURICE SIMON, M.A.

RABBAH

ECCLESIASTES

TRANSLATED BY

REV. DR. A. COHEN, M.A., PH.D.

THE SONCINO PRESS
LONDON • NEW YORK

THIRD EDITION 1983

ISBN: 0-900689-38-2

MANUFACTURED IN THE UNITED STATES OF AMERICA
PRINTED BY NOBLE OFFSET PRINTERS, INC.

CONTENTS

Introduction	*page* vii
Chapter I	1
Chapter II	51
Chapter III	74
Chapter IV	110
Chapter V	127
Chapter VI	158
Chapter VII	166
Chapter VIII	213
Chapter IX	226
Chapter X	260
Chapter XI	284
Chapter XII	299

INTRODUCTION

THE time and place of the composition of Ḳoheleth Rabbah[1] cannot be exactly determined. There is nothing definite in its contents to serve as a clue to the identity of the author or the country of his residence, although Weiss[2] is of the opinion that the style and language are reminiscent of the Palestinian School of expositors. With regard to the date, a general reading gives an impression of comparative lateness which is confirmed by several considerations.

(1) The comment on v, 8 f is derived from a Talmudical source, viz., Ber. 5*a*, where it is declared that the teachings contained in the Mishnah and Gemara are to be considered as having been given to Moses on Sinai. Our Midrash, however, goes farther and includes in the enumeration such late treatises as Aboth d'R. Nathan and the tractates *Gerim*, *'Abadim*, *Ẓiẓith*, *Tefillin*, and *Mezuzah.*

(2) A considerable proportion of the contents is extracted from other parts of the Midrash Rabbah, in particular Genesis, Leviticus, Numbers, Song of Songs, and Lamentations. That the author borrowed from these sources, and not *vice versa*, is clearly demonstrated in two instances to be found in XII, 7, one with its ending inappropriate to Ecclesiastes, and the other with its reference to Jeremiah (!) uttering '*Vanity of vanities*', which is an alteration of '*How sitteth solitary*!'

(3) A noteworthy feature of the present Midrash is the absence of lengthy introductions so common in the others and the fact that it approaches nearer to a commentary on the Biblical text than is usual in the Midrash Rabbah. The author is often an exegete rather than a homilist.

These characteristics point to the early Geonic era (the seventh century) as the probable period in which it was written.

The Hebrew text of Ecclesiastes was, according to an ancient arrangement, divided into four 'orders' or sections.[3]

[1] This is the name given to the work in the printed edition of Pesaro, 1519. The Venice edition of 1545 calls it 'Midrash Ḳoheleth.'

[2] *Dor*, 4th ed., III, p. 242.

[3] The division of the Biblical Books into chapters is later.

The first began at I, I, the second at III, 13, the third at VII, I, and the fourth at IX, 7. In the editions of the Midrash, Chapter VII has the superscription 'Second Section', after IX, 6 there is the note 'Ended is the Second Section', and before IX, 7 the heading 'The Third Section' is inserted. Some scholars[1] have concluded that the author of the Midrash had before him a different arrangement, viz., into three sections. This view is open to doubt. It is to be noted that he nowhere marks the end of the first section, and according to this opinion the book falls into three very unequal divisions.

The more probable view is that he possessed the arrangement into four sections. There is in the extant version of the Midrash no commentary on III, 12. If we assume that there was one originally, it is likely that when it was erroneously omitted by a copyist, the note 'Ended is the First Section' dropped out with it. A later copyist, finding no mention of this, altered the subsequent 'Third Section' and 'Fourth Section' into 'Second' and 'Third' respectively.

The Midrash to Ecclesiastes owes its inclusion in the 'Rabbah' collection to the fact that the Biblical Book is read in the Synagogue on the Sabbath during the Festival of Tabernacles or the Eighth Day of Solemn Assembly if it be the Sabbath. That this custom is late may be deduced from Sopherim XIV, 3, which does not name Ecclesiastes with the '*Megilloth*' Ruth, Song of Songs, Lamentations, and Esther. When the practice of reading the Book was established,[2] its Midrash increased in importance and took its place in the Midrash Rabbah.

A. COHEN.

[1] Zunz, *Gottes. Vor.*, 2nd ed., p. 277; Weiss, *loc. cit.*

[2] When this was done is uncertain. The earliest reference appears to be in the Maḥzor Vitry (c. 1100); cf. *J.E.* VIII, p. 429. Elbogen, however, holds that Ḳoheleth was read on Tabernacles in early times, v. *Der jüd. Gottesdienst*, p. 185.

ECCLESIASTES

CHAPTER I

1. THE WORDS OF ḲOHELETH, THE SON OF DAVID, KING IN JERUSALEM (I, 1). That is what Scripture declares by the Holy Spirit through Solomon, king of Israel: *Seest thou a man diligent in his business? he shall stand before kings* (Prov. XXII, 29). Once R. Ḥanina b. Dosa saw the inhabitants of his city taking vowed offerings and free-will offerings[1] up to Jerusalem. He exclaimed, 'All are taking vowed offerings and free-will offerings up to Jerusalem, but I take nothing!' What did he do? He went out to the waste land of his city and saw there a stone which he chipped, chiselled, and polished. He then said, 'Behold, I take it upon myself to convey it to Jerusalem.'[2] He sought to hire workmen, and five men chanced to come his way. He asked them, 'Will you carry up this stone for me to Jerusalem?' They answered, 'Give us five *sela*'s and we will carry it up to Jerusalem.' He wanted to give them the money, but he had none with him at the time; so they left him and departed. The Holy One, blessed be He, arranged for five angels to appear to him in the likeness of men. He asked them, 'Will you carry up this stone for me?' They answered, 'Give us five *sela*'s and we will carry your stone up for you to Jerusalem, but on condition that you place your hand and finger with ours.'[3] He placed his hand and finger with theirs and they found themselves standing in Jerusalem. He wanted to pay them their hire but could not find them. He entered the Hall of Hewn Stone[4] and inquired about them. [The men in the Hall] said to him, 'Probably Ministering Angels carried your stone up to Jerusalem'; and they applied to him this text,

[1] The Mishnah (Ḳin. I, 1) defines them as follows: A vowed offering is when one says, 'I vow to dedicate a burnt-offering'; a free-will offering when one says, 'This animal is to be a burnt-offering.' In the latter case the animal is specified. [2] To present it to the Temple.
[3] Probably a hint that religion demands personal service.
[4] A hall in the Temple where the Great Sanhedrin held its sessions.

'*Seest thou a man diligent in his business? he shall stand before kings*' (melakim)—read the phrase as 'He shall stand before *angels*' (mal'akim).

R. Simon said in the name of R. Simeon b. Ḥalafta: It may be likened to a councillor who became great in the royal palace. The king said to him, 'Ask what you will and I shall give it you.' The councillor thought to himself, 'If I ask for silver and gold, or precious pearls, or garments, he will give them to me; but I will ask for his daughter [in marriage] and then everything will be given to me included with his daughter.' Similarly, *In Gibeon the Lord appeared to Solomon in a dream by night; and God said: Ask what I shall give thee* (I Kings III, 5). Solomon thought to himself, 'If I ask for silver and gold and pearls, He will give them to me; but I shall ask for wisdom and then everything will be included.' That is what is written, *Give Thy servant therefore an understanding heart* (*ib.* 9). The Holy One, blessed be He, said to him: 'Thou hast asked for wisdom and didst not ask riches, honour, and the life of thine enemies for thyself; therefore wisdom and knowledge will be granted thee and thereby riches and possessions also will I give thee' (cf. *ib.* 11 ff.). Immediately, *Solomon awoke, and, behold it was a dream* (*ib.* 15). R. Isaac said: A dream stands upon its foundation.[1] [Solomon became so wise that] when a bird chirped he knew for what it chirped, and when an ass brayed he knew for what it brayed. At once, *He came to Jerusalem, and stood before the ark of the covenant of the Lord, and offered up burnt-offerings, and offered peace-offerings, and made a feast to all his servants* (*ib.*). (R. Isaac said: We learn from this that a feast should be held after completing [the study of] the Torah.)[2] Forthwith the Holy Spirit alighted upon him and he composed the following three Books: Proverbs, Song of Songs, and Ecclesiastes. Hence it is written, THE WORDS OF ḲOHELETH, THE SON OF DAVID.

[1] It is not an empty experience. [2] It is the prevailing custom to hold such a festive gathering after finishing the study of a Talmudic Tractate. Possibly too he refers to the completion of the Pentateuch.—Solomon offered all these sacrifices because he had completed the acquisition of knowledge.

2. Another interpretation of THE WORDS OF ḲOHELETH, THE SON OF DAVID: There were three prophets to whom, because it consisted of words of reproach, their prophecy was attributed personally, viz. '*The words of Ḳoheleth*,' *The words of Amos* (Amos I, 1), and *The words of Jeremiah* (Jer. I, 1).[1] Why was Jeremiah's name so called? Because in his days Jerusalem became a desolation (*eremiah*). Why was Amos's name so called? R. Phinehas said: Because he was heavy (*'amus*) of tongue.[2] His contemporaries exclaimed, 'The Holy One, blessed be He, passed over all His creatures and only caused His *Shechinah* to alight upon this stammerer, this tongueless person!' Why was Ḳoheleth's name so called? Because his words were uttered in public (*hiḳḳahel*), as it is stated, *Then Solomon assembled* (yaḳhel) *the elders of Israel* (I Kings VIII, 1). R. Aḥa said in the name of R. Huna: One band of them went in as another went out in order to hear Solomon's wisdom. That is what the Queen of Sheba said to him: *Happy are thy men, happy are these thy servants, that stand continually before thee, and that hear thy wisdom* (*ib.* x, 8); and it is likewise written, *And there came of all peoples to hear the wisdom of Solomon* (*ib.* v, 14).

He was called by three names: Jedidiah (II Sam. XII, 25), Ḳoheleth, and Solomon. R. Joshua said: He had seven names: Agur, Jaḳeh, Lemuel, Ithiel[3] [in addition to the three mentioned]. R. Samuel said: The proper, authentic names among them are Jedidiah, Ḳoheleth, and Solomon. R. Samuel admits the other four, but [he maintains that] Solomon received them as surnames and they were given to him for expository reasons. He was called 'Agur' because he was stored (*agur*) with words of Torah. He was called 'Jaḳeh' because he discharged (*meḳi'*) words [of wisdom] like a bowl that is filled at one time and emptied at another time; similarly did Solomon learn

[1] In contrast: *The word of the Lord that came to Joel* (Joel I, 1), *The word of the Lord that came to Micah* (Micah I, 1).
[2] A stammerer. [3] Cf. Prov. XXX, 1, XXXI, 1.

Torah at one time and forget it at another time.[1] He was called Lemuel because he spoke against God[2] in his heart, saying, 'I can multiply [wives] without sinning.'[3] He was called 'Ithiel' because he said, 'God is with me (*itti el*), and I can do so, seeing that I am David's son, a king and a king's son, a wise man and a wise man's son, righteous and the son of a righteous man, a nobleman and a nobleman's son.' R. Judan said in the name of R. Alexandri: An ox, before its tendons are cut, can be drawn by even one of its tendons[4]; but when they have been cut, how many ropes and nails are needed to drag it along! Similarly, while Solomon had not yet sinned he depended on his own merit; but when he had sinned the merit of his ancestors had to be drawn upon for him. That is what is written, *For David My servant's sake* (I Kings XI, 13).[5] R. Simeon b. Yoḥai taught: Happy is he who is worthy to reign in the place of kingship.[6] Elsewhere it is written, *Og, the king of Bashan, who dwelt in Ashtaroth, at Edrei* (Deut. I, 4); but here [it is written], KING IN JERUSALEM, in a place of kingship.

1. VANITY OF VANITIES (I, 2). R. Huna said in the name of R. Aḥa: David used a phrase without explaining it and its exposition was given by his son Solomon; and Solomon used a phrase without explaining it and its exposition was given by his father David. David said, *Man is like unto a breath* (Ps. CXLIV, 4). To what breath? If he were like the steam[7] from an oven, there is substance in it[8]; if like the steam of a stove, there is substance in it! His son Solomon came and explained it; for that is what is written, VANITY OF VANITIES, SAITH ḲOHELETH

[1] As a punishment for marrying foreign wives.
[2] שנם לאל, the dotted letters correspond to all but one in 'Lemuel'.
[3] In defiance of Deut. XVII, 17.
[4] Since it can move of its own accord, one rope is sufficient by which to lead it. When its tendons are severed it cannot walk and its whole weight has to be pulled.
[5] God will not rend the kingdom from Solomon, but defer the partition until after his death.
[6] Jerusalem.
[7] *Breath*, 'steam', and 'vanity' are all translations of the word '*hebel*'.
[8] It is created from the food which is cooking.

[is man]. R. Samuel b. Naḥman taught in the name of R. Joshua b. Ḳorḥah: It may be likened to a man who sets on the fire seven pots[1] one on top of the other, and the steam from the topmost one has no substance in it, [and such is man].

Solomon said, *For who knoweth what is good for man in his life, all the days of his vain life which he spendeth as a shadow?* (Eccl. VI, 12)—as a shadow of what? If life is like the shadow cast by a wall, there is substance in it; if like the shadow cast by a date-palm, there is substance in it![2] David came and explained, *His days are as a shadow that passeth away* (Ps. *loc. cit.*). R. Huna said in the name of R. Aḥa: Life is like a bird which flies past and its shadow passes with it. Samuel said: It is like the shadow of bees in which there is no substance at all.

R. Samuel b. R. Isaac taught in the name of R. Samuel b. Eleazar: The seven '*vanities*' mentioned by Ḳoheleth correspond to the seven worlds which a man beholds.[3] At a year old he is like a king seated in a canopied litter, fondled and kissed by all. At two and three he is like a pig, sticking his hands in the gutters. At ten he skips like a kid. At twenty he is like a neighing horse, adorning his person and longing for a wife. Having married, he is like an ass.[4] When he has begotten children, he grows brazen like a dog to supply their food and wants. When he has become old, he is [bent] like an ape.[5] What has just been said holds good only of the ignorant; but of those versed in the Torah[6] it is written, *Now king David was old* (I Kings I, 1)—although he was '*old*', he was still a '*king*'.

R. Judah b. R. Simon said: The seven '*vanities*' mentioned by Ḳoheleth correspond to the seven days of creation. On the first day, *In the beginning God created*

[1] Ḳoheleth refers to seven '*vanities*' in the verse, since the plural connotes two. [2] In the sense that they enjoy a certain permanence.
[3] I.e. the seven stages of life. Cf. *As You Like It*, Act II, sc. 7.
[4] Working hard for a livelihood. [5] Radal explains: he loses the appearance of a human being and his senses. [6] Lit. 'sons of the Torah'.

the heavens and the earth (Gen. I, 1); but it is written, *For the heavens shall vanish away like smoke, and the earth shall wax old like a garment* (Isa. LI, 6). On the second day, *Let there be a firmament* (Gen. I, 6); but it is written, *And the heavens shall be rolled together like a scroll* (Isa. XXXIV, 4). On the third day, *Let the waters under the heaven be gathered together* (Gen. I, 9); but it is written, *The Lord shall utterly destroy the tongue of the Egyptian sea* (Isa. XI, 14). On the fourth day, *Let there be lights in the firmament of the heaven* (Gen. I, 14); but it is written, *Then the moon shall be confounded and the sun ashamed* (Isa. XXIV, 23). On the fifth day, *Let the waters swarm with swarms of living creatures* (Gen. I, 20); but it is written, *I will consume the fowls of the heaven, and the fishes of the sea* (Zeph. I, 3). On the sixth day, *And God said: Let us make man in our image* (Gen. I, 26); but it is written, *And I will cut off man from off the face of the earth* (Zeph. *loc. cit.*). With regard to the Sabbath what is there for you to say?[1] *Every one that profaneth it shall surely be put to death* (Ex. XXXI, 14).[2] [The penalty of death] only applies to one who deliberately profanes it, but one who does so inadvertently brings an offering and obtains atonement.[3] R. Berekiah said: When Adam perceived the excellence of the Sabbath, that [for its unintentional desecration] one could bring an offering and gain atonement, he began to sing to the Holy One, blessed be He, praise and a psalm concerning it. That is what is written, *A Psalm, a Song. For the Sabbath day* (Ps. XCII, 1). R. Levi said: Adam composed that Psalm.

1. WHAT PROFIT HATH MAN OF ALL HIS LABOUR WHEREIN HE LABOURETH UNDER THE SUN (I, 3)? R. Benjamin said: The Sages sought to suppress[4] the Book of Ḳoheleth because they discovered therein words which savour of heresy. They declared: Behold all the wisdom of Solomon which he aims at teaching [in this

[1] Is it not a holy institution with no '*vanity*' in it?
[2] It may be the cause of death, and therefore there is '*vanity*' in it.
[3] Consequently the Sabbath is practically without '*vanity*', and is a blessing to man.
[4] Lit. 'hide', i.e. exclude from the Scriptural canon.

Book] is, WHAT PROFIT HATH MAN OF ALL HIS LABOUR? It is possible that the words may also be applied to man's labour in the Torah! On reconsidering the matter they declared: He did not say 'Of all labour' but OF ALL *HIS* LABOUR—In HIS LABOUR[1] one should not labour,[2] but one should toil in the labour of the Torah!

R. Samuel b. Isaac said: The Sages sought to suppress the Book of Ḳoheleth because they discovered therein words which savour of heresy. They declared: All the wisdom of Solomon is contained in the statement, *Rejoice, O young man, in thy youth, and let thy heart cheer thee in the days of thy youth, and walk in the ways of thy heart, and in the sight of thine eyes* (Eccl. XI, 9). Now Moses said, *That ye go not about after your own heart and your own eyes* (Num. XV, 39), whereas Solomon said, '*Walk in the ways of thy heart, and in the sight of thine eyes!*' Is restraint to be abolished?[3] Is there no judgment and no Judge? But since he continued, *But know thou, that for all these things God will bring thee into judgment*, they exclaimed, Well has Solomon spoken.

R. Huna and R. Aḥa said in the name of R. Ḥilfai: A man's labour is UNDER THE SUN, but his treasury of reward is above the sun.[4] R. Judan said: UNDER THE SUN he has no profit, but he has it above the sun.[5] R. Levi and the Rabbis comment. R. Levi said: [The meaning of the phrase is]: What advantage should there be for human beings who lay up a store of pious and benevolent acts? Sufficient for them that I [God] cause light to shine upon them.[6] The Rabbis say: [The meaning is]: What advantage should there be for the righteous who lay up a store of pious and benevolent acts? Sufficient for them that I will renew their faces like the sun, as it is

[1] I.e. labour for his personal needs, his *secular* pursuits.
[2] For it is vanity. [3] Lit. 'is the strap to be loosened?'
[4] In heaven in the after-life.
[5] Commentaries: for labour under the sun—i.e. for worldly striving—he has no profit; but for labour above the sun—i.e. for religious striving—he has profit.
[6] That itself is ample reward; all else that I give them is additional bounty.

written, *They that love Him shall be as the sun when he goeth forth in his might* (Judg. V, 31).[1]

R. Jannai said: Usually when a person buys a pound of meat, how much trouble and labour he goes through before he has cooked it! I [God], however, cause the winds to blow for you, clouds to ascend, rain and dew to fall, make plants to grow and ripen, and prepare a table before every individual and supply the needs of every individual and every person sufficient for his wants; and yet you refuse to bring me the *omer*![2] R. Phinehas said: Usually when a person washes his garment in winter, how much trouble and labour he goes through before he has dried it! I, however, cause the winds to blow for you, clouds to ascend, rain and dew to fall, make plants to grow, wash, ripen, and dry them, and prepare a table before every individual and every person sufficient for his wants, and yet you refuse to bring me the *omer*! R. Berekiah said: [God declared]: 'I am your purveyor, and you will not let Me taste My own food so that I may know what it requires!' R. Joshua of Siknin said in the name of R. Levi: [God declared]: 'I am your steward [guarding your crops] and you refuse to pay Me My wages [for guarding them]!'

R. Eleazar said: It is written, *Neither say they in their heart: Let us now fear the Lord our God, who giveth the former rain, and the latter in due season: who keepeth for us the appointed weeks of the harvest* (Jer. V, 24). [God declared to them]: 'Guilty creatures that you are! Think ye that now ye have no need of Me?'[3] Therefore it is stated, '*Who keepeth for us the appointed weeks of the harvest*,' i.e. who protects it for us from scorching heat and injurious dews. That is what David says, *A rain of charity*[4] *didst Thou pour down, O God* (Ps. LXVIII, 10)—if it [the crop]

[1] Mah.: renders thus: What profit has man for all his toil (i.e. for laying up a store of good deeds)? To which the answer is: what he receives under the sun—the light of the sun.

[2] V. Lev. XXIII, 9 ff. Or: and would you not bring Me the *omer*!—that is the least return that you can make (Y.T.). Similarly the following passages.

[3] 'Now'—after I have given you the former and the latter rain.

[4] So understood by the Midrash. E.V. '*A bounteous rain*'.

needs rain, it [the rain] is [of Thy] charity; and if it needs dew, then do '*Thou pour* [it] *down, O God*'.

R. Ḥiyya learnt: It is written, *Seven weeks shall there be complete* (Lev. XXIII, 15)[1]—when [are they complete]?[2] When the levitical watches of Jeshua and Shecaniah[3] are not between them.[4] R. Abba said: Come and see how much trouble and labour [the Israelites] experience before they bring the *omer*; as we have learnt: How do they prepare it? The agents of the *Beth Din* go out on the eve of the Festival [of Passover] and tie the corn in bundles while it is still uncut[5] so that it should be easier to reap. All the population of the towns in the neighbourhood assemble there in order that it may be reaped with great ceremony.

R. Levi said: The Holy One, blessed be He, says to you, 'O man, behold you have ploughed, sown, reaped, tied into bundles and formed many stacks; but if I do not produce a little wind for you are you able to winnow? And even the payment for that wind you refuse to give Me!' Alas! what profit is there that He troubled the wind [to blow]![6]

Rabbi [Judah ha-Nasi] made a wedding feast for his son. He invited all the Rabbis, but forgot to extend an invitation to Bar Ḳappara. The latter went and wrote above the door [of the banqueting hall], 'After all your rejoicing is death, so what is the use of your rejoicing?' Rabbi inquired, 'Who has done this to us?' They said,

[1] Between the Festivals of Passover and Pentecost.
[2] I.e. each beginning on the first day of the week.
[3] V. I Chron. XXIV, 11.
[4] M.K. quotes a very complicated explanation from the 'Rokeaḥ' showing how the rotation of the twenty-four levitical orders was affected according as the first day of Passover fell on a Sabbath or week-day. There is another reading which omits the negative, and this is preferred by Jast. who explains: When the divisions of J. and S. are between them (meaning, they officiate between Passover and Pentecost), i.e. when there are ten Sabbaths between the first of the month of Nisan on the first Sabbath of which the turn (viz. of the levitical orders) commences, and the sixth of Sivan (on which Pentecost occurs).
[5] Lit. 'attached to the ground'. The quotation is from Men. X, 3.
[6] Thus showing that the verse 'what profit', etc., can apply even to God.

'It was Bar Ḳappara whom you forgot to invite. He was concerned about himself.'[1] He thereupon arranged another banquet to which he invited all the Rabbis including Bar Ḳappara. At every course which was placed before them Bar Ḳappara related three hundred fox-fables, which were so much enjoyed by the guests that they let the food become cold and did not taste it. Rabbi asked his waiters, 'Why do our courses go in and out without the guests partaking of them?' They answered, 'Because of an old man who sits there, and when a course is brought in, he relates three hundred fox-fables; and on that account the food becomes cold and they eat none of it.' Rabbi went up to him and said, 'Why do you act in this manner? Let the guests eat!' He replied, 'So that you should not think that I came for your dinner, but because you did not invite me with my colleagues. Did not Solomon declare, WHAT PROFIT HATH A MAN OF ALL HIS LABOUR seeing that *One generation passeth away and another generation cometh?*' When they had apologised to each other and become reconciled, Abba bar Ḳappara said to Rabbi, 'If the Holy One, blessed be He, has given you bounteous wealth in this world which does not belong to you, how much more [will He grant you] in the World to Come which is wholly yours!'[2]

R. Bana'ah said: The Holy One, blessed be He, said to Israel: 'My sons, know what the difference is between Me and you. What is written? *Gather ye of it* [the manna] *every man according to his eating; an omer a head, according to the number of your persons, shall ye take it* (Ex. XVI, 16). You, however, have to give one *omer* for all of you, and not an *omer* of wheat but of barley. Nevertheless, be careful to bring it in its proper time.' Therefore Moses exhorted Israel and said to them, *Ye shall bring the sheaf*[3] *of the first-fruits of your harvest unto the priest* (Lev. XXIII, 9).

[1] I.e. about the affront caused by his not being invited.
[2] Mah.: this world was not his, since he did not wish to enjoy aught of it. Perhaps: man enjoys this world without having earned it, but the next world is his—he has earned it in this world. [3] Lit. '*omer*'.

1. ONE GENERATION PASSETH AWAY, AND ANOTHER GENERATION COMETH (I, 4). R. Judan said in the name of R. Levi: There is not a single day on which sixty myriads are not born and sixty myriads do not die. What is the reason [for his remark? As it is written], ONE GENERATION PASSETH AWAY, AND ANOTHER GENERATION COMETH. THE SUN ALSO RISETH, AND THE SUN GOETH DOWN (*ib.* 5): R. Berekiah, R. Jacob b. Abuna, and R. Ḥiyya b. Abba said in the name of R. Levi b. Sisi: Between sunrise and sunset one generation passes away and another comes. Whence do we know that a 'generation' numbers sixty myriads? As it is stated, *Surely there shall not one of these men, even this evil generation, see the good land* (Deut. I, 35), and that generation numbered sixty myriads.[1] R. Berekiah said: When a potter places [a number of vessels] in his furnace, what he puts in first he takes out last. Here, on the other hand, [with the generations] what passes away first comes first and what passes away last comes last.

2. R. Levi and R. Jacob of Gebal[2] said in the name of R. Ḥanina: As a generation passes away so it comes [at the Resurrection]; i.e. if one dies lame or blind he comes lame or blind, so that people shall not say, 'Those He allowed to die are different from those He restored to life.' For it is written, *I kill and I make alive* (*ib.* XXXII, 39)—having declared that He performs the more difficult act, He then declares that He performs the easier act! For '*I kill and I make alive*' is the harder act, so how much more is it with the easier act, viz. *I wound and I heal* (*ib.*)?[3] But [the meaning is]: I raise them [from the grave] with their blemishes, so that people shall not say, 'Those He allowed to die are different from those He restored to life.' '*I kill and I make alive, I wound,*' then will I heal them [after Resurrection].

[1] Cf. Num. XI, 21. [2] Northern part of Mount Seir (cf. Ps. LXXXIII, 8).
[3] Why is the latter clause added since it is implied in the former? Hence the interpretation which follows.

3. Another interpretation of '*I wound and I heal*': R. Ḥanina said in the name of R. Simeon b. Laḳish, R. Joshua of Siknin in the name of R. Joḥanan, and R. Levi in the name of R. Joḥanan: It is not written here 'I smite', but '*I wound*' (maḥaẓti)—i.e. the distinction (*meḥiẓah*) which I made between the celestial creatures and the terrestrial, viz. that the former endure while the latter die, holds good only in this world, but in the Messianic future there will be no death at all; as it is stated, *He will swallow up death for ever* (Isa. xxv, 8). R. Abba said: That distinction too will I [God] heal. '*Maḥaẓti*' (I made a distinction), and the distinction which I made '*I heal*'.[1]

4. R. Abba b. Kahana said (another version is: he said it in the name of R. Adda b. Ḥunia): The generation which comes should be esteemed by you as the generation which has passed, that you should not say, 'If R. Akiba were now living I would study Scripture under him; if R. Zera and R. Joḥanan were now living I would study Mishnah under them.' But the generation which comes in your days and the Sage who is in your days should be like the generation which has passed and the former Sages who preceded you. R. Joḥanan said: It is written, *The Lord that made Moses and Aaron*, etc. (1 Sam. XII, 6), and it is written, *And the Lord sent Jerubbaal, and Bedan, and Jephthah and Samuel* (*ib.* 11). (Jerubbaal is Gideon, Bedan is Samson, while Jephthah is the man of that name.)[2] It is also written, *Moses and Aaron among His priests, and Samuel among them that call upon His name* (Ps. XCIX, 6). The text puts three insignificant men on a level with three of the great men[3] of the world to teach

[1] Mah. makes this refer to the distinction of trouble: the trouble and sorrow which distinguish the life of terrestrial beings from that of the heavenly beings will be 'healed'—vanish—after the Resurrection.

[2] Cf. R.H. 25*a*: Why was Gideon called Jerubbaal? Because he waged strife (*meribah*) with Baal. Why was Samson called Bedan? Because he came from the tribe of Dan.

[3] Gideon, Samson, Jepthah are likened to Samuel in v. 11, while Samuel in turn is compared with Moses and Aaron. Thus the former three are likened to the latter three.

you that the *Beth Din* of Jerubbaal is as great and important before the Holy One, blessed be He, as the *Beth Din* of Moses, the *Beth Din* of Samson as that of Aaron, and the *Beth Din* of Jephthah as that of Samuel. This is to teach you that whoever is appointed leader of the community, though he be the lowliest of the lowly, is the equal of the most celebrated of the former celebrities; as it is said, *And thou shalt come unto the priests, the Levites, and unto the judge that shall be in those days* (Deut. XVII, 9). There is only mention of your own generation; whence do we know that it applies to a judge who is not of your generation?[1] i.e. why is it stated, '*Unto the judge that shall be in those days*'? This indicates that the judge of your generation in his time is the equal of the judge of former times. It is similarly declared, *Say not thou: How was it that the former days were better than these?* (Eccl. VII, 10). R. Simeon b. Laḳish said: You must only listen to the judge in your own generation. It is written, *And the heads of the fathers'* (ha'aboth) *houses of the family of the children of Gilead . . . came near, and spoke before Moses, and before the princes, the heads of fathers'* (aboth) *houses of the children of Israel* (Num. XXXVI, 1). R. Judan said: [It is first written], '*ha'aboth*' and then '*aboth*'! The fact is that [the children of Gilead] were entering upon their term of office whereas [Moses and the princes] were being relieved of office[2]; for that reason the text detracts from their dignity [by omitting the definite article].

R. Berekiah said: It is written, *And Jehoiada was the leader of Aaron* (I Chron. XII, 27).[3]

Was, then, Jehoiada the leader of Aaron! The meaning, however, is: If Aaron had lived in the same generation as Jehoiada, the latter in his time would have been superior to him. R. Simai said: It is written, *But Aaron and his sons offered upon the altar of burnt-offerings* (*ib.* VI, 34).

[1] The more correct form occurs in Sifre §153: Can it enter your mind that a man would go to a judge who did not exist in his own days? Therefore it is stated, etc.

[2] They belonged to the generation which was to die in the wilderness.

[3] So lit. E.V. '*Of the house of Aaron*'.

Were, then, Aaron and his sons living? Surely Zadok and his sons were officiating at that time! The purpose is to teach you that had Aaron and his sons been living Zadok in his time would have been superior to them.[1] R. Hillel, the son of R. Samuel b. Naḥman, deduces the same idea from the following: *And all the congregation of them that were come back out of the captivity made booths, and dwelt in the booths; for since the days of Joshua the son of Nun unto that day had not the children of Israel done so. And there was very great gladness* (Neh. VIII, 17). The text shows less respect to that righteous man in his grave[2] for the sake of a So-and-so then living [viz. Ezra]. The Rabbis deduce the same idea from the following: *The son of Abishua, the son of Phinehas, the son of Eleazar, the son of Aaron the chief priest. This Ezra went up from Babylon* (Ezra VII, 4 f.). This[3] indicates that if Aaron had been living, Ezra in his time would have been superior to him.

AND THE EARTH ABIDETH FOR EVER. R. Judah b. Ḳorḥah said: The verse should have read rather, 'The earth passeth away and the earth cometh, and the generation abideth for ever'; because what was created for the sake of what? Was earth created for the sake of a generation or vice versa? Is it not a fact that earth was created for the sake of a generation?[4] But a generation, for the reason that it does not abide by the commands of the Holy One, blessed be He, decays, whereas the earth which abides by the commands of the Holy One, blessed be He,[5] does not decay.

R. Simeon b. Yoḥai said: It is written, *For as the days of a tree shall be the days of My people* (Isa. LXV, 22), and '*tree*' means nothing else than Torah, as it is stated,

[1] 'E.J.: though Aaron in fact was greater, yet since Zadok was the leader in his generation, Aaron would have submitted to his authority.
[2] By spelling his name ישוע instead of the usual and more dignified יהושע.
[3] The phrase *This Ezra* instead of simply '*Ezra*'; this emphasises that Ezra and none other was the leader.
[4] The world was created to be the abode of man. Hence he should have said that even if the earth passes away yet the generation of man will remain. [5] By producing fruits annually.

She is a tree of life to them that lay hold upon her (Prov. III, 18). Now what was created for the sake of what? Was Torah created for the sake of Israel or vice versa? Surely Torah was created for the sake of Israel. Since, then, Torah which was created for the sake of Israel endures for all eternity, how much more must Israel, for whose sake it was created, [endure for all eternity]!

R. Isaac said: A kingdom comes and a kingdom goes but Israel abides for ever; this is the meaning of AND THE EARTH ABIDETH FOR EVER.[1] R. Samuel, in the name of R. Paltia of Naveh,[2] derives [the identification of EARTH with Israel] from the following verse: *And Jonathan, the son of Gershom, the son of Manasseh, he and his sons were priests to the tribe of the Danites until the day of the captivity of the land* (Judg. XVIII, 30).[3] Can, then, the '*land*' go into captivity or be moved! It alludes in fact to Israel who is called 'land', as it is said, *And all nations shall call you happy, for ye shall be a delightsome land* (Mal. III, 12).

R. Berekiah said in the name of R. Simeon b. Lakish: To whatever the Holy One, blessed be He, created in man He created a parallel in the earth. Man has a head and so has the earth, as it is said, *Nor the head*[4] *of the dust of the world* (Prov. VIII, 26). Man has eyes and so has the earth, as it is said, *And they shall cover the eye*[5] *of the earth* (Ex. X, 5). Man has ears and so has the earth, as it is said, *Give ear, O earth* (Isa. I, 2). Man has a mouth and so has the earth, as it is said, *And the earth opened her mouth* (Num. XVI, 32). Man eats and so does the earth, as it is said, *A land that eateth up the inhabitants thereof* (*ib.* XIII, 32). Man drinks and so does the earth, as it is said, *A land of hills and valleys, and drinketh water as the rain of heaven cometh down* (Deut. XI, 11). Man vomits and so does the earth, as it is said, *That the land vomit not you out also* (Lev. XVIII, 28). Man has hands and so

[1] '*Earth*' referring to Israel, as the Midrash proceeds to explain.
[2] A town in Galilee. [3] The Heb. for '*earth*' and '*land*' is the same.
[4] E.V. '*beginning*'. [5] So lit. E.V. '*face*'.

has the earth, as it is said, *The land is broad of hands*[1] *for them* (Gen. XXXIV, 21).

Man has thighs and so has the earth, as it is said, *I will gather them from the uttermost parts*[2] *of the earth* (Jer. XXXI, 8). Man has a navel and so has the earth, as it is said, *That dwell in the navel*[3] *of the earth* (Ezek. XXXVIII, 12). Man has nakedness and so has the earth, as it is said, *To see the nakedness of the land ye are come* (Gen. XLII, 9). Man has feet and so has the earth, as it is said, THE EARTH ABIDETH[4] FOR EVER. What means ABIDETH? It preserves.[5] R. Aḥa and the Rabbis comment. R. Aḥa said: [It preserves] its commands.[6] The Rabbis said: [It preserves] its produce.[7]

R. Simeon the son of Jose b. Lekunia said: Since in this world one man builds a house and another has the use of it,[8] one man plants a tree and another eats of it, in the Hereafter [Israel] shall not build and another inhabit, nor plant and another eat; as it is said, *For as the days of a tree shall be the days of My people, and Mine elect shall long enjoy the work of their hands* (Isa. LXV, 22).

1. THE SUN ALSO RISETH (I, 5). R. Berekiah said in the name of R. Abba b. Kahana: Do we not know that the sun riseth and sets! What it means, however, is that before the sun of one righteous man sets, He causes the sun of another righteous man to rise. On the day that R. Akiba died Rabbi [Judah ha-Nasi] was born,[9] and this verse was applied to him, THE SUN ALSO RISETH, AND THE SUN GOETH DOWN. On the day that R. Adda b. Ahaba died his son, R. Hamnuna, was born, and there was applied to him, THE SUN ALSO RISETH, AND THE SUN GOETH DOWN. On the day

[1] So lit. E.V. '*large enough*'.
[2] The Hebrew word is similar to that for 'thighs'.
[3] E.V. '*middle*'. [4] Lit. 'standeth'. [5] Lit. 'causes to stand'.
[6] As mentioned above, viz. the Divine decree that it should produce fruit annually. [7] Earth has to be stored along with produce in order to keep it from rotting. Cf. Gen. R. XC, 5. [8] Lit. 'uses it up.'
[9] This and the following statements are not to be understood too literally. R. Akiba died in 132 C.E. and Rabbi was born in 135.

that R. Hamnuna died his son, R. Abin, was born, and there was applied to him, THE SUN ALSO RISETH, AND THE SUN GOETH DOWN. On the day that R. Abin died Abba Hoshaiah of Ṭirya[1] was born, and there was applied to him, THE SUN ALSO RISETH, AND THE SUN GOETH DOWN. Before He caused the sun of Sarah to set, He made the sun of Rebekah to rise; that is what is written, *And Bethuel begot Rebekah* (Gen. XXII, 23), after which *Sarah died in Kiriath-Arba* (*ib.* XXIII, 2), and it is written, *And Isaac brought her into his mother Sarah's tent* (*ib.* XXIV, 67).[2] Before He caused the sun of Moses to set, He made the sun of Joshua to rise. Before He caused the sun of Joshua to set, He made the sun of Othniel, i.e. Jabez,[3] to rise; and so with them all, in generation after generation. That is the meaning of THE SUN ALSO RISETH, AND THE SUN GOETH DOWN.[4]

2. It has been taught in the name of R. Nathan: The globe of the sun has a sheath, as it is written, *In them hath He set a tent for the sun* (Ps. XIX, 5), and therefore it is a lake of water. Whenever the sun desires to come forth it flames, and the Holy One, blessed be He, weakens its force with the water in order that it should not burn up the world. In the Hereafter, however, the Holy One, blessed be He, will strip its sheath and uncover it and cause it to consume the wicked; as it is said, *For, behold, the day cometh, it burneth as a furnace; and all the proud, and all that work wickedness, shall be stubble; and the day that cometh shall set them ablaze* (Mal. III, 19). R. Jannai and R. Ishmael both declared: There is no Gehinnom in the Hereafter; but the sun will come forth and the righteous derive benefit from it. Whence do we know this? As it is said, *But unto you that fear My name shall the sun of righteousness arise with healing in its wings* (*ib.* 20). The wicked, on the other hand, will be punished

[1] A village near Mount Carmel.
[2] The point is that she completely resembled Sarah (Gen. R. LX, 16) and thus worthily filled her place.
[3] They are identified in Tem. 16*a*.
[4] Cf. Gen. R. LVIII, 2.

by it, as it is said, '*And the day that cometh shall set them ablaze.*'

1. THE WIND GOETH TOWARD THE SOUTH, AND TURNETH ABOUT UNTO THE NORTH (I, 6). IT GOETH TOWARD THE SOUTH, by day; TURNETH ABOUT UNTO THE NORTH, by night; IT TURNETH ABOUT CONTINUALLY IN ITS CIRCUIT, AND THE WIND RETURNETH AGAIN TO ITS CIRCUITS, towards the east and west. AND THE WIND RETURNETH AGAIN TO ITS CIRCUITS. R. Joshua b. Ḥananiah said: When the wind goes forth into the world, the Holy One, blessed be He, reduces its violence by means of the mountains and breaks its force by means of the hills, saying to it, 'Take heed that you harm not My creatures.' Why does He act so? *For a wind becomes faint* (ya'aṭof) *before Me* (Isa. LVII, 16)[1], the meaning of the phrase being 'He tires' it [the wind], as the word is used in *When my soul fainted* (hith'aṭṭef) *within me* (Jonah II, 8). For what purpose [does He break the force of the wind]? For the sake of, *And the souls I have made* (Isa. *loc. cit.*).[2]

R. Huna said: On three occasions the wind went forth without check and sought to destroy the whole world with its inhabitants, viz. in the days of Job, of Elijah, and of Jonah. In the days of Job, as it is said, *And, behold, there came a great wind from across the wilderness* (Job I, 19); in the days of Elijah, as it is said, *And, behold, the Lord passed by, and a great and strong wind rent the mountains, and broke in pieces the rocks* (I Kings XIX, 11); and in the days of Jonah, as it is said, *But the Lord hurled a great wind into the sea* (Jonah I, 4). R. Judah b. Shallum said: The wind which blew in the days of Job only came into the world because of that house [which was to be destroyed], and he wind which blew in the days of Jonah only came into the world because of that ship [in which he was

[1] E.V. '*For the spirit that enwrapped itself is from Me*'.
[2] E.V. '*Which I have made*'. God made the souls of men, and He protects them from the violence of Nature's forces.

journeying].[1] The only wind which embraced the whole universe was that connected with Elijah; as it is stated, *And He said: Go forth, and stand upon the mount before the Lord*, etc. (I Kings *loc. cit.*).

R. Ḥiyya b. Tanḥum said (some report that he said it in the name of R. Joḥanan): King Messiah will not come until all the souls have appeared [on earth] which under the Divine plan were to be created, and they are the souls mentioned in the book of Adam[2]; as it is said, *This is the book of the generations of Adam* (Gen. v, 1).

1. ALL THE RIVERS RUN INTO THE SEA (I, 7). From whence does the earth drink? R. Eliezer and R. Joshua offer answers. R. Eliezer says: It drinks from the waters of the ocean, because it is written, *But there went up a mist*[3] *from the earth, and watered the whole face of the ground* (Gen. II, 6). R. Joshua said to him, 'But are not the waters of the ocean salty!'[4] He answered, 'They are sweetened by the clouds; as it is written, *Which the skies pour down* (Job XXXVI, 28). Where are the waters distilled?[5] In the skies.' R. Joshua, on the other hand, says: The earth drinks from the upper waters, because it is written, *Drinketh water as the rain of heaven cometh down* (Deut. XI, 11). The clouds raise themselves from earth to heaven and receive the waters as from the mouth of a bottle; as it is written, *Which distil rain from His vapour* (Job XXXVI, 27). And [the clouds] distil it as through a sieve and one drop does not touch another; as it is written, *Darkness of waters, thick clouds of the skies* (Ps. XVIII, 12). Why does it call the skies *sheḥaḳim*? Because they grind (*shoḥeḳim*) the water [into separate drops]. R. Abba b. Kahana said: In the same manner that the stomach [grinds food]; R. Samuel b. Naḥman said: As the small intestines of an animal [grind food].[6] For R. Joshua said:

[1] In Gen. R. XXIV, 4, R. Judan apparently states that these winds were confined to the ship and to Job's house, and the same is probably meant here. [2] V. Gen. R. XXIV, 4, note *ad loc.* [3] Caused by evaporation of the sea. [4] And rain-water is not salty. [5] The Heb. *nazal* means 'pour down' and 'be distilled'. [6] Cf. Gen. R. XIII, 10.

Wonderful is the day on which rain descends, because [a rainfall] is equal [in its marvellous character] to the whole of Creation. What is the reason for his statement? *Who doeth great things and unsearchable, marvellous things without number* (Job v, 9). How? *Who giveth rain upon the earth* (*ib.* 10).

2. How did the earth drink [before rain was created]? R. Judah, R. Simon, and the Rabbis offer answers. R. Judah says: As it does now from the Nile, which periodically inundates the land. R. Simon said: By means of a flood as it does now from the River Ḳabriel, which rises and inundates the land. The Rabbis say: As it does now from the Babylonian river Tuvay. Why is it called 'Tuvay'? Because it returns and inundates once in forty years. At first the earth obtained its water in this way, as it is said, *But there went up a mist*[1] *from the earth, and watered the whole face of the ground* (Gen. II, 6); then the Holy One, blessed be He, made a change so that the earth should only drink from above. R. Samuel b. Naḥman said in the name of R. Ḥanina of Sepphoris (another version is: R. Ḥanin of Sepphoris said in the name of R. Samuel b. Naḥman): For four reasons the Holy One, blessed be He, made a change so that the earth should only drink from above, viz. because of men of violence,[2] to wash away the injurious dew [from plants], that one who lives on high land should drink equally with one who lives on low land, and that all should turn their eyes toward heaven; as it is said, *So that those who are low may turn* [their eyes] *upward* (Job v, 11).[3]

3. Another interpretation of ALL THE RIVERS RUN INTO THE SEA: i.e. the ocean; YET THE SEA IS NOT

[1] The Heb. אד is understood as 'inundation', which is the correct meaning. This paragraph is repeated from Gen. R. XIII, 9.
[2] That they should not deprive the weak of their supply of water.
[3] *Those who are low* = man. E.V.: '*So that He setteth up on high those that are low*'.

FULL refers to the ocean,[1] which is never filled. Once R. Eliezer and R. Joshua were travelling on the great sea.[1] The ship entered a place where the water did not flow.[2] R. Eliezer said to R. Joshua, 'We have only come here so as to be able to make a test.'[3] They filled a cask with water from that place. When they arrived at Rome, Hadrian asked them, 'What are the waters of the ocean?' They replied, 'It consists of water which absorbs water.'[4] He said to them, 'Is it possible that the rivers should run into it without it becoming full?' They answered, 'It absorbs all the water in the world.' He said to them, 'I will not believe you until you prove it to me.' They took the water which they had drawn from the ocean, filled a flask with it and then poured further water into it which was absorbed by the ocean-water. According to the opinion of R. Eliezer [all water] is drawn from the ocean; according to the opinion of R. Joshua [all water] returns there.[5]

4. Another interpretation of ALL THE RIVERS RUN INTO THE SEA: a man's whole wisdom is in the heart; YET THE SEA IS NOT FULL: but the heart is never filled. Do you mean to say that when a man pours forth wisdom from his heart[6] it never returns to him? Therefore the text continues, THITHER THEY GO AGAIN.[7]

5. Another interpretation of ALL THE RIVERS: all the Torah which a man studies is only in his heart; YET THE SEA IS NOT FULL: but the heart is not full nor the appetite ever satisfied, as it is said, *And yet the appetite is not filled* (Eccl. VI, 7). Do you mean to say that when a man imparts his learning to another, it never returns to him? Therefore the text continues, THITHER THEY

[1] As a rule this means the Mediterranean. [2] A shallow spot.
[3] The experiment which they later carried out in their interview with Hadrian. [4] The water absorbs any water added to it, so that the ocean does not become full. [5] The passage is difficult. v. Gen. R. XIII, 9, for notes. [6] In the act of teaching others.
[7] By teaching he adds to his wisdom, because his understanding of the subject is thereby clarified.

GO AGAIN, as it is written, *And these words, which I command thee this day shall be*[1] *upon thy heart* (Deut. VI, 6).

A matron asked R. Jose b. Ḥalafta, 'What means that which is said, *He giveth wisdom unto the wise* (Dan. II, 21)? The text should have stated, "He giveth wisdom unto them that are not wise and knowledge to them that know not understanding"!' He answered her, 'I will explain with a parable. If two persons came to borrow money from you, one rich and the other poor, to whom would you lend, the rich man or the poor?' She replied, 'To the rich man.' 'Why?' he asked; to which she answered, 'Because if the rich man loses my money he has wherewith to repay me; but if the poor man loses my money, from where can he repay me?' He said to her, 'Do your ears hear what you have uttered with your mouth? If the Holy One, blessed be He, gave wisdom to fools, they would sit and meditate upon it[2] in privies, theatres, and bath-houses; but the Holy One, blessed be He, gave wisdom to the wise who sit and meditate upon it in Synagogues and Houses of Study. Hence "*He giveth wisdom unto the wise, and knowledge to them that know understanding*".'

6. Another interpretation of ALL THE RIVERS RUN INTO THE SEA: proselytes only enter the fold of Israel; YET THE SEA IS NOT FULL: but Israel fall short of their full number,[3] as it is said, *Who hath counted the dust of Jacob?* (Num. XXIII, 10). Perhaps, then, you mean to say that one who does not become a proselyte in this world can become such in the next? Therefore the text states, *Behold! the proselyte will become a convert* (Isa. LIV, 15)[4];

[1] I.e. will always be, even when you teach them to others.
[2] The Torah, with which wisdom is identified.
[3] Israel does not require these additions to be 'full', since nobody can count *the dust of Jacob*, i.e. born Israelites.
[4] The word *behold* is understood to point to the present: only now, in this world, can he become a convert. E.V. '*Behold they may gather together*'.

but from now onwards *They are not by Me* (*ib.*), meaning, they are kept apart from Me.[1] Who then will be with Me [in the Hereafter]? *Whoever is converted to thee* (*ib.*) in this world *Shall be attached to thee* (*ib.*)[2] in the World to Come. R. Johanan said: Not only so, but from the place where a person becomes a proselyte he will take his portion; as it is stated, *In what tribe the proselyte becomes a convert*,[3] *there shall ye give him his inheritance* (Ezek. XLVII, 23).

7. Another interpretation of ALL THE RIVERS RUN INTO THE SEA: All the dead enter Sheol, but Sheol is never full; as it is said, *The nether-world* (Sheol) *and Destruction are never satisfied* (Prov. XXVII, 20). Do you mean to say that once they die in this world they will never live again in the World to Come? Therefore the text states, UNTO THE PLACE WHITHER THE RIVERS GO, THITHER THEY CAN GO AGAIN; i.e. to the place where the dead assemble in the World to Come they return and will utter a song in the days of the Messiah. What is the reason for this statement? *From the uttermost part of the earth have we heard songs* (Isa. XXIV, 16), and *Thy dead shall live, my dead bodies shall arise, awake and sing* (*ib.* XXVI, 19).

8. Another interpretation of ALL THE RIVERS RUN INTO THE SEA: All Israel assemble only at Jerusalem and come up yearly at the pilgrim-festivals.[4] YET THE SEA IS NOT FULL; for we have learnt: They stood closely packed yet prostrated themselves with plenty of room.[5] R. Samuel b. Ḥobah said in the name of R. Aḥa: There was a space of four cubits between each and a cubit on every side so that one should not overhear the prayer

[1] They cannot be accepted in the World to Come.
[2] E.V.: '*Whoever shall gather together against thee shall fall because of thee*'. The Midrash, however, understands *fall* here in the sense of 'to become attached'; cf. I Chron. XII, 19, where it is used in that sense. [3] E.V. '*The stranger sojourneth*'. [4] V. Deut. XVI. [5] Ab. V, 5 (Sonc. ed., p. 62).

of the person next to him and make a mistake [in his own prayer]. UNTO THE PLACE WHITHER THE RIVERS GO: in the place where Israel assemble in this world [Jerusalem] they will assemble in the World to Come, in the Hereafter; as it is said, *And it shall come to pass in that day, that a great horn shall be blown; and they shall come that were lost in the land of Assyria, and they that were dispersed in the land of Egypt; and they shall worship the Lord in the holy mountain at Jerusalem* (*ib.* XXVII, 13).

9. Another interpretation of ALL THE RIVERS RUN INTO THE SEA: All wealth only goes to the kingdom of Edom,[1] and the kingdom of Edom is never filled; for R. Levi said: It is written, *So the eyes of man* (adam) *are never satiated* (Prov. XXVII, 20), i.e. the eyes of Edom are never satiated. Do you mean to say that when wealth enters Edom it never returns to its owners? Therefore the text states, UNTO THE PLACE WHITHER THE RIVERS GO, THITHER THEY GO AGAIN. From the place where wealth accumulates, viz. the kingdom of Edom, in this world, thence it will be dispersed in the days of the Messiah; as it is written, *And her gain and her hire shall be holiness to the Lord* (Isa. XXIII, 18). R. Ishmael b. R. Jose asked Rabbi [Judah ha-Nasi], 'What means that which is written, *For her gain shall be for them that dwell before the Lord* (*ib.*)?' He answered, 'For example, you and your companions, and those two men wrapped in linen sheets[2] like yourselves, because you do not hold yourselves in high esteem.' R. Jeremiah b. Eleazar said: The Holy One, blessed be He, will in the Hereafter renew the light of the faces of the righteous; as it is stated, *But they that love Him be as the sun when he goeth forth in his might* (Judg. V, 31). In the same manner that He will renew their faces, so will He renew their garments, to-day half-silken garments and to-morrow pure silk. [R. Ishmael] asked [Rabbi], 'What means that which is written, *To*

[1] Rome, the conqueror of the then known world.
[2] Referring to two Sages who were very humble.

eat their fill and for stately clothing (Isa. *loc. cit.*)?' He replied, 'To-day cotton and to-morrow pure silken garments.'[1]

1. ALL THINGS TOIL TO WEARINESS,[2] MAN CANNOT UTTER IT (I, 8). Idle talk wearies a man [as e.g. when he makes such remarks as]: 'The partridge to-day is pickled with garlic,' 'The side [of the animal] is like lead,' 'Cut thin slices,' 'Roasted with mustard,' 'Portions which deserve to be called portions,' 'Ox of judgment with poor mountain' [which is a pun for] 'beet with mustard'.[3]

R. Jonathan's hair kept falling out and he went to Magdala of the Dyers[4] to be cured. There was a barber in the place who said to him, 'Have you come here on account of your hair to be cured?' He replied, 'My hair is falling out, and I heard that there was a remedy for it here. I have journeyed here to hasten a cure.' [The barber] arose, knelt at his feet and said to him, 'I only spoke with Rab [about this remedy] last night.'[5]

2. Another interpretation of ALL THINGS TOIL TO WEARINESS: handicrafts weary. R. Eleazar said in the name of R. Abbahu: It happened that a woman took her son to a baker in Cæsarea and said to him, 'Teach my son the trade.' He replied to her, 'Let him stay with me five years and I will teach him five hundred confections with wheat.' He stayed with him five years and was taught five hundred confections with wheat. The baker said to her, 'Let him stay with me another five years and I will

[1] This question and answer should precede the passage beginning 'R Jeremiah b. Eleazar said'.

[2] The Heb. could be translated, 'All words are weary.'

[3] 'Idle talk' is illustrated by remarks about food. Some of the phrases involve punning. E.g. 'roasted' is really the Heb. word for 'pray' which in Aramaic is צלי; but this word is in Heb. 'roasted'. The last phrase, 'ox of judgment with poor mountain,' is also a pun, and occurs in 'Er. 53*b*. 'Ox of judgment' in Aramaic is תור דין, but as one word it is תרדין 'beet'. 'Poor mountain' is הר דל, by which חרדל 'mustard' is intended.

[4] A place near Tiberias.

[5] This is quoted as an example of 'idle talk'.

teach him a thousand confections with wheat.' But how many confections are possible with wheat? The Rabbis say: With wheat of *minnith*[1] they are numberless. R. Aḥa said: There are five hundred confections with wheat according to the numerical value of the letters of the word *minnith*. R. Ḥanina and R. Jonathan were both sitting and reckoning [how many ways there were of baking wheat] and stopped at sixty.[2] R. Eleazar further said in the name of R. Jose[3]: A woman of Cæsarea once took her son to a cook[4] and said to him, 'Teach my son the trade.' He replied to her, 'Let him stay with me for four years and I will teach him a hundred dishes made from eggs.' He stayed with him four years and was taught a hundred dishes made from eggs. The cook said to her, 'Let him stay with me another four years and I will teach him another hundred dishes made from eggs.' Rabbi [Judah ha-Nasi] heard this and exclaimed, 'We do not know what good living is!'[5]

3. Another interpretation of ALL THINGS TOIL TO WEARINESS: Words of heresy weary man. R. Eliezer was once arrested because of heresy,[6] and the governor took him and made him ascend a dais to be tried. He said to him, 'Rabbi, can a great man like you occupy himself with those idle matters?' He answered him, 'Faithful is the Judge concerning me.'[7] [The governor] thought that he was alluding to him, whereas he said

[1] V. Ezek. XXVII, 17. The negative of 'numberless' has fallen out of the text. This story occurs in Lam. R. III, 17, with some variations.
[2] They could not think of any more.
[3] Emend to 'R. Eleazar b. R. Jose said', as in Lam. R.; so also here in Warsaw ed. [4] V. Lam. R. *loc. cit.*
[5] He lived in the period after the destruction of the Temple when the people suffered privation. These stories illustrate the weariness of trades where there is so much to learn.
[6] During the Roman persecution under Trajan in 109 C.E. R. Eliezer b. Hyrcanus was arrested on suspicion of adhering to the sect of Christians. v. R. T. Herford, *Christianity in Talmud and Midrash*, pp. 140 ff., J. Klausner, *Jesus of Nazareth*, pp. 37 ff. The story is related with variations in A. Z. 16*b* (Sonc. ed., pp. 84 f.).
[7] He protested his innocence.

it with reference to God. He thereupon said to him, 'Since I have been acknowledged right by you, I too have been thinking and say, "Is it possible that these Academies[1] should go astray with such idle matters!" You are consequently acquitted and free.'[2] After R. Eliezer had left the dais, he was sorely grieved at having been arrested because of heresy. His disciples visited him to console him, but he would not accept [their words of comfort]. R. Akiba visited him and said to him, 'Rabbi, perhaps one of the *minim* expounded something in your presence which was acceptable to you.'[3] He answered, 'By heaven, you have reminded me! Once I was walking up the main street of Sepphoris when there came toward me a man named Jacob of Kefar Sekaniah[4] who told me something in the name of So-and-so[5] which pleased me, viz. "It is written in your Torah, *Thou shalt not bring the hire of a harlot, or the price of a dog, into the house of the Lord thy God for any vow* (Deut. XXIII, 19). What is to be done with them?" I told him that they were prohibited [for every use]. He said to me, "They are prohibited as an offering, but is it permissible to destroy them?" I retorted, "In that case, what is to be done with them?" He said to me, "Let bath-houses and privies be made with them." I exclaimed, "You have said an excellent thing," and the law [not to listen to the words of a *min*] escaped my memory at the time. When he saw that I acknowledged his words, he added, "Thus said So-and-so[5]: From filth they came and on filth they should be expended; as it is said, *For the hire of a harlot hath she gathered them and unto the hire of a harlot they shall return* (Micah I, 7). Let them be spent on privies for the public," and the thought pleased me. On that account I was arrested for heresy. More than that, I transgressed what

[1] Where R. Eliezer was a teacher.
[2] Levy (*Wörterbuch*) renders: By God! you are free.
[3] And having innocently repeated it, he was suspected of sharing the heresy and was arrested.
[4] Identified with Suchnin in Galilee. The man was a disciple of Jesus and may be James the son of Alphaeus (Mark III, 18) or James the little (*ib.* XV, 40).
[5] Sc. Jesus the Nazarene; v. A.Z. (Sonc. ed.), p. 85.

is written in the Torah, *Remove thy way far from her, and come not nigh the door of her house* (Prov. v, 8)—"*Remove thy way far from her,*" i.e. heresy, "*And come not nigh the door of her house,*" i.e. immorality. Why? *For she hath cast down many wounded, yea, a mighty host are all her slain'* (*ib.* VII, 26). Up to what distance [must one remove himself]? Four cubits.

It was for this[1] that R. Eleazar b. Dama, the son of R. Ishmael's sister, met his death. He had been bitten by a serpent and Jacob of Kefar Sekaniah came to heal him, but R. Ishmael would not allow him, saying to him, 'You are not permitted, Ben Dama, [to accept the help of this *min*].' He said to him, 'Permit me, and I will cite a proof to you from the Torah that it is allowed'; but he had not sufficient time to cite the proof to him before he died. R. Ishmael rejoiced and exclaimed, 'Happy art thou, Ben Dama, that thou didst expire in a state of purity and didst not break down the fence erected by the Sages! For whoever breaks down a fence erected by the Sages will eventually suffer penalties; as it is stated, *Whoso breaketh through a fence, a serpent shall bite him'* (Eccl. x, 8). But had he not been bitten by a serpent! [The meaning is] a serpent will not bite him in the Hereafter. What could he have quoted [as a proof from the Torah]? *Which if a man do, he shall live by them* (Lev. XVIII, 5)—'*He shall live by them,*' i.e. and not die by them.[2]

4. A woman once came to R. Eliezer to be made a proselyte, saying to him, 'Rabbi, receive me.' He said to her, 'Recount your acts to me.' She told him, 'My youngest son [was conceived] through my eldest son.' He stormed at her; so she went to R. Joshua, who received her. His disciples said to him, 'R. Eliezer drove her away and you accept her!' He replied, 'When she set her mind

[1] For having disobeyed the law about conversing with a *min*. What follows is narrated in A.Z. 27*b* (Sonc. ed., p. 137).

[2] He might have argued that to save a life, the law against intercourse with a *min* did not apply.

on being a proselyte, she no longer lived to the world,[1] as it is written, *None that go unto her return* (Prov. II, 19); and if they do return [to their evil ways] *Neither do they attain unto the paths of life'* (*ib.*).

Ḥanina, the son of R. Joshua's brother, came to Capernaum,[2] and the *minim* worked a spell on him and set him riding upon an ass on the Sabbath. He went to his uncle, Joshua, who anointed him with oil and he recovered [from the spell. R. Joshua] said to him, 'Since the ass of that wicked person[3] has roused itself against you, you are not able to reside in the land of Israel.' So he went down from there to Babylon where he died in peace.

One of R. Jonathan's disciples ran away [to the *minim*]. He came and found him in subjection to them.[4] The *minim* sent the following message after him: 'Is it not written thus, *Cast in thy lot among us; let us all have one purse'* (Prov. I, 14)? He fled and they pursued him. They said to him, 'Rabbi, do an act of kindness to a certain bride.' He went and found them ravishing a girl. He exclaimed, 'Is this the way for Jews to behave!' They replied to him, 'But is it not written in the Torah, "*Cast in thy lot among us; let us all have one purse?*"'[5] He fled and they pursued him till he came to the door [of his house] and shut it in their faces. They said, 'R. Jonathan, go, tell your mother that you have not turned and looked upon us; for if you had turned and looked upon us, more than we pursue you would you have pursued us!'[6]

The *minim* used to have dealings with R. Judah b. Naḳosa. They used constantly to ask him questions which he was always able to answer. He said to them, 'In vain you bring your trifling arguments. Let us agree among ourselves that whoever overcomes his opponent [in debate]

[1] 'The woman by her repentance died to her past life and would never live in it again' (Herford, *op. cit.*, p. 190).
[2] A town in Galilee (Matt. IV, 13). [3] An allusion to Jesus.
[4] So Herford translates (*op. cit.*, p. 215). Jast. renders: found him doing the cooking [for the *minim* who shared all things in common].
[5] The early Christians were accused of indulging in free love.
[6] You would have been tempted to join us.

shall split his head open with a mallet.' He defeated them and rained blows on their heads until they were filled with cracks. When he returned his disciples said to him, 'Rabbi, they helped you from heaven and you conquered!'[1] He replied to them, 'In vain! go and pray for me[2] and for this bag[3] which was full of precious stones and pearls but is now filled with ashes.'

5. Another interpretation of ALL THINGS TOIL TO WEARINESS: even words of Torah weary a man. At first a man enters [the House of Study] to learn Torah. There they teach him that what he thought unclean is clean and vice versa. But he does not know that through all this weakening of his strength[4] he will eventually be able to deduce by *a fortiori* reasoning and by analogy, and decide issues concerning what is unclean or clean, what is forbidden or permitted.

6. THE EYE IS NOT SATISFIED WITH SEEING. Samuel b. Naḥman said: All the good things, blessings, and consolations which the prophets beheld in this world were not seen by them for nothing, but in virtue of having meditated and performed precepts and righteous acts. Now if you say that they did see these things, has it not been already stated, *Neither hath the eye seen except Thee, O God* (Isa. LXIV, 3)?[5] But if you argue that they did not see them [at all], they surely did see a part, as it is stated, *For the Lord God will do nothing, but He revealeth His counsel unto His servants the prophets* (Amos III, 7).[6] How did they see? R. Berekiah said: As [one peeps]

[1] Although you disobeyed the law by having dealings with the *minim*.
[2] He was conscious that he had done wrong.
[3] Referring to his head. 'Apparently his mind had been contaminated with heresy, and was filled with evil thoughts in place of his former learning and piety' (Herford, *op. cit.*, p. 219).
[4] This weakens him intellectually, raising doubts in his mind.
[5] E.V. '*Neither hath the eye seen a God beside Thee*'.
[6] The passage apparently means that they did not see the *whole* of the future, but on the other hand it is untrue to suggest that they saw nothing at all.

through a crack in the door. R. Levi said: They saw the reward [which was in store for others] but did not see [their own reward].[1] R. Simeon b. Ḥalafta said: All the good things, blessings, and consolations which the prophets beheld in this world were seen for the repentant; but as for him who never experienced sin in his lifetime, '*Neither hath the eye seen except thee, O God, what He worketh for him that waiteth for Him.*'

1. THAT WHICH HATH BEEN IS THAT WHICH SHALL BE (I, 9). The Rabbis say: In the Hereafter the generations will assemble in the presence of the Holy One, blessed be He, and say before Him, 'Lord of the Universe, who shall utter a song before Thee first?' He will answer them, 'In the past none but the generation of Moses uttered a song before Me, and now none but that generation shall utter a song before Me.' What is the proof? As it is said, *Sing unto the Lord a new song, and His praise from the end of the earth; ye that go down to the sea* (Isa. XLII, 10).[2]

Once [the Roman] government dispatched a message to our Rabbis, saying, 'Send us one of your torches.' They said, 'They possess ever so many torches and they want one torch from us! (What multitudes of torches they have; what abundance of precious stones and pearls!)[3] It seems to us that they want of us nothing else than somebody who enlightens faces with legal decisions.' They sent R. Meir to them, and they asked him many questions, all of which he answered. Finally they asked him why the pig is called [in Hebrew] '*ḥazir*', and he replied, 'Because it is destined to restore (*lehaḥazir*) the sovereignty to its owners.'[4] R. Meir continued to sit

[1] This is the explanation of M.K. Radal quotes a different reading from a parallel version: They saw the banquet (arranged for the righteous) but not their reward. Another explanation is offered: They saw (matters connected with this world), but did not see the reward (which is due in the World to Come). [2] Referred to the Israelites who crossed the Red Sea. [3] The words in brackets should be omitted as an interpolation. [4] I.e. on the downfall of Rome, Israel will again come into his own. For the designation of Rome as 'pig', cf. Lev. R. XIII, 5. This is quoted as an illustration of '*That which hath been is that which shall be*'.

and expound: A time will come when the wolf will have a fleece of fine wool and the dog a coat of ermine.[1] They said to him, 'Enough R. Meir! THERE IS NOTHING NEW UNDER THE SUN.'[2]

The Rabbis say: In the Hereafter the Holy One, blessed be He, will send forth a herald to announce, 'Whoever has not partaken of swine's flesh in his lifetime, let him come and take his reward'; and many who belonged to the Gentile peoples who never partook of swine's flesh will come to receive their reward. At that time the Holy One, blessed be He, will declare, 'These wish to be rewarded in both worlds. Not enough for them that they enjoyed their world [upon earth], but they also seek to enjoy the world of My children!'[3] At that time the Holy One, blessed be He, will send forth a herald a second time to announce, 'Whoever has not partaken of the flesh of animals which had not been ritually slaughtered or of animals disqualified for food or of the animals and reptiles prohibited by the Torah,[4] [let him come and receive his reward.' But there were none, apart from Israel, because] if [a Gentile] had not partaken of the flesh of such animals which belonged to himself he did so of animals which belonged to another. Hence, why is the pig called '*ḥazir*'? Because it is destined to restore greatness and sovereignty to those to whom they are due.[5]

What were *sealskins*?[6] R. Judah said: They were violet-coloured skins; R. Nehemiah says: They were ermine; R. Joḥanan says: The Holy One, blessed be He, showed Moses a large species of animal, the skin of which he

[1] To provide garments for the righteous.

[2] Since such a phenomenon had never occured, they argued that it could not happen in the future.

[3] The meaning seems to be: The Gentiles who abstained from swine's flesh did so for their personal benefit and were rewarded by immunity from the ills which result from the consumption of such meat. The Israelites, on the other hand, were actuated solely by the desire to obey God's prohibition, and are accordingly entitled to a reward in the Hereafter. [4] V. Lev. XI.

[5] 'Pig' is here typical of all prohibited foods; and it will be the criterion whereby Israel will be rewarded in the Hereafter.

[6] Required to form the covering of the Tabernacle, Ex. XXVI, 14.

used for the requirements of the Temple. [God] then stored it away.[1] R. Abin said: The name of the animal was *ḳeresh*.[2] R. Hoshaiah learnt: It had one horn on its forehead, as it is said, *It shall please the Lord better than a bullock that hath horns and hoofs* (Ps. LXIX, 32). But should we not infer from the word '*maḳrin*' (that hath horns) that it possesses two horns! R. Ḥanina b. Isaac said: The word is written defectively.[3]

R. Berekiah said in the name of R. Isaac: As the first redeemer was, so shall the latter Redeemer be. What is stated of the former redeemer? *And Moses took his wife and his sons, and set them upon an ass* (Ex. IV, 20). Similarly will it be with the latter Redeemer, as it is stated, *Lowly and riding upon an ass* (Zech. IX, 9). As the former redeemer caused manna to descend, as it is stated, *Behold, I will cause to rain bread from heaven for you* (Ex. XVI, 4), so will the latter Redeemer cause manna to descend, as it is stated. *May he be as a rich cornfield*[4] *in the land* (Ps. LXXII, 16). As the former redeemer made a well to rise,[5] so will the latter Redeemer bring up water, as it is stated, *And a fountain shall come forth of the house of the Lord, and shall water the valley of Shittim* (Joel IV, 18).

1. IS THERE A THING WHEREOF IT IS SAID: SEE, THIS IS NEW (I, 10)? It is written, *And the Lord delivered unto me the two tables of stone written with the finger of God; and on them was written according to all the words which the Lord spoke with you* (Deut. IX, 10). R. Joshua b. Levi said: [The text has not] 'on them' but '*and on them*', [not] 'all' but '*according to all*', [not] 'words' but '*the words*', [not] 'the commandment' but '*all the commandments*'.[6] This is to teach you that Scripture,

[1] For the Hereafter when its skin would be used as clothing for the righteous. This is an instance of '*That which hath been*, etc.'
[2] Probably the antelope (v. Lewysohn, *Zoologie des Talmuds*, p. 114), although the text understands it as the unicorn.
[3] With a *yod* missing. In Rabbinic exegesis this implies limitation, and is therefore understood to imply an animal with one horn.
[4] פסת is read as פתת 'pieces of bread'. [5] V. Num. XXI, 17 f.
[6] This last phrase does not occur in the Biblical text.

Mishnah, *halachoth*, oral laws not included in the Mishnah, homiletical expositions, and the decisions to be hereafter given by eminent scholars already existed and were communicated as a law to Moses from Sinai.[1] Whence do we know this? From what is written, IS THERE A THING WHEREOF IT IS SAID: SEE, THIS IS NEW? [Were a scholar to maintain this], behold his colleague can prove to him IT HATH BEEN ALREADY. R. Berekiah said in the name of R. Ḥelbo: It is like one who has a coin wrapped up in the hem of his garment and it falls out.[2] If he were to put a larger coin there, the space could not contain it, a small coin would not fill the space, but a similar coin does fill it. Similarly, if you have heard Torah from the mouth of a scholar, let it be in your estimation as if your ears had heard it from Mount Sinai. That is what the prophet rebukes the people for when he tells them, *Come ye near unto me, hear ye this: From the beginning I have not spoken in secret; from the time that it was, there am I* (Isa. XLVIII, 16).[3] They said to him, '[If you were present at the Revelation] why have you not told us [this teaching before]?' He replied to them, 'Because chambers [for the reception of prophecy] had not been created within me, but now that they have been created within me, *Now the Lord God hath sent me, and His spirit'* (*ib.*).[4]

1. THERE IS NO REMEMBRANCE OF THEM OF FORMER TIMES (I, 11). R. Aḥa said: THERE IS NO REMEMBRANCE OF THEM OF FORMER TIMES alludes to the generation of the Flood; NEITHER SHALL THERE BE ANY REMEMBRANCE OF THEM IN LATTER TIMES alludes to the people of Sodom. To whom does AMONG

[1] The meaning is that all the later teachings were only a development of the Torah revealed to Moses. They are not innovations.
[2] But the coin, having been there for some time, left its impression on the garment.
[3] I.e. the prophet was (figuratively) present at Sinai when the Torah was revealed, and consequently he was not delivering a new message.
[4] His prophecy was from the days of Moses, but he had to wait for the opportune time to deliver it.

THOSE THAT SHALL COME AFTER refer? To Israel,[1] as it is said, *They shall set forth hindmost* [2] *by their standards* (Num. II, 31).

R. Judan said in the name of R. Simeon b. Shaḳfa: THERE IS NO REMEMBRANCE OF THEM OF FORMER TIMES alludes to the Egyptians; NEITHER SHALL THERE BE ANY REMEMBRANCE OF THEM OF LATTER TIMES alludes to the Amalekites; and to whom [was it commanded] to blot out the remembrance of Amalek? To Israel, as it is said, *Thou shalt blot out the remembrance of Amalek* (Deut. XXV, 19).[3]

How many miracles were worked for Israel after they left Egypt and before they went out! Concerning these [miracles] it is said, THERE IS NO REMEMBRANCE OF THEM OF FORMER TIMES, NEITHER SHALL THERE BE ANY REMEMBRANCE OF THEM OF LATTER TIMES. To what, then, shall I give remembrance? To the miracles of the World to Come, as it is written, *They shall no more say: As the Lord liveth, that brought up the children of Israel out of the land of Egypt; but: As the Lord liveth that brought up and that led the seed of Israel out of the north country, and from all the countries whither I had driven them* (Jer. XXIII, 7 f.).[4]

Many prophets arose in Israel whose names have not been specified; but in the Hereafter the Holy One, blessed be He, will come and bring them with Him. That is what is written, *And the Lord my God shall come, and all the holy ones with Thee* (Zech. XIV, 5).

R. Zera said: How many pious men and sons of the Torah deserve to be numbered as, e.g., Judah b. R. Hezekiah[5]; yet concerning them it states NEITHER SHALL THERE BE ANY REMEMBRANCE OF THEM OF

[1] Unlike the others, the remembrance of Israel will endure.
[2] The Heb. for *hindmost* is the same for '*after*' in Eccl., and the phrase refers to the journey of Israel.
[3] This is apparently intended to prove that AMONG THOSE THAT SHALL COME AFTER must refer to Israel, since it was Israel that was commanded to blot out THEM OF LATTER TIMES—the Amalekites.
[4] The miracles of the latter time will overshadow those of the former time.
[5] He is nowhere else mentioned in Rabbinic literature.

LATTER TIMES. In the Hereafter, however, the Holy One, blessed be He, will number for Himself a band of righteous men of His own and seat them by Him in the Great Academy[1]; as it is said, *Then the moon shall be confounded and the sun ashamed; for the Lord of hosts will reign in mount Zion, and in Jerusalem, and before His elders*[2] *shall be glory* (Isa. XXIV, 23). It is not written here 'Before His angels, His troops, or His priests' but '*Before His* elders *shall be glory*'.

R. Abin said in the name of R. Simeon b. Yoḥai: The Holy One, blessed be He, will in the Hereafter sit [in an Academy shaped] like a threshing-floor and the righteous will be seated before Him, as it is written in connection with Jehoshaphat, *Now the king of Israel and Jehoshaphat the king of Judah sat . . . in a threshing-floor* (II Chron. XVIII, 9). Did they, then, sit in a threshing-floor! But it is as we have learnt: The Sanhedrin sat in the form of a semi-circular threshing-floor, so that they might see one another.[3] Therefore Solomon said, 'I saw Him squeezed in between them'; as it is written, *Her husband*[4] *is known in the gates, when He sitteth among the elders of the land* (Prov. XXXI, 23).

R. Berekiah, R. Ḥelbo, Ulla of Berai,[5] R. Bibi, and R. Eleazar said in the name of R. Ḥanina: In the Hereafter the Holy One, blessed be He, will be appointed leader of the chorus of the righteous, as it is stated, *Mark ye well her ramparts* (Ps. XLVIII, 14). The word for '*ramparts*' (ḥelah) is written as *ḥolah* (chorus),[6] i.e. the chorus in which [the righteous] will dance before Him as maidens, pointing at Him with the finger and exclaiming, *For such is God, our God, for ever and ever; He will guide us eternally* (*ib.* 15)—'*'al-muth*' (eternally) means with quickness, or it means like maidens (*'alamoth*), as in the

[1] According to tradition there was an Academy of learning in heaven.
[2] *Elder* (זקן) is explained by the Rabbis as one who has acquired (זה קנה) wisdom. [3] Sanh. 36*b* (Sonc. ed., p. 230).
[4] Figuratively of God in His relationship to Israel; and '*elders*' as above denotes the learned. [5] A town in Babylon.
[6] This reading does not occur in the received text of the Heb. Bible.

phrase *Damsels playing upon timbrels* (*ib.* LXVIII, 26). Aquila[1] renders *''al-muth'* by *'athanasia'*.[2] [Another interpretation of] *''al-muth'* is: in two worlds (*'alamoth*)—He will guide us in this world and in the World to Come.

1. I ḲOHELETH HAVE BEEN KING OVER ISRAEL IN JERUSALEM (I, 12). R. Samuel b. R. Isaac said: This ought to have been written as a superscription at the beginning of the Book; why then is it written here? The fact is that the Torah does not follow a chronological order. Another instance is as R. Ishmael learnt: *The enemy said: I will pursue, I will overtake* (Ex. XV, 9)—this should have been at the beginning of the song; why then is it written here? The fact is that the Torah does not follow a chronological order. Another instance is: *And it came to pass on the eighth day* (Lev. IX, 1)—this should have been at the beginning of the Book[3]; why then is it written here? The fact is that the Torah does not follow a chronological order. Another instance is: *Ye are standing this day all of you before the Lord your God* (Deut. XXIX, 9)—this should have been at the beginning of the Book, only the Torah does not follow a chronological order. Another instance is: *And the Lord said unto Joshua: This day will I begin to magnify thee in the sight of all Israel* (Josh. III, 7)—this should have been at the beginning of the Book, only the Torah does not follow a chronological order. Another instance is: *Hear, O ye kings; give ear, O ye princes* (Judg. V, 3)—this should have been at the beginning of the song, only the Torah does not follow a chronological order. Another instance is: *In the year that king Uzziah died* (Isa. VI, 1)—this should have been at the beginning of the Book,[4] only the Torah does not follow a chronological order. Another instance is: *Go, and cry in the ears of Jerusalem* (Jer. II, 2)—this should

[1] Translator of the Bible into Greek.
[2] A deathless [world]. על מות is taken as the equivalent of אל מות 'not death'. [3] Since it relates the inauguration of the service of the Tabernacle. [4] The chapter tells of the prophet's call.

have been at the beginning of the Book,[1] only the Torah does not follow a chronological order. Another instance is: *Son of man, put forth a riddle* (Ezek. XVII, 2)—this should have been at the beginning of the Book,[2] only the Torah does not follow a chronological order. Another instance is: *But I was brutish and ignorant, I was as a beast before Thee* (Ps. LXXIII, 22)—this should have been at the beginning of the Book,[3] only the Torah does not follow a chronological order. Like these examples is: I ḲOHELETH HAVE BEEN KING OVER ISRAEL IN JERUSALEM—this should have been at the beginning of the Book, only the Torah does not follow a chronological order.

I ḲOHELETH HAVE BEEN KING OVER ISRAEL IN JERUSALEM. I was [somebody] when I was [king over Israel], but now I am nobody. R. Ḥanina b. Isaac said: When I was [king over Israel] I was [somebody], but now I am worth nothing. Three worlds[4] did he behold in his lifetime. On this statement R. Judan and R. Oniah comment. R. Judan said: He had been king, commoner, and again king; wise, foolish, and again wise; rich, poor, and again rich. What is the proof? It is written, *All things have I seen in the days of my vanity* (Eccl. VII, 15). A man does not speak of his destitution save in the time of his ease when he has returned to his prosperity. R. Oniah said: He had been commoner, king, and again commoner; foolish, wise, and again foolish; poor, rich, and again poor. What is the proof? It is written, I ḲOHELETH HAVE BEEN KING OVER ISRAEL IN JERUSALEM.[5]

1. AND I APPLIED MY HEART TO SEEK AND TO SEARCH OUT BY WISDOM (I, 13). What means To

[1] That was the first message the prophet was to deliver.
[2] The chapter narrates the devastation of Jerusalem, whereas chap. I is dated the fifth year of Jehoiachin's captivity.
[3] As Radal explains, this probably means the beginning of Book III of the Psalms which commences with Ps. LXXIII. This verse would have been an appropriate opening of this Psalm.
[4] Three turns of fortune.
[5] Since he speaks of himself as having been king in the past, it follows that he was now in reduced circumstances.

SEARCH OUT (LA-THUR) BY WISDOM? To search for wisdom, to become an explorer of wisdom, as the word is employed in, *Send thou men, that they may spy out* (yathuru) *the land of Canaan* (Num. XIII, 2); i.e. I will sit in the presence of him who teaches Scripture well or expounds Mishnah well.[1] Another interpretation of TO SEEK AND TO SEARCH OUT is to understand LA-THUR as *le-hothir*, 'to leave over'. When a poet composes a poem as an alphabetical acrostic, sometimes he completes it and sometimes he fails to complete it; but when Solomon composed an alphabetical acrostic he exceeded it by five letters. Thus it is written, *And his songs* (shiro) *were a thousand* (elef) *and five* (I Kings V, 12), which means that he exceeded (*shiyuro*) his parable by five letters in addition to the alphabet (*alef*).[2] Not alone in matters of Torah was Solomon a spy [for wisdom], but *Concerning all things that are done under heaven* (*ib.*); e.g. how to sweeten mustard or lupins, and how to prepare a hot brew consisting of a third part each of wine, water, and pepper.

IT IS A SORE TASK THAT GOD HATH GIVEN TO THE SONS OF MEN TO BE EXERCISED THEREWITH. R. Bun says: This is the nature of wealth.[3] R. Judan said in the name of R. Aibu: Nobody departs from the world with half his desire gratified. If he has a hundred he wants to turn them into two hundred, and if he has two hundred he wants to turn them into four hundred.

(TO BE EXERCISED THEREWITH. R. Phinehas said in the name of R. Joḥanan: Since he is dealing with the subject of idolatry, immorality, and homicide, he tells you that nothing is worse than these except robbery.)[4] R. Judah said in the name of R. Levi: If a man is worthy and uses his wealth for pious purposes, when he prays he

[1] In this way he was a spy to discover knowledge.

[2] A play on *elef* (a thousand) which is read *alef*, the first letter of the alphabet, and thus standing for the whole alphabet (Mah.). By 'parable' the acrostic is meant.

[3] The more man has the more he wants.

[4] This sentence is out of place here and should come later in the paragraph in connection with the futility of robbery.

is answered. That is what is stated, *So shall my righteousness answer for me* (Gen. XXX, 33).[1] Should he not use his wealth in this manner, it will testify against him and accuse him; as it is said, *To bear perverted witness against him* (Deut. XIX, 16).

R. Joḥanan said: [The phrase, IT IS A SORE TASK, etc.,] refers to the peculiar character of robbery; because R. Simeon b. Abba said in the name of R. Joḥanan: When, e.g., the measure of iniquities is full, which accuses first of all [before the judgment-throne of God]? Robbery; for R. Judah said in the name of R. Joḥanan: It is written, *And their unlawful gain at the head of all of them* (Amos IX, 1).[2] R. Jacob b. Aḥa said in the name of R. Joḥanan: Twenty-four sins did Ezekiel enumerate, and out of all of them he concluded only with robbery; as it is written, *Behold, therefore, I have smitten My hand at thy dishonest gain which thou hast made* (Ezek. XXII, 13).

R. Ḥunia related this verse to the Prophets and Hagiographa, for if the Israelites had been worthy they would have read the Pentateuch alone[3]; and the Prophets and Hagiographa were only given to them to labour in these as well as in the Pentateuch and perform the precepts and righteous acts so as to receive a good reward. The Rabbis say: Nevertheless[4] [Scripture says], TO BE EXERCISED THEREWITH, which intimates that they receive a reward for them as for the Pentateuch.[5]

R. Abbahu said: [The phrase, IT IS A SORE TASK, etc]., refers to the peculiar character of [the study of] the Torah, which is that a man learns Torah and forgets

[1] E.V. '*Witness against me*'. The word for '*witness*' is the same root as '*to be exercised*'. [2] E.V. '*And break them in pieces on the head of all of them*', reading *ubiẓ'am* for *ubeẓa'am*.

[3] Most of the prophets and the Hagiographa contain rebukes to Israel for their wrong-doing, and would therefore have been unnecessary had they been righteous (cf. Ned. 22*b*). Hence that too IS A SORE TASK ... TO BE EXERCISED THEREWITH.

[4] In spite of the fact that the books of the Prophets, etc., owe their existence to Israel's sinning. [5] How this follows is not clear. M.K.: THEREWITH is in the singular (*bo*), and so intimates that all the Books of the Bible count as one, and are equal, and as there is reward for studying the Pentateuch, so is there reward for the rest.

it. The Babylonian Rabbis in the name of R. Isaac the Palestinian[1] and R. Tobiah in the name of R. Isaac said: It is for man's good that he learns Torah and forgets it; because if a man studied Torah and never forgot it, he would occupy himself with learning it for two or three years, resume his ordinary work and never pay further attention to it. But since a man studies Torah and forgets it, he will not entirely abandon its study.[2]

The Rabbis say: [The phrase, IT IS A SORE TASK, etc.,] refers to the peculiarity of robbery. Know this, because from the fact that the former generations[3] were engaged in and addicted to robbery—as it is written, *There are that remove the landmarks, they violently take away flocks and feed them* (Job XXIV, 2)—behold, they were blotted out from the world by water; but since the tribes of Reuben and Gad kept themselves aloof from robbery, the Holy One, blessed be He, gave them an inheritance in a place which was free from robbery, as it is said, *Behold, the place was a place for cattle* (Num. XXXII, 1). This is similar to the statement, 'Sixteen miles square from Mahir.'[4]

1. I HAVE SEEN ALL THE WORKS THAT ARE DONE UNDER THE SUN; AND BEHOLD, ALL IS VANITY AND A STRIVING AFTER WIND (I, 14). R. Abba b. Kahana said: It may be likened to an old man who was sitting at the cross-roads. Before him were two paths, one which was even at its beginning but with thorns, cedars, and reeds at the end, while the other began with thorns, cedars, and reeds but ended in an even road. He warned the passers-by and told them that the beginning of this path was even but that it had thorns, cedars, and reeds at the end. As for the other, its beginning was thorns,

[1] Lit. 'The Rabbis of there in the name of R. Isaac of here'. v. Introduction. [2] And earn the reward for his study.

[3] In the period of the Flood.

[4] There is here an allusion to the law in Bekh. IX, 2.: 'What is the distance that cattle wander while pasturing? Sixteen miles.' In J. Pes. 30*d* Mahir is mentioned as a place where the pasture-land was not less than sixteen miles from the next town, so that the cattle of its inhabitants would not unlawfully devour the produce of neighbours.

cedars, and reeds, but its end was even. Ought not people to be thankful to him for warning them for their good so that they should not weary themselves? In like manner, ought not people to be thankful to Solomon who sits by the gates of wisdom and warns Israel,[1] I HAVE SEEN ALL THE WORKS THAT ARE DONE UNDER THE SUN; AND BEHOLD, ALL IS VANITY AND A STRIVING AFTER WIND, except repentance and good deeds? The Rabbis say: It is like an astrologer who was sitting at the entrance of a harbour and advised all passers-by, telling them that such-and-such wares could be sold in such-and-such a place[2]; ought not people to be thankful to him? Similarly with Solomon who said, I HAVE SEEN, etc., except repentance and good deeds.

1. THAT WHICH IS CROOKED CANNOT BE MADE STRAIGHT; AND THAT WHICH IS WANTING CANNOT BE NUMBERED (I, 15). In this world he who is crooked can be made straight and he who is wanting can be numbered[3]; but in the Hereafter he that is crooked cannot be made straight and he that is wanting cannot be numbered. There were certain wicked men who were companions one to the other in this world. One of them repented in good time during his life before he died, but the other did not repent before his death. The one who had done this during his lifetime was in reward stationed by the side of the band of righteous, while the other stood by the side of the band of the wicked; and beholding his companion he exclaimed, 'Is there perhaps favouritism in this world![4] Woe to me! He and I were on earth together and were alike. We stole together, robbed together, and did all the evil deeds in the world together. Why, then, is he with the band of righteous, while I am with the band of the wicked!' 'You great fool!' comes the answer, 'you were a repulsive object after your death for three days, and people did not put you in a coffin but dragged

[1] The words, *I returned, and saw under the sun* (Eccl. IX, 11), are inserted here in error. [2] And so warning them not to send them elsewhere.
[3] The number can be made up.—I.e. in this world one can reform if he is wicked. [4] Viz. the world after death.

you to the grave with ropes.[1] *The maggot is spread under thee, and the worms cover thee* (Isa. XIV, 11). Your companion saw your vileness and swore to turn from his way of wickedness. He repented like a righteous man, and his repentance caused him to receive here life, honour, and a portion with the righteous. Why has all this [happened to you]? Because you had the opportunity to repent; and if you had done so, it would have been well with you.' He thereupon cries to them, 'Let me go and do penance'; but he is answered, 'You great fool! do you not know that this world is like the Sabbath and the world from which you came like the Sabbath-eve? If a man does not make preparation on the Sabbath-eve what will he eat on the Sabbath! And do you not know that the world from which you came is like dry land and this world like the sea? If a man does not make preparation for himself while he is on dry land, what will he eat when at sea! And do you not know that this world is like a wilderness and the world from which you came like inhabited land? If a man does not make preparation for himself from the inhabited territory, what will he eat in the wilderness!' Forthwith he gnashes his teeth and gnaws his flesh, as it is said, *The fool foldeth his hands together, and eateth his own flesh* (Eccl. IV, 5). He then cries, 'Let me behold the glory of my companion'; but they tell him, 'You great fool! we are commanded by the Almighty that the righteous shall not stand among the wicked nor the wicked among the righteous, the pure among the unclean nor the unclean among the clean. Concerning what have we been commanded? Concerning this gate,[2] as it is said, *This is the gate of the Lord, the righteous shall enter into it'* (Ps. CXVIII, 20). Forthwith he rends his garments and pulls out his hair; as it is said, *The wicked shall see, and be vexed* (*ib.* CXII, 10).

2. Another interpretation of THAT WHICH IS CROOKED CANNOT BE MADE STRAIGHT: From the time the

[1] Owing to his bad reputation, he was not given the kind of burial accorded to a respectable person.
[2] To permit the righteous alone to enter.

waters became degraded during the six days of Creation,[1] they have never been rectified. AND THAT WHICH IS WANTING CANNOT BE NUMBERED: Since the Holy One, blessed be He, made for the lunar year eleven days less than the solar year,[2] how many years and cycles, and how many intercalations,[3] have occurred without the solar year overtaking the lunar![4]

Another interpretation of THAT WHICH IS CROOKED CANNOT BE MADE STRAIGHT: From the time the generation of the Flood became crooked in their evil deeds they have never been rectified. AND THAT WHICH IS WANTING CANNOT BE NUMBERED: From the time the Holy One, blessed be He, reduced their years—as it is said, *Therefore shall his days be a hundred and twenty years* (Gen. VI, 3)—they have never been restored to their original number.

Another interpretation of THAT WHICH IS CROOKED CANNOT BE MADE STRAIGHT: If a man diverts himself from the words of Torah, can he make himself straight? AND THAT WHICH IS WANTING CANNOT BE NUMBERED: If a man lets himself go short of[5] words of Torah, is he able to make up the deficiency? From the time that a man diverts himself from words of Torah, he cannot make himself straight: and from the time that a man lets himself go short of words of Torah, he is unable to make up the deficiency. It is like the case of R. Judah and R. Eleazar who studied together. R. Judah married, and R. Eleazar had a start over him of the seven days of the wedding-festivities. Several years passed during which the former endeavoured to catch up to him, but did not succeed in doing so. That is the meaning of AND THAT WHICH IS WANTING CANNOT BE NUMBERED.

[1] Cf. Ex. R. XV, 22. [2] This alludes to the legend that the moon was originally as large as the sun, and subsequently God ordered it to diminish in size (Gen. R. VI, 3.: Ḥul. 60*b*).

[3] The periodical insertion of an extra month in the lunar year, so that the Festivals should fall in their proper season.

[4] This should apparently be reversed; with the lunar year overtaking the solar year—i.e. in spite of all additions the lunar year remains shorter.

[5] Emended text (M.K.).

If the time of the recital of the *shema'* arrived and a man did not recite it in its proper time, concerning him Scripture states, THAT WHICH IS CROOKED CANNOT BE MADE STRAIGHT.[1] If the time of saying the Prayer[2] arrived and he did not offer the prayer, concerning him it is stated, AND THAT WHICH IS WANTING CANNOT BE NUMBERED.

We have learnt: R. Simeon b. Menasia says: What is a case of that which is crooked and cannot be made straight? When a man has illicit intercourse and begets a bastard by a woman. Should you think to apply the words to a robber or a thief—he is able to make restitution.

R. Simeon b. R. Jose says: We only call him CROOKED who was straight at first and then became crooked.[3] Who is he? The disciple of the sages who abandons the Torah.

R. Simeon b. Menasia says: If a man steals, it is possible for him to restore the theft; if he robs with violence he can restore what he robbed; so concerning such an instance it is not said, THAT WHICH IS CROOKED CANNOT BE MADE STRAIGHT. If, however, a man has intercourse with a married woman, he has torn his life from the world and she is prohibited from cohabitation with her husband.

R. Simeon b. Yoḥai says: People do not remark, 'Examine this camel or pig lest it has a blemish.'[4] Which do they examine? Animals qualified as sacrifices. To whom does this apply? A disciple of the Sages who abandons the Torah.[5] Judah b. Laḳish said in the name of R. Simeon b. Gamaliel: Concerning such a person Scripture states, *As a bird that wandereth from her nest, so is a man that wandereth from his place* (Prov. XXVII, 8). He further remarked: A thousand generations were included in the Divine Plan to be created, and how many of them were

[1] He cannot rectify the omission if it was done intentionally. v. Ber. 26*a* The times, morning and evening, during which the *shema'* must be recited are prescribed by law. [2] I.e. the Eighteen Benedictions, also called the *'Amidah*; v. A.P.B., pp. 44 ff.

[3] The Heb. *me'uwath* denotes: that which has been rendered crooked.

[4] Because they are prohibited as sacrifices even if unblemished.

[5] Such a man is more culpable than one who has never studied, and will be severely punished in the Hereafter.

eliminated? Nine hundred and seventy-four. What is the proof? It is written, *The word which He commanded to a thousand generations* (Ps. cv, 8). To what does this allude? To the Torah.[1] R. Levi said in the name of R. Samuel b. Naḥman: Nine hundred and eighty were eliminated. What is the proof? It is written, '*The word which He commanded to a thousand generations*,' and this refers to circumcision.[2]

R. Jacob b. Aḥa said in the name of R. Joḥanan: A man should never hold back from going to the House of Study; for on several occasions this *Halachah* was debated in Jabneh[3] in connection with the Jordan boats. Why can the Jordan boat become unclean?[4] Nobody stood up to speak about it until R. Ḥanina b. Akabia expounded it in his city as follows: Why does the Jordan boat become unclean? Because they load it on dry land and then let it down into the water.[5] The Rabbis raised the objection against him: Do not the sailors of Ashkelon let down [their boat from the land to the sea, and it does not become unclean]![6] R. Eleazar b. Jose replied: This is different, because part of the boat only is grounded.[7] Another matter he expounded was: Branches of date-palm which have been lopped, whether to form a mattress or a hut, must be bound together.[8]

1. I SPOKE WITH MY OWN HEART (I, 16). The heart sees, as it is said, *My heart hath seen much.*[9] It hears, as it is said, *Give Thy servant therefore a heart that hears*

[1] It was revealed after twenty-six generations from the Creation, whereas, according to the Psalmist, it should have been given to the thousandth generation. Therefore 974 were eliminated from the Divine Plan.
[2] Abraham, who first performed the rite, lived in the twentieth generation.
[3] The famous school in Palestine created by R. Joḥanan b. Zakkai after the destruction of the Temple. [4] An ordinary boat cannot become unclean. The Jordan boat was small and portable.
[5] It is therefore like an object used on *land*, and such becomes unclean; cf. Shab. 83*b*. [6] Quoted (not verbally) from J. Shab. 7*a*.
[7] It is never completely out of water, and is only pulled partially ashore to load and unload. It is consequently an ordinary boat. [8] On the Friday if the man intends to move them on the Sabbath. v. Shab. 50*a*.
[9] The continuation of the text. E.V.: '*My heart hath had great experience.*'

(I Kings III, 9).[1] It speaks, as it is said, I SPOKE WITH MY OWN HEART.[2] It walks, as it is said, *Went not my heart?* (II Kings V, 26). It falls, as it is said, *Let no man's heart fail*[3] *within him* (I Sam. XVII, 32). It stands, as it is said, *Can thy heart stand?* (Ezek. XXII, 14).[4] It rejoices, as it is said, *Therefore my heart is glad and my glory rejoiceth* (Ps. XVI, 9). It cries, as it is said, *Their heart cried unto the Lord* (Lam. II, 18). It is comforted, as it is said, *Bid Jerusalem take heart* (Isa. XL, 2). It is troubled, as it is said, *Thy heart shall not be grieved* (Deut. XV, 10). It becomes hard, as it is said, *The Lord hardened the heart of Pharaoh* (Ex. IX, 12). It grows faint, as it is said, *Let not your heart faint* (Deut. XX, 3). It grieves, as it is said, *It grieved Him at His heart* (Gen. VI, 6). It fears, as it is said, *For the fear of thy heart* (Deut. XXVIII, 67). It can be broken, as it is said, *A broken and contrite heart* (Ps. LI, 19). It becomes proud, as it is said, *Thy heart be lifted up* (Deut. VIII, 14). It rebels, as it is said, *This people hath a revolting and rebellious heart* (Jer. V, 23). It invents, as it is said, *Even in the month which he had devised of his own heart* (I Kings XII, 33). It cavils, as it is said, *Though I walk in the stubbornness of my heart* (Deut. XXIX, 18). It overflows, as it is said, *My heart overfloweth with a goodly matter* (Ps. XLV, 2). It devises, as it is said, *There are many devices in a man's heart* (Prov. XIX, 21). It desires, as it is said, *Thou hast given him his heart's desire* (Ps. XXI, 3). It goes astray, as it is said, *Let not thy heart decline to her ways* (Prov. VII, 25). It lusts, as it is said, *That ye go not about after your own heart* (Num. XV, 39). It is refreshed, as it is said, *Stay ye your heart* (Gen. XVIII, 5). It can be stolen, as it is said, *And Jacob stole Laban's heart* (*ib.* XXXI, 20).[5] It is humbled, as it is said, *Then perchance their uncircumcised heart be humbled* (Lev. XXVI, 41). It is enticed, as it is said, *He spoke enticingly unto*[6] *the damsel* (Gen. XXXIV, 3). It errs, as it is said, *My heart is bewildered*

[1] Lit. translation. E.V. '*An understanding heart*'.
[2] Understood to mean, by means of my heart.
[3] Lit. 'fall'. [4] E.V. '*endure*'. [5] Lit. E.V. '*outwitted Laban*'.
[6] Lit. 'upon the heart of'.

(Isa. XXI, 4). It trembles, as it is said, *His heart trembled* (I Sam. IV, 13). It is awakened, as it is said, *I sleep, but my heart waketh* (S.S. V, 2). It loves, as it is said, *Thou shalt love the Lord thy God with all thy heart* (Deut. VI, 5). It hates, as it is said, *Thou shalt not hate thy brother with thy heart* (Lev. XIX, 17). It envies, as it is said, *Let not thy heart envy sinners* (Prov. XXIII, 17). It is searched, as it is said, *I the Lord search the heart* (Jer. XVII, 10). It is rent, as it is said, *Rend your heart, and not your garments* (Joel II, 13). It meditates, as it is said, *The meditation of my heart shall be understanding* (Ps. XLIX, 4). It is like a fire, as it is said, *There is in my heart as it were a burning fire* (Jer. XX, 9). It is like a stone, as it is said, *I will take away the stony heart out of thy flesh* (Ezek. XXXVI, 26). It turns in repentance, as it is said, *That turned to the Lord with all his heart* (II Kings XXIII, 25). It becomes hot, as it is said, *While his heart is hot* (Deut. XIX, 6). It dies, as it is said, *His heart died within him* (I Sam. XXV, 37). It melts, as it is said, *The hearts of the people melted* (Josh. VII, 5). It takes in words, as it is said, *And these words, which I command thee this day, shall be upon thy heart* (Deut. VI, 6). It is susceptible to fear, as it is said, *I will put My fear into their hearts* (Jer. XXXII, 40). It gives thanks, as it is said, *I will give thanks unto the Lord with my whole heart* (Ps. CXI, 1). It covets, as it is said, *Lust not after her beauty in thy heart* (Prov. VI, 25). It becomes hard, as it is said, *He that hardeneth his heart shall fall into evil* (*ib.* XXVIII, 14). It makes merry, as it is said, *It came to pass when their hearts were merry* (Judg. XVI, 25). It acts deceitfully, as it is said, *Deceit is in the heart of them that devise evil* (Prov. XII, 20). It speaks from out of itself, as it is said, *Now, Hannah, she spoke in her heart* (I Sam. I, 13). It loves bribes, as it is said, *But thine eyes and thy heart are not but for thy covetousness* (Jer. XXII, 17). It writes words, as it is said, *Write them upon the table of thy heart* (Prov. III, 3). It plans, as it is said, *A heart that deviseth wicked thoughts* (*ib.* VI, 18). It receives commandments, as it is said, *The wise heart will receive commandments* (*ib.* X, 8). It acts with pride, as it is said, *The pride of thy heart hath beguiled thee* (Obad. 3). It makes arrangements, as it is said, *The preparations of the heart are man's* (Prov. XVI, 1). It aggrandises itself, as it is said, *Will thy heart therefore lift thee up?* (II Chron. XXV, 19). Hence, I SPOKE WITH MY OWN HEART, SAYING: LO, I HAVE GOTTEN GREAT WISDOM.

1. FOR IN MUCH WISDOM IS MUCH VEXATION (I, 18). All the time that a man increases wisdom he increases vexation, and all the time that he increases knowledge he increases sufferings.[1] Solomon said: Through increasing wisdom I have increased vexation, and through increasing knowledge I have increased sufferings.

Rab said: With a disciple of the Sages warning is unnecessary.[2] R. Samuel b. Naḥman said: [His reputation] is like the fine linen garments which come from Beth Shean[3]; if one of them becomes soiled, think for what a high price was it made! But as to the coarse flaxen garments which come from Arbel,[4] should one of them become soiled, what is it and what is its value![5] To what may the matter be likened? To two men who entered a shop. One ate coarse bread and vegetables, while the other ate fine bread and fat meat, and drank old wine and partook of an oily sauce and came out feeling ill. The man who had fine food suffered harm, while he who had coarse food escaped harm.[6] Similarly, have you ever seen an ass or a camel in convulsions? By whom are pains experienced? By human beings. R. Ishmael learnt: According to the camel is the load.[7]

[1] V. Gen. R. XIX, 1.
[2] To make him liable to punishment for a misdemeanour. With an ordinary person a warning is required (cf. Sanh. 8*b*, Sonc. ed., p. 37). In this way increase of knowledge is a cause of vexation.
[3] A town in Galilee. [4] A Galilean town near Sepphoris.
[5] Its cost is small and not much loss is incurred. Similarly nobody takes much notice if an ordinary person does wrong; but the matter is serious if it happens to be a scholar.
[6] The scholar, who feeds his mind with much learning, is in the same way more likely to suffer than the ignorant man.
[7] A proverb indicating that the more eminent a person the greater is his responsibility.

It was taught in the name of R. Meir: Because the wisdom of the serpent was so great, therefore was the penalty inflicted upon it proportionate to its wisdom, as it is said, *Now the serpent was more subtle than any beast of the field* (Gen. III, 1). Consequently he was cursed above all cattle and all beasts of the field.[1]

There have been some who increased wisdom to their advantage and others who increased it to their disadvantage. They who increased it to their advantage were Moses and Solomon, and they who increased it to their disadvantage were Doeg and Ahitophel.[2] There have been some who increased their strength to their advantage and others who increased it to their disadvantage. They who increased it to their advantage were David and Judah, and they who increased it to their disadvantage were Samson and Goliath. There have been some who increased wealth to their advantage and others who increased it to their disadvantage. They who increased it to their advantage were David and Solomon, and they who increased it to their disadvantage were Korah and Haman.[3] There have been some who had many children to their advantage and others who had many to their disadvantage. It was an advantage in the case of the sons of Jacob and David, but a disadvantage in the case of the sons of Ahab and Eli, as it is said, *Now the sons of Eli were base men* (I Sam. II, 12); and as for the sons of Ahab,[4] they received not the yoke of Heaven upon themselves and *They knew not the Lord* (*ib.*), declaring, 'There is no Kingship in Heaven.'

[1] *Ib.* 14. [2] The former shed much blood (I Sam. XXII, 18 ff.), the latter strangled himself (II Sam. XVII, 23).
[3] They became ambitious for power and this led to their downfall.
[4] They numbered seventy and were put to death by Jehu (II Kings X). It is assumed that their doom was the consequence of their impiety.

Chapter II

1. I SAID IN MY HEART: COME NOW, I WILL TRY YOU WITH MIRTH (II, 1). R. Phinehas and R. Hezekiah in the name of R. Simon b. Zabdi commented on this. R. Phinehas said: [The text can be read as] *anassekah* (I will try thee) and *anuskah* (I will flee thee). I will make a test with words of Torah and I will make a test with words of heresy; I will flee from words of heresy to words of Torah. AND ENJOY PLEASURE: i.e. the pleasure of Torah. AND, BEHOLD, THIS ALSO WAS VANITY! The verse should have stated nothing else than 'And, behold, this also was *pleasure*'; but it declares, AND, BEHOLD, THIS ALSO WAS VANITY! R. Hezekiah said in the name of R. Simon b. Zabdi: All the Torah which you learn in this world is 'vanity' in comparison with Torah [which will be learnt] in the World to Come; because in this world a man learns Torah and forgets it, but with reference to the World to Come what is written there? *I will put My law in their inward parts* (Jer. XXXI, 33).[1] The Rabbis, however, say: [The word *anassekah* indicates], the Evil Inclination will yet be dissolved (*yinnathek*) before the Good Inclination. AND ENJOY PLEASURE: i.e. the pleasure of the World to Come. R. Jonah said in the name of R. Simon b. Zabdi: All the prosperity which a man experiences in this world is 'vanity' in comparison with the prosperity of the World to Come; because in this world a man dies and bequeaths his prosperity to another, but in connection with the World to Come it is written, *They shall not build, and another inhabit* (Isa. LXV, 22).

1. I SAID OF LAUGHTER: IT IS MAD (II, 2). R. Abba b. Kahana said: [The meaning is], How confounded[2] [senseless] is the laughter in which the heathen peoples

[1] Having been placed there by God, it can never be forgotten.
[2] מהולל 'mad' is understood as מהול 'mixed', whence confounded or confused.

indulge in their circuses and theatres! AND OF MIRTH: WHAT DOTH IT ACCOMPLISH? What cause can a disciple of the Sages[1] have to enter such places?

Another interpretation of I SAID OF LAUGHTER: IT IS MAD: How mixed was the laughter in which the Attribute of Justice indulged over the generation of the Flood![2] That is what is written, *Their seed is established in their sight with them . . . their houses are safe, without fear . . . they send forth their little ones like a flock, and their children dance. They sing to the timbrel and harp, and rejoice at the sound of the pipe. They spend their days in prosperity, and peacefully they go down to the grave* (Job XXI, 8–13).[3] How does it continue? *Yet they said unto God: Depart from us* (*ib.* 14). Since they declared, *What is the Almighty, that we should serve Him ?* (*ib.* 15), the Holy One, blessed be He, retorted, 'AND OF MIRTH: WHAT DOTH IT ACCOMPLISH? I swear by your lives that I will blot you out of the world.' That is what is written, *And He blotted out every living substance* (Gen. VII, 23).

Another interpretation of I SAID OF LAUGHTER: IT IS MAD: How mixed was the laughter in which the Attribute of Justice indulged over the men of Sodom! As it is stated, *As for the earth, out of it cometh bread, and underneath it is turned up as it were by fire. The stones thereof are the place of sapphires, and it hath dust of gold. That path no bird of prey knoweth, neither hath the falcon's eye seen it* (Job XXVIII, 5 ff.). But when they said, 'Let us cause the practice of hospitality to wayfarers to be forgotten among ourselves,'[4] as it is written, *He breaketh open a shaft away from where men sojourn, they are forgotten of the foot that passeth by* (*ib.* 4)—the Holy One, blessed

[1] Who can enjoy the delights of the Torah.
[2] I.e. how the divine indulgence towards the sinful generation was abused! (Jast.). Or, how dire was the laughter of Justice in knowing that their prosperity would be but short-lived. This is in the same strain as Ps. II, 4: *He that sitteth in Heaven laugheth, the Lord hath them in derision* ('E.J.).
[3] This is a description of the wicked as depicted by Job, and it is applied to the generation of the Flood.
[4] Lit. 'let us cause the law of the foot (i.e. travellers) to be forgotten'.

be He, said to them, 'I swear by your lives that I will cause you to be forgotten from the world'; as it is stated, *Then the Lord caused to rain upon Sodom and upon Gomorrah brimstone and fire* (Gen. XIX, 24).

2. Another interpretation of I SAID OF LAUGHTER: IT IS MAD: How mixed was the laughter in which the Attribute of Justice indulged over Elisheba, the daughter of Amminadab.[1] Elisheba, the daughter of Amminadab, experienced four joys in one day: her brother-in-law, Moses, was a king; her brother, Nahshon, was the chief of all the princes; her husband, Aaron, was [High] Priest, wearing the stones of the ephod; and her two sons were deputy High Priests. When these, however, entered [the Tabernacle] to burn incense without permission, they were burnt, and her joy was turned to mourning. That is what is written, AND OF MIRTH: WHAT DOTH IT ACCOMPLISH?—as it is said, *After the death of the two sons of Aaron, when they drew near before the Lord, and died* (Lev. XVI, 1).

3. Another interpretation of I SAID OF LAUGHTER: IT IS MAD: How mixed is laughter! For R. Aḥa said in the name of Samuel: Three acts [connected with Solomon] the Attribute of Justice allowed to succeed for a time[2] but in the end confounded and confused. It is written, *Neither shall he multiply wives to himself* (Deut. XVII, 17), yet *He had seven hundred wives, princesses, and three hundred concubines* (I Kings XI, 3). It is written, *He shall not multiply horses to himself* (Deut. XVII, 16), yet *Solomon had forty stalls of horses* (I Kings V, 6). It is written, *Neither shall he greatly multiply to himself silver and gold* (Deut. XVII, 17), yet *The king made silver to be in Jerusalem as stones* (I Kings X, 27). Were none of the stones stolen? R. Jose b. R. Ḥanina said: Some stones measured ten cubits and others eight cubits.[3] It has been

[1] Aaron's wife (Ex. VI, 23).
[2] Although they involved a breach of an ordinance of the Torah. The rendering is that of M.K. [3] So they were too huge to be stolen.

taught in the name of R. Simeon b. Yoḥai: Even the weights which were used in the days of Solomon were of gold; as it is stated, *None were of silver; it was nothing accounted of in the days of Solomon* (*ib.* 21). The Holy One, blessed be He, said, 'AND OF MIRTH: WHAT DOTH IT ACCOMPLISH? How has this crown fared in thy possession! Descend from My throne!' At that time an angel descended in the likeness of Solomon and sat on his throne. [Solomon] went about to the Synagogues, Academies, and the houses of the eminent men of Israel, saying, 'I, ḲOHELETH, HAVE BEEN KING'; but they smote him with a rod,[1] and set before him a dish of grits. At that time he wept and exclaimed, '*This was my portion from all my labour*' (Eccl. II, 10).

4. Another interpretation of I SAID OF LAUGHTER: IT IS MAD: R. Phinehas said: If a man's feasting is disturbed, what is the use of rejoicing? It happened once that the son of one of the eminent men of Babylon married on the fourth day of the week. The father made a dinner for the Sages and said to his son, 'Go up to the attic and bring us some good wine from a certain cask.' He went up to bring the old wine from the attic; a serpent bit him and he died. The father waited for him to descend and, as he failed to do so, said, 'I will see what is the reason that my son is delayed.' He went up, and found that he had been bitten by a serpent and was lying dead among the casks. The pious man waited up there until his guests had eaten and drunk and finished the meal and were about to say Grace. Then he spoke to them, 'My masters, not to say the blessing for a bridegroom[2] have you come to my house, to bless therewith my son; say now over him the benediction for mourners.[3] Not to conduct him under the marriage-canopy have you come; convey him to the grave.' R. Zakkai went in and delivered a funeral oration over him on the text, I SAID OF

[1] For claiming to be Solomon, and then fed him like a beggar.
[2] V. Keth. 8*a* (Sonc. ed., p. 31 f.) and A.P.B., p. 299.
[3] V. Keth. 8*b* (Sonc. ed., p. 39 f.) and A.P.B., p. 282 f.

LAUGHTER: IT IS MAD; AND OF MIRTH: WHAT DOTH IT ACCOMPLISH?

1. I SEARCHED IN MY HEART HOW TO PAMPER MY FLESH WITH WINE (II, 3). Solomon said, I SEARCHED IN MY HEART HOW TO PAMPER MY FLESH WITH WINE—to pamper my heart with the wine of the Torah. AND MY HEART CONDUCTING ITSELF WITH WISDOM—with the wisdom of the Torah. HOW YET TO LAY HOLD ON FOLLY: R. Judan asked R. Aḥa, 'What is the meaning of the phrase, HOW YET TO LAY HOLD ON FOLLY (SIKLUTH)?' He replied, 'To grasp intelligence.'[1]

1. I MADE ME GREAT WORKS (II, 4). Solomon said: I made greater works than did my ancestors. I MADE ME GREAT WORKS: that is what is written, *Moreover the king made a great throne of ivory* (I Kings X, 18). I BUILDED ME HOUSES: that is what is written, *And it came to pass at the end of twenty years, wherein Solomon had built the two houses, the house of the Lord and the king's house* (*ib.* IX, 10). I PLANTED ME VINEYARDS: as it is said, *Solomon had a vineyard at Baal-hamon* (S.S. VIII, 11).

1. I MADE ME GARDENS AND PARKS (II, 5): this is to be understood literally. AND I PLANTED IN THEM ALL KINDS OF FRUITS: even pepper.[2] R. Abba b. Kahana said: Solomon made use of the spirits and sent them to India from where they brought him water with which to water [the pepper-plant] here [in the land of Israel] and it produced fruit. R. Jannai b. R. Simeon said to him: If you hold that opinion you attribute much labour to Solomon [in connection with his plantations]; the truth is that Solomon in his wisdom stood upon the

[1] סכלות 'folly' is connected with שכל 'intelligence'. The Midrashic rendering is thus the opposite of E.V.

[2] Typical of exotic plants which do not grow in Palestine. For that reason Indian water had to be brought so that such plants should be productive

centre[1] of the earth, and saw which root branched off to a particular country.[2] He planted upon the root of that country and in this way produced fruits.

1. I MADE ME POOLS OF WATER: (II, 6): i.e. reservoirs. TO WATER THEREFROM THE WOOD SPRINGING UP WITH TREES: i.e. the land of Israel, as it is said, *And the king put them in the house of the forest of Lebanon* (1 Kings X, 7).[3]

1. I ACQUIRED MEN-SERVANTS AND MAID-SERVANTS (II, 7): as it is written, *All the Nethinim, and the children of Solomon's servants, were three hundred ninety and two* (Neh. VII, 60). AND HAD SERVANTS BORN IN MY HOUSE[4]: as it is said, *And those officers provided victual for king Solomon, and for all that came unto king Solomon's table . . . they let nothing be lacking* (1 Kings V, 7). What means '*They let nothing be lacking*'? R. Ḥama b. Ḥanina said: Never did Solomon's table lack anything, neither roses in summer nor cucumbers in winter; but he enjoyed these the whole year.

ALSO I HAD GREAT POSSESSIONS OF HERDS AND FLOCKS: It mentions [that these included] *barburim abusim*—fatted fowl (*ib.* 3). What were they? The Rabbis say: A species of birds from Barbaria.[5] R. Berekiah said in the name of R. Judah: A rare and precious bird which used to come and sit on his table daily. From where did it come? It came from Barbaria every day.

1. I GATHERED ME ALSO SILVER AND GOLD (II, 8). That is what is written, *And the king made silver to be in*

[1] Lit. 'foundation'. There was an ancient belief that Jerusalem was the geographical centre of the world and the Temple-area the centre of Jerusalem.

[2] The idea is that the roots in all countries were connected with the centre of the world. Solomon was thereby able to plant, e.g., on the Palestinian end of the root of the pepper-tree which grew in India, and so made it grow also in his country. [3] Since Solomon stored the gold in his country, the words are taken as descriptive of the land of Israel.

[4] Lit. 'I had sons of the house', which is understood as his household.

[5] Term applied to countries beyond the Roman Empire.

Jerusalem as stones (I Kings X, 27). Can they possibly have been like the stones one finds in roadways and courts? Were they then not stolen! They were in fact huge in size, stones measuring eight or ten cubits. It has been taught that even the weights which were used in the days of Solomon were of gold,[1] and they employed golden balances weighing a *centenarium*.[2] Every weight, large and small alike, was of gold.

AND TREASURES SUCH AS KINGS HAVE AS THEIR OWN: as it is said, *And all the kings of the earth sought Solomon* (II Chron. IX, 23). AND THE PROVINCES (MEDINOTH): this alludes to the Queen of Sheba who came and contested (*medayyeneth*) with him with her wisdom and questions but was unable to conquer him; as it is said, *She came to prove him with hard questions . . . and Solomon told her all the questions* (I Kings X, 1 ff.).[3]

I GOT ME MEN-SINGERS AND WOMEN-SINGERS: the words mean male and female singers. AND THE DELIGHTS OF THE SONS OF MEN: i.e. public baths and lavatories.[4] WOMEN VERY MANY: i.e. numerous demonesses to heat them.[5]

R. Ḥiyya b. Nehemiah said: Does Scripture merely inform us of Solomon's material wealth? Behold, it speaks of nothing else than [the riches he acquired] in connection with matters of Torah. I MADE ME GREAT WORKS: that is what is written, *And the tables were the* work *of God* (Ex. XXXII, 16). I BUILDED ME HOUSES: viz. Synagogues and Houses of Study. I PLANTED ME VINEYARDS: this refers to the rows of disciples who sat in tiers as in a vineyard; as we have learnt: This exposition was made by R. Eleazar b. 'Azariah in the presence of

[1] V. on v. 2. [2] A Latin weight, the equivalent of the Hebrew 'talent'.
[3] The Midrash actually quotes two half verses, viz, vv. 1 and 3.
[4] Considered in those times to be great luxuries.
[5] The Heb. שדה ושדות is obscure. The Midrash identifies the word with the fem. of שד 'demon'. Evil spirits were popularly believed to haunt baths and privies; according to the Midrash he pressed even these into his service.

the Sages in the vineyard of Jabneh[1]—was it, then, a vineyard? Only it was so called because of the disciples who sat in tiers as in a vineyard. I MADE ME GARDENS AND PARKS: this refers to the great collections of Mishnah, as, e.g., that of R. Ḥiyya the elder, and of Bar Ḳappara.[2] AND I PLANTED TREES IN THEM OF ALL KINDS OF FRUIT: this is the Talmud [dialectic] which is contained in them. I MADE ME POOLS OF WATER: R. Ḥiyya the elder said: these are the expositions. TO WATER THEREFROM THE WOOD SPRINGING UP WITH TREES: these are the pupils who study. (R. Naḥman said: POOLS OF WATER is an allusion to the Talmud; TO WATER THEREFROM THE WOOD SPRINGING UP WITH TREES is a reference to the disciples who study.) I ACQUIRED MEN-SERVANTS AND MAID-SERVANTS: these are the heathen nations, as it is said, *And also upon the servants and upon the handmaids in those days will I pour out My spirit* (Joel III, 2). In the Messianic future they will become servants of Israel, as it is written in Isaiah, *And strangers shall stand and feed your flocks, and aliens shall be your plowmen and your vinedressers* (LXI, 5). AND HAD SERVANTS BORN IN MY HOUSE: this is the Holy Spirit.[3] ALSO I HAD GREAT POSSESSIONS OF HERDS AND FLOCKS: these are the sacrifices, as it is written, *Ye shall bring your offering of the cattle, even of the herd or flock* (Lev. I, 2). I GATHERED ME ALSO SILVER AND GOLD: this refers to the words of the Torah, as it is said, *More to be desired are they than gold* (Ps. XIX, 11). AND TREASURES SUCH AS KINGS HAVE AS THEIR OWN: (These are the princes of the Torah),[4] as it is said, *By me* [wisdom] *kings reign* (Prov. VIII, 15). AND THE PROVINCES (MEDINOTH): these are the disciples who contend (*medayyenim*) in *halachah*. I GOT

[1] Keth. 49*a* (Sonc. ed., p. 281). The continuation occurs in J. Ber. 7*d*.
[2] Attempts to codify the Oral Law made by the Rabbis named. The codification by R. Judah ha-Nasi became generally acknowledged and superseded the others. [3] Those who studied in 'MY HOUSE', i.e. the Academy, were worthy to receive the Holy Spirit.
[4] These words are to be inserted from the Yalḳuṭ.

ME MEN-SINGERS AND WOMEN-SINGERS: these are the *Toseftoth*.[1]

(The singers were male and female.)[2] AND DELIGHTS: these are the *Haggadoth* which are delightful expositions of Scripture. WOMEN VERY MANY: this alludes to male and female judges.[3]

2. R. Joshua b. Levi interpreted the passage as alluding to Israel when they entered the Holy Land. I MADE ME GREAT WORKS: i.e. *When ye are come into the land of your habitations, which I give unto you, and will make an offering by fire unto the Lord* (Num. XV, 2 f.). I BUILDED ME HOUSES: i.e. *And houses full of all good things* (Deut. VI, 11). I PLANTED ME VINEYARDS: i.e. *Vineyards and olive-trees, which thou didst not plant* (*ib.*). I MADE ME GARDENS AND PARKS: The accursed Hadrian asked R. Joshua b. Ḥanania, 'It is written in the Torah, *A land wherein thou shalt eat bread without scarceness, thou shalt not lack anything in it* (*ib.* VIII, 9). Are you able to bring me three things if I ask for them?' 'What are they?' he asked. He replied, 'Pepper, pheasants, and silk.' He brought him pepper from Niẓhana,[4] pheasants from Zidon[5] (others say, from Akbrin),[6] and silk from Gush Ḥeleb.[7] I MADE ME POOLS OF WATER: as it is said, *A land of brooks of water* (*ib.* 7). TO WATER THEREFROM THE WOOD SPRINGING UP WITH TREES: R. Levi said: The land of Israel did not even lack reeds to be made into arrows. I ACQUIRED MEN-SERVANTS AND MAID-SERVANTS: i.e. *And a mixed multitude went up also with them* (Ex. XII, 38). AND HAD SERVANTS BORN IN MY

[1] Lit. 'additions', Rabbinical dicta not included in the Mishnah, and separately collected in a work called 'Tosefta'.

[2] This sentence is printed in brackets in the text and is an explanatory gloss on the words in Eccl.

[3] Since a woman could not act as judge in the legal sense, it must mean 'supervisors'. Or perhaps actual judges were meant, as we find Deborah acting as a judge in Scriptural times. How this meaning is read into the Heb. of Eccl. is doubtful.

[4] The place is nowhere else mentioned. It may be a corruption of Nazareth. [5] A Phœnician town. [6] A town in Upper Galilee.

[7] Giscala in Galilee.

HOUSE: these are the Gibeonites whom Joshua made hewers of wood and drawers of water, as it is said, *And Joshua made them that day hewers of wood and drawers of water for the congregation* (Josh. IX, 27). ALSO I HAD GREAT POSSESSIONS OF HERDS AND FLOCKS: i.e. *Now the children of Reuben and the children of Gad had a great multitude of cattle* (Num. XXXII, 1). I GATHERED ME ALSO SILVER AND GOLD: as it is said, *And He brought them forth with silver and gold* (Ps. CV, 37). AND TREASURES SUCH AS KINGS AND THE PROVINCES HAVE AS THEIR OWN: this refers to the spoils of Og and Midian.[1] I GOT ME MEN-SINGERS AND WOMEN-SINGERS: the terms imply male and female singers. AND THE DELIGHTS OF THE SONS OF MEN: i.e. the enjoyment of Israel [in the Holy Land]. WOMEN VERY MANY: [the Hebrew words denote] all kinds of luxuries.

1. SO I WAS GREAT, AND INCREASED MORE THAN ALL THAT WERE BEFORE ME IN JERUSALEM (II, 9). Who was before him in Jerusalem? Was it not his father David![2] Four men are called '*maneh* son of *peras*',[3] viz. On, the son of Peleth,[4] the son of Zippor,[5] the son of Beor,[6] and Hezekiah.[7] Two men are called '*maneh* son of *maneh*', viz. Ben 'Aḳish[8] and Solomon.

ALSO MY WISDOM STOOD ME IN STEAD. R. Aḥa said: Solomon declared: Of all the Torah which I learnt,

[1] Num. XXI, 35, and XXV, 17 ff.
[2] Solomon exceeded even him in greatness.
[3] *Maneh* is a coin of the value of 100 shekels, and *peras* was half a *maneh*. The phrase means that the son was more distinguished than the father.
[4] Num. XVI, 1. In Sanh. 109*b* (Sonc. ed., p. 753) 'On' is explained as 'he sat in lamentations' for having joined Korah's rebellion, and 'Peleth' that 'wonders were wrought for him' because he dissociated himself from the conspiracy.
[5] I.e. Balak, king of Moab. In Num. XXIII, 18, he is called בנו צפר instead of the more usual בן צפר. For the reason v. the next note.
[6] I.e. Balaam who is so denominated in Num. XXIV, 3. In Sanh. 105*a* (Sonc. ed., p. 715) the form of the name is explained as implying that the father was a prophet, but his son was greater.
[7] His father, Ahaz, was an evil-doer (II Kings XVI, 2).
[8] Possibly a corruption of 'the son of Kish', viz. king Saul.

there remained with me in my old age [only what I acquired through] the blows [which my teacher gave me] in anger.[1]

1. AND WHATSOEVER MINE EYES DESIRED I KEPT NOT FROM THEM. I WITHHELD NOT MY HEART FROM ANY JOY (II, 10): this is the joy which comes from wealth. FOR MY HEART HAD JOY OF ALL MY LABOUR, AND THIS WAS MY PORTION FROM ALL MY LABOUR. Some say that this was his pitcher,[2] others his girdle. Another interpretation is: AND WHATSOEVER MY EYES DESIRED: viz. of women; I KEPT NOT FROM THEM. I WITHHELD NOT MY HEART FROM ANY JOY: this is the joy of women. FOR MY HEART HAD JOY OF ALL MY LABOUR: this is the separation of the dough, while others say it was the separation of wine for the drink-offerings.[3]

1. AND I TURNED (PANITHI) MYSELF TO BEHOLD WISDOM (II, 12). Read the word as *pinnithi*, i.e. 'I emptied myself' like this bowl which at times is filled and at other times emptied. Similarly Solomon learnt Torah at one time and forgot it another time.[4]

TO BEHOLD WISDOM AND MADNESS AND FOLLY. R. Ḥanina b. Papa and R. Simon comment. R. Ḥanina b. Papa says: MADNESS refers to the intrigues of rulership[5] and FOLLY to trouble [caused by lack of wisdom].[6] R. Simon says: MADNESS refers to the madness of heresy and FOLLY means inanity.

FOR WHAT CAN THE MAN DO THAT COMETH AFTER THE KING? If a man tells you, 'I can stand upon the foundation of the world,'[7] answer him, 'You are unable

[1] The text is doubtful and the translation emends פסטירין to מסטרין. The word ALSO (*af*) is understood in the sense of 'anger'. Levi (*Wörterbuch*) renders: which I learnt later in my old age, in the additional years (those which exceed the normal span), remained with me. Thus אף (E.V. '*also*') is rendered the additional (years).

[2] Which was all that was left to him after he had been deposed. v. Sanh. 20*b* (Sonc. ed., p. 110).

[3] V. on IX, 7.

[4] V. on I, 1, p. 3 f.

[5] I.e. the intrigues of Court life.

[6] Or, to the heavy cares (of government).

[7] I.e. I can fathom Nature to its depths.

to understand a human king; how then can you comprehend the supreme King of kings, the Holy One, blessed be He!' R. Naḥman made two comparisons—one to a thicket of reeds which nobody could penetrate. What did a certain shrewd man do? He kept on cutting them down and entering as he cut and then came out by way of the clearing. The other comparison of R. Naḥman was to a huge palace with so many doors that whoever entered it lost his way. A shrewd man was there who on entering took a rope of reed-grass which he tied to the entrance. All were then able to enter and depart by the guidance of the rope.[1] R. Simeon b. Yoḥai said: To what may the matter be likened? To a human king who built a palace which all passers-by entered and which they criticised, saying, 'If its pillars were taller it would be more beautiful,' 'If its walls were taller it would be more beautiful,' 'If its roof were loftier it would be more beautiful.' But would any man come and say, 'If I had three hands, or three eyes, or three ears, or three legs, I would be more beautiful'? Therefore the text states, EVEN THAT WHICH HATH ALREADY BEEN THEY HAVE MADE[2]—it is not written here 'He has made' but THEY HAVE MADE. If it is possible to say so, the Holy One, blessed be He, and His *Beth Din* made it.[3] They took a vote concerning every one of your limbs and made you perfect. Should you, then, argue that there were two creative powers,[4] has it not been already stated, *Hath* He *not made thee, and established thee?* (Deut. XXXII, 6)!

R. Levi b. Ḥayetha said: When a human king builds a palace, if he placed its water-spout over its entrance, it would not be beautiful or commendable; but the Holy One, blessed be He, created man and placed his spout over his entrance, viz. his nose, and it constitutes his

[1] This is a comment on the beginning of the verse, AND I TURNED MYSELF TO BEHOLD WISDOM, which R. Naḥman explains as meaning that he (Solomon) illuminated and clarified the tangled paths of knowledge (Mah. on Gen. R. XII, 1, where the whole passage is repeated); cf. S.S. R. I, 1, §8. [2] So lit. E.V. '*already been done*'.
[3] Therefore everything has been made after consultation and is perfect.
[4] God and His *Beth Din*.

beauty and excellence. R. Isaac b. Marion said: It is written, *Then the Lord God formed man* (Gen. II, 7); why, then, is it stated in the next verse, *The man whom He had formed* (yaẓar)? Its purpose is to indicate that the Creator (*ẓur*)[1] is a skilful artist (*ẓayyar*); He, as it were, boasts of His universe and exclaims, 'Behold the creation which I have created and the form which I have constructed!' R. Isaac b. Marion also said: *These are the generations of the heaven and of the earth when they were created (ib.* 4)[2]—*He* created them and *He* praises them [as His handiwork], so who would presume to decry them! When their Creator lauds them, who would dare to defame them! But they are beautiful and worthy of praise; concerning them it is stated, '*These are the generations of the heaven and of the earth.*'[3] R. Phinehas said in the name of R. Levi: '*When they were created*'—i.e. He created them with the letter *hé*.[4]

1. THEN I SAW THAT WISDOM EXCELLETH FOLLY (II, 13). It has been taught in the name of R. Meir: As there is superiority of light over darkness, so there is superiority of words of Torah over words of vanity.

1. THE WISE MAN, HIS EYES ARE IN HIS HEAD (II, 14). Has the wise man his eyes in his head and the fool in his feet! The meaning, however, is that while the wise man is still at the beginning of an enterprise he knows how it will turn out. R. Meir called the end of a matter its 'head'.[5] Another interpretation of THE WISE MAN, HIS EYES ARE IN HIS HEAD: this alludes to the patriarch Abraham; BUT THE FOOL WALKETH IN

[1] Lit. 'the Rock', a designation of God.
[2] בהבראם instead of בבראם. The ה is interpreted as indicating הוא 'He'.
[3] The point probably lies in the Rabbinic exposition of '*these*' as indicating that '*these*' are of value, whereas the earlier ones were unsatisfactory; v. Gen. R. XII, 3. [4] I.e. with absolute ease, like the utterance of the letter *hé*, which requires a mere breath. v. Gen. R. XII, 2.
[5] Because in the case of a wise man its end was in his thought before he began it. 'Head' is understood in the sense of 'the beginning' which may indeed be the meaning of the Hebrew.

DARKNESS: this alludes to Nimrod.[1] AND I ALSO PERCEIVED THAT ONE EVENT HAPPENETH TO THEM ALL.[2]

1. THEN I SAID IN MY HEART: AS IT HAPPENETH TO THE FOOL, SO WILL IT HAPPEN EVEN TO ME (II, 15). I[3] have been called 'king' and the wicked Nimrod is called 'king'. Both alike died; in that case, WHY WAS I THEN MORE WISE? Why did I [Abraham] jeopardise my life for the sanctification of the name of the Holy One, blessed be He, and warn people, saying, 'There is no God like Him among those above or below'? Then I said further, FOR THERE IS NO REMEMBRANCE OF THE WISE MAN TOGETHER WITH THE FOOL FOR EVER,[4] SEEING THAT IN THE DAYS TO COME ALL WILL LONG AGO HAVE BEEN FORGOTTEN. Why [should he have said so]? When adversity befalls Israel they cry, '*Remember Abraham, Isaac, and Israel, Thy servants*' (Ex. XXXII, 13); but do the heathen nations [in their distress] cry, 'Remember the deeds of Nimrod!' That is what is written, SO HOW SHALL THE WISE MAN DIE EVEN AS THE FOOL![5]

2. Another interpretation of THE WISE MAN, HIS EYES ARE IN HIS HEAD: i.e. Moses. BUT THE FOOL WALKETH IN DARKNESS: i.e. the wicked Balaam. AND I ALSO PERCEIVED THAT ONE EVENT HAPPENETH TO THEM ALL. THEN SAID I IN MY HEART, etc. Each of them was called 'prophet'; in that case WHY WAS I THEN MORE WISE? Why did I [Moses] give my life to the Torah? Then I said, FOR THERE IS NO REMEMBRANCE OF THE WISE MAN TOGETHER WITH THE FOOL FOR EVER, SEEING THAT IN THE DAYS TO COME ALL WILL LONG AGO HAVE BEEN FORGOTTEN.

[1] Who tried to compel Abraham to idolatry; v. Gen XXXVIII, 13.
[2] In the end they both died. [3] Abraham, v. Gen R. XLII, 5.
[4] E.V. '*For of the wise man, even as of the fool, there is no remembrance for ever*'.
[5] The wise man lives in the memory of others. E.V. '*And how must the wise man*'. He probably renders: for the wise man being remembered whereas the fool is not.

In the future Israel will suffer adversity and cry, '*Then His people remembered the days of old, the days of Moses,* etc.' (Isa. LXIII, 11); but do the heathen nations [in their distress] cry, 'Then he remembered the days of old, the days of Balaam!' That is what is written, SO HOW SHALL THE WISE MAN DIE EVEN AS THE FOOL!

3. Another interpretation of THE WISE MAN, HIS EYES ARE IN HIS HEAD: i.e. David, king of Israel; BUT THE FOOL WALKETH IN DARKNESS: i.e. the wicked Nebuchadnezzar. AND I ALSO PERCEIVED THAT ONE EVENT HAPPENETH TO THEM ALL. THEN SAID I IN MY HEART . . . FOR THERE IS NO REMEMBRANCE OF THE WISE MAN TOGETHER WITH THE FOOL FOR EVER, SEEING THAT IN THE DAYS TO COME ALL WILL LONG AGO HAVE BEEN FORGOTTEN —the former built the Temple[1] and reigned forty years, while the latter destroyed it and reigned forty years. In that case, WHY WAS I THEN MORE WISE? Why did I [David] devote myself to the building of the Temple? Then I said, FOR THERE IS NO REMEMBRANCE OF THE WISE MAN TOGETHER WITH THE FOOL FOR EVER, SEEING THAT IN THE DAYS TO COME ALL WILL LONG AGO HAVE BEEN FORGOTTEN. Subsequently Solomon was to arise, build the Temple, and say, *Remember the good deeds of David Thy servant* (II Chron. VI, 42); but could Evil-Merodach[2] stand up and say, 'Remember the good deeds of Nebuchadnezzar Thy servant!' That is what is written, SO HOW SHALL THE WISE MAN DIE EVEN AS THE FOOL!

4. Another interpretation of THE WISE MAN, HIS EYES ARE IN HIS HEAD: i.e. he who purchases wheat for three years; BUT THE FOOL WALKETH IN DARKNESS: i.e. he who purchases wheat for one year.[3] AND I ALSO PERCEIVED . . . THEN SAID I IN MY HEART, etc.—each alike eats; so in that case WHY WAS I THEN

[1] Since he planned it, its erection is attributed to him although executed by his son. [2] II Kings XXV, 27. [3] V. Est. R. I, I.

MORE WISE? Why did I [the buyer of wheat for three years] pawn the furniture of my room to provide myself with food? Then I said, FOR THERE IS NO REMEMBRANCE OF THE WISE MAN TOGETHER WITH THE FOOL FOR EVER, etc. Subsequently a year of drought may come and the latter will eat food at a great cost while the former eats it at a cheap price. That is what is written, SO HOW SHALL THE WISE MAN DIE EVEN AS THE FOOL!

5. Another interpretation of THE WISE MAN, HIS EYES ARE IN HIS HEAD: i.e. a disciple who is diligent in his study.[1] AND I ALSO PERCEIVED . . . THEN I SAID IN MY HEART, etc. Each is alike called 'Rabbi', each alike is a 'Sage', each alike wraps himself in his *tallith*; so in that case, WHY WAS I THEN MORE WISE? Why did I devote myself to my study of Torah? Then I said, FOR THERE IS NO REMEMBRANCE OF THE WISE MAN TOGETHER WITH THE FOOL FOR EVER. Some day they may both enter a House of Assembly or some other place and question each other. One is questioned and answers, the other is questioned but is unable to answer. That is what is written, SO HOW SHALL THE WISE MAN DIE EVEN AS THE FOOL!

R. Ḥiyya b. Nehemiah said: If a disciple [thinks there is] no necessity to quote a teaching in the name of his master, his knowledge of Torah will in the future be forgotten; and shall not the master apply himself to his disciple for this reason![2]

1. SO I HATED LIFE (II, 17). Imiḳanṭron[3] wrote to the emperor Hadrian, saying, 'If it is the circumcised you hate, there are also the Ishmaelites[4]; if it is the Sabbath-observers, there are also the Samaritans.[5] Behold, you

[1] We must insert some words like: BUT THE FOOL, etc., i.e. one who neglects his study. (It is so inserted in Warsaw ed.).
[2] To impress upon him the necessity of quoting the author of a teaching that his name may live after he is dead.
[3] The name of a certain Jew otherwise unknown.
[4] Who practise circumcision but are not persecuted.
[5] Who observe many Jewish rites, including the Sabbath.

only hate this people [Israel]; and their God will exact punishment from you.' Hadrian issued a decree that the man who had done this should disclose his identity to the king, who would give him something. A certain person went and disclosed himself [as the writer of the letter]. The king ordered that he should be beheaded. The king asked him, 'Why did you speak in this manner?'[1] He replied, 'Because you free me from three evil experiences.' 'What are they?' he inquired. 'My appetite desires to eat morning and evening but I have nothing to give it; and the same applies to my wife and children.' Hadrian said, 'Since you lead such an unhappy life, abandon it [and die],' and the man applied the text to himself, SO I HATED LIFE.

There was a certain glutton who worked all the days of the year on weekdays, yet on the Sabbath he had nothing to eat. What did he do? He once donned his working clothes,[2] went to the top of the roof and threw himself down and died, applying to himself the text, SO I HATED LIFE.

People came and told R. Hoshaia, 'The judges whom you appointed drink wine publicly,'[3] but he did not believe them. He once went out and found his judges drinking wine publicly. [In his distress] he applied the text to himself, SO I HATED LIFE, and died peacefully.

R. Huna said: *And man became a living soul* (Gen. II, 7): He made him a slave indentured to himself,[4] so that if he does not work he does not eat. That is the opinion of R. Huna[5]; because R. Huna said: *The Lord hath delivered me into their hands, against whom I am not able to stand* (Lam. I, 14), because if I do not work by day I am not able to stand by night.

[1] In the present state of the text this can only refer to the wording of the letter. Probably part of the conversation has dropped out, and the man expressed his hatred of life and readiness to be executed. [2] According to Jast., lit. 'garments of leather'. The commentators explain it as 'best garments'. [3] Contrary to *It is not for kings* (i.e. judges) *to drink wine* (Prov. XXXI, 4). [4] V. Gen. R. XIV, 10, for the explanation of this passage. [5] The passage has no connection with the context and possibly belongs to the next verse. In Lam. R. *ad loc.* the name is Ḥanina.

1. AND I HATED ALL MY LABOUR WHEREIN I LABOURED UNDER THE SUN (II, 18). R. Meir was a skilful scribe and used to earn three *sela's* a week. He spent one *sela'* on food and drink, another on clothing, and the third on the support of Rabbinical scholars. His disciples asked him, 'What are you doing to provide for your children?' He answered, 'If they are righteous, then it will be as David said, *Yet have I not seen the righteous forsaken, nor his seed begging bread* (Ps. XXXVII, 25). If they are not righteous, why should I leave my possessions to the enemies of the Omnipresent!' Therefore Solomon said, AND WHO KNOWETH WHETHER HE WILL BE A WISE MAN OR A FOOL? (II, 19).

1. THEREFORE I TURNED ABOUT TO CAUSE MY HEART TO DESPAIR (II, 20): from toiling, but I reconsidered and said, 'Just as others toil for me, so I must toil for others.'

The accursed Hadrian was once walking along the roads of Tiberias, when he saw an old man standing and cutting down shrubs to set plants. He said to him, 'Old man, old man, what is your age to-day?' He answered, 'I am a hundred.' The king said to him, 'You, a hundred years old, and you stand cutting shrubs to set plants! Do you think you will eat of their fruit?' He replied, 'If I am worthy, I shall eat; if not, just as my forefathers toiled for me, so I toil for my children.' He told him, 'By your life, if you are fortunate enough to eat of their fruit, let me know.' In due course they produced figs, and he said, 'Now is the time to inform the king.' What did he do? He filled a basket with figs, and went up and stood at the palace-gate. He was asked, 'What do you want?' He said to them, 'Go and tell the king, "An old Jew whom you once met wishes to greet you."' They went and informed the king, 'An old Jew wishes to greet you.' He said, 'Bring him in.' When he entered, the king asked, 'What do you want?' He replied, 'I am the old man whom you met when I was cutting shrubs to set plants, and you said to me that if I was fortunate enough to eat of the fruits I should inform you. Behold, I have been worthy to eat of them and these figs are the fruits they produced.' Hadrian thereupon said, 'I order that his basket be emptied of the figs and filled with *denarii*.' His attendants asked him, 'You display all this honour to this old Jew?' He answered, 'His Creator has honoured him, so shall not I?'

The wife of the neighbour [of this old man] was a worthless woman. She said to her husband, 'O you cause of my troubles! See how fond the king is of figs, and how he exchanges them for *denarii*!' What did he do? He filled his sack with figs and stood in front of the palace. He was asked, 'What do you want?' He said to them, 'I heard that the king is fond of figs and exchanges them for *denarii*.' They went in and informed the king, 'There is an old man standing at the palace-gate carrying his sack full of figs. We asked him what he wanted, and he told us, "I heard that the king is fond of figs and exchanges them for *denarii*."' He said, 'I order that you make him stand at the palace-gate, and whoever comes in and goes out shall throw a fig in his face.' By nightfall they had emptied his sack and he returned home. He said to his wife, 'I have to thank you for all this honour!' She retorted, 'Go and tell it to your mother! [You are fortunate] that they were figs and not citrons, and were ripe and not hard!'

1. FOR THERE IS A MAN WHOSE LABOUR IS WITH WISDOM (II, 21). R. Judan b. R. Simon said: Great is the power [of imagination] of the prophets who liken the creature to its Creator. That is what is written, *And I heard the voice of a man*[1] *between the banks of the Ulai* (Dan. VIII, 16). R. Judan b. R. Simon also said: There is another text which shows this still more clearly, viz. *And upon the likeness of the throne was a likeness as of the appearance of a man* (Ezek. I, 26).

WITH WISDOM: as it is written, *The Lord by wisdom*

[1] Understood as a reference to God who is here called *man*. Similarly MAN in Eccl. is explained as God. Cf. Gen. R. XXVII, 1.

founded the earth (Prov. III, 19). AND WITH KNOWLEDGE: as it is written, *By His knowledge the depths were broken up* (*ib.* 20). AND WITH SKILL: R. Berekiah said in the name of R. Judah b. R. Simon: Not with toil or with labour did the Holy One, blessed be He, create His universe, for it is written, *By the* word *of the Lord the heavens were made* (Ps. XXXIII, 6). YET TO A MAN THAT HATH NOT LABOURED THEREIN SHALL HE LEAVE IT FOR HIS PORTION: this refers to the generation of Enosh[1] and the generation of the Flood. THIS ALSO IS VANITY AND A GREAT EVIL: for it is written, *And the Lord saw that the wickedness of man was great in the earth*, etc. (Gen. VI, 5 ff.).

1. FOR ALL HIS DAYS ARE PAINS (II, 23): this alludes to the generation of the Flood who pained the Holy One, blessed be He, with their evil deeds. AND HIS OCCUPATION VEXATION: because they vexed the Holy One, blessed be He, with the work of their hands. EVEN IN THE NIGHT HIS HEART TAKETH NO REST: because His heart did not rest by reason of their transgressions[2] Whence do we know [that His heart did not rest] also by day? As it is said, *And that every imagination of the thoughts of his heart was only evil all* day (Gen. *loc. cit.*).[3] Likewise the Holy One, blessed be He, brought punishment upon them by day and night, as it is said, *And the rain was upon the earth forty days and forty nights* (*ib.* VII, 12).

Another interpretation of EVEN IN THE NIGHT HIS HEART TAKETH NO REST: this refers to the Holy One, blessed be He, who thought in His heart to bring punishment upon them by day and night, as it is said, *And He blotted out every living substance* (*ib.* 23).

Another interpretation of FOR ALL HIS DAYS ARE

[1] Gen. IV, 26, is interpreted by the Rabbis to mean that in the days of Enosh men 'profaned' the name of the Lord.

[2] Or, the hearts of the generation of the Flood did not rest from evil. There is probably a merging of subjects here, first 'God' being the subject and then 'the generation of the Flood'.

[3] E.V. '*continually*'.

PAINS: this is an allusion to the men of Sodom who pained the Holy One, blessed be He, with their evil deeds. AND HIS OCCUPATION VEXATION: because they vexed the Holy One, blessed be He, with the work of their hands. EVEN IN THE NIGHT HIS HEART TAKETH NO REST: to bring punishment upon them by day and night, as it is said, *Then the Lord caused to rain upon Sodom and upon Gomorrah brimstone and fire* (*ib.* XIX, 24).[1]

Another interpretation of FOR ALL HIS DAYS ARE PAINS: this is an allusion to the Egyptians who pained the Holy One, blessed be He, with their evil deeds. AND HIS OCCUPATION VEXATION: because they vexed the Holy One, blessed be He, with the work of their hands. EVEN IN THE NIGHT HIS HEART TAKETH NO REST: because when an Israelite finished his work, the Egyptian would say to him, 'Hoe me a couple of fields and chop a couple of logs for me.' Another interpretation of EVEN IN THE NIGHT HIS HEART TAKETH NO REST: this refers to the Holy One, blessed be He, who thought in His heart to bring punishment upon them by night and by day, as it is said, *And it came to pass at midnight that the Lord smote all the firstborn in the land of Egypt* (Ex. XII, 29).

1. THERE IS NOTHING BETTER FOR A MAN THAN THAT HE SHOULD EAT AND DRINK (II, 24). R. Tanḥuma in the name of R. Naḥman, the son of R. Samuel b. Naḥman, and R. Menaḥma said (another version: R. Jeremiah and R. Meyasha said in the name of R. Samuel b. R. Isaac): All the references to eating and drinking in this Book signify Torah and good deeds. R. Jonah said: The most clear proof of them all is, *A man hath no better thing under the sun than to eat and drink, and to be merry, and that this should accompany him in his labour*—'amalo (Eccl. VIII, 15). The last word should be read as *'olamo* (his world)—in this world; All *the days*

[1] Since this happened during the day (Gen. XIX, 23), Radal suggests that the punishment by night was the blindness with which they were struck (*ib.* 11).

of his life (*ib.*) alludes to the grave. Are there, then, food and drink in the grave which accompany a man to the grave? It must then mean Torah and good deeds.

1. FOR WHO WILL EAT, OR WHO WILL ENJOY, IF NOT I (II, 25)? Solomon said: Who has eaten as I have eaten, who has drunk as I have drunk, and who has done as I have done? R. Jeremiah said in the name of R. Samuel b. R. Isaac: Solomon possessed a large eagle upon which he rode and travelled to Tadmor[1] in the wilderness and returned in one day That is what is written, *And he built Tadmor in the wilderness* (II Chron. VIII, 4).

1. FOR TO THE MAN THAT IS GOOD IN HIS SIGHT HE GIVETH WISDOM, AND KNOWLEDGE, AND JOY (II, 26). FOR TO THE MAN THAT IS GOOD IN HIS SIGHT: i.e. the patriarch Abraham, HE GIVETH WISDOM, AND KNOWLEDGE, AND JOY. BUT TO THE SINNER HE GIVETH THE TASK TO GATHER AND TO HEAP UP: this refers to Nimrod. And of whom is it said, THAT HE MAY LEAVE TO HIM THAT IS GOOD IN THE SIGHT OF GOD? Of Abraham, as it is stated, *And Abraham was old, well stricken in age, and the Lord had blessed Abraham in all things* (Gen. XXIV, 1).

Another interpretation of FOR TO THE MAN THAT IS GOOD IN HIS SIGHT: i.e. Isaac, HE GIVETH WISDOM, AND KNOWLEDGE, AND JOY. BUT TO THE SINNER HE GIVETH THE TASK TO GATHER AND TO HEAP UP: this refers to Abimelech. And of whom is it said, THAT HE MAY LEAVE TO HIM THAT IS GOOD IN THE SIGHT OF GOD? Of Isaac, as it is stated, *And Isaac sowed in that land, and found in the same year a hundredfold; and the Lord blessed him* (*ib.* XXVI, 12).

Another interpretation of FOR TO THE MAN THAT IS GOOD IN HIS SIGHT: i.e. Jacob, HE GIVETH WISDOM, AND KNOWLEDGE, AND JOY. BUT TO THE

[1] Palmyra, an oasis in the Syrian desert.

SINNER HE GIVETH THE TASK TO GATHER AND TO HEAP UP: this refers to Laban. And of whom is it said, THAT HE MAY LEAVE TO HIM THAT IS GOOD IN THE SIGHT OF GOD? Of Jacob, as it is stated, *For I have seen all that Laban doeth unto thee* (*ib.* XXXI, 12).

Another interpretation of FOR TO THE MAN THAT IS GOOD IN HIS SIGHT: i.e. Israel in Egypt, HE GIVETH WISDOM, AND KNOWLEDGE, AND JOY. BUT TO THE SINNER HE GIVETH THE TASK TO GATHER AND TO HEAP UP: this refers to the Canaanites. (R. Levi said: None of them would even put a drop of oil in his grits, and even if an egg of his was broken he would not eat it, but he sold it and turned it into money, so that when the Israelites should enter the land, they would find it full of blessings.) And of whom is it said, THAT HE MAY LEAVE TO HIM THAT IS GOOD IN THE SIGHT OF GOD? Of Israel, as it is stated, *Unto these the land shall be divided* (Num. XXVI, 53).

Another interpretation of FOR TO THE MAN THAT IS GOOD IN HIS SIGHT: i.e. Hezekiah, HE GIVETH WISDOM, AND KNOWLEDGE, AND JOY. BUT TO THE SINNER HE GIVETH THE TASK TO GATHER AND TO HEAP UP: this refers to Sennacherib. And of whom is it said, THAT HE MAY LEAVE TO HIM THAT IS GOOD IN THE SIGHT OF GOD? Of Hezekiah, as it is stated, *So that he was exalted in the sight of all nations* (II Chron. XXXII, 23).

Another interpretation of FOR TO THE MAN THAT IS GOOD IN HIS SIGHT: i.e. Mordecai, HE GIVETH WISDOM, AND KNOWLEDGE, AND JOY. BUT TO THE SINNER HE GIVETH THE TASK TO GATHER AND TO HEAP UP: this refers to Haman. And of whom is it said, THAT HE MAY LEAVE TO HIM THAT IS GOOD IN THE SIGHT OF GOD? Of Mordecai, as it is stated, *On that day did the king Ahasuerus give the house of Haman the Jews' enemy unto Esther the queen* (Est. VIII, 1).

Chapter III

1. To every thing there is a season (iii, 1). There was a time for Adam to enter the Garden of Eden, as it is said, *And He put him into the Garden of Eden* (Gen. ii, 15), and a time for him to leave it, as it is said, *Therefore the Lord God sent him forth from the Garden of Eden* (*ib.* iii, 23). There was a time for Noah to enter the ark, as it is said, *Come thou and all thy house into the ark* (*ib.* vii, 1), and a time for him to come out, as it is said, *Go forth from the ark* (*ib.* viii, 16). There was a time for Abraham to receive the commandment of circumcision, as it is said, *And as for thee, thou shalt keep My covenant* (*ib.* xvii, 9), and there was a time for some of his descendants to be circumcised in two localities, viz. in Egypt and in the wilderness, as it is said, *For all the people that came out were circumcised; but all the people that were born in the wilderness by the way as they came forth out of Egypt, had not been circumcised* (Josh. v, 5).[1]

And a time to every purpose under the heaven. There was a time for the Torah to be given to Israel. R. Bibi said: There was a time for a certain thing to be found above the heaven, and now it was to be found beneath the heaven. What was it? The Torah, as it is stated, *And God spoke all these words saying* (Ex. xx, 1).

1. A time to be born, and a time to die (iii, 2). R. Berekiah said: Is then all the wisdom which Solomon uttered simply that there is A time to be born, and a time to die? What then is its meaning? Happy the man whose hour of death is like the hour of his birth; as he was pure in the hour of his birth so should he be pure in the hour of his death. A time to be born, and a time to die: when a woman is at the time of

[1] This seems unintelligible. v. Gen. R. xlvi, 2 (Th's. ed.) for a different and more intelligible reading.

childbirth they call her '*ḥayetha*'. Why do they call her that? Because she is nearly dying but revives (*ḥayah*). And why do they call her '*meḥabbalta*'?[1] Because she is given in pledge in the hand of death, as the word is used in the sentence, *If thou at all take thy neighbour's garment to pledge*—ḥabol (Ex. XXII, 25). R. Simon said in the name of R. Nathan of Beth Gubrin[2]: It is written, *The grave and the barren womb* (Prov. XXX, 16). Why is '*the grave*' mentioned next to the '*womb*'? To tell you that as [the child] is brought forth from the womb with loud cries, so will [the dead] be brought forth from the grave [at the resurrection] with loud cries.[3]

2. Another interpretation of A TIME TO BE BORN AND A TIME TO DIE: [The travailing woman is in such danger] because even the Angel of Death becomes her accuser. R. Samuel b. Naḥman said: [The Mishnah states]: For three transgressions do women die in the time of childbirth: because they are not careful with regard to their periodic separation, to *ḥallah*, and to the lighting of the [Sabbath] lamp.[4] And in three circumstances do men die[5]: when dwelling in a dilapidated house, travelling by road alone, and sailing on the ocean, because then Satan brings accusations against them. For R. Levi said: In three circumstances is Satan present to accuse: when a man dwells in a dilapidated house, when he travels by road alone, and when he sails on the ocean. R. Simeon b. Abba said in the name of R. Ḥanina: All roads are presumed to be dangerous.[6] Whenever R. Jannai went out into the open street he first left orders in his house.[7] R. Ḥelbo and R. Simeon b. Abba said in the name of R. Joshua b. Levi: All invalids are presumed to be in danger of death. R. Nathan the *kohen*, brother of R.

[1] Lit. 'travailing woman'; but the root *ḥabal* also denotes 'pledge'. She incurs the danger of death in the act of giving birth.
[2] N.W. of Hebron. [3] Cf. Sanh. 92*a*. [4] Shab. II, 6.
[5] I.e. are in danger of death, and if not meritorious succumb to it.
[6] Any kind of travelling was dangerous in those times.
[7] How his property was to be disposed of should he meet with an accident.

Ḥiyya b. Abba, was about to journey by sea. He said to his brother, 'Pray on my behalf.' He replied to him, 'What shall I pray for you? When you tie your *lulab* tie your boat[1]; and if you enter a Synagogue and hear the voice of the congregation praying for rain, do not rely on my prayer.'[2]

R. Joshua, the son of R. Ḥiyya of Kefar-Agun, was in Asya[3] and wanted to make a journey by sea between the Festival of Sukkoth and Ḥanukkah.[4] A matron said to him, 'Do people make sea voyages during these days?' but he paid no attention to what she said. Then his father appeared to him in a dream and said, 'My son, [you will die] without burial,' [as it is written], *And moreover he have no burial* (Eccl. VI, 3). He paid no attention to the words of either of them and so it happened to him.[5]

3. Another interpretation of A TIME TO BE BORN, AND A TIME TO DIE: it means, from the time of birth is the time to die. From the hour a person is born it is decreed for him how many years he is to live. If he is worthy, he completes his years, but if he is unworthy they are reduced in number for him; as it is written, *The fear of the Lord prolongeth days, but the years of the wicked shall be shortened* (Prov. X, 27). So says R. Akiba; but the Rabbis say: If he is worthy, the number is increased for him, but if he is unworthy, they are reduced in number for him. 'If he is worthy, the number is increased for him,' as it is stated, *Behold, I will add unto thy days fifteen years* (Isa. XXXVIII, 5). R. Akiba replied to them: The addition was only from his own years.[6] Know that it is so, because it is written, *Behold, a son shall be born unto the house of David, Josiah by name* (I Kings XIII, 2), and

[1] The *lulab* is used at the Harvest Festival in the Autumn, and that is the time to stop travelling by sea so as to escape the dangerous storms.
[2] This prayer was offered in the Synagogue on the eighth day of the Harvest Festival. If he ventured to sea after that, he was not to depend for safety on the prayer of an individual. [3] V. Gen. R. VI, 5.
[4] I.e. between the Harvest Festival and the Feast of Dedication which occurs in December. [5] He perished by drowning.
[6] He did not die before his allotted time, but he did not exceed it.

Manasseh had not yet entered the world![1] He said to them[2]: Is it then written, '*A son shall be born to the house of David*' from Hezekiah? It is not stated thus, but simply '*To the house of David*', i.e. from the rest of the royal house of David.[3] The following supports the view expressed by the sages our Rabbis. One of the eminent men of Sepphoris once had occasion to celebrate the circumcision of his son, and the men of 'En Te'enah[4] came up to honour him [with their presence], among them being R. Simeon b. Ḥalafta. When they arrived at the city-gate they heard the sound of some children standing and playing in front of a house. On beholding R. Simeon b. Ḥalafta, who was a distinguished-looking[5] and handsome man, they exclaimed, 'You will not move from here until you dance a little for us.' He said to them, 'You cannot have this from me because I am an old man.' He railed at them, but they were not frightened or cowed. He lifted up his face and saw the house about to overturn [on the children]; so he said to them, 'Repeat[6] after me what I say to you. Go and tell the owner of this house that if he is asleep, he should wake up, because the beginning of a sin is sweet but its end bitter.'[7] At the sound of their voices the owner of the house awakened, and he came out and fell before the Rabbi's feet,[8] saying, 'My master, I beg of you not to pay attention to their words because they are young and foolish.' He replied, 'What can I do for

[1] Josiah was the grandson of Manasseh. The latter was born three years after his father's illness (II Kings XXI, 1); and since the birth of his son Josiah was prophetically announced long before the birth of his father Hezekiah, it is obvious that the years allotted to Hezekiah at his birth extended beyond the year of his illness (to include the year of Manasseh's birth). Consequently, the original number must have been reduced at his illness; and, at his recovery, only that was added which was first subtracted (Yeb. 50*a*, Sonc. ed., p. 325, n. 14).

[2] In Yeb. 50*a* the argument that follows is that of the Rabbis. The reading should therefore be: 'They said to him,' viz. to R. Akiba.

[3] And not necessarily of Hezekiah.

[4] Lit. 'well of the fig tree'; name of a place in the vicinity of Sepphoris.

[5] Radal emends עולין to אלים 'fat'. [6] The text is uncertain.

[7] Apparently the boys were his children, and he would suffer for having reared them so badly that they were disrespectful to an old man.

[8] He was terrified at the house threatening to fall down.

you seeing that it is decreed [that the house should collapse]? I will, however, wait for you until you bring out all that you have in the house.' When he had removed all that he had in the house, it reared itself and collapsed.[1]

[R. Simeon and his companions] proceeded to fulfil the commandment of circumcision, and the father of the child gave them old wine to drink, saying, 'Drink some of this old wine, and I trust in the Lord of heaven that He will grant me to offer you drink at his wedding feast.' They responded, 'As you have brought him into the covenant [of Abraham], so may you bring him to Torah and the marriage-canopy.' After this had been said, R. Simeon b. Ḥalafta went out into the darkness [to return home], and the messenger of men[2] met him and said to him, 'Because you rely on your good deeds you go out at a time which is not a time.'[3] He asked him, 'Who are you?' 'I am the messenger of men,' was the reply. The Rabbi asked him, 'Why do you look so upset?' He answered, 'Because of the hard things I hear from human beings every day.' 'What are they?' the Rabbi inquired. He replied, 'This child whom you circumcised to-day was fated to be taken away from here by me when he is thirty days old; but his father gave you wine and said, "Drink this good wine, for I trust in the Lord of heaven that He will grant me to offer you drink at his wedding feast." I heard this and grieved, because your prayer annuls the decree against him.' He exclaimed, 'By your life, reveal my fate to me.' He replied, 'I have no jurisdiction over you and your colleagues.' 'Why?' he asked. 'Because every day you labour in the Torah and the commandments, and perform righteous acts, and the Holy One, blessed be He, adds to your days.' He said to him, 'May it be pleasing before the Holy One, blessed be He, that as you have no power over our fate, so may

[1] Apparently it collapsed because R. Simeon cast his eye on it and cursed it; hence he stated that he could not revoke his curse but could suspend it ('E.J.). [2] The Angel of Death.

[3] Not a proper time for a journey, viz. at night when evil spirits are abroad.

you have no permission to overrule our words.' They prayed for mercy from Heaven and the child lived.[1]

R. Akiba said: What use have we for such a tale as this! I have no anecdote but an explicit text, viz. *The number of thy days I will fulfil* (Ex. XXIII, 26)[2]; for behold, Moses performed many commandments and many righteous acts, but finally it was said to him, *Behold, thy days approach that thou must die* (Deut. XXXI, 14). Hence it is stated, A TIME TO BE BORN, AND A TIME TO DIE.

Another interpretation of A TIME TO BE BORN, AND A TIME TO DIE: When a person is born, the Holy One, blessed be He, looks to him to marry before the age of twenty. If he reaches that age without marrying, the Holy One, blessed be He, says to him, 'It was for you a time [for children] to be born and you were unwilling, so there is nothing else than a time to die.' There are some who say that he who anticipates [the age of marrying] a little will be pure.[3]

A TIME TO PLANT: in the time of peace; AND A TIME TO PLUCK UP THAT WHICH IS PLANTED: in the time of war.

1. A TIME TO KILL (III, 3): in the time of war; AND A TIME TO HEAL: in the time of peace. A TIME TO BREAK DOWN: in the time of war; AND A TIME TO BUILD UP: in the time of peace.

1. A TIME TO WEEP (III, 4): in the time of mourning; AND A TIME TO LAUGH: after the mourning. A TIME TO MOURN: in the time of mourning; AND A TIME TO DANCE: after the mourning.

1. A TIME TO CAST AWAY STONES (III, 5)[4]: at the time when your wife is ritually clean; AND A TIME TO

[1] This anecdote supports the Rabbi's view that the allotted span may be increased.
[2] But they will not be increased beyond the allotted span.
[3] This follows the emended reading of Radal. The text is corrupt. The age of 18 is accordingly recommended for marriage (Ab. V, 21).
[4] Understood in the sense of marital intercourse.

GATHER STONES TOGETHER: at the time when your wife is ritually unclean. A TIME TO EMBRACE: if you see a band of righteous men standing anywhere, do you stand, embrace, kiss, and show them affection; AND A TIME TO REFRAIN FROM EMBRACING: if you see a band of wicked men, keep far away from them and those like them.

1. A TIME TO SEEK (III, 6): in the time of peace; AND A TIME TO LOSE: in the time of war. A TIME TO KEEP: in a favourable time; AND A TIME TO CAST AWAY: in an unfavourable time. A trader once made a voyage with his son, taking with him chests filled with *denarii*. [The captain] gave them quarters in a dark [part of the ship].[1] The man heard the voices of the sailors, saying, 'When we are out on the high sea we will kill them, throw them overboard and take that store of *denarii* from him.' What did he do? He pretended to be angry with his son, took hold of the chests and threw them into the sea. When they landed, he went and charged them before the emperor's proconsul, who imprisoned them and condemned them to give the man his store of *denarii*. They said to the proconsul, 'How do you judge us to be guilty?' He answered them, 'From what Solomon, King of Israel, said, A TIME TO CAST AWAY.'[2]

1. A TIME TO REND (III, 7): in the time of war; AND A TIME TO SEW: in the time of peace. A TIME TO KEEP SILENCE, AND A TIME TO SPEAK: The wife of R. Mana died in Sepphoris. R. Abun went up to visit him, and said to him, 'Would the master care to expound something of the Torah to us?' He replied, 'Behold the time mentioned by the Torah has come when one should keep silent and give preference to silence.'[3]

[1] The text is uncertain. Radal offers two alternatives: (1) He sat upon them in the dark [to guard them]; (2) He began to handle coins in the dark [and so the sailors knew that he had a large sum of money with him].
[2] To save his life the man had been compelled to throw his money overboard, and they were responsible for his loss.
[3] A time of mourning was inopportune for expounding Torah.

A TIME TO LOVE (III, 8): in the time of peace; AND A TIME TO HATE: in the time of war; A TIME FOR WAR: in the time of war; AND A TIME FOR PEACE: in the time of peace.

2. R. Joshua of Siknin expounded the text in connection with Israel. A TIME TO BE BORN, AND A TIME TO DIE: The Holy One, blessed be He, said: 'In a brief space of time I caused thy children to give birth'[1]; for it is written, *And as for thy nativity in the day thou wast born* (Ezek. XVI, 4). AND A TIME TO DIE: for it is written, *In this wilderness they shall be consumed, and there they shall die* (Num. XIV, 35). *And there was not left a man of them, save Caleb the son of Jephunneh, and Joshua the son of Nun* (*ib.* XXVI, 65). A TIME TO PLANT: as it is said, *And I will plant them upon their land* (Amos IX, 15); AND A TIME TO PLUCK UP THAT WHICH IS PLANTED: for it is written, *And the Lord rooted them out of their land* (Deut. XXIX, 27). A TIME TO KILL: for it is written, *And He hath slain all that were pleasant to the eye* (Lam. II, 4); AND A TIME TO HEAL: for it is written, *Behold, I will bring it healing and cure* (Jer. XXXIII, 6). A TIME TO BREAK DOWN: for it is written, *And ye shall go out at the breaches, every one straight before her* (Amos IV, 3); AND A TIME TO BUILD UP: for it is written, *And I will build it as in the days of old* (*ib.* IX, 11). A TIME TO WEEP: for it is written, *She weepeth sore in the night* (Lam. I, 2); AND A TIME TO LAUGH: for it is written, *Then was our mouth filled with laughter* (Ps. CXXVI, 2). A TIME TO MOURN: for it is written, *And in that day did the Lord, the God of hosts, call to weeping and to lamentation* (Isa. XXII, 12); AND A TIME TO DANCE: for it is written, *And the broad places of the city shall be full of boys and girls playing in the broad places thereof* (Zech. VIII, 5). A TIME TO CAST AWAY STONES: for it is written, *The hallowed stones are poured out at the head of every street* (Lam. IV, 1); AND A TIME TO

[1] Probably: they did not travail long.

GATHER STONES TOGETHER: for it is written, *Behold, I lay in Zion for a foundation a stone* (Isa. XXVIII, 16). A TIME TO EMBRACE: as it is said, *And his right hand embrace me* (S.S. II, 6); AND A TIME TO REFRAIN FROM EMBRACING: as it is said, *And the Lord have removed men far away* (Isa. VI, 12). A TIME TO SEEK: for it is written, *But from thence ye will seek the Lord thy God* (Deut. IV, 29). AND A TIME TO LOSE: for it is written, *Take heed to yourselves, lest your heart be deceived . . . and ye perish quickly* (*ib.* XI, 16 f.). A TIME TO KEEP: for it is written, *Behold, He that keepeth Israel doth neither slumber nor sleep* (Ps. CXXI, 4); AND A TIME TO CAST AWAY: for it is written, *And He cast them into another land* (Deut. XXIX, 27). A TIME TO REND: for it is written, *The Lord hath rent the kingdom of Israel* (I Sam. XV, 28); AND A TIME TO SEW: for it is written, *Then they may become one in thy hand* (Ezek. XXXVII, 17). A TIME TO KEEP SILENCE: for it is written, *I have long time held my peace* (Isa. XLII, 14); AND A TIME TO SPEAK: for it is written, *Speak upon the heart of Jerusalem* (*ib.* XL, 2).[1] A TIME TO LOVE: for it is written, *I have loved you, saith the Lord* (Mal. I, 2); AND A TIME TO HATE: for it is written, *She hath uttered her voice against Me, therefore I have hated her* (Jer. XII, 8). A TIME FOR WAR: for it is written, *Therefore He was turned to be their enemy, Himself fought against them* (Isa. LXIII, 10); AND A TIME FOR PEACE: for it is written, *Behold I will extend peace to her like a river* (*ib.* LXVI, 12).

1. WHAT PROFIT HATH HE THAT WORKETH IN THAT HE LABOURETH (III, 9)? Solomon said: Since there are times for all things, what advantage has the labourer in his work and the upright man in his uprightness?[2] Another interpretation of WHAT PROFIT (YITHRON): They do not allow a man to dwell (*mathrin*) except with his fellow-craftsman.[3]

[1] E.V. '*Bid Jerusalem take heart*'. [2] He will be subject to turns of fortune, good and bad, whether he is industrious or not, upright or not. [3] Explained below as referring to the Hereafter.

R. Isaac b. R. Marion said: *But the righteous shall live by his faith* (Hab. II, 4) means that even the Righteous One who lives for ever lives from His faith. The Holy One, blessed be He, said: 'First I slew the firstborn of Egypt (as it is stated, *And it came to pass at midnight, that the Lord smote all the firstborn in the land of Egypt* (Ex. XII, 29)); therefore every firstborn that is born to you sanctify unto Me,' as it is stated, *Sanctify unto Me all the firstborn* (*ib.* XIII, 2), i.e. sanctify unto Me the firstborn by faith in Me. That is the meaning of '*But the righteous shall live by his faith*'.

R. Phinehas said in the name of R. Reuben: To what may the matter be likened? To a king who arranged a meal and invited guests to come to him. The king issued an order, saying, 'Let each man bring what he is to sit upon.' Some brought rugs; others brought mats, mattresses, wrappers, and chairs; while others brought logs of wood and stones. The king took note and said, 'Every man shall sit on what he brought.' Those who sat on wood or stone grumbled at the king and exclaimed, 'Is it to the honour of a king that we should sit on wood or stone?' When the king heard it, he said to them, 'Not enough that you have disgraced with stone and wood the palace which was erected for me at great cost, but you have the impudence to level criticisms against me. For your honour nobody but yourselves is responsible!' Similarly, in the Hereafter the wicked are condemned to Gehinnom; and they grumble at the Holy One, blessed be He, saying, 'Behold, we looked for the salvation of the Holy One, blessed be He, and this is what happens to us!' The Holy One, blessed be He, replies to them, 'In the world in which you spent your life were you not quarrelsome, slander-mongers, and evil-doers; did you not indulge in strife and violence? That is what is written, *Behold, all ye that kindle a fire, that gird yourselves with firebrands; therefore begone in the flame of your fire, and among the brands that ye have kindled* (Isa. L, 11). And should you say, *This ye have*[1] *of* My

[1] E.V. '*shall ye have*'.

hand (*ib.*), no, you did it to yourselves, and therefore *Ye shall lie down in sorrow* (*ib.*), for *This hath been of* your *doing'* (Mal. I, 9).

R. Simeon b. Laḳish was studying Torah as much as he required in a cave at Tiberias,[1] and a potter used to prepare a drink of water for him every day. He used to come in feeling very tired, and take and drink it. On one occasion the man entered, sat down by the Rabbi and stayed with him a short while to rest. He said to him, 'Master, do you remember that you and I used to go to school together; but whereas you were worthy [to devote yourself to the study of the Torah], I was not so worthy. Pray for me that my portion may be with you in the World to Come.' He replied to him, 'How can I pray for you since it will be your lot to go with your fellow-craftsmen? Because they do not allow a man to dwell except with his fellow-craftsmen.'

1. I HAVE SEEN THE TASK WHICH GOD HATH GIVEN TO THE SONS OF MEN TO BE EXERCISED THEREWITH (III, 10). R. Aibu said: This is the peculiarity of wealth; for R. Judan said in the name of R. Aibu: Nobody departs from the world with half his desire gratified. If he has a hundred he wants to turn them into two hundred, and if he has two hundred he wants to turn them into four hundred. TO BE EXERCISED THEREWITH: R. Joshua of Siknin said in the name of R. Levi: If a man is worthy and uses his wealth in accordance with the precepts of the Torah, when he prays he is answered. That is what is stated, *So shall my righteousness answer for me* (Gen. XXX, 33). Should he not use his wealth in this manner, it will testify against him and accuse him, for it is written, *To bear perverted witness against him* (Deut. XIX, 16). R. Joḥanan said: It refers to the peculiarity of robbery; because R. Simeon b. Laḳish said in the name of R. Joḥanan: For instance when the measure of iniquities is full, which accuses first of all [before the judgment-throne

[1] In a time of persecution when the study of Torah was forbidden.

of God]? Robbery; for R. Huna said in the name of R. Joḥanan: It is written, *And their unlawful gain at the head of them all* (Amos IX, 1). R. Phinehas said in the name of R. Joḥanan: Since he is dealing with the subject of idolatry, immorality, and homicide he lets us know that nothing is worse than these except robbery. R. Jacob b. Aḥa said in the name of R. Joḥanan: Twenty-four sins did Ezekiel enumerate, and out of them all he concluded only with robbery; as it is written, *Behold, therefore, I have smitten My hand at thy dishonest gain which thou hast made* (Ezek. XXII, 13). R. Ḥunia related this verse to the Prophets and Hagiographa, for if the Israelites had been worthy they would have read the Pentateuch alone; and the Prophets and Hagiographa were only given to them that they might labour in these as well as the Pentateuch and perform the precepts and righteous acts so as to receive a good reward. The Rabbis say: Nevertheless [Scripture says], TO BE EXERCISED THEREWITH, which intimates that they receive a reward as in the case of the Pentateuch.

R. Abbahu said: It refers to the peculiarity of [the study of] the Torah, which is that a man learns Torah and forgets it. The Babylonian Rabbis in the name of R. Isaac the Palestinian[1] and R. Ṭobiah in the name of R. Isaac said: It is for man's good that he learns Torah and forgets it; because if a man studied Torah and never forgot it, he would occupy himself with learning it for two or three years, resume his ordinary work and never pay further attention to it. But since a man studies Torah and forgets it, he will not abandon its study.

The Rabbis say: It refers to the peculiarity of robbery. Know this, since it was because the former generations were engaged in and addicted to robbery—as it is written, *There are that remove the landmarks, they violently take away flocks and feed them* (Job. XXIV, 2)—that they were blotted out from the world by water; but because

[1] Lit. 'the Rabbis of there in the name of R. Isaac of here'. V. Introduction.

the tribes of Reuben and Gad kept themselves aloof from robbery, the Holy One, blessed be He, gave them an inheritance in a place which was free from robbery, as it is said, *Behold, the place was a place for cattle* (Num. XXXII, 1). This is similar to the statement, 'Sixteen miles square from Mahir.'[1]

1. HE HATH MADE EVERY THING BEAUTIFUL IN ITS TIME (III, 11). R. Tanḥuma said: In its due time was the universe created. It was not meet to be created before then, but it was created in its proper time, as it is said, HE HATH MADE EVERY THING BEAUTIFUL IN ITS TIME. R. Abbahu said: From this [we learn] that the Holy One, blessed be He, kept on constructing worlds and destroying them until he constructed the present one and said, 'This pleases Me, the others did not.'

R. Eleazar said: This is a door which is opened to the depths,[2] as it is stated, *And God saw everything that He had made, and, behold, it was very good* (Gen. I, 31). If another had declared, HE HATH MADE EVERY THING BEAUTIFUL IN ITS TIME, I might have said that this man who had never eaten a piece of bread declares, HE HATH MADE EVERY THING BEAUTIFUL IN ITS TIME[3]; but for Solomon, of whom it is written, *And Solomon's provision for one day was thirty measures of fine flour*, etc. (1 Kings V, 2), it was appropriate to declare, HE HATH MADE EVERY THING BEAUTIFUL IN ITS TIME. In like manner if another had declared, *Vanity of vanities, saith Ḳoheleth* (Eccl. I, 2), I might have said that this man who had never owned two farthings in his life makes light of the wealth of the world and declares, '*Vanity of vanities*'; but for Solomon it was appropriate to declare '*Vanity of vanities*' because of him it is written,

[1] Repeated from I, 13, with a few minor changes.
[2] The declaration, HE HATH MADE EVERY THING BEAUTIFUL, is a principle to be applied to every phase of God's creation.
[3] As he possesses little or nothing, any trifling thing would appear wonderful to him.

And the king made silver to be in Jerusalem as stones (I Kings x, 27). They were not stolen because some stones measured ten cubits and others eight cubits, and even the weights which were used in the days of Solomon were of gold, as it is stated, *None were of silver, it was nothing accounted of in the days of Solomon* (*ib.* 21).[1] Why, then, did he say, '*Vanity of vanities*'? He saw the world [as it is] and what it would finally be.[2] If, further, another had declared, *And all the inhabitants of the earth are reputed as nothing* (Dan. IV, 32), I might have said that this man who had never ruled over two flies declared, '*And all the inhabitants of the earth are reputed as nothing*'; but it was appropriate for the wicked Nebuchadnezzar to say so who ruled over the whole world, as it is stated, *And I have given him the beasts of the field also*—to serve him (Jer. XXVIII, 14), as is evident from what is written, *And wheresoever the children of men, the beasts of the field, and the fowls of the heaven dwell, hath He given them into thy hand and hath made thee to rule over them all* (Dan. II, 38).

If another of the wise men of the heathen peoples had uttered this verse, *Now I know that the Lord is greater than all gods* (Ex. XVIII, 11), I might have said that this man who does not understand the real nature of idolatry declared, '*Now I know that the Lord is greater than all gods*'; but Jethro who uttered it had worshipped many idols. For R. Ishmael learnt: Reuel, i.e. Jethro, did not omit a single form of idolatry in the world without turning to it and serving it, for it is written, *Woe unto us! Who shall deliver us out of the hand of these mighty gods? These are the gods that smote the Egyptians with all manner of plagues* (I Sam. IV, 8)[3]; but finally he declared, '*Now I know that the Lord is greater than all gods,*' became a proselyte and acknowledged the Holy One, blessed be He. For such a man it was proper to say, '*Now I know that the Lord is greater than all gods.*' He turned in

[1] V. on II, 2. [2] He therefore concluded that the good things of this world were only '*vanities*'.

[3] This quotation is apparently irrelevant. M.K. gives a forced explanation but on the whole it seems best to delete it (אות אמת).

repentance before the Holy One, blessed be He, who accepted him and established him in Israel for generations.

If another prophet and sage had stood up to declare, *The Rock, His work is perfect* (Deut. XXXII, 4), [the statement would have no force]; but it was appropriate for Moses our teacher to declare it since it is written of him, *He made known His ways unto Moses, His doings unto the children of Israel* (Ps. CIII, 7).

If another man had come and reproved Israel, I would have exclaimed, Shall one who had partaken of their food and drink and derived benefit from them presume to reprove them! But for Moses, of whom it is written, *I have not taken one ass from them* (Num. XVI, 15), it was proper to reprove Israel. That is what is written, *These are the words*[1] *which Moses spoke unto all Israel beyond the Jordan*, etc. (Deut. I, 1).

2. Another interpretation of HE HATH MADE EVERY THING BEAUTIFUL IN ITS TIME: R. Bun explained it in two ways. R. Bun said: Abraham deserved to be created before Adam; but the Holy One, blessed be He, said: 'If I create Abraham first, should he act corruptly there would be nobody to follow him and make amends; but I will create Adam, and if he acts corruptly Abraham will follow him and make amends.' R. Bun also said: It is written, *The greatest man among the Anakim* (Josh. XIV, 15).[2] Abraham should have been created the first man, as it is said, '*The greatest man among the Anakim.*' Why was he called '*greatest*'? Because it was proper for him to be created first. Only the Holy One, blessed be He, said: 'If I create him first, should he act corruptly there would be nobody to follow him and make amends; but I will create Adam first, and if he acts corruptly, Abraham will follow him and make amends.'

[1] Explained by Sifre *ad loc.* as 'words of rebuke'.

[2] The text mentions that Hebron was previously called Kiriath-Arba, i.e. the city of Arba. Since Abraham was connected with that city (Gen. XIII, 18), he is identified with Arba who is described as *The greatest man among the Anakim.*

R. Abba b. Kahana said: There are some who illustrate as follows. To what is the matter like? To one who had a smoothly planed trunk of a tree in his dwelling-place. Where will he set it? Will it not be in the middle of the living-room so that it can support the beams in front of it and behind it? Similarly, why did the Holy One, blessed be He, create the patriarch Abraham in the centre [of the generations]? So that he might support the generations that preceded and those that follow him. R. Levi said: [The reason is] because a virtuous woman is brought into the house of a depraved woman but not vice versa.[1]

R. Judah b. R. Simon said: By rights the Torah should have been given through Adam, as it is stated, *This book* [pertains to] *the generations of Adam* (Gen. V, 1).[2] The Holy One, blessed be He, said: 'Should I not give the Torah to Adam, the creature of My hands, so that he may occupy himself therewith?' He reconsidered the matter and said: 'If six commandments[3] were given to him and he was unable to abide by them and observe them, were I to give him six hundred and thirteen commandments,[4] comprising two hundred and forty-eight positive precepts and three hundred and sixty-five prohibitions, how much less would he abide by them!' Therefore it is written, *And unto man He said* (Job. XXVIII, 28), which is to be read as 'not man',[5] i.e. not to [the first] man will I give them; but to whom will I give them? To his descendants.

R. Jacob of Kefar-Ḥanan said: By rights twelve tribes should have issued from Adam, for it is written, '*This is the book of the generations of Adam.*' The word for '*this*', viz. *zeh*, consists of two letters with the numerical value of seven and five respectively; hence twelve tribes, that being

[1] So that the latter may benefit by the good example. Abraham lived at a time when people were bad so that they might learn from him.

[2] Making 'this book' refer to the Torah. E.V. '*This is the book of the generations of Adam*'. [3] V. Gen. R. XVI, 6.

[4] The total of the commandments in the Pentateuch.

[5] Since the text has לאדם instead of אל אדם, it is read as אל אדם.

the number of '*Zeh* [should have been the] *generations of Adam*.' The Holy One, blessed be He, said: 'Adam is the creature of My hands, so shall I not give him twelve tribes?' He reconsidered the matter and said: 'If, when I gave him two sons, one of them arose and killed his brother, how much more [bloodshed will there be] if I give him twelve sons!' Therefore it is written, '*And unto man He said*,' which is to be read as 'not man', i.e. I will not give them to Adam; but to whom will I give them? To Jacob the righteous man.

R. Isaac said: By rights Israel should have been given the Torah immediately on their departure from Egypt; but the Holy One, blessed be He, said: 'The bloom of My children has not yet returned. From slaving with clay and bricks have they just emerged, and they are unable to receive the Torah at once.' To what is the matter like? To a king whose son arose from his sick-bed, and people said to him, 'Let your son go to his school.' He replied, 'The bloom of my son has not yet returned and you say that he should go to his school! Let my son recuperate for two or three months with food and drink and get well; after that he will go to his school.' Similarly spake the Holy One, blessed be He: 'The bloom of My children has not yet returned. From slaving with clay and bricks have they just been released, can I then give them the Torah! Let my children recuperate for two or three months with the manna, the well of water and the quails[1]; after that I will give them the Torah.' When was it given? *In the third month* (Ex. XIX, 1).

R. Bibi, R. Aibu and R. Huna said in the name of R. Isaac b. Marion; Israel should by rights have entered the Holy Land immediately after their departure from Egypt, only the trees had become old from the waters of Noah.[2] The Holy One, blessed be He, said: 'Shall I bring Israel into a desolate land! Rather will I lead them round the way of the wilderness for forty years

[1] Ex. XVI, XVII.
[2] And had ceased to yield fruit, while the Canaanites had not planted fresh ones. Therefore the land was not ready to receive the Israelites.

so that the Canaanites may arise, and cut down the old trees and plant new ones, and Israel may enter the land and find it full of blessings.'

Rabbi [Judah ha-Nasi] says: Even of a transgression we can say that it is beautiful in its time.[1]

3. Another interpretation of HE HATH MADE EVERY THING BEAUTIFUL IN ITS TIME: R. Berekiah reported that R. Abbahu said in the name of R. Eleazar: The schism between Rehoboam and Jeroboam should have been between David and Sheba the son of Bichri[2]; but the Holy One, blessed be He, said: 'The Temple is not yet built, so shall I allow a schism to be introduced into the kingdom of the House of David! Let the Temple first be erected, and then let be what must be.' (Rabbi said: Even of a transgression it may be said that it is beautiful in its time.)[3]

R. Benjamin said in the name of R. Levi: ALSO HE HATH SET THE WORLD IN THEIR HEART: i.e. a love of the world He set in their heart.[4] R. Nathan said: A dread of the Angel of Death He set in their heart.[5] Nehemiah, the son of R. Samuel b. Naḥman, said: *And, behold, it was very good* (Gen. I, 31)—'*And, behold, it was good*' alludes to the creation of man and the Good Inclination, '*very*' alludes to the Evil Inclination. Is, then, the Evil Inclination '*very good*'! It is in truth to teach you that were it not for the Evil Inclination, nobody would build a house, marry and beget children; and

[1] The printed ed. attaches this sentence to the end of the paragraph, but its proper place, as Radal remarks, is after 'Another interpretation . . . ITS TIME' 'E.J. explains: sometimes even a transgression is necessary to achieve a noble purpose, and quotes Ps. CXIX, 126: *When it is time to work for the Lord, they have made void Thy law*. (This is the Rabbinical rendering of the verse.)

[2] Who led a revolt against David which proved unsuccessful (II Sam. XX).

[3] If the passage is correctly inserted here, it may mean that even in a matter like a revolution there is a time when its effects will not be so disastrous. But it is bracketed in the edd. and is probably out of place.

[4] To develop the resources of the world.

[5] Were it not for the fear of death, man might defer begetting children to perpetuate his name.

thus Solomon says, *That it is a man's rivalry with his neighbour* (Eccl. IV, 4).[1]

R. Berekiah and R. Abbahu said in the name of R. Jonathan: ALSO HE HATH SET THE WORLD IN THEIR HEART: i.e. a love of the world and a love of children He set in their heart. To what is the matter like? To a king who had two sons, one big and the other small. The elder treated him with respect while the younger relieved himself upon him; nevertheless his love for the younger child exceeds that of the elder.

R. Aḥwah b. R. Zera said: HA'OLAM (THE WORLD) should be read as *hu'alam* (concealed), i.e. the Ineffable Name was hidden from them.[2] It may be likened to a king who held a banquet to which he invited guests. After they had eaten and drunk, they said to him, 'Give us swords and spears to play with'; but he gave them myrtle-branches, and they struck and wounded one another with them. The king exclaimed, 'If you acted so when I gave you myrtle-branches, how much damage would there have been had I given you swords and spears!' Similarly the Holy One, blessed be He, said: 'If at a time when I concealed the Ineffable Name, men slay by a substituted name of Mine,[3] how much more so had I given and revealed My Ineffable Name!' A Persian woman once cursed her son with one syllable of the Ineffable Name. Samuel heard her and said to her, 'Go, prepare shrouds for him.'[4] R. Ḥanina possessed the secret of the Ineffable Name, and when his time arrived to die, he said: 'Is there anybody here [who is worthy] that I should transmit it to him?' They answered, 'Anini b. Naḥshon is here.' He sent for him and he came, and Anini's son also entered and hid under the bed. When R. Ḥanina was about to transmit the Name, the child sneezed, and the

[1] The ambition to excel is a motive force in keeping the world going.
[2] The true pronunciation of the Tetragrammaton was kept a secret and *Adonai* substituted for it.
[3] It was thought possible to slay by means of the Divine Name used in incantations.
[4] He is certain to die.

father said,[1] 'Go out from here because he is not worthy to hear it, nor you[2] to receive it.'[3]

A physician in Sepphoris possessed the secret of the Ineffable Name. When he was about to die, he asked, 'Is there anybody here [who is worthy] that I should transmit it to him?' They answered, 'There is R. Phinehas b. Ḥama.' He sent for him, and when he came the physician asked him, 'Have you ever taken anything from a Jew?' He replied, 'I accepted *ma'aser*'; whereupon he refused to transmit the Name to him, saying, 'This man might want something from a person who declined to give it to him, and he will kill him in his anger [by using the Name].'

It has been taught: The Name may not be transmitted to every man, nor to one who is not in his prime, but only to one who has lived most of his years. It may only be transmitted when the persons are standing, in a clean place and upon the water.[4] At first they used to transmit it to everyone [in the priesthood]; but when sinners increased in number it was instituted that it should be transmitted only to the well-conducted among the priests, and they used to muffle it amidst the chanting of the other priests.[5] R. Ṭarfon said: I once went up with my uncle Samson upon the dais,[6] and I inclined my ears towards the High Priest [to catch the Name], but he muffled it amidst the chanting of the priests. R. Ṭarfon further said: I once did hear it and fell upon my face [in awe]. Those who were near [the High Priest], when they heard it, fell upon their faces and exclaimed, 'Blessed be the name of His glorious kingdom for ever and ever.' Neither

[1] The text should read: He [R. Ḥanina] said.
[2] The father.
[3] The Rabbi assumed that the father conspired with the son to hide himself. Or possibly it was the father who said this: the child's sneeze at that moment proved that he himself was not worthy of receiving it.
[4] Where there could be no eavesdroppers.
[5] So that it should not be audible to others when they pronounced it in the priestly benediction.
[6] Where the priests stood to utter the benediction.

these nor the others[1] departed from there until it had become concealed from them, as it is said, *This is My name for ever*—le'olam (Ex. III, 15). The last word is written so that it can be read as *le'elem* (for concealment). Why was all this precaution necessary? SO THAT MAN CANNOT FIND OUT THE WORK THAT GOD HATH DONE FROM THE BEGINNING EVEN TO THE END.[2]

1. I KNOW THAT THERE IS NOTHING BETTER FOR THEM THAN TO REJOICE, AND TO GET PLEASURE SO LONG AS THEY LIVE. BUT ALSO THAT EVERY MAN SHOULD EAT AND DRINK (III, 12 f.). R. Tanḥuma in the name of R. Naḥman, the son of R. Samuel b. Naḥman, and R. Menaḥma said (another version: R. Jeremiah and R. Meyasha in the name of R. Samuel b. R. Isaac): All the eating and drinking mentioned in this Book refer to Torah and good deeds. R. Jonah said: The most clear proof of them all is, *A man hath no better thing under the sun than to eat and to drink, and to be merry, and that this should accompany him in his labour*—'amalo (Eccl. VIII, 15). The last word should be read as *'olamo* (his world)—in this world; *All the days of his life* (*ib.*) alludes to the grave. Are there, then, food and drink in the grave which accompany a man to the grave! But it means the Torah and good deeds which a man does.[3]

1. I KNOW THAT, WHATSOEVER GOD DOETH, IT SHALL BE FOR EVER (III, 14). R. Judah b. R. Simon said: By rights the first man should have lived and endured for ever[4]; why, then, was the penalty of death imposed on him? GOD HATH SO MADE IT, THAT MEN SHOULD FEAR BEFORE HIM.

[1] The text is faulty and must be corrected according to the version in J. Yoma 40*d*: Those who were standing near fell upon their faces, while those who were too far away [to hear the Name] exclaimed, 'Blessed,' etc. Neither of these two classes departed, etc. I.e. even those who heard it from the High Priest miraculously forgot it before they descended.
[2] I.e. that he should not be able to penetrate the future.
[3] Repeated from II, 24.
[4] Since Ḳoheleth declares that what God makes lasts for ever.

R. Eleazar said: At the beginning of the world's creation it is stated, *Let the waters under the heaven be gathered together unto one place* (Gen. I, 9). For what purpose? *And let the dry land appear* (*ib.*). Why is it written twice, *He hath called for the waters of the sea, and poureth them out upon the face of the earth; the Lord is His name* (Amos v, 8; IX, 6)? Once with reference to the generation of the Flood and the other with reference to the generation of the Dispersion[1]; and GOD HATH SO MADE IT, THAT MEN SHOULD FEAR BEFORE HIM.

R. Simeon b. Laḳish said: It is written, *All this word which I command you, that shall ye observe to do; thou shalt not add thereto, nor diminish from it* (Deut. XIII, 1). But the righteous do add to and do not[2] diminish from it! R. Jose b. R. Ḥanina said: [It is written, *Take heed to thyself that thou offer not thy burnt-offerings in every place that thou seest* (*ib.* XII, 13)][3]; from this it is seen that a high place was not permitted except by a prophet, yet Elijah stood and offered at the top of Carmel[4]; and, as R. Simlai of Beroiara[5] remarked: Elijah said to Him, *I have done all these things*[6] *at Thy word* (I Kings XVIII, 36).

R. Ḥanina said: It is written, *And thy house and thy kingdom shall be made sure for ever before thee* (II Sam. VII, 16). When? *If thy children keep My covenant . . . their children also for ever shall sit upon thy throne* (Ps. CXXXII, 12); but if not, *Then will I visit their transgression with the rod* (*ib.* LXXXIX, 33).[7] R. Judan said: Great is the fear [of God], because heaven and earth were only created through the merit of such fear; as it is written, GOD HATH SO MADE IT, THAT MEN SHOULD FEAR BEFORE HIM. R. Jeremiah said: Great is the fear [of God], since

[1] The builders of the Tower of Babel. [2] Radal deletes the negative.
[3] The Scriptural text is added from Lev. R. XXII, 9.
[4] His action apparently contravened the Torah; but since it is impossible to think this, it is inferred that the prophets had the power to suspend the law temporarily in an emergency, by adding to it or diminishing from it.
[5] The place cannot be identified.
[6] The erection of an otherwise illegal altar.
[7] This is an illustration of the idea that God establishes something for ever as an incentive for man to fear Him.

Solomon concluded the two Books which he wrote with nothing else than a reference to fear; as it is written in the Book of Proverbs, *Grace is deceitful, and beauty is vain; but a woman that feareth the Lord she shall be praised* (Prov. XXXI, 30), and in the present Book it is written, *Fear God and keep His commandments* (Eccl. XII, 13).

R. Simeon b. Laḳish was coming back from Ḥamath-Gerah[1] when R. Jonathan met him and asked, 'How does my master explain the following passages?' which he proceeded to quote to him; and these are the passages which he cited for him.[2] Thus did the Holy One, blessed be He, decree, that the celestial beings shall be above in heaven and that the terrestrial creatures should be below. Moses, however, arose and reversed them; that is what is written, *And Moses went up to God* (Ex. XIX, 3), *And the Lord came down upon Mount Sinai* (*ib.* 20). Similarly the Holy One, blessed be He, decreed that the terrestrial creatures should eat and drink whereas the celestial beings should not eat and drink. Abraham, however, arose and made celestial beings eat and drink; as it is written, *He stood by them under the tree and they did eat* (Gen. XVIII, 8). But did they really eat? R. Nathan said: They pretended to eat and the courses disappeared one after the other. Moses arose and made terrestrial creatures [himself] not to eat and drink; as it is written, *And he was there with the Lord forty days and forty nights; he did neither eat bread, nor drink water* (Ex. XXXIV, 28). Similarly the Holy One, blessed be He, decreed that the sea should remain sea and the dry land should remain dry land; but Moses arose and made the sea into dry land, as it is written, *And the children of Israel went into the midst of the sea upon the dry ground* (*ib.* XIV, 22). Elisha, the disciple of his disciple, arose and made the dry land into sea; as it is written, *Make this valley full of trenches* (II Kings III, 16). In like manner the Holy One, blessed be He, decreed that the heavens should praise Him, as

[1] Radal reads 'Ḥamath-Geder'. The name indicates a hot spring near Geder (Josh. XII, 13). [2] Read מקרי for מקרתה.

it is said, *The heavens declare the glory of God* (Ps. XIX, 2); but Moses stood up and silenced them, as it is said, *Give ear, ye heavens, and I will speak* (Deut. XXXII, 1). Similarly the Holy One, blessed be He, decreed that the sun and moon should praise Him, as it is said, *From the rising of the sun unto the going down thereof the Lord's name is to be praised* (Ps. CXIII, 3)—the last word is written so that it can be read as *mehallel*.[1] His disciple, Joshua, stood up and silenced them, as it is said, *Sun, stand thou still upon Gibeon, and thou, Moon, in the valley of Aijalon* (Josh. X, 12). Similarly the Holy One, blessed be He, decreed that summer should be summer and winter be winter; but Samuel stood up and turned summer into winter, as it is said, *Is it not wheat harvest to-day? I will call unto the Lord, that He may send thunder and rain* (I Sam. XII, 17). Elijah arose and turned winter into summer, as it is said, *There shall not be dew nor rain these years, but according to my word* (I Kings XVII, 1).[2] Similarly the Holy One, blessed be He, decreed that day should be day and night be night; but Jacob arose and made day into night, as it is said, *And he lighted upon the place, and tarried there all night, because the sun was set*—ki ba' (Gen. XXVIII, 11)—actually He extinguished (*kibbah*) the sun.[3] The Rabbis explain that the Holy One, blessed be He, caused the sun to set before its time and spoke with him secretly [in his dream]. It may be likened to the friend of a king who visited him at stipulated times; and if the king was engaged with his subjects,[4] he gave an order for his sake, 'Extinguish the lamps and lights that I may converse with my friend in secret.' In like manner the Holy One, blessed be He, caused the sun to set before its time and spoke with the patriarch Jacob in secret.

[1] Instead of *mehullal* 'to be praised' the word is read as *mehallel*, i.e. 'it [the sun] praises the Lord's name'.

[2] In Palestine the heavy rain only fell in winter. Therefore a rainless winter was the equivalent of summer.

[3] Made it set before its time.

[4] Or perhaps: and for his sake the king showed favour to all his subjects. He would order: Extinguish, etc. 'And for . . . his subjects' is omitted in the parallel version in Gen. R. LXVIII, 10, *q.v.*

Deborah and Barak arose and made night into day, as it is written, *Then sang Deborah and Barak the son of Abinoam on that day*, etc. (Judg. v, 1).[1] R. Phinehas and R. Hilkiah said in the name of R. Simon: Six miracles were performed on that day.[2] On the same day they both came, she sent for him and he for her, they fought the battle, Sisera was slain, they shared the spoil, and uttered a song, as it is said, '*Then sang Deborah and Barak the son of Abinoam on that day*,' etc.

1. THAT WHICH IS HATH BEEN LONG AGO (III, 15). R. Judah and R. Nehemiah[3] comment. R. Judah declares: Should anybody say to you, 'Is it possible that [before the work of Creation] the whole world was water in the midst of water?' answer him that the whole of the ocean is likewise water in the midst of water. AND THAT WHICH IS TO BE HATH ALREADY BEEN: Should anybody say to you, 'Is it possible that the Holy One, blessed be He, will make sea into dry land?' answer him that it has already been done; for did He not do so by the hand of Moses, as it is said, *And the children of Israel walked upon dry land in the midst of the sea* (Ex. XIV, 29)? It is written, *Lift thou up thy rod*, etc. (*ib.* 16) and *The children of Israel went into the midst of the sea upon the dry ground* (*ib.* 22). Should anybody say to you, 'Is it possible that if Adam had not sinned, he would have existed for ever?' answer him that it has happened in the case of Elijah (may he be remembered for good) who was sinless and exists for ever. Should anybody say to you, 'Is it possible that the Holy One, blessed be He, will revive the dead for us?' answer him that He has already done so through Elijah, Elisha, and Ezekiel.[4] R. Aha said in the name of R. Halafta: Everything which the Holy One, blessed be He, will do or renew in His world in the Messianic

[1] Rendering: Then sang Deborah *on account of* that day, viz. because night had been turned to day ('E.J.).
[2] And the day was prolonged into the night for the purpose.
[3] R. Nehemiah's statement is omitted from the text.
[4] I Kings XVII, 17 ff., II Kings IV, 32 ff., Ezek. XXXVII, 1 ff.

future He has already done in part through the medium of a prophet in this world. I am He who will make the sea into dry land, and I have already done so in this world, as it is written, '*Lift thou up thy rod,*' etc. I am He who will remember the barren as I have already done through Abraham, as it is stated, *And the Lord remembered Sarah as He had said* (Gen. XXI, 1). I am He who will revive the dead as I have already done through Elijah, Elisha, and Ezekiel. I am He who will make kings to bow down before you as I have already done for you through Daniel to whom Nebuchadnezzar prostrated himself, as it is said, *Then the king Nebuchadnezzar fell upon his face and worshipped Daniel* (Dan. II, 46). I am He who will make the blind to see in the Messianic era as I have already done through Elisha, as it is said, *And the Lord opened the eyes of the young man* (II Kings VI, 17).

AND GOD SEEKETH THAT WHICH IS PURSUED. R. Huna said in the name of R. Jose: God always seeks that which is pursued. You find that when a righteous man pursues a righteous man, God seeks him who is pursued; and when a wicked man pursues a righteous man, God seeks him who is pursued; and when a wicked man pursues a wicked man, God seeks the pursued. In every instance He seeks the pursued. R. Judah b. R. Simon said in the name of R. Jose b. R. Nehorai: The Holy One, blessed be He, always demands the blood of the pursued from the pursuers. Know that it is so, because Abel was pursued by Cain and the Holy One, blessed be He, chose only Abel, as it is said, *And the Lord had respect unto Abel and his offering* (Gen. IV, 4). Noah was pursued by his generation and the Holy One, blessed be He, chose only Noah, as it is said, *For thee have I seen righteous before Me in this generation* (*ib.* VII, 1). Abraham was pursued by Nimrod and the Holy One, blessed be He, chose Abraham, as it is said, *Thou art the Lord the God, who didst choose Abram* (Neh. IX, 7). Isaac was pursued by the Philistines and the Holy One, blessed be He, chose Isaac, as it is said, *We saw plainly that the Lord was with thee* (Gen. XXVI, 28). Jacob was pursued by Esau and the Holy One, blessed be He, chose Jacob, as it is said, *For the Lord hath chosen Jacob unto Himself, and Israel for His own treasure* (Ps. CXXXV, 4). Joseph was pursued by his brothers and the Holy One, blessed be He, chose Joseph, as it is said, *He appointed it in Joseph for a testimony, when He went forth against the land of Egypt* (*ib.* LXXXI, 6). Moses was pursued by Pharaoh and the Holy One, blessed be He, chose Moses, as it is said, *Had not Moses His chosen stood before Him in the breach* (*ib.* CVI, 23). David was pursued by Saul and the Holy One, blessed be He, chose David, as it is said, *He chose David also His servant, and took him from the sheepfolds* (*ib.* LXXVIII, 70). Saul was pursued by the Philistines and the Holy One, blessed be He, chose Saul, as it is said, *See ye him whom the Lord hath chosen* (I Sam. X, 24). Israel was pursued by the nations and the Holy One, blessed be He, chose Israel, as it is said, *The Lord thy God hath chosen thee to be His own treasure* (Deut. VII, 6). R. Eleazar, the son of R. Jose b. Zimra, said: It is the same with the offerings. The Holy One, blessed be He, said: 'The ox is pursued by the lion, the goat by the leopard, the lamb by the wolf. Do not bring Me offerings from the pursuers but from the pursued'; as it is said, *When a bullock, or a sheep, or a goat, is brought forth*, etc. (Lev. XXII, 27).

1. AND MOREOVER I SAW UNDER THE SUN, IN THE PLACE OF JUSTICE, THAT WICKEDNESS WAS THERE (III, 16). R. Eleazar and R. Joshua b. Levi said: IN THE PLACE OF JUSTICE, THAT WICKEDNESS WAS THERE—in the place where the Great Sanhedrin sit and adjudicate (*ḥotekin*) for Israel WICKEDNESS WAS THERE, as it is said, *All the princes of the king of Babylon came in, and sat in the middle* (hatawek) *gate* (Jer. XXXIX, 3), which means, in the place where *halachoth* were decided, WICKEDNESS WAS THERE: there sat *Nergal-sarezer, Samgar-nebo, Sarsechim, Rab-saris, Nergal-sarezer, Rab-mag, with all the residue of the princes of the king of Babylon* (*ib.*). The proverb declares, 'Where the master hung up his weapons, there the shepherd has hung up

his wallet'[1]; and the Holy Spirit cried, IN THE PLACE OF JUSTICE, THAT WICKEDNESS WAS THERE. It is a place of which it is said, *Righteousness lodged in her, but now murderers* (Isa. I, 21). There were murders committed; there they slew Zechariah and Uriah.[2]

R. Jonathan asked R. Aḥa, 'Where did the Israelites slay Zechariah, in the Court of Israel or the Court of Women?' He replied, 'In neither of these, but it was in the Court of the Priests. Nor did they treat his blood like the blood of a hind or ram; for in regard to the blood of these animals it is written in the Torah, *He shall pour out the blood thereof and cover it with dust* (Lev. XVII, 13). They did not treat the blood of the righteous Zechariah as the blood of a ram or hind, but poured it upon the stones; as it is written, *For her blood is in the midst of her, she set it upon the bare rock; she poured it not upon the ground, to cover it with dust* (Ezek. XXIV, 7). And for what purpose was all this? *That it might cause fury to come up, that vengeance might be taken* (*ib.*). Therefore it is written, *Remember then thy Creator in the days of thy youth, before the evil days come* (Eccl. XII, 1).[3] You find that when Nebuzaradan came up to destroy Jerusalem, the Holy One, blessed be He, hinted to that blood that it should seethe and bubble for two hundred and fifty-two years from the reign of Joash to that of Zedekiah.[4] What did they do? They scraped quantities of dust to throw on it and made heaps and heaps over it, but it did not become still, and the blood kept seething and foaming. The Holy One, blessed be He, said to the blood: "The time has come for you to collect your debt." When Nebuzaradan came up and saw it, he asked, "What kind of blood is this which seethes in this manner?" They answered, "The

[1] B.M. 84*b* (Sonc. ed., p. 484). The place formerly used for an honourable purpose is now put to a dishonourable use.
[2] II Chron. XXIV, 20; Jer. XXVI, 20 ff.
[3] I.e. the evils brought by Nebuzaradan.
[4] The murder of Zechariah occurred just before the death of Joash (II Chron. XXIV, 21 f.). Then followed Amaziah who reigned 29 years, Uzziah 52, Jotham 16, Ahaz 16, Hezekiah 29, Manasseh 55, Amon 2, Josiah 31, Jehoiakim 11, Zedekiah 11. The total is 252.

blood of bulls, rams, and lambs which are slaughtered and offered as sacrifices." He had bulls, rams, and lambs brought and slaughtered alongside of it, but it did not become still or rest or stop seething. He forthwith took and hanged them on the gallows, saying to them, "Tell me what is the nature of this blood, otherwise I will comb your flesh with an iron comb." They replied, "Since the Holy One, blessed be He, is determined to demand punishment from us for his blood, we will reveal to you what happened. There was a priest-prophet and judge who prophesied against us all that you are doing with us; but we did not believe him, and we arose against him and killed him because he reproved us." Nebuzaradan immediately had eighty thousand priestly novitiates brought and slew them by it. The blood did not stop, but gushed forth until it reached the grave of Zechariah. He took the Great Sanhedrin and Minor Sanhedrin and slew them by it; but it did not stop. Then the villain went and exclaimed over the blood, "Are you and your blood better than these men's? Do you wish me to destroy all your people on its account!" At that moment the Holy One, blessed be He, was filled with compassion and said, "If this wicked and cruel person, the son of a wicked father, who came up to destroy My house, is filled with compassion for them, how much more should I be so of whom it is written, *The Lord, the Lord, God, merciful and gracious* (Ex. XXXIV, 6) and *The Lord is good to all, and His tender mercies are over all His works* (Ps. CXLV, 9)!" Then the Holy One, blessed be He, hinted to the blood and it was absorbed in that same place.' R. Judan said: Seven transgressions were committed by Israel at that time: they killed a priest, a prophet, and a judge, they shed innocent blood, they defiled the Temple Court, and this was done on the Sabbath which was also the Day of Atonement.[1]

R. Joshua interpreted the verse as referring to the golden calf. IN THE PLACE OF JUSTICE, THAT

[1] Cf. Lam. R. Proem XXIII.

WICKEDNESS WAS THERE: in the place where Moses practised the Attribute of Justice, as it is said, *Go to and fro from gate to gate throughout the camp, and slay every man his brother* (Ex. XXXII, 27), WICKEDNESS WAS THERE: there it is written, *And the Lord smote the people, because they had made the calf* (*ib.* 35)[1]; and the Holy Spirit cried, IN THE PLACE OF JUSTICE, THAT WICKEDNESS WAS THERE — in the place where I declared them righteous and ascribed godliness to them, as it is stated, *I said: Ye are godlike beings, and all of you sons of the Most High* (Ps. LXXXII, 6), WICKEDNESS WAS THERE, there they acted wickedly and made the calf, as it is stated, *And worshipped it* (Ex. XXXII, 8).[2]

R. Judah interpreted the verse in connection with the incident at Shittim. IN THE PLACE OF JUSTICE, THAT WICKEDNESS WAS THERE: in the place where the Attribute of Justice functioned, viz. at Shittim, as it is said, *Take all the chiefs of the people, and hang them up unto the Lord in face of the sun* (Num. XXV, 4), WICKEDNESS WAS THERE, as it is said, *And those that died by the plague were twenty and four thousand* (*ib.* 9)[1]; and the Holy Spirit cried, IN THE PLACE OF JUSTICE, THAT WICKEDNESS WAS THERE—in the place where I vindicated them against Balaam's curses, which I turned into blessings, as it is stated, *But the Lord thy God turned the curse into a blessing unto thee* (Deut. XXIII, 6), WICKEDNESS WAS THERE, there they acted wickedly and were guilty of immorality, as it is said, *And Israel abode in Shittim, and the people began to commit harlotry with the daughters of Moab* (Num. XXV, 1).[2]

R. Levi and R. Isaac make statements. R. Levi said: Two things are in the hand [of God] and two in His right hand. 'Two things are in the hand [of God],' as it is said, *In whose hand is the soul of every living thing* (Job XII, 10), and it is written, *My hand take hold on judgment* (Deut. XXXII, 41). 'And two in His right hand,' as it is

[1] Interpreting 'wickedness' as the punishment for wickedness (Y.T.).
[2] There are apparently two interpretations here merged into one.

said, *At His right hand was a fiery law unto them* (*ib.* XXXIII, 2), and it is written, *Thy right hand is full of righteousness* (Ps. XLVIII, 11). R. Isaac said: The Holy One, blessed be He, spake to the soul: 'O soul, although I strengthened thee and commanded thee, saying, *Only be stedfast in not eating the blood* (Deut. XII, 23), behold, thou goest forth, robbest, dost violence, sinnest and standest in the [power of the] Attribute of Justice,[1] yet thou goest forth from the Attribute of Justice and sinnest again'; as it is said, *Speak unto the children of Israel, saying: If a soul*[2] *shall sin through error* (Lev. IV, 2).

1. I SAID IN MY HEART: THE RIGHTEOUS AND THE WICKED GOD WILL JUDGE (III, 17). R. Ḥanina b. Papa said: The meaning is, God will judge the righteous and wicked alike. A robber ascends the scaffold and R. Akiba ascended the scaffold.[3] Rabbi [Judah ha-Nasi] said: [The meaning is,] God judges a righteous man through a wicked man.[4] Thus Tineius Rufus[5] judged R. Akiba.

When Trajan executed Julianus and his brother Pappus in Laodicea, he said to them, 'If you are of the people of Hananiah, Mishael and Azariah,[6] and I am a descendant of Nebuchadnezzar, let their God come and save you from my hand!' They replied, 'Hananiah, Mishael, and Azariah were upright men, and king Nebuchadnezzar a worthy king and fit that a miracle should be wrought through him. We, however, are sinners against the Omnipresent and you are a sinful king and unfit that a miracle should be wrought through you. Moreover, we are [because of our sins] condemned to death. If you slay us, well and good; if not, the Omnipresent has many lions, bears, serpents, and scorpions by which men are killed. Should you slay us, you will be reckoned as one of them; but the Holy One, blessed be He, will exact vengeance for our

[1] You receive punishment. [2] E.V. '*any one*'. For this paragraph cf. Lev. R. IV, 1. [3] The latter to suffer martyrdom.
[4] Any evil committed by the former is punished by wrong done to him by the latter. [5] Roman governor of Judea. [6] Dan. I, 7; III, 16 ff.

blood of you.' It is reported that before he had time to move from there two deputies came against him from Rome who split his skull with clubs.

FOR THERE IS A TIME THERE FOR EVERY PURPOSE AND FOR EVERY WORK. For every purpose there is a time, and for every time there is a purpose, AND FOR EVERY WORK [judgment is] THERE [in the Hereafter][1]: a man can do what he pleases in this world, but in the Hereafter there will be judgment and reckoning.

1. I SAID IN MY HEART: IT IS BECAUSE OF THE SONS OF MEN, THAT GOD MAY SIFT THEM, AND THAT THEY MAY SEE THAT THEY THEMSELVES ARE BUT AS BEASTS (III, 18). IT IS BECAUSE (DIBRATH) means the manner (*middaberoth*) in which the wicked conduct themselves in this world, in that they revile and blaspheme in this world; nevertheless the Holy One, blessed be He, grants them abundant peace. For what purpose? THAT GOD MAY SIFT THEM (LE-BARAM): i.e. to make manifest to them (*le-barer lahem*) what is the Attribute of Judgment for the wicked. AND THAT THEY MAY SEE THAT THEY THEMSELVES ARE BUT AS BEASTS: that they should recognise and demonstrate to the world that the wicked are likened to the beast. In the same way that a beast is condemned to death[2] and does not enter the life of the World to Come, so are the wicked condemned to death like a beast and do not enter the World to Come.

Another interpretation of IT IS BECAUSE OF THE SONS OF MEN: because of the manner in which the righteous conduct themselves in this world, with privation, fastings, and sufferings. For what purpose? THAT GOD MAY SIFT THEM: to make manifest to them the quality of their righteousness. AND THAT THEY MAY

[1] This is the comment on the verse and apparently means that man has an opportunity at some time or other of doing whatever he desires (including sin), but that on the other hand for every purpose (i.e. pleasure indulged in by man) there is a time for judgment (cf. Eccl. VIII, 6) sc. in the Hereafter. [2] V. Sanh. I, 1 (Sonc. ed., p. 2).

SEE THAT THEY THEMSELVES ARE BUT AS BEASTS: that they should recognise and demonstrate to the peoples of the world how Israel is drawn after Him like a beast [which follows its owner], as it is said, *And ye My sheep, the sheep of My pasture, are men, and I am your God* (Ezek. XXXIV, 31). Furthermore, just as a beast stretches forth its neck for slaughter, so is it with the righteous, as it is said, *Nay, but for Thy sake are we killed all the day, we are accounted as sheep for the slaughter* (Ps. XLIV, 23). [Apart from this derivation from texts] you have this traditional teaching: If one performs a precept when near to his end, it is as though his quality of righteousness lacked only that precept and is completed thereby; and if one commits a transgression when near to his end, it is as though his quality of wickedness lacked only that transgression and is completed thereby. Both of them depart [from the world] fully consummated, one in the quality of righteousness and the other in the quality of wickedness.

R. Bun and R. Isaac make statements. R. Bun said: The Holy One, blessed be He, spake: 'As I raised prophets from Israel who are called "men", as it is stated, "*Ye . . . are men*" (Ezek. *loc. cit.*), shall I not similarly raise prophets from the heathens who are called "cattle", as it is stated, *And also* much cattle!' (Jonah IV, 11).[1] R. Isaac said: *For that which befalleth the sons of men befalleth beasts* (Eccl. III, 11), i.e. as it happens to man shall it not happen to the beast? The Holy One, blessed be He, spake: 'As I decreed and said concerning man, *And in the eighth day the flesh of his foreskin shall be circumcised* (Lev. XII, 3), have I not made a similar decree concerning beasts, as it is stated, *But from the eighth day and thenceforth it may be accepted for an offering made by fire unto the Lord* (*ib.* XXII, 27)?'

SO THAT MAN HATH NO PRE-EMINENCE ABOVE

[1] This occurs in God's justification for His sparing Nineveh, viz. because it contained much cattle. The Rabbis assume that human beings are meant.

A BEAST[1]; FOR ALL IS VANITY. What means NO? R. Naḥman b. R. Isaac said: He made for man an ornament[2] in the lower part of the body so that he should not be degraded like a beast. R. Jannai and R. Judan comment. One said: He made for him certain coverings over his buttocks so that he should not be degraded like a beast; while the other said that He made for him fleshy protuberances in the lower part of the body so that he should not feel pain at the time of sitting. R. Levi and R. Ammi comment. One said: He ordained burial for him; the other said that He ordained the use of a coffin for him. One says[3]: He ordained the use of a coffin and shrouds for him.

1. ALL GO UNTO ONE PLACE; ALL ARE OF THE DUST, AND ALL RETURN TO DUST (III, 20). R. Eliezer and R. Joshua make statements. R. Eliezer says: All that the Holy One, blessed be He, created in heaven has its origin in heaven, and all that He created on earth has its origin in the earth. On what is this statement based? *Praise ye the Lord from the heavens, praise Him in the heights. Praise ye Him, all His angels . . . Praise the Lord from the earth, ye sea-monsters, and all deeps; fire and hail, snow and vapour*, etc., to the end of the Psalm (Ps. CXLVIII, 1 ff.).[4] R. Joshua says: All that the Holy One, blessed be He, created in heaven and on earth has its origin in heaven. Although it is written concerning snow, *For He saith to the snow: Be of the earth* (Job XXXVII, 6),[5] nevertheless its origin is only from heaven, as it is stated, *For as the rain cometh down and the snow from heaven* (Isa. LV, 10).

[1] Interpreted by the Midrash: the pre-eminence which a man hath above a beast is 'no'—i.e. that man is not in some respects as a beast, as the Midrash proceeds to explain.

[2] The Heb. is נוי and for NO is אין. There is a play on the letters. The meaning is that God arranged that the function of evacuation should not be objectionable in man.

[3] Read probably 'the Rabbis say'. Man's superiority over the animal consists in the manner of disposing the body after death.

[4] In this Psalm, angels, sun, moon, and all heavenly bodies are described as being from heaven; while 'sea-monsters, deeps, etc.' until man are described as being from the earth.

[5] E.V. '*Fall thou on the earth*'.

R. Ḥiyya b. Joseph says: All that is in heaven and on earth has its origin from the earth. Although it is written concerning rain, '*For as the rain cometh down and the snow from heaven,*' nevertheless its origin is only from the earth. What is the ground of this view? *But there went up a mist from the earth* (Gen. II, 6). R. Judan derives the teaching from the present verse, ALL GO UNTO ONE PLACE, ALL ARE OF THE DUST. R. Naḥman said: Even the sun was only created from the earth, as it is written, *Who commandeth the sun, and it riseth not* (Job IX, 7).[1]

1. WHO KNOWETH THE SPIRIT OF MAN WHETHER IT GOETH UPWARD, AND THE SPIRIT OF THE BEAST[2] WHETHER IT GOETH DOWNWARD TO THE EARTH (III, 21)? It has been taught: Both the souls of the righteous and those of the wicked alike ascend above, but the souls of the righteous are placed in the Divine treasury, while those of the wicked are cast about on earth. For Abigail said to David by the Holy Spirit, *The soul of my lord shall be bound in the bundle of life* (I Sam. XXV, 29). It might be thought that this will happen also to the souls of the wicked; therefore it is stated, *And the souls of thine enemies, them shall He sling out as from the hollow of a sling* (*ib.*).

A matron asked R. Jose b. Ḥalafta, 'What is the meaning of the text, WHO KNOWETH THE SPIRIT OF MAN WHETHER IT GOETH UPWARD?' He replied, 'It refers to the souls of the righteous which are placed in the Divine treasury. For so spake Abigail to David by the Holy Spirit, "*The soul of my lord shall be bound in the bundle of life.*" It might be thought that this will also happen to the souls of the wicked; therefore it is stated, "*And the souls of thine enemies, them shall He sling out as from the hollow of a sling.*"' She asked him, 'What, then, is the meaning of the text, AND THE SPIRIT OF THE

[1] The preceding verse reads, *Who shaketh the earth out of her place,* which is understood as the general clause, and all that follows as particular parts of '*the earth*'. [2] I.e. the wicked, as in v. 18.

BEAST WHETHER IT GOETH DOWNWARD TO THE EARTH?' He replied, 'It refers to the souls of the wicked which descend to Gehinnom below, as it is stated, *In the day when he went down to the netherworld I caused the deep to mourn and cover itself for him'* (Ezek. XXXI, 15).[1]

1. WHEREFORE I PERCEIVED THAT THERE IS NOTHING BETTER THAN THAT A MAN SHOULD REJOICE IN HIS WORKS; FOR THAT IS HIS PORTION; FOR WHO SHALL BRING HIM TO SEE WHAT SHALL BE AFTER HIM (III, 22)? Who will bring David [back to life] to see what Solomon made?[2] Who will bring Solomon back to see what will happen to him through what Rehoboam did?[3]

[1] In these interpretations the text is regarded as a positive statement, viz. that the souls of the righteous and of the unrighteous go up to heaven and down to Gehinnom respectively, and not as a question.
[2] The Temple and the grandeur of his kingdom.
[3] He caused the kingdom to be split.

CHAPTER IV

1. BUT I RETURNED AND CONSIDERED ALL THE OPPRESSIONS THAT ARE DONE UNDER THE SUN (IV, 1). R. Judah, R. Nehemiah, and the Rabbis comment. R. Judah says: It refers to the children who are buried early in life through the sins of their fathers in this world. In the Hereafter they will range themselves with the band of the righteous, while their fathers will be ranged with the band of the wicked. They will speak before Him: 'Lord of the universe, did we not die early only because of the sins of our fathers? Let our fathers come over to us through our merits.'[1] He replies to them, 'Your fathers sinned also after your death, and their wrongdoings accuse them.' R. Judah b. R. Ilai said in the name of R. Joshua b. Levi: At that time Elijah (may he be remembered for good) will be there to suggest a defence. He will say to the children: 'Speak before Him, "Lord of the universe, which Attribute of Thine predominates, that of Grace or Punishment? Surely the Attribute of Grace is great and that of Punishment small, yet we died through the sins of our fathers. If then the Attribute of Grace exceeds the other, how much more should our fathers come over to us!"' Therefore he says to them, 'Well have you pleaded; let them come over to you'; as it is written, *And they shall live with their children, and shall return* (Zech. X, 9), which means that they returned from the descent to Gehinnom and were rescued through the merit of their children. Therefore every man is under the obligation to teach his son Torah that he may rescue him from Gehinnom.

R. Ḥanina[2] interpreted the verse as referring to the martyrs[3] who enter the life of the World to Come even if they do not confess [their sins before death].

[1] Let our early death be an expiation for their sins. Cf. Soṭ. 49*a* (Sonc. ed., p. 262). [2] This should probably be 'Nehemiah' as in the beginning of the last paragraph. [3] Lit. 'slain by the government'. The form of confession is given in A.P.B., p. 317.

R. Benjamin interpreted the verse of one who pretends to have a knowledge of Torah. Everybody thinks he is a Bible-scholar but he is not, or a Mishnah-scholar but he is not. He wraps himself in his *ṭallith* and has the phylactery on his head.[1] AND BEHOLD THE TEARS OF SUCH AS WERE OPPRESSED, AND THEY HAD NO COMFORTER: the Holy One, blessed be He, spake, 'It is for Me to punish them,' as it is stated, *Cursed be he that doeth the work of the Lord deceitfully* (Jer. XLVIII, 10).

The Rabbis interpreted the verse of the heathen peoples. AND BEHOLD THE TEARS OF SUCH AS WERE OPPRESSED, AND THEY HAD NO COMFORTER: the Holy One, blessed be He, spake, 'It is for Me to remonstrate with them,' as it is written, *Their Redeemer is strong, the Lord of hosts is His name; He will thoroughly plead their cause* (*ib.* L, 34).

Daniel the tailor interpreted the verse as referring to the illegitimate. These are the actual illegitimate. Now what wrong has such a person done? A man has illicit intercourse and begets this child; how has the latter sinned and how is he responsible![2] R. Judah b. Pazzi said: Even illegitimates enter the World to Come; for it is written, AND BEHOLD THE TEARS OF SUCH AS WERE OPPRESSED, AND THEY HAD NO COMFORTER. The Holy One, blessed be He, spake, 'Since they were under a disability in this world, as regards the Hereafter Zechariah says, "I see that they have seats [of pure gold],"[3] as it is stated, *Behold a candlestick all of gold, with a bowl* (gullah) *upon the top of it . . . and two olive-trees by it'* (Zech. IV, 2 f.).[4] Two teachers differ about the meaning of the world '*gullah*'. One said that it signifies 'captivity' (*golah*), while the other said that it signifies 'redemption' (*ge'ulah*). He who said that it

[1] He apes the manners of the scholar. [2] He is therefore cited as an example of the innocent victim of another's sin.

[3] 'Of pure gold' is added from Lev. R. XXXII *ad fin.* Levi renders: I will regard them as of pure gold; the word in the text meaning pure gold. [4] Referred now to the Hereafter (or the Messianic era), when all will be as of pure gold.

signifies 'captivity' refers it to the exile to Babylon and the exile of the *Shechinah* with them. He who said that it signifies 'redemption' refers it to the Redeemer, for it is written, *Our Redeemer the Lord of hosts is His name* (Isa. XLVII, 4) and *The breaker is gone up before them . . . and their king is passed on before them, and the Lord at the head of them* (Micah II, 13).

1. WHEREFORE I PRAISED THE DEAD THAT ARE ALREADY DEAD (IV, 2): i.e. the generation of Enosh[1] and the generation of the Flood, MORE THAN THE LIVING THAT ARE YET ALIVE: i.e. the men of Sodom and the Egyptians.[2]

1. BUT BETTER THAN THEY BOTH IS HE THAT HATH NOT YET BEEN (IV, 3). This refers to the thousand generations which were included in the Divine plan to be created. How many of them were eliminated? R. Joḥanan said in the name of R. Eliezer the son of R. Jose the Galilean: Nine hundred and seventy-four generations, as it is stated, *The word which He commanded to a thousandth generation* (Ps. CV, 8).[3]

R. Joshua interpreted the verse as referring to Israel when they stood before Mount Sinai. Since they participated in the act [of making the golden calf], Moses left no piece of ground on the mountain upon which he did not prostrate himself and beg mercy for Israel, but he was not answered; and five destroying angels attached themselves to him,[4] viz. Ḳeẓef (Wrath), Mashḥith (Destruction), Hashmed (Annihilation), Af (Anger), and Ḥemah (Hot Displeasure).[5] Moses was at once afraid of them; so what did he do? He had recourse to the deeds of the patriarchs. He immediately recalled them and said, '*Remember Abraham, Isaac, and Israel, Thy servants*' (Ex. XXXII, 13). The Holy One, blessed be He, spake

[1] V. p. 70, n. 1. [2] Who were living when the former were dead.
[3] Cf. I, 15. Here the reference is to the 26th generation to whom the Torah was revealed. [4] To punish Israel with destruction.
[5] Wrath, Destruction, etc., are personified as angels.

to him: 'Moses, what claims have the patriarchs of old upon Me? If I come to examine them, I have grievances against them: against Abraham for saying, *Whereby shall I know that I shall inherit it?* (Gen. XV, 8)[1]; against Isaac, as it is stated, *Now Isaac loved Esau* (*ib.* XXV, 28) whereas I hated him, as it is stated, *But Esau I hated* (Mal. I, 3); against Jacob for saying, *My way is hid from the Lord* (Isa. XL, 27).' When, however, Moses said, *To whom Thou didst swear by Thine own self* (Ex. *loc. cit.*), the Holy One, blessed be He, was filled with compassion for them, as it is stated, *The Lord repented of the evil which He said He would do unto His people* (*ib.* 14). Forthwith three of the destroying angels, viz. Ḳeẓef, Mashḥith, and Hashmed, departed from him, and two were left, viz. Af and Ḥemah, as it is written, *For I was in dread of* Af *and* Ḥemah (Deut. IX, 19). Moses said before Him: 'Lord of the universe, can I stand against the two of them? Do Thou tackle one and I the other'; that is what is written, *Arise, O Lord, against Thine* Af (Ps. VII, 7).[2] Whence is it known that Moses stood against one, viz. the angel Ḥemah? As it is stated, *Therefore He said that He would destroy them, had not Moses His chosen stood before Him in the breach, to turn back His* Ḥemah (*E.V. 'hot displeasure'*), *lest it*[3] *should destroy them* (Ps. CVI, 23). Concerning that time it declares, WHEREFORE I PRAISED THE DEAD THAT ARE ALREADY DEAD MORE THAN THE LIVING THAT ARE YET ALIVE, as, e.g., myself [Moses] and my contemporaries.[4]

R. Samuel b. Naḥman interpreted the verse in connection with David. When Solomon built the Temple, he wanted fire to descend from heaven [to consume the offerings], but it did not descend. He offered a thousand sacrifices, but it did not descend. He offered twenty-four prayers, but it did not descend. Finally he said, *Remember the good deeds of David Thy servant* (II Chron. VI, 42), and immediately fire descended, as it is stated, *Now when*

[1] By that question he evinced lack of faith.
[2] E.V. '*In Thine anger*'. [3] E.V. '*He*'. [4] The dead patriarchs were able to secure mercy for Israel whereas Moses had been unsuccessful.

Solomon had made an end of praying, the fire came down from heaven (*ib.* VII, 1). R. Judah b. R. Ilai and the Rabbis differ in their explanation. R. Judah b. R. Ilai said: David came to life at that time; the Rabbis said: Solomon brought his coffin. They are, however, not really at variance[1]; because he who said that David came to life at that time is supported by what David declared with his own mouth, viz. *O Lord, Thou broughtest up my soul from the nether-world* (Ps. XXX, 4),[2] and another verse declares, *O Lord God, turn not away the face of Thine anointed* (II Chron. VI, 42), i.e. who liveth before Thee.[3] The other opinion, that Solomon brought David's coffin, is supported by the text, '*Remember the good deeds of David Thy servant.*'[4] Concerning that occasion it is said, WHEREFORE I PRAISED THE DEAD THAT ARE ALREADY DEAD MORE THAN THE LIVING THAT ARE YET ALIVE, as, e.g., myself [Solomon] and my contemporaries.[5]

R. Judah b. R. Simon interpreted the verse in connection with Ezekiel. When he stood in the valley and said, *O ye dry bones, hear the word of the Lord* (Ezek. XXXVII, 4), immediately *The bones came together, bone to bone* (*ib.* 7). He said to them, 'At first I told you, *Hear ye the word of the Lord, O house of Jacob* (Jer. II, 4), and you did not listen, but now you have listened. When you were alive you did not listen, but now that you are dead you have listened!' Concerning that time it is stated, WHEREFORE I PRAISED THE DEAD THAT ARE ALREADY DEAD MORE THAN THE LIVING THAT ARE YET ALIVE, as, e.g., I [Ezekiel] and my contemporaries.[6]

1. THE FOOL FOLDETH HIS HANDS TOGETHER, AND EATETH HIS OWN FLESH (IV, 5). The matter may

[1] This seems to mean that both agree that the body of David was present, one opinion being that his coffin was brought and the other that he was revived for the occasion. Y.T. explains differently.
[2] The title of the Psalm is, '*A Song at the Dedication of the House*,' i.e. Solomon's Temple. [3] And the continuation of the verse mentions David. [4] The presence of the coffin adding force to the prayer.
[5] Solomon was unable to get the fire to descend, but David succeeded.
[6] 'As I, etc.' is out of place here and should be deleted ('E.J.).

be likened to two men who were labouring in the Torah. One laboured and improved while the other laboured and then abandoned the study. The latter saw the other standing with the band of the righteous [in the Hereafter] whereas he stood with the band of the wicked. He at once folds his hands together and eats his own flesh.

1. BETTER IS A HANDFUL OF QUIETNESS, THAN BOTH THE HANDS FULL OF LABOUR AND STRIVING AFTER WIND (IV, 6). Better is he who learns *halachoth* and is familiar with them than he who learns *halachoth* and rules of exegesis but does not rehearse them and become familiar with them. A proverb declares, 'Better is one bird caged than a hundred in flight.' AND A STRIVING AFTER WIND: his striving to be called a master of legal treatises.[1]

Another interpretation of BETTER IS A HANDFUL OF QUIETNESS: Better is he who practises charity to only a small extent from his own possessions than one who steals, robs, and oppresses [the poor] and gives much charity from what belongs to others. A proverb declares, 'She prostitutes herself for apples and distributes them among the sick.' AND A STRIVING AFTER WIND: his striving to be called a philanthropist.

Another interpretation of BETTER IS A HANDFUL OF QUIETNESS: Better is he who possesses ten gold pieces with which he does business and maintains himself than he who takes money from others which he loses and causes to vanish [in business]. A proverb declares, 'Not enough that he loses his own but he loses also what belongs to others, both what is his and what is not his.' AND A STRIVING AFTER WIND: his striving to be called a business-man.

Another interpretation of BETTER IS A HANDFUL OF QUIETNESS: Better is he who leases one garden and eats its fruits than he who leases many gardens and neglects them. A proverb declares, 'Who leases a garden

[1] Or, of traditional interpretations (i.e. interpretations according to the traditional rules of exegesis—Levy).

eats birds, who leases gardens will be eaten by birds.' AND A STRIVING AFTER WIND: his striving to be called a landed proprietor.

R. Jacob b. R. Ḳurshai said: BETTER IS A HANDFUL OF QUIETNESS in the World to Come, THAN BOTH THE HANDS FULL OF LABOUR AND STRIVING AFTER WIND in this world. He used to say: More beautiful is one hour of the soul tranquillity in the World to Come than all the life of this world; and more beautiful is one hour spent in repentance and good deeds in this world, than all the life of the World to Come.[1] The reason is that the World to Come only results from the effect of this world.

R. Ḥiyya b. Abba said: BETTER IS A HANDFUL OF QUIETNESS, viz. the Sabbath, THAN BOTH THE HANDS FULL OF LABOUR AND STRIVING AFTER WIND, viz. the six working-days. For R. Ḥiyya b. Abba said: Israel will only be redeemed through the merit of the Sabbath, as it is stated, *In sitting still and rest shall ye be saved* (Isa. XXX, 15), i.e. in the Sabbath and resting shall be your salvation. AND A STRIVING AFTER WIND: his striving to be called one who toils and eats. R. Berekiah said: Better is one step made by the Holy One, blessed be He, in the land of Egypt—as it is stated, *I will go through the land of Egypt in that night* (Ex. XII, 12)—THAN BOTH THE HANDS, i.e. *The handfuls of soot of the furnace* (*ib.* IX, 8).[2] Why? Because Israel was delivered by the former but not by the latter.

R. Isaac interpreted the verse in connection with the tribes of Gad and Manasseh who came to the land of Israel and saw how many sown fields and plantations were there. They said: 'BETTER IS A HANDFUL OF QUIETNESS in the land of Israel, THAN BOTH THE HANDS FULL OF LABOUR on the other side of the Jordan.' On reflection they said, 'Are we not ourselves

[1] The two parts of the saying are in reversed order in Ab. IV, 17 (Sonc. ed., p. 53, v. notes *ad loc.*).
[2] Used for bringing the plague of boils.

responsible?[1] Did we not say, *Let this land be given unto thy servants for a possession* (Num. XXXII, 5)?' R. Isaac said: It is written, *That the cloud of the incense may cover* (Lev. XVI, 13). We did not know what the purpose of this covering was until David came and explained it; as it is stated, *Thou hast forgiven the iniquity of Thy people, Thou hast pardoned all their sin* (Ps. LXXXV, 3). Likewise spake the Holy One, blessed be He: 'More dear to Me is the handful of flour brought by a poor man as a voluntary meal-offering than the two handfuls of incense offered by the High Priest.' Why? Because the latter is brought to secure atonement but not the former; as it is written, *And when any one bringeth a meal-offering unto the Lord*, etc. (Lev. II, 1).[2]

1. THEN I RETURNED AND SAW VANITY UNDER THE SUN (IV, 7): this is the mantle of the angel of death.[3]

1. THERE IS ONE THAT IS ALONE, AND HE HATH NOT A SECOND (IV, 8). THERE IS ONE: i.e. the Holy One, blessed be He, of whom it is said, *The Lord our God, the Lord is one* (Deut. VI, 4). AND HE HATH NOT A SECOND: He has no partner in His universe. YEA, HE HATH NEITHER SON NOR BROTHER: since He has no brother, whence should He have a son?[4] But the Holy One, blessed be He, displayed love for Israel and called them 'sons', as it is said, *Ye are the children of the Lord your God* (*ib.* XIV, 1). He likewise called them

[1] That our portion is to be on the other side of the Jordan and not in the land of Israel.
[2] The poor man's offering is brought from a disinterested motive. The statement of R. Isaac should come at the end of the paragraph and is meant as a proof that the incense offered by the High Priest was for the purpose of securing atonement. The whole of the paragraph occurs with variations in Lev. R. III, 1.
[3] Under this mantle the souls are conveyed from earth when persons die, and death renders all the things of this world vain.
[4] Commentaries explain that *aḥ* (E.V. '*brother*') is understood in the sense of consort (from *aḥah* 'to join'), and the question is: since He has no consort, whence is He to have a son?

'brothers', as it is said, *For My brethren and companions' sake, I will now say: Peace be within thee* (Ps. CXXII, 8).[1]

YET IS THERE NO END OF ALL HIS LABOUR: to all that He made during the six days of creation. FOR WHOM THEN DO I LABOUR, AND BEREAVE MY SOUL OF PLEASURE? Is it not for those who cleave to His ways? If the righteous do not endeavour to store up pious acts and good deeds before Him, then is it not vanity which the Holy One, blessed be He, created in His universe?[2]

Another interpretation: THERE IS ONE refers to Abraham, as it is said, *Abraham was one* (Ezek. XXXIII, 24); AND HE HATH NOT A SECOND: he has no equal. YEA, HE HATH NEITHER SON NOR BROTHER: he had neither son nor brother when he descended into the furnace.[3] When the Holy One, blessed be He, said to him, *Take now thy son, thine only son* (Gen. XXII, 2), he did not see that he had a son; and when He said to him, *Get thee out of thy country* (*ib.* XII, 1), he did not see that he had a brother.[4] YET IS THERE NO END OF ALL HIS LABOUR: in the performance of precepts and good deeds. FOR WHOM THEN DO I LABOUR, AND BEREAVE MY SOUL OF PLEASURE? Is it not to cleave to His ways,[5] because whoever does not act like Him, THIS ALSO IS VANITY.

Another interpretation of THERE IS ONE THAT IS ALONE: it alludes to the tribe of Levi. YEA, HE HATH NEITHER SON NOR BROTHER: when Moses said to them, *Go to and fro from gate to gate throughout the*

[1] *My* being related to God. This apparently contradicts the text under discussion. Perhaps the idea is that because we find that God has a son and a brother (or, consort; v. preceding note) in a spiritual sense, viz. Israel, the text insists that He has none in a physical sense. Thus the passage may have an anti-Christian bearing.

[2] The world would then have been created to no avail.

[3] Actually he had a brother, Nahor. The idea is probably that he had none to support him. V. Gen. R. XXXVIII, 13.

[4] He did not allow son or brother to stand in the way of fulfilling God's command.

[5] Or, to his (not His) ways, the reference being to Abraham. Similarly in the next paragraph 'his ways' may refer to the tribe of Levi.

camp, and slay every man his brother (Ex. XXXII, 27), and it is written, *Who said of his father, and of his mother, I have not seen him, neither did he acknowledge his brethren* (Deut. XXXIII, 9). YET IS THERE NO END OF ALL HIS LABOUR: in the service of the Tabernacle. NEITHER IS HIS EYE SATISFIED WITH RICHES refers to the sacrifices. FOR WHOM THEN DO I LABOUR? Is it not to cleave to His ways,[1] and whoever does not act like Him, THIS ALSO IS VANITY, YEA, IT IS A GRIEVOUS BUSINESS.

Another interpretation of THERE IS ONE THAT IS ALONE: it alludes to the Evil Inclination. AND HE HATH NOT A SECOND: it has no equal for the performance of a transgression. YEA, HE HATH NEITHER SON NOR BROTHER: when a man goes to perform a transgression he does not consider that he has a son who may die for his iniquities, nor does he consider that he has a brother who will be ashamed of him and disgraced by him. YET IS THERE NO END OF ALL HIS LABOUR in evil deeds. NEITHER IS HIS EYE SATISFIED WITH RICHES refers to his bad actions. FOR WHOM THEN DO I LABOUR? Surely it is *not* to cleave to his ways,[2] and whoever does not so,[3] THIS ALSO IS VANITY.

Another interpretation of THERE IS ONE THAT IS ALONE: it alludes to [such as] Gebini b. Ḥarson.[4] AND HE HATH NOT A SECOND: he has no equal [for wealth]. YEA, HE HATH NEITHER SON NOR BROTHER: because he was his mother's only child. YET IS THERE NO END OF ALL HIS LABOUR from the estate which his father left him. NEITHER IS HIS EYE SATISFIED WITH RICHES because he was blind in one eye. FOR WHOM THEN DO I LABOUR, AND BEREAVE MY SOUL OF PLEASURE? It is related that when his father died, he said to his mother, 'Show me all the silver and

[1] Cf. n. 5, p. 118.
[2] Man's labours must be *not* to cleave to the ways of the Tempter.
[3] But does cleave to the Tempter.
[4] His father was a man of immense wealth.

gold which my father left me.' She went and showed him a heap of *denarii* [so vast] that she stood at one end and he at the other and they were unable to see one another. R. Levi said in the name of R. Simeon b. Laḳish: On the day that Gebini b. Ḥarson died, Belshazzar, the governor of Babylon, was born.[1]

1. TWO ARE BETTER THAN ONE (IV, 9 ff.). TWO ARE BETTER when they study Torah together, THAN ONE who labours alone. FOR IF THEY FALL, THE ONE WILL LIFT UP HIS FELLOW (*ib.* 10): if one of them forgets a *halachah* the other can restore it to him. AND A THREEFOLD CORD IS NOT QUICKLY BROKEN (*ib.* 12): this refers to the teacher who corrects their mistake for them.

Another interpretation of TWO ARE BETTER THAN ONE: TWO ARE BETTER when they transact business [in partnership], THAN ONE, each for himself. FOR IF THEY FALL (*ib.* 10): if one of them falls and is in danger, his fellow can raise him up. AND A THREEFOLD CORD IS NOT QUICKLY BROKEN when there are three [in partnership].

When R. Meir saw a man go into the open street alone, he used to cry out to him, 'Go in peace, O master of death!'[2] When he saw two, he used to cry out to them, 'Peace be with you, O masters of strife!'[3] When he saw three, he used to cry out to them, 'Peace be with you, O masters of peace!'[4]

R. Joḥanan made two statements in this connection. He said: TWO ARE BETTER, i.e. a husband and wife, THAN ONE, than each separately. AND A THREEFOLD CORD: this alludes to the Holy One, blessed be He, who grants them children. His other remark was: TWO ARE BETTER alludes to Amram and Jochabed. BECAUSE THEY HAVE A GOOD REWARD FOR THEIR LABOUR,

[1] The latter plundered all the gold. Hence the wealth was 'vanity' to its owner. [2] By going about alone he places himself in danger.
[3] Two men together are likely to quarrel.
[4] When there are three, if two fall out, the third can reconcile them.

i.e. Moses who is called 'good', as it is stated, *And when she saw that he was a goodly child*—ṭob hu (Ex. II, 2), i.e. his name was Ṭobiah because he was born circumcised.[1]

R. Judah, R. Nehemiah, and the Rabbis comment. R. Judah says: [Two] refers to David and Bath-sheba, and A THREEFOLD CORD to Nathan the prophet who told her, *I also will come in after thee, and confirm thy words* (I Kings I, 14).[2] When they came into David's presence, he agreed with them and said, *Cause Solomon my son to ride upon mine own mule* (*ib.* 33). R. Nehemiah said: TWO ARE BETTER refers to Jehoiada and Jehoshabeath,[3] THAN ONE, i.e. than if each had acted separately. AND A THREEFOLD CORD is the Sanhedrin which agreed with them, as it is written, *Then they brought out the king's son, and put upon him the crown* (II Chron. XXIII, 11). The Rabbis said: TWO ARE BETTER refers to Mordecai and Esther, THAN ONE, i.e. than if each had acted separately. AND A THREEFOLD CORD is Ahasuerus who agreed with them and issued a decree, *Write ye also concerning the Jews, as it liketh you in the king's name* (Est. VIII, 8).

R. Levi b. Ḥama said in the name of R. Ḥanina: TWO ARE BETTER, i.e. the two whom Mordecai and Esther caused to be hanged,[4] THAN ONE, i.e. the one whom Joseph caused to be hanged[5]; because through the former miracles were performed for all Israel[6] but not through the latter. AND A THREEFOLD CORD is the Holy One, blessed be He, who is above them all, because He caused

[1] Cf. Soṭ. 12*a* (Sonc. ed., p. 61).

[2] The effect of their combined effort was securing the throne for Solomon.

[3] Who conspired to make Joash king (II Chron. XXII, 11).

[4] Bigthan and Teresh, whom Mordecai discovered plotting against the king (Est. II, 23).

[5] The king's baker, whose dream Joseph interpreted in that sense (Gen. XL, 22). 'E.J. suggests that תלו (hanged) should be emended to עלו (rose to greatness). The text will then read: the two who rose to greatness, viz. Esther and Mordecai, were better, etc. This seems more plausible.

[6] It was the record of this service rendered by Mordecai that was the cause of Haman's downfall (Est. VI). But v. preceding note, which makes this explanation unnecessary.

the enemy to fall, as it is written, *So they hanged Haman on the gallows that he had prepared for Mordecai* (*ib.* VII, 10).

R. Isaac said: Better is a Biblical section spoken through two than a section spoken through one. A section spoken through two is Exodus XII, beginning, *And the Lord spake* unto Moses and Aaron *in the land of Egypt, saying: This month shall be unto you the beginning of months*, [which is better] than the sections, beginning, *And the Lord spoke* unto Moses, *saying*. A THREEFOLD CORD is, e.g., Leviticus XI, beginning, *And the Lord spoke* unto Moses and Aaron, *saying unto them*,[1] [these words indicating] to his sons, Eleazar and Ithamar. As R. Ḥiyya taught: '*Saying unto them*,' i.e. to Eleazar and Ithamar, and they were to speak unto all Israel.

Another interpretation of TWO ARE BETTER: it refers to Moses and Aaron, THAN ONE, than if each had acted separately. You find that when Moses came and blessed Israel, the *Shechinah* did not rest [upon Israel] through him; but when they both came and blessed Israel, the *Shechinah* at once rested [upon Israel] through them, as it is written, *And* Moses and Aaron *went into the tent of meeting, and came out, and blessed the people* (Lev. IX, 23); they blessed Israel, and then *The glory of the Lord appeared unto all the people*, i.e. the *Shechinah* rested [upon Israel] through them.

R. Zeira said: There are various kinds of families. A family of scholars[2] produces scholars; a family of students of Torah produces students of Torah; a family of rich men produces rich men. It was objected, 'Behold there is the third generation of a certain family which became reduced and ceased to be wealthy!' He replied to them, 'Is it written, "A threefold cord[3] is *never* broken?" It is written, IS NOT QUICKLY BROKEN! If [the third generation] is hard upon us [students of Torah],[4] it ceases to be rich.' This agrees with what Bar Ḳappara said: If

[1] Ex. XIII. [2] Lit. 'scribes'.
[3] Representing three generations. [4] And does not support them.

not he,[1] then his son will; and if not his son, then his grandson will.

1. BETTER IS A POOR AND WISE CHILD THAN AN OLD AND FOOLISH KING (IV, 13). BETTER IS A POOR AND WISE CHILD, i.e. the Good Inclination. Why is it called CHILD? Because it attaches itself to man only from the age of thirteen years and onward.[2] And why is it called POOR? Because all do not obey it. And why is it called WISE? Because it teaches human beings the right way. THAN AN OLD AND FOOLISH KING, i.e. the Evil Inclination. Why does he call it KING? Because all obey it. Why does he call it OLD? Because it attaches itself to man from youth to old age. Why does he call it FOOLISH? Because it teaches man the way of evil.

WHO KNOWETH NOT HOW TO RECEIVE ADMONITION ANY MORE: because man does not know how much trouble and suffering come upon him, and he is not admonished by them.[3]

1. FOR OUT OF PRISON (HA-SURIM) HE CAME FORTH TO BE KING (IV, 14). [The Evil Inclination is so described] because it entangles human beings as if among thorns (*seriatha*). ALTHOUGH IN HIS KINGDOM HE WAS BORN POOR: in the dominion of the Good Inclination the poverty of the Evil Inclination is born.[4]

Another interpretation of BETTER IS A POOR AND WISE CHILD, i.e. Abraham, THAN AN OLD AND FOOLISH KING, i.e. Nimrod. What means *At the vale of Shaveh* (Gen. XIV, 17)? It was so called because there they became unanimous (*hushewu*) and cut down cedars and constructed from them a high platform on which they seated Abraham, praising him and saying, *Hear us*,

[1] If that man does not become reduced in circumstances. V. Shab. 151*b*.
[2] Then the age of discretion and personal responsibility is reached.
[3] The purpose of suffering is correction, but few learn the lesson.
[4] As the former grows stronger the other becomes weaker.

my lord, thou art a mighty prince among us (*ib.* XXIII, 6). ALTHOUGH IN HIS KINGDOM HE WAS BORN POOR: in the dominion of Abraham the poverty of Nimrod was born.

Another interpretation of BETTER IS A POOR CHILD, i.e. Joseph; AND WISE, because through his wisdom he saved the whole world in the time of famine. THAN AN OLD AND FOOLISH KING, i.e. Potiphar. He is called FOOLISH because he witnessed ever so many miracles performed on account of Joseph, yet was not admonished![1] FOR OUT OF PRISON HE CAME FORTH TO BE KING: from Pharaoh's fortress he came out a king, as it is said, *I am Pharaoh, and without thee shall no man lift up his hand or his foot in all the land of Egypt* (*ib.* XLI, 44).

1. I SAW ALL THE LIVING THAT WALK UNDER THE SUN (IV, 15). This alludes to the actions of the righteous. What caused them to be LIVING? That they WALK UNDER THE SUN with THE CHILD, THE SECOND, viz. the Good Inclination.[2]

1. THERE WAS NO END OF ALL THE PEOPLE, EVEN OF ALL THEM WHOM HE DID LEAD (IV, 16). There is no end to all the generations which the Evil Inclination destroyed. YET THEY THAT COME AFTER SHALL NOT REJOICE IN HIM: because they give obedience to the Evil Inclination.

1. GUARD THY FOOT WHEN THOU GOEST TO THE HOUSE OF GOD (IV, 17). It has been taught: Nobody may enter the Temple Mount with money tied up in his garment, with the dust upon his feet, or with his wallet girded to him on the outside; that is what is written, GUARD THY FOOT WHEN THOU GOEST TO THE HOUSE OF GOD. R. Jose b. Judah says: It is written, *And he came even before the king's gate; for none might*

[1] And believed the accusation of his wife against Joseph.
[2] As explained on V. 13, where CHILD denotes the Good Inclination.

enter within the king's gate clothed with sackcloth (Est. IV, 2). If this may not be done on account of the honour due to a human king, how much more may it not be done on account of the honour due to the supreme King of kings![1]

R. Adda b. R. Simeon said in the name of R. Nathan: A man should never stand on an elevated place and pray, but in a lowly place. What is the reason? It is written, *Out of the* depths *have I called thee, O Lord* (Ps. CXXX, 1). Rabbi [Judah ha-Nasi] said: A man should not pray if he feels the need to relieve himself, as it is stated, *Prepare to meet thy God, O Israel* (Amos IV, 12). R. Alexandri said: Because it is written, GUARD THY FOOT.[2] R. Ḳruspedai said in the name of R. Joḥanan: GUARD THY FOOT means, from the drops [of urine] which are between your legs. WHEN THOU GOEST TO THE HOUSE OF GOD be clean. To what does this refer? To the minor function [of urinating]; but in the case of the major function, if he is able to contain himself he should.[3] R. Abba said: It is written, *Let thy fountain* (meḳoreka) *be blessed* (Prov. V, 18)—i.e. be blessed in the house to which you are called (*meḳor'aka*)[4]; again, may your summons (*miḳra'ka*) to the grave be blessed.[5]

Simeon of Siknin was a shrewd man, and he used to dig wells, trenches, and caves in Jerusalem. He said to R. Joḥanan b. Zakkai, 'I am as great a man as you.' 'How is that?' he asked, to which he replied, 'I work on behalf of the public as well as you. If a man comes to you for a decision or with an inquiry, you tell him to drink from a certain well whose waters are pure and cold. Or if a woman questions you concerning her ritual impurity, you tell her to immerse herself in a certain well whose

[1] Quoted from Tosefta Ber. VII, 19—i.e. one must not enter in his workaday clothes. [2] A euphemistic expression for 'relieve thyself'.

[3] He should not allow this need, unless it is urgent, to interfere with his attendance in the Synagogue.

[4] To pray and study, viz. in the Synagogue, while 'be blessed' in the sense of internal physical cleanness, in the same strain as the whole passage (M.K., Mah.).

[5] May you die in a state of purity. The passage is quoted from J. Ber. 4*d*.

waters cleanse.'[1] The Rabbi thereupon applied this verse to him, AND BE READY TO HEARKEN: IT IS BETTER THAN WHEN FOOLS GIVE SACRIFICES, FOR THEY KNOW NOT THAT THEY DO EVIL.[2]

Huna b. Geniba said: More beloved [by God] is the recital of the *shema'*[3] in its proper time than a thousand sacrifices which a fool offers. Why? FOR THEY KNOW NOT THAT THEY DO EVIL, i.e. the fool does not know how to distinguish between the various kinds of vows. Whence do we derive this? From the instance of Jephthah.[4]

R. Simeon b. Ḥalafta said: If the weak one is above and the strong below, who conquers? He who is above. How much more so [will the victory be assured] when the one above is He who lives eternally, for He is mighty and above and you are below. Moreover the text confronts you, *God is in heaven, and thou upon earth* (Eccl. v, 1).[5]

[1] He meant that he provided the necessary well, and so co-operated with the Rabbi.
[2] The Rabbi implied that this well-digger, being ignorant, did not know what was ritually clean or unclean; and it was presumptuous for him to claim equality.
[3] The words BE READY TO HEARKEN, lit. 'be near to hear', are understood as: be near the time to say *shema'* (lit. 'hear').
[4] Who was unaware that his vow, involving human life, was invalid.
[5] This paragraph belongs to the first verse of Chap. V.

Chapter V

1. FOR A DREAM COMETH[1] THROUGH A MULTITUDE OF BUSINESS (V, 2). All the pains and sufferings which the Holy One, blessed be He, brought upon the generation of the Flood were THROUGH THE MULTITUDE OF evil BUSINESS which was in their hand. AND A FOOL'S VOICE THROUGH A MULTITUDE OF WORDS: on account of the multitude of words which they put forth from their mouths, saying, *What is the Almighty, that we should serve Him?* (Job XXI, 15).

Another interpretation of FOR A DREAM COMETH THROUGH A MULTITUDE OF BUSINESS: All the pains and sufferings which the Holy One, blessed be He, brought upon the generation of the Dispersion were THROUGH THE MULTITUDE OF evil BUSINESS which was in their hand. AND A FOOL'S VOICE THROUGH A MULTITUDE OF WORDS: because they said, *And let us make us a name, lest we be scattered abroad upon the face of the whole earth* (Gen. XI, 4).

Another interpretation of FOR A DREAM COMETH THROUGH A MULTITUDE OF BUSINESS: All the pains and sufferings which the Holy One, blessed be He, brought upon the men of Sodom were THROUGH THE MULTITUDE OF evil BUSINESS which was in their hand. AND A FOOL'S VOICE THROUGH A MULTITUDE OF WORDS: because they said, 'Let us cause the practice of hospitality to wayfarers to be forgotten among ourselves,' as it is written, *And forgetteth that the foot may crush them, or that the wild beast may trample them* (Job XXXIX, 15).[2]

Another interpretation of FOR A DREAM COMETH THROUGH A MULTITUDE OF BUSINESS: All the pains and sufferings which the Holy One, blessed be He, brought upon the Egyptians were THROUGH THE

[1] By the system of Noṭariḳon, i.e. taking the syllables of a word to build up other words, the Heb. for this phrase is made to indicate 'all pains'.
[2] Cf. on II, 2.

MULTITUDE OF evil BUSINESS which was in their hand. AND A FOOL'S VOICE THROUGH A MULTITUDE OF WORDS: because they said, *Who is the Lord, that I should hearken unto His voice to let Israel go?* (Ex. V, 2).

Another interpretation of FOR A DREAM COMETH THROUGH A MULTITUDE OF BUSINESS: All the pains and sufferings which the Holy One, blessed be He, brought upon Sisera were THROUGH THE MULTITUDE OF evil BUSINESS which was in his hand. AND A FOOL'S VOICE THROUGH A MULTITUDE OF WORDS: as it is said, *And twenty years he mightily oppressed the children of Israel* (Judg. IV, 3).

Another interpretation of FOR A DREAM COMETH THROUGH A MULTITUDE OF BUSINESS: All the pains and sufferings which the Holy One, blessed be He, brought upon Sennacherib were THROUGH THE MULTITUDE OF evil BUSINESS which was in his hand. AND A FOOL'S VOICE THROUGH A MULTITUDE OF WORDS: for he defied and blasphemed Him, as it is said, *Who are they among all the gods of these countries, that have delivered their country out of my hand, that the Lord should deliver Jerusalem out of my hand* (Isa. XXXVI, 20)?

Another interpretation of FOR A DREAM COMETH THROUGH A MULTITUDE OF BUSINESS: All the pains and sufferings which the Holy One, blessed be He, brought upon the tribes of Judah and Benjamin were THROUGH THE MULTITUDE OF evil BUSINESS which was in their hand. [AND A FOOL'S VOICE THROUGH A MULTITUDE OF WORDS:] as it is said, *They have belied the Lord* (Jer. V, 12).

Another interpretation of FOR A DREAM COMETH THROUGH A MULTITUDE OF BUSINESS: All the pains and sufferings which the Holy One, blessed be He, brought upon Nebuchadnezzar were because he said, *Who is the God that shall deliver you out of my hands* (Dan. III, 15)?

Another interpretation of FOR A DREAM COMETH

THROUGH A MULTITUDE OF BUSINESS: All the pains and sufferings which the Holy One, blessed be He, brought upon Belshazzar were THROUGH THE MULTITUDE OF evil BUSINESS which was in his hand; as it is written, *They drank wine, and praised the gods of gold and silver* (*ib.* V, 4). You find the same with Pharaoh, as it is said, *And it came to pass at the end of two full years*, etc. (Gen. XLI, 1). Pharaoh said, 'Who will raise himself above whom? I above my god or my god above me? No, I will raise myself above my god.' That is what is written, '*And it came to pass at the end of two full years' that Pharaoh dreamed; and, behold, he stood over the river.*[1] You also find the same with Ahasuerus. R. Judah b. R. Simon said: All the night Ahasuerus kept seeing Haman [in a dream] standing over him, with his sword drawn in his hand, stripping him of his purple garments and removing his crown from his head, and seeking to kill him. He woke and exclaimed, 'Was this a mere dream or a revelation?' How long [was he in a state of uncertainty]? Until the morning dawned, when the king asked, *Who is in the court* (Est. VI, 4)? and was told, *Behold, Haman standeth in the court* (*ib.* 5). Then he said, 'That is the dream I saw, FOR A DREAM COMETH THROUGH A MULTITUDE OF BUSINESS.' *Now Haman was come into the outer court of the king's house, to speak unto the king to hang Mordecai on the gallows that he had prepared for him* (*ib.* 4) and for his associates.[2]

It is written, *He hath also prepared for him the weapons of death, yea, His arrows which he made sharp*—ledoleḳim (Ps. VII, 14). What means '*ledoleḳim*'?[3] Rabbi [Judah ha-Nasi] said: It alludes to the wicked who[4] hurled fire upon them. R. Jacob of Kefar-Ḥanan said: It alludes to those who set fire [to the edifice] in the destruction of

[1] Over the Nile, which the Egyptians worshipped; hence he stood over his god. Cf. Gen. R. LXXXIX, 3.

[2] Perhaps the Midrash renders, for himself: Haman had unconsciously prepared a gallows for himself and his associates.

[3] The root of the word means 'to kindle'.

[4] The Romans who, in the siege of Jerusalem, used flame-throwers.

the Temple. The Rabbis say: It alludes to the persecutors of Israel; for it is written, *They chased us* (delaḳunu) *upon the mountains* (Lam. IV, 19).

Now Haman said in his heart (Est. VI, 6). The wicked are under the control of their heart, as it is stated, *And Esau said in his heart* (Gen. XXVII, 41), *And Jeroboam said in his heart* (I Kings XII, 26). The righteous, however, have their heart under their control; as it is written, *Now Hannah, she spoke upon*[1] *her heart* (I Sam. I, 13), *And David said to*[1] *his heart* (*ib.* XXVII, 1), *But Daniel purposed in*[2] *his heart* (Dan. I, 8). In this respect they resemble their Creator, as it is stated, *The Lord said to*[1] *His heart* (Gen. VIII, 21). R. Levi and the Rabbis[3] comment. R. Levi said: [God said]: 'They devise evil in their heart, so shall I devise good in My heart? They devise evil in their heart, so I shall punish them in their heart'; as it is said, *Their sword shall enter into their own heart* (Ps. XXXVII, 15).

'*Now Haman said in his heart*': Haman immediately answered and said, *Let royal apparel be brought* (Est. VI, 8)—he said to the king, 'You have many robes, but let it be "*royal apparel*", viz. that which you wore on the day when you became king.' *And the horse that the king rideth upon* (*ib.*)—he said to him, 'You have many horses, but let it be the horse upon which you rode on the day when you became king.' *And on whose head a crown royal is set* (*ib.*)—when he mentioned the crown, the king's face changed and he exclaimed, 'Behold, his time has come [to die].'[4] That is what is written, FOR A DREAM COMETH THROUGH A MULTITUDE OF BUSINESS; AND A FOOL'S VOICE THROUGH A MULTITUDE OF WORDS.

1. BETTER IS IT THAT THOU SHOULDEST NOT VOW (V, 4). R. Meir said: Better than both is not to vow

[1] So lit. E.V. '*in*'. [2] Lit. 'placed upon'.
[3] The comment of the Rabbis is omitted.
[4] He recognised the danger which threatened him as forboded in his dream.

at all[1]; rather let the man bring his lamb[2] to the Temple, dedicate it and have it slain, as it is said, *But if thou shalt forbear to vow, it shall be no sin in thee* (Deut. XXIII, 23).[3] R. Huna said: Once a man vowed and did not fulfil it; he went on a voyage, his ship was wrecked and he died. R. Samuel said: Whoever vows without fulfilling brings upon himself the death of his wife; for it is written, *And as for me, when I came from Paddan, Rachel died unto me* (Gen. XLVIII, 7).[4] R. Samuel b. Isaac said: Whoever vows without fulfilling causes [others] to fall into the power of four transgressions, viz. idolatry, immorality, bloodshed, and slander; and all of them he learnt from the instance of Jacob. Idolatry, for it is written, *Put away the strange gods that are among you* (*ib.* XXXV, 2); immorality, for it is written, *He had defiled Dinah his daughter* (*ib.* XXXIV, 5); bloodshed, for it is written, *Two of the sons of Jacob, Simeon and Levi, Dinah's brethren, took each man his sword, and came upon the city unawares, and slew all the males* (*ib.* 25); and slander, for it is written, *And he heard the words of Laban's sons* (*ib.* XXXI, 1).

R. Mana said: Whoever vows without fulfilling brings death upon himself, as it is said, *For the Lord thy God will surely require it of thee* (Deut. XXIII, 22).[5] R. Ammi said: There is no death without sin [to cause it] and no suffering without iniquity. 'There is no death without sin,' as it is said, *The soul that sinneth, it shall die* (Ezek. XVIII, 4); 'and no suffering without iniquity,' as it is said, *Then will I visit their transgressions with the rod, and their iniquity with strokes* (Ps. LXXXIX, 33).

1. SUFFER NOT THY MOUTH TO BRING THY FLESH INTO GUILT (V, 5). R. Joshua b. Levi interpreted the verse as alluding to those who publicly

[1] Ned. 9*a* (Sonc. ed., p. 21). 'Both' refers to vowing and not paying and even vowing and paying.
[2] Without previously making a vow to bring it.
[3] On which the Rabbis comment: hence if one does *not* forbear to vow, it is a sin in him (Ned. 77*b*).
[4] On Jacob not fulfilling his vow. Cf. Gen. R. LXX, 4.
[5] V. Lev. R. XXXVII, 1.

undertake to subscribe to charity but do not pay. NEITHER SAY THOU BEFORE THE MESSENGER, i.e. the official [who comes to collect the money], THAT IT WAS AN ERROR, saying, 'I am sorry [I cannot pay].' WHEREFORE SHOULD GOD BE ANGRY AT THY VOICE? at the voice with which you said [that you would give the money]? AND DESTROY THE WORK OF THY HANDS: on the few pious acts which are in the hand of that man, the Holy One, blessed be He, brings a curse and causes them to be lost to him.

R. Benjamin interpreted the verse as alluding to those who make a pretence of knowledge of the Torah.[1] SUFFER NOT THY MOUTH: give not permission to your mouth, TO BRING THY FLESH INTO GUILT: to make your body sin in the matter of your study. NEITHER SAY THOU BEFORE THE MESSENGER, i.e. the teacher, THAT IT WAS AN ERROR: he makes himself out to be a Bible-scholar but is not one, or a Mishnah-scholar but he is not one. WHEREFORE SHOULD GOD BE ANGRY AT THY VOICE: at the voice with which you said, 'This *halachah* he told me, this teaching he told me.'[2] AND DESTROY THE WORK OF THY HANDS: even on the few *halachoth* which that man possesses the Holy One, blessed be He, brings forgetfulness and a curse and causes them to be lost to him.

The Rabbis interpret the verse as alluding to one who vows. BEFORE THE MESSENGER: this is the Sage.[3] THAT IT WAS AN ERROR: saying, 'I made no vow.' WHEREFORE SHOULD GOD BE ANGRY: because you did utter a vow, AND DESTROY THE WORK OF THY HANDS: even on the small amount of money which is in the possession of that man the Holy One, blessed be He, brings a curse and causes it to be lost to him.

R. Huna interpreted the verse as alluding to a slanderer. SUFFER NOT THY MOUTH to speak slander. BEFORE THE MESSENGER: i.e. the body. THAT IT WAS AN

[1] Cf. IV, 1.
[2] 'He'—a great Rabbi; thus falsely claiming to have studied under teachers. [3] Who had the power to absolve a person from his vow.

ERROR: saying, 'I did not speak slander.' AND DESTROY THE WORK OF THY HANDS: these are the sinews and bones in that man's body; the Holy One, blessed be He, brings consumption and inflammation into them and causes them to perish from him.

R. Manni interpreted the verse as alluding to Miriam. SUFFER NOT THY MOUTH, i.e. Miriam, TO BRING THY FLESH INTO GUILT: in that she spoke slander against Moses, saying, *Hath the Lord indeed spoken only by Moses* (Num. XII, 2)? BEFORE THE MESSENGER: i.e. Moses, as it is said, *And sent a messenger* (*ib.* XX, 16).[1] THAT IT WAS AN ERROR: as it is written, *For that we have done foolishly, and for that we have sinned* (*ib.* XII, 11). WHEREFORE SHOULD GOD BE ANGRY AT THY VOICE? i.e. *And Miriam . . . spoke against Moses* (*ib.* 1). AND DESTROY THE WORK OF THY HANDS: Miriam spoke slander with her mouth, but all her limbs were punished. R. Joshua learnt: A word for a *sela'*, but silence for two *sela's*; [let your words be] like a precious stone.[2] Rabbi [Judah ha-Nasi] said: Best of all is silence; as we have learnt in the *Ethics of the Fathers:* Simeon his son used to say: All my days I grew up among the Sages, and I have found nothing better for a person than silence.[3]

1. FOR THROUGH A MULTITUDE OF DREAMS AND VANITIES THERE ARE ALSO MANY WORDS; BUT FEAR THOU GOD (V, 6). Rabbi [Judah ha-Nasi] said: If you have seen ill-omened dreams and ill-omened and confusing visions of which you are afraid, take hold of three things and you will be delivered from them. For R. Judan said in the name of R. Eliezer: Three things annul evil decrees, viz. prayer, charity, and repentance, and the three of them are mentioned in one verse, as it is written, *If My people, upon whom My name is called, shall humble themselves, and pray, and seek My face, and turn from their evil ways; then will I hear from heaven, and will*

[1] E.V. '*an angel*'.
[2] Carefully guarded, and not brought out thoughtlessly.
[3] Ab. I, 17 (Sonc. ed., p. 9).

forgive their sin, and will heal their land (II Chron. VII, 14). '*And pray,*' i.e. prayer; '*And seek My face.*' i.e. charity, as it is stated, *I shall behold Thy face in righteousness* (Ps. XVII, 15)[1]; '*And turn from their evil ways,*' i.e. repentance. Following on these '*Then will I hear from heaven,*' etc. R. Mana said: Fasting also [annuls evil decrees], as it is stated, *The Lord answer thee in the day of trouble* (*ib.* XX, 2).[2] R. Ḥiyya and R. Jose say: Likewise a change of name and a change of conduct [annul evil decrees]; and some add: Also a change of place, for it is written, *Get thee out of thy country . . . and I will make of thee a great nation* (Gen. XII, 1 f.). 'A change of name' [is learnt from the instance of] our father Abraham, as it is said, *Neither shall thy name any more be called Abram, but thy name shall be called Abraham* (*ib.* XVII, 5)—Abram cannot beget a child but Abraham can, Sarai cannot bear a child but Sarah can.[3] 'A change of conduct' [is learnt from the instance of] Nineveh, as it is said, *And God saw their works, that they turned from their evil way, and God repented of the evil which He said He would do unto them, and He did it not* (Jonah III, 10). Rabbah b. Meḥasya and Ḥama b. Guria said: Fasting is as effective against a dream[4] as fire against tow. R. Ḥisda remarked: [The fast must be] on the same day [as the dream], to which R. Joḥanan added: Even on the Sabbath.[5]

Thus do we find it with Hezekiah, king of Judah. When Hezekiah fell ill, the Holy One, blessed be He, said to Isaiah, 'Go, and tell him, *Set thy house in order, for thou shalt die and not live*' (Isa. XXXVIII, 1). Hezekiah said to Isaiah, 'Isaiah, it is usual when a person visits an invalid to say to him, "May mercy be shown you from Heaven," and the physician comes and tells him, "Eat this and do not eat that; drink this and do not drink that." Even when he sees him near to death he does not say to him, "Set thy house in order," that his mind be not upset.

[1] The same Heb. word denotes '*righteousness*' and 'charity'.
[2] I.e. a day which you make one of trouble by self-imposed privation.
[3] Cf. Gen. R. XLIV, 10, 12. [4] To destroy its bad effects.
[5] When a fast, other than the Day of Atonement, is disallowed.

You, however, tell me, "*Set thy house in order, for thou shalt die and not live!*" I pay no attention to what you say, nor will I listen to your advice. I hold on to nothing else than what my ancestor said, FOR THROUGH THE MULTITUDE OF DREAMS AND VANITIES THERE ARE ALSO MANY WORDS; BUT FEAR THOU GOD.' Immediately *Hezekiah turned his face to the wall* (*ib.* 2). To which wall did he turn his face? R. Joshua b. Levi said: To Rahab's wall, of which it is written, *Her house was upon the side of the wall* (Josh. II, 15). He spoke before Him: 'Lord of the universe, she saved two lives for Thee and Thou savedst many lives for her!' (R. Simeon b. Yoḥai learnt: Even if there were two hundred men in her family and they were connected with two hundred families, they were all saved through her merit; for it is not written here 'her family' but *All her families*[1] *also they brought out* (*ib.* VI, 23).) 'How much more [shouldest Thou spare me] seeing that my ancestors gathered unto Thee all proselytes!'[2] R. Samuel b. Naḥman said: He turned his face to the wall of the Shunammite of which it is written, *Let us make, I pray thee, a little chamber on the wall* (II Kings IV, 10).[3] He spoke before Him: 'Lord of the universe, this Shunammite made one [little chamber on the] wall for Elisha and Thou revivedst her son; how much more [shouldest Thou spare me] seeing that my ancestors made all this glory[4] for Thee!' R. Huna said in the name of R. Jose: He turned his eyes to the chambers[5] of his heart, as it says, *My bowels, my bowels! I writhe in pain! The chambers of my heart! My heart moaneth!* (Jer. IV, 19). (The *k'tib* is 'his heart'.)[6] He spoke before Him: 'Lord of the universe, I have examined the two hundred and forty limbs which Thou didst create in me, and I have not

[1] So lit. E.V. '*kindred*'. The plural denotes remote relatives by marriage.
[2] II Chron. II, 16 f., where the 'strangers' numbered by Solomon are understood as converts. [3] So lit. E.V. '*roof*'. [4] The Temple.
[5] Lit. 'walls'. The verse from Jer. is quoted to illustrate the phrase 'the walls of my heart' used in the sense of 'chambers of my heart'.
[6] M.K. remarks that the variant reading is noted only for information and no lesson is deduced from it. Actually this variant does not occur in the received text.

found that I provoked Thee with any one of them. How much more, then, shouldest Thou grant me my life!' The Rabbis say: He turned his eyes to the walls of the Temple of which it is written, *In their setting of their threshold by My threshold . . . and there was but the wall between Me and them* (Ezek. XLIII, 8). He spoke before Him: 'Lord of the universe, my forefathers were great men; yet they were unable to pray at all times[1] in the Temple, but they would stand and pray inside their house with only the wall between them and the Sanctuary. With me, however, there is no wall intervening between me and the Temple when I pray, so how much more shouldest Thou grant me my life!' Forthwith, *Then came the word of the Lord to Isaiah, saying: Go, and say to Hezekiah . . . I have heard thy prayer* (Isa. XXXVIII, 4). He had not gone out from there [when he received the message of reprieve]. Isaiah spoke before Him: 'Lord of the universe, at first Thou sayest one thing to me and now another thing; how can I go and tell him this?' He replied to him: 'Hezekiah is a humble man and he will receive it from thee. Furthermore, the report has not yet gone out [to the ears of the people]'[2]; as it is written, *And it came to pass, before Isaiah was gone out of the inner court of the city*, etc. (II Kings XX, 4).[3] When Isaiah went to him [with the second message], Hezekiah exclaimed, 'Did I not tell you from the beginning, "I pay no attention to what you say, nor will I listen to your advice, but to what my ancestor said, FOR THROUGH A MULTITUDE OF DREAMS AND VANITIES THERE ARE ALSO MANY WORDS; BUT FEAR THOU GOD"?'

1. IF THOU SEEST THE OPPRESSION OF THE POOR (V, 7). If you see the oppression of the lowly and the needy, and the Righteous One who liveth for ever granting prosperity and comfort to the oppressor, [DO THOU

[1] Occasionally they were prevented from entering the Sanctuary because they were ritually unclean. [2] Who might find it difficult to understand the two different messages brought in the name of God.
[3] But not into the public places of the city.

SEE] IN THE STATE (BAMMEDINAH)—see at work on him the judgment (*bo'dinah*) of Gehinnom.[1] FOR ONE HIGHER THAN THE HIGH WATCHETH: viz. the angels, AND THERE ARE HIGHER THAN THEY: viz. the Holy One, blessed be He.

R. Jose b. Ḥaninah interpreted the verse as applying to Esau [i.e. Rome]. If you see Esau[2] in the great city of Rome oppressing the lowly and robbing the poor, and the Holy One, blessed be He, granting him prosperity, see at work on him the Attribute of Justice. MARVEL NOT at what the ancient [Isaac] said and that his desire was fulfilled, as it is stated, *Behold, of the fat places of the earth shall be thy dwelling* (Gen. XXVII, 39). FOR ONE HIGHER THAN THE HIGH WATCHETH: viz. the commanders, captains, and lieutenants; AND THERE ARE HIGHER THAN THEY: viz. the King who liveth for ever.

R. Aḥa said: From the 'behold' of a human king you may infer the 'behold' of the Holy One, blessed be He. If the 'behold' of a human being gave life to a whole people in this world, as it is stated, *Behold, I have given Esther the house of Haman* (Est. VIII, 7),[3] how much more will it be so when the 'behold' of the Holy One, blessed be He, is fulfilled, as it is stated, *Behold, a day of the Lord cometh* (Zech. XIV, 1)!

1. MOREOVER THE PROFIT OF THE EARTH IS IN ALL THINGS (V, 8 f.).[4] R. Judah says: Even things which you deem superfluous in the world are essential parts of its composition. E.g. palm-fibre for the making of ropes and twigs for the formation of garden-hedges are essential parts of the world's composition. A KING MAKETH HIMSELF SERVANT TO THE FIELD: Even if a king has dominion from one end of the earth

[1] The oppressor's prosperity is only temporary and punishment awaits him. [2] Warsaw ed. reads 'Romulus' (the legendary founder of Rome).
[3] The downfall of Haman saved the Jews of Persia from the massacre planned for them.
[4] This almost follows A.V. and is the Midrashic rendering.

to the other, he is enslaved to the field; for if the soil produces he can achieve something, but if the soil is unproductive he can accomplish nothing.[1] Therefore HE THAT LOVETH SILVER SHALL NOT BE SATISFIED WITH SILVER; NOR HE THAT LOVETH ABUNDANCE WITHOUT [EARTH] PRODUCE[2]: THIS ALSO IS VANITY: whosoever is greedy and covetous for money, but has no land—what benefit does he derive?[3] R. Judah b. R. Jose and R. Ḥanin said: It is written, *And all that handle the oar, the mariners, and all the pilots of the sea, shall come down from their ships, they shall stand upon the land* (Ezek. XXVII, 29). Do we, then, now know that they stand upon the land? But the meaning is, should the ship of one of them sink, then if he possesses landed property, it supports him, but if he has no such asset, there is no greater vanity than this.[4]

2. R. Nehemiah says: MOREOVER THE PROFIT OF THE EARTH IS IN ALL THINGS: Those subjects which you deem additional to the Torah—e.g. the addenda of the School of Rabbi [Judah ha-Nasi] and of R. Nathan, *halachoth* concerning proselytes and slaves[5]—they too were given to Moses on Sinai, and like the laws [Tractates] of *Ẓiẓith*, *Ṭefillin* and *Mezuzah* are an integral part of the Torah; as it is written, *The Lord delivered unto me the two tables of stone written with the finger of God, and on*

[1] The text here is corrupt and has been emended according to the reading in Lev. R. XXII, 1.

[2] Heb. תבואה must be understood in this sense here; THIS ALSO IS VANITY is absent from the text, but must be added (Radal in Lev. R. *ad loc.*).

[3] According to the Midrash the text praises the solid value of land as opposed to the fleeting nature of coin. Abundance of money without earth produce (i.e. land) is vanity—ephemeral and uncertain.

[4] The whole passage shows how deeply the Jew was rooted in the soil originally.

[5] I.e. additions to the Mishnah (the so-called *Baraithoth*), Aboth de R. Nathan (an expanded version of the Pirke Aboth) and the Tractates on Proselytes and Slaves, which were added to the official Mishnah; similarly the post-Talmudic tractates on *Ẓiẓith*, etc., which he goes on to mention. The reference can hardly be to the actual laws on these subjects, as there would be no point in mentioning that these are not superfluous, for it is obvious.

them was written according to all the words (Deut. IX, 10), and it is written, *All the commandment which I command thee this day shall ye observe to do* (*ib.* VIII, 1). [The text has not] 'all' but '*according to all*', [not] 'words' but '*the words*', [not] 'commandment' but '*the commandment*'. [This is to teach that] Scripture, Mishnah, *halachah*, oral laws not included in the Mishnah, homiletical expositions, and even what an eminent disciple was in the future to say in the presence of his teacher were all given as a law to Moses on Sinai.[1] A KING: i.e. a master of Talmud; MAKETH HIMSELF SERVANT TO THE FIELD: i.e. to a master of Mishnah who sifts[2] the *halachah* before him. R. Jacob b. Abuna said in the name of R. Jose: If he studies and does not teach there is no greater vanity than this.[3]

The Rabbis say: Even things which you deem superfluous in the world, as, e.g., flies, fleas, and gnats, are also an essential part of the world's constitution, as it is said, *And the heaven and the earth were finished* (Gen. II, 1).[4]

3. A KING: i.e. the Holy One, blessed be He; MAKETH HIMSELF SERVANT TO THE FIELD: i.e. to Zion, as it is said, *Therefore shall Zion for your sake be plowed as a field* (Micah III, 12).[5] Therefore, HE THAT LOVETH SILVER, i.e. he who loves the precepts, SHALL NOT BE SATISFIED with the precepts[6]; but if he has no commandment which is established for future generations, what profit has he?[7] For behold, Moses performed many precepts and righteous acts, but he had a commandment established for future generations, as

[1] Cf. on I, 10.
[2] Lit. 'hoes'. Lev. R. *loc. cit.*, reads סודר 'arranges'. The point is that scholarship in Talmud must be based on the correct understanding of the Mishnah.
[3] This is a comment on the end of the verse, which is rendered: nor he who loveth abundance (to amass—a great store of learning) without increase, i.e. without increasing knowledge by disseminating it. That is vanity.
[4] V. Gen. R. X, 7. [5] God is attached to Zion.
[6] He will never think that he has performed sufficient and need perform no more. [7] Cf. Deut. R. II, 27.

it is written, *Then Moses separated three cities* (Deut. IV, 41).

4. Another interpretation of MOREOVER THE PROFIT OF THE EARTH, etc.: The Holy One, blessed be He, spake to the prophets: 'Do you imagine that if you do not go on My mission, I have no other messenger? Behold, THE PROFIT OF THE EARTH IS IN ALL THINGS: I can carry out My purpose through all things.' R. Aḥa said: Even through a serpent, a scorpion, a flea, or a frog.

The wicked Titus entered the Holy of Holies with a drawn sword in his hand and slashed the curtain. He then took two harlots and had intercourse with them upon the altar. When he came out his sword was dripping with blood, some say from the blood of the sacrificial offerings and others say from the blood of the goat used on the Day of Atonement.[1] He began blaspheming and defying God, saying, 'He who wages war with a king in the desert and conquers him is not like him who wages war with a king in his very house[2] and conquers him.' What did Titus do? He collected all the vessels of the Temple into a net and boarded a ship. When he had sailed, a gale struck the sea, and he said, 'Apparently the might of this people's God is only on the water. He punished the generation of Enosh only with water[3]; and also when I was in His house He could not withstand me, but now He attacks me here.' The Holy One, blessed be He, exclaimed, 'O you villain, son of a villain! By your life, I will punish you with the most insignificant creature which I created during the six days of Creation.' Forthwith the Holy One, blessed be He, rebuked the sea and it became still from its raging. Titus went ashore, and when he reached

[1] In the Talmudic version, Giṭ. 56*b* (Sonc. ed., p. 259), the sword was bloodstained through slashing the curtain.

[2] I.e. the capital of his kingdom. Titus boasted that he was able to gain the victory in Jerusalem, where Israel's King reigned.

[3] The Flood. The 'generation of Enosh' is used loosely for that of the Deluge (in Noah's days) because according to the Rabbis (v. Gen. R. XXIII, 6 and 7) wickedness then began.

Rome all the population came out and greeted him with cries of 'O conqueror of the barbarians!' They immediately kindled the fire of the bath-house for him and he bathed. On leaving the bath, they mixed for him a vial of *poterion*[1] and wine. The Holy One, blessed be He, arranged that there should be in the goblet a gnat which entered Titus's nose and reached his brain. It began piercing his brain, devouring it, and growing in size until it became as large as a young dove and weighed two pounds. He ordered, 'Summon the physicians to split my brain open so that I may know with what the God of this people has punished me.' They summoned the physicians who split his brain open and found a kind of young dove weighing two pounds. R. Eleazar b. R. Jose said: I was in Rome at the time, and they placed the young dove on one scale and two pounds on the other, and they balanced. They set it in a dish, and as it altered so did he alter.[2] When the gnat flew away, the soul of Titus flew to destruction and everlasting abhorrence. This is an illustration of THE PROFIT OF THE EARTH [as interpreted above].

5. R. Tanḥuma and R. Menaḥma related the following incidents.[3] A man was once standing by the river and he saw a frog carrying a scorpion and conveying it across the river. He exclaimed, 'Surely it is engaged on performing its mission.' The frog conveyed the scorpion across; the latter performed its mission and was carried back to its place. Then a sound of wailing was heard in the city, 'A scorpion has stung So-and-so and he has died.' R. Phinehas said in the name of R. Ḥanin of Sepphoris: A man was once reaping in the valley of Beth Ṭofeth[4] and he saw some grass from which he made a garland for his head.

[1] Extract of a shrub taken medicinally after a bath.

[2] 'E.J. it gradually resumed its normal size, and as it did so, Titus too shrank as it were and his strength ebbed away.

[3] The moral they teach is that God employs insignificant creatures to bring His punishment on wrongdoers.

[4] A variant is 'Valley of Neṭofah', near Bethlehem.

A serpent appeared, but he struck and killed it. A man came and stood by him. He glanced at the serpent and said, 'I wonder who killed it.' 'I did,' said the other. He then noticed the grass on his head and asked, 'Are you able to take off the crown of grass from your head?' 'Yes,' he replied. The man then asked, 'Are you able to touch the serpent with this rod?' 'Yes,' he replied. As soon as he touched the serpent, his limbs immediately fell to pieces.[1]

R. Jannai was sitting and teaching by the city-gates. He saw a serpent coming towards him very excitedly. He drove it away from one side and it reappeared on another side. He exclaimed, 'It is certainly engaged on the performance of its mission.' At once a cry of alarm occurred in the city, 'So-and-so has been bitten by a serpent and died.'

R. Eleazar was sitting in a privy. A Roman came, made him stand up and himself sat down. The former exclaimed, 'Not for nothing did this man come [and act so to me].' Forthwith a serpent appeared and bit him so that he died. R. Eleazar applied to him this verse, *Therefore will I give a man* (adam) *in place of thee* (Isa. XLIII, 4),[2] [which is to be read,] 'I will give Edom [a Roman] in place of thee.'

R. Isaac b. R. Eleazar was walking on the cliffs by the sea at Cæsarea. He saw a thigh bone[3] rolling towards him, and twice he hid it [in the earth], but it kept rolling up to him. He exclaimed, 'This is engaged on the performance of its mission.' Some days later a Government courier passed that spot, and it rolled between his feet, so that he stumbled, fell and died. They went and searched in his bag and found that he was carrying documents with bad tidings for the Jews of Cæsarea.

R. Simeon b. Ḥalafta was an experimenter. He possessed a garden in which was a sycamore trunk, and a hoopoe came and built its nest in it. R. Simeon arose and upset it. What did he do? He took a plank, placed it in front of the nest, struck a nail through it and fixed it.[4] What did

[1] V. Gen. R. x, 7. [2] E.V. '*Give men for thee*'.
[3] So in Gen R. *loc. cit.*
[4] Thus hiding the nest—he wanted to see what the bird would do.

the hoopoe do? It went and brought a certain herb which it placed on the nail and destroyed it. What did R. Simeon do? He exclaimed, 'It is well that I should conceal this herb, lest thieves go and do this and destroy human beings.'

The she-ass of R. Jannai ate a certain herb and became blind; she then ate another herb and her sight was restored. Later two men happened to walk along the road of Tiberias, one blind and the other able to see, and the latter was leading the blind man. They sat down by the road to eat something, and by chance they ate of these herbs. The blind man had his sight restored and the man who had been able to see became blind. They did not depart from there until the man who had originally been blind was leading the man who could originally see.

A man who was coming up from Babylon [to Palestine] sat down by the road to eat something when he saw two birds fighting. One killed the other, and it went and brought a certain herb which it placed on the dead bird and it revived. He exclaimed, 'It is well for me to take this herb with which to revive the dead in the land of Israel.' He hastened on his journey and saw a dead fox lying in the road. He said, 'It is well for me to experiment with this fox.' He placed the herb on it and revived it. He continued his journey until he reached the Ladder of Tyre.[1] When he arrived at the Ladder of Tyre he saw a dead lion lying in the road. He said, 'It is well for me to experiment with this.' He placed the herb on it and revived it. The lion sprang upon him and devoured him. That is what people say: 'Do no good to an evil person and harm will not come to you; for if you do good to an evil person, you have done wrong.'

R. Tanḥuma said: Even with water the Holy One, blessed be He, fulfils His mission. It happened that a person who was afflicted with boils went down to bathe in the Lake of Tiberias. Now it chanced that just at that moment Miriam's well gushed up in that spot, and he

[1] A hill south of Tyre.

washed therein and was healed. But where is Miriam's well? R. Ḥiyya b. Abba said: It is written, *Which looketh down upon the desert*—yeshimon (Num. XXI, 20); because whoever ascends Mount Yeshimon[1] sees a sieve-like object in the Lake of Tiberias, and that is Miriam's well. R. Joḥanan said: The Rabbis made a calculation and found that it was directly facing the middle gate of the old Synagogue of Sergunieh.[2]

R. Huna b. Papa said: The Israelites used to offer sacrifices on prohibited altars in the wilderness (until the Tabernacle was set up).[3] We learn in the Mishnah: Before the Tabernacle was set up [in the wilderness] the high places were permitted and the service was conducted by the firstborn; but when the Tabernacle was set up, the high places were forbidden and the service was conducted by the priests.[4] Nevertheless the Israelites used to offer sacrifices on prohibited altars in the wilderness and the penalties they incurred wrought havoc among them. The heathen peoples remarked, 'They do service in His name and yet He slays them in the wilderness!' Therefore the Holy One, blessed be He, spake to Moses, *What man soever there be of the house of Israel, that killeth an ox, or lamb . . . and hath not brought it unto the door of the tent of meeting . . . blood shall be imputed unto that man* (Lev. XVII, 3 f.).

1. WHEN GOODS INCREASE, THEY ARE INCREASED THAT EAT THEM (V, 10). R. Ḥananiah and R. Jonathan asked Menaḥem the cake-baker (R. Berekiah said in the name of R. Jose b. Ḥananiah that Menaḥem the cake-baker asked them): 'What means, *He afflicted thee and suffered thee to hunger and fed thee with manna* (Deut. VIII, 3)? Was it a starvation diet that the Holy One, blessed be He, gave Israel in the manna!' What did he do? He set before them two cucumbers, one whole and the other broken, and said, 'How much does this whole one

[1] Shab. 35*a* reads 'Mount Carmel'. [2] Near Tiberias.
[3] The words in brackets are to be deleted. [4] Zeb. XIV, 4.

cost?' They answered, 'Two *maneh.*' 'And how much does this broken one cost?' They answered, 'One *maneh.*' He said to them, 'But is not the fate of this [whole one] to be made the same as the other?'[1] They answered, '[The broken one] is not like [the whole one], because just as one derives enjoyment from taste, so does one enjoy appearance.'[2]

R. Eleazar said in the name of R. Jose b. Zimra: Three things are said about the inside of the fig, viz., it is good to eat, it is fair to behold, and it increases wisdom. All three are mentioned in one verse, viz., *And when the woman saw that the tree was good for food*, hence it was good to eat, *And that it was a delight to the eyes*, hence it was fair to behold, *And that the tree was to be desired to make one wise* (Gen. III, 6), hence it increases wisdom. That is what is written, *Maschil of Ethan*[3] *the Ezrahite* (Ps. LXXXIX, 1). Similarly[4] said Isaac, *And make me savoury food* (Gen. XXVII, 4)—he said to his son, 'Previously I used to enjoy the sight [of the venison], but now [that my eyes are dim] I only enjoy its savour.' In like manner said Solomon, WHEN GOODS INCREASE, THEY ARE INCREASED THAT EAT THEM, i.e. he who sees his basket empty and is hungry is not like him who sees his basket full and is [consequently] sated.[5]

A Cuthean asked R. Meir, 'Do the dead live again?' He answered, 'Yes.' He then asked, ['Do they come back to life] secretly or in public?' He answered, 'In public.' 'How can you prove it to me?' he asked, to which R. Meir replied: 'Not from Scripture nor from the Mishnah, but from everyday life I will answer you. There was a

[1] It will be broken into pieces, so why should its price be higher?

[2] Similarly the Israelites were unable to have full enjoyment from the manna. Although, according to tradition, it imparted the flavour of several species of food, those who ate it did not have the satisfaction which they would have experienced from seeing the different articles of diet. [3] *Maschil* means 'makes intelligent' and *Ethan* contains all the letters but one of *te'enah*, 'fig'.

[4] This refers to the end of the last paragraph about the enjoyment of the sight of food. [5] Mere sight and the knowledge that one has food sometimes relieve hunger.

trustworthy man in our city with whom everyone deposited [money] secretly and he restored it to the owners in public. Somebody came and deposited it with him in public; so how should he restore it to him, in secret or publicly? Will he not do it publicly?' 'Certainly,' was the reply. Then said R. Meir to him, 'Let your ears hear what your lips speak. Men deposit a white drop [in secret] with their wives, and the Holy One, blessed be He, restores that drop publicly in the form of a beautiful and perfect creature. How much more will a dead person who departs [from the world] publicly return publicly? As he departs with loud cries so will he return with loud cries.' (R Jonathan said in the name of R. Jonathan of Beth Gubrin: It is written, *The grave and the barren womb* (Prov. XXX, 16)—what has one to do with the other? In truth as the barren womb yields [the child] with loud cries, so will Sheol yield [the dead] with loud cries.)[1]

The Cuthean asked, 'How will they come [from the grave], naked or clothed?' He answered, 'Clothed.' 'How can you prove it to me?' he inquired. He replied, 'Not from Scripture nor from the Mishnah, but from everyday life I will answer you. Have you ever sown beans?' 'Yes.' 'How did you sow them, naked or clothed?' 'Naked.'[2] 'How did they come up, clothed or naked?' 'Clothed.' R. Meir said to him, 'Do not your ears hear what your mouth speaks? If beans, when a person sows them naked, come up clothed, how much more will the dead which depart clothed [in shrouds] return clothed!' (R. Aibu—another version: in the name of R. Nathan—said: It is written, *It is changed as clay under the seal, and they stand as a garment* (Job XXXVIII, 14), i.e. the garment which descends [to the grave] with a man in this world will come back with him in the Hereafter.) The Cuthean asked him, 'Since [the dead] come back alive and clothed, who supplies them with food?'[3] He said to him,

[1] Cf. III, 2.
[2] The seed has no outer shell, but the bean has one when grown.
[3] How will one find sufficient food for all who have existed since the Creation?

'Have you ever been to the hot spring of Gadara?'[1] 'Yes.' 'In the season or out of the season?' 'Both.' 'Were supplies of food obtainable there?' 'They were obtainable.' 'In the season or out of it?'[2] 'Both in and out of the season, because crowds bring foodstuff there to buy and sell.' R. Meir said to him, 'As He brings the crowds [of the dead], so does He bring their sustenance, as it was written by Solomon, WHEN GOODS INCREASE, THEY ARE INCREASED THAT EAT THEM, i.e. when they who are to eat the good things increase in number, the good things are increased in quantity [to meet the need].' The Cuthean asked, 'Since [the dead] come back to life, clothed and fed, why do you weep over them [when they die]?' He answered, 'A curse upon you! Shall a man lose something that is precious to him and not weep? As the human being comes [into the world] with loud cries, so he departs with loud cries [from the bereaved].'

2. It has been taught: When the child is formed in its mother's womb there are three partners concerned with it, viz., the Holy One, blessed be He, the father and mother. The father provides the white semen from which are formed the white substances [of the embryo], the brain, the nails, the white of the eyes, the bones, and sinews. The mother provides the red element from which are formed the blood, skin, flesh, hair, and the black in the eyes. The Holy One, may His name be blessed and His memorial exalted, gives him ten things, viz., spirit and soul, beauty of features, sight of the eyes, hearing of the ears, speech of the lips, the ability to raise the hands and to walk with the feet, wisdom and understanding, counsel, knowledge, and strength. When its time comes to die, the Holy One, blessed be He, takes His portion and leaves the portion contributed by the father and mother before them, and they weep. The Holy One, blessed be He,

[1] V. Sanh. 108*a* (Sonc. ed., p. 740, n. 8).
[2] People resorted to the hot spring usually at certain times of the year.

says to them, 'Why do you weep? Have I taken anything of yours? I have only taken what belongs to Me!' They say before Him, 'Lord of the universe, so long as Thy portion was mingled with ours, our portion was preserved from the maggot and worm; but now that Thou hast taken away Thy portion from ours, behold our portion is cast away and given to the maggot and worm.'

R. Judah the Prince used to cite this parable: To what is the matter like? To a king who possessed a vineyard which he handed over to a tenant.[1] The king said to his servants, 'Go, cut down the grapes of my vineyard, take away my portion and leave behind the portion which belongs to the tenant.' They at once went and carried out his order. The tenant began to cry and lament; so the king said to him, 'Have I taken anything of yours? I have only taken my own!' He replied to him, 'My lord king, so long as your portion was with mine, my portion was guarded from plunder and theft; but now that you have removed your portion, behold my portion is exposed to plunder and theft!' The king is the supreme King of kings, the Holy One, blessed be He; the tenant is the father and mother. So long as the soul is within the human being, he is preserved; but when he dies he is for the maggot and worm, as it is said, *How much less man, that is a worm!* (Job xxv, 6), i.e. the vermin upon him during his lifetime, *And the son of man that is a maggot!* (*ib.*), i.e. the maggots which swarm under him when he is dead.

Simeon b. Eleazar says: Even a child of one day does not require guarding while he is alive against weasels, mice, and snakes; the dog sees it and flees and so does the serpent. When, however, a human being is dead, though he be as huge as Og, king of Bashan, he needs to be guarded against weasels, mice, and snakes. So long as a man is alive the fear of him is cast upon all created things, beasts, and reptiles, as it is said, *The fear of you and the dread of you shall be upon every beast of the earth*, etc. (Gen. IX, 2);

[1] *Aris*, a tenant who undertakes to cultivate the land for a portion of the produce as his wage.

but when he is dead, the fear of him is removed and he needs to be watched. Furthermore, a child of one day, while it is alive, may have the Sabbath desecrated for it[1]; but when David, king of Israel, died the Sabbath could not be desecrated for him, even as Solomon said, *For a living dog is better than a dead lion* (Eccl. IX, 4). It is like that which R. Judah said in the name of Rab; for R. Judah said in the name of Rab: What means that which is written, *Lord, make me to know mine end, and the measure of my days, what it is; let me know how short-lived I am* (Ps. XXXIX, 5)? David spoke before the Holy One, blessed be He, 'Lord of the universe, "*Make me to know mine end.*"'[2] He replied, 'It is a decree from before Me that a human being is not informed what his end is to be.' [David said, 'Let me know] "*The measure of my days, what it is*".' He replied, 'It is a decree from before Me that the human being is not informed what the measure of his days is to be.' [David said,] '*Let me know how short-lived I am.*'[3] He told him, '[You will die] on the Sabbath.' He spoke before Him, 'Let me die on the first day of the week.'[4] He replied to him, 'Already has the time of the kingship of your son Solomon arrived, and one reign may not overlap another even a hair's breadth.' 'Then let me die on the eve of the Sabbath,' he pleaded. He replied, '*For a day in Thy courts is better than a thousand* (*ib.* LXXXIV, 11), i.e. better to Me is one day in which you are engaged in Torah before Me than a thousand sacrifices which your son Solomon will offer before Me on the altar.'[5] David used to sit and study every Sabbath throughout the day. He had a garden at the rear of his house, and on that day [when he was to die] the Angel of Death came and shook the trees. He went out to see what it was, but as he ascended a step it broke under him, and he was silenced [in death]

[1] To save its life in an emergency.
[2] This probably means, my future, my fate (not when I am to die).
[3] Understood as 'on what day I am to die'; lit. 'how I am to cease'.
[4] So that his body could at once be prepared for burial. This is prohibited on the Sabbath.
[5] I cannot shorten your life even by one day, as it is precious to Me.

and his soul had peace. Solomon sent a message to the House of Study: 'My father is dead, lying in the sun, and the dogs of my father's house are hungry; what shall I do?' They sent back the reply, 'Cut up the carcass of an animal and place it before the dogs. As for your father, set a loaf of bread or a child upon him[1] and then you may move the body.' Did not, then, Solomon truly say, '*A living dog is better than a dead lion*'?[2]

1. SWEET IS THE SLEEP OF A LABOURING MAN, WHETHER HE EAT LITTLE OR MUCH (V, 11): Rabbi [Judah ha-Nasi] came out of the bath, wrapped himself in his garments and sat down to attend to the people [who brought to him their difficulties]. His servant mixed for him a cup [of wine and water]; but being busy with attending to the people, he had no leisure to receive it from him, and the servant became drowsy and fell asleep. Rabbi turned, and gazing at him exclaimed, 'Rightly did Solomon say, SWEET IS THE SLEEP OF A LABOURING MAN, WHETHER HE EAT LITTLE OR MUCH; BUT THE SATIETY OF THE RICH WILL NOT SUFFER HIM TO SLEEP—like me who am busy attending to the needs of the people; I am not even allowed to sleep.'

R. Berekiah said: To what may the matter be likened? To a king who had a park which he handed over to his son. So long as his son did his bidding, the king used to look out for the finest plants in the world and plant them in his son's park; but when his son did not do his bidding, he used to look for the most beautiful and gorgeous plant in the park and uproot it. Thus the king is the Holy One, blessed be He; the park is the world or, as some say, Israel. So long as they do His bidding, the Holy One, blessed be He, looks out for a righteous person among the

[1] It would be permissible to move the child or loaf, and the body could be moved with it.
[2] Whereas his first question was about his father, they answered first about the dogs, a living dog being more important than a dead king.

peoples of the world as, e.g., Jethro, Rahab, Ruth, or Antoninus,[1] whom He brings and attaches to Israel; but when they do not do His bidding, He looks for a righteous man in Israel and removes him from their midst.

2. What is the difference between the death of the young and the death of the old? R. Judah and R. Nehemiah give answers. R. Judah says: When a lamp is extinguished of its own accord, it is good for the lamp and for the wick; but when it is not extinguished of its own accord, it is bad for the lamp and for the wick.[2] R. Nehemiah says: When the fig is gathered in its due season it is good for the fig and for the tree; but when it is not gathered in its due season, it is bad for the fig and for the tree. Here is an illustration. R. Ḥiyya the elder and his disciples (other versions: R. Simeon b. Ḥalafta and his disciples, R. Akiba and his disciples) were sitting and studying beneath a fig-tree. The owner of the tree arose early to gather its fruit. They said, 'Let us change our place lest he suspect us [of stealing his figs]'; so they sat in another place. On the morrow the owner of the tree arose early to gather his figs but did not find the Sages there. He went after them and, on finding them, said, 'You performed a pious act for me,[3] and now you withhold it from me.' 'Heaven forfend!' they exclaimed. He asked them, 'Why, then, did you leave your place and sit elsewhere?' They answered, 'We said, "Lest he suspect us."' He said to them, 'Heaven forfend [that I should think so of you]! But I tell you why I arose early to gather the fruit; it is because it becomes wormy when the sun shines upon it.' That day he left the fruit without gathering it, and they found that when the sun shone upon it the figs became wormy. They remarked,

[1] Frequently mentioned in Rabbinic literature as a friend of R. Judah ha-Nasi. He is usually identified with Marcus Aurelius; but S. Krauss, *Antoninus und Rabbi*, identifies him with Avidius Cassius, a famous general of Marcus Aurelius and Procurator of Judea.

[2] So it is good for a person to die in the fulness of years, and not to be cut off in youth like a lamp blown out by a gust of wind.

[3] By studying beneath his tree

'The owner of the fig-tree knows well which is the proper time for the figs to be gathered and gathers them accordingly. Similarly the Holy One, blessed be He, knows when is the proper time for a righteous man [to die] and then removes him.'

3. Ḥiyya b. R. Adda, the son of Bar Ḳappara's sister, died. They told R. Joḥanan to go in and deliver an oration over him. He said to them, 'Let R. Simeon b. Laḳish go in because he knows what were the good qualities of the deceased.' R. Simeon went in and delivered this oration over him: *My beloved is gone down to his garden* (S.S. VI, 2)—the Holy One, blessed be He, knows the deeds of R. Ḥiyya b. Adda and has removed him [from the world].[1]

4. When R. Simon b. Zebid died, R. Ila went in and delivered a funeral oration over him on the verses, *But wisdom, where shall it be found? And where is the place of understanding? Man knoweth not the price thereof; neither is it found in the land of the living. The deep saith: It is not in me . . . it is hid from the eyes of all living* (Job XXVIII, 12 ff.). If this be so, when a Sage dies, whence are we to replace him? Four things are of service to the world, but all of them, if they are lost, can be replaced, viz. *There is a mine for silver, and a place for gold which they refine. Iron is taken out of the dust, and brass is molten out of the stone* (*ib.* 1 f.). But if a Sage dies who can bring us a substitute for him? We have lost R. Simon; who can bring a substitute for him? R. Levi said: [The progenitors of the twelve] tribes made a discovery [of money in their sacks] and were astounded and their heart failed them, as it is said, *And their heart failed them and they turned trembling one to another* (Gen. XLII, 28). We who have lost R. Simon b. Zebid, how much more [should our heart fail us]!

[1] 'E.J.: God knows that he has achieved all that it was possible for him to achieve on earth, and so has removed him that he should not be exposed to the Tempter; cf. Gen. R. IX, 5.

5. When R. Bun b. R. Ḥiyya died, R. Zera went in and delivered a funeral oration over him on the present verse, SWEET IS THE SLEEP OF A LABOURING MAN. To whom was R. Bun b. R. Ḥiyya like? To a king who possessed a vineyard and hired many labourers to work it. Among them was one labourer far more skilful in his work than the rest; so what did the king do? He took him by the hand and walked with him up and down. Towards evening the labourers came to receive their wages and this labourer came with them, and he gave him the full amount. The others began to grumble, saying, 'We toiled all the day, whereas this man toiled for two hours, and yet the king has given him his full wage!' The king said to them, 'What cause have you for grumbling? This man in two hours did more good work than you in a whole day.' Similarly did R. Bun b. R. Ḥiyya learn in twenty-eight years[1] more Torah than an eminent scholar could learn in a hundred years. R. Joḥanan said: Whoever has laboured in the Torah in this world is not allowed to sleep [in the Hereafter] but is taken to the Academy of Shem and Eber,[2] and of Abraham, Isaac and Jacob, Moses and Aaron. For how long? *Until I will make thee a great name, like unto the name of the great ones that are in the earth* (II Sam. VII, 9).

1. THERE IS A GRIEVOUS EVIL WHICH I HAVE SEEN UNDER THE SUN (V, 12). Is there, then, a grievous evil and a good evil! But what is a grievous evil? For instance, gout, poverty, debility, nakedness, and hunger. NAMELY, RICHES KEPT BY THE OWNER THEREOF TO HIS HURT: R. Joshua said: It alludes to Korah.[3] R. Samuel said: It alludes to Naboth the Jezreelite.[4] R. Judah said: It alludes to Haman. R. Isaac said: It alludes to the sons of Reuben and Gad.[5] The Rabbis say:

[1] Or perhaps: by the age of twenty-eight. [2] V. Gen. R. LXIII, 6.
[3] V. p. 50, n. 3. [4] I Kings XXI.
[5] Num. XXXII. Because of the abundance of their cattle, they did not have an inheritance in Canaan and were exiled before the other tribes.

It alludes to Job who was rich, became impoverished, and returned to his former status.

R. Gamaliel b. R. Ḥanina asked R. Mana, 'What means that which is written, RICHES KEPT BY THE OWNER THEREOF TO HIS HURT?' He replied, 'The upshot of his wealth is [the payment of] his fine. When the Government imposes a fine upon him, he will give whatever is demanded.'[1]

1. AND THOSE RICHES PERISH BY EVIL ADVENTURE (V, 13). R. Haggai said in the name of R. Isaac: By the evil adventure which he planned against the poor man [do his riches perish. When asked for help] he says to him, 'Is it not better for you to work and eat? Look at your legs,[2] look at your knees, look at your muscles! So is it not better for you to work and eat?' The Holy One, blessed be He, exclaims, 'Not enough that you give him nothing of your own, but you even cast an evil eye upon what I have given him!' Therefore, IF HE HATH BEGOTTEN A SON, THERE IS NOTHING IN HIS HAND: of the money which he possessed he will leave nothing to his son.

1. AS HE CAME FORTH OF HIS MOTHER'S WOMB (V, 14). Genibah said: It is like a fox who found a vineyard which was fenced in on all sides. There was one hole through which he wanted to enter, but he was unable to do so. What did he do? He fasted for three days until he became lean and frail, and so got through the hole. Then he ate [of the grapes] and became fat again, so that when he wished to go out he could not pass through at all. He again fasted another three days until he became lean and frail, returning to his former condition, and went out. When he was outside, he turned his face and gazing at the vineyard, said, 'O vineyard, O vineyard, how good are you and the fruits inside! All that is inside is beautiful

[1] It is implied that charges are invented against a rich man as a pretext for confiscating his wealth. [2] How strong they are.

and commendable, but what enjoyment has one from you? As one enters you so he comes out.' Such is this world.

Another interpretation of AS HE CAME FORTH OF HIS MOTHER'S WOMB, NAKED SHALL HE GO BACK AS HE CAME: It has been taught: As a man enters [the world] so he departs. He enters it with a cry and departs from the world with a cry. He enters the world with weeping and takes leave of it with weeping. He enters the world in love and takes leave of it in love. He enters the world with a sigh and takes leave of it with a sigh. He enters the world devoid of knowledge and takes leave of it devoid of knowledge. It has been taught in the name of R. Meir: When a person enters the world his hands are clenched as though to say, 'The whole world is mine, I shall inherit it'; but when he takes leave of it his hands are spread open as though to say, 'I have inherited nothing from the world.' For thus said Solomon, AS HE CAME FORTH OF HIS MOTHER'S WOMB, NAKED SHALL HE GO BACK AS HE CAME, AND SHALL TAKE NOTHING FOR HIS LABOUR.

1. AND THIS ALSO IS A GRIEVOUS EVIL, THAT IN ALL POINTS AS HE CAME, SO SHALL HE GO (V, 15). As he comes [into the world so weak that he must be fed] with slops, so when he goes [in his old age he must be fed] with slops. R. Phinehas said: As the world opened with four kingdoms, so will it close with four kingdoms. It opened with four kingdoms, as it is said, *Amraphel king of Shinar, Arioch king of Ellasar, Chedorlaomer king of Elam, and Tidal king of Goiim* (Gen. XIV, 1); and it will close with four kingdoms, viz., Babylon, Greece, Media, and Edom [Rome].[1]

AND WHAT PROFIT HATH HE THAT HE LABOURETH FOR THE WIND? The Holy One, blessed be He, said to man, 'You have ploughed, sown, reaped, tied into bundles, threshed, and gathered the produce into stacks; but if I do not produce wind to winnow for you, from

[1] V. Gen. R. XLII, 2 and notes *ad loc.*

where would you exist? Behold you refuse to give the *omer* as payment for that wind!'[1] Hence WHAT PROFIT HATH HE [GOD] THAT HE LABOURETH FOR THE WIND?

1. ALL HIS DAYS ALSO HE EATETH IN DARKNESS (V, 16): it speaks of the generation of the Judges.[2] AND HE HATH MUCH VEXATION: in that they provoked the Holy One, blessed be He, with their evil deeds. AND SICKNESS AND WRATH: SICKNESS refers to sufferings,[3] AND WRATH to their rousing the Holy One, blessed be He, to anger by saying, *O Lord, the God of Israel, why is this come to pass in Israel, that there should be to-day one tribe lacking in Israel?* (Judg. XXI, 3).[4]

Another interpretation of ALL HIS DAYS ALSO HE EATETH IN DARKNESS: it speaks of the generation of Samuel. AND HE HATH MUCH VEXATION: in that they provoked the Holy One, blessed be He, with their evil deeds. AND SICKNESS refers to sufferings, AND WRATH to their rousing the Holy One, blessed be He, to anger by saying, *Wherefore hath the Lord smitten us to-day before the Philistines?* (I Sam. IV, 3). The ten tribes were exiled and none of them remained; the tribes of Judah and Benjamin were exiled and some of them remained.[5]

1. BEHOLD THAT WHICH I HAVE SEEN: IT IS GOOD, YEA, IT IS COMELY FOR ONE TO EAT AND TO DRINK (V, 17). R. Tanḥuma said: All the eating and drinking mentioned in this Book refers to Torah and good deeds. R. Jonah said: The most clear proof of them all is, *A man hath no better thing under the sun than to eat and to drink, and to be merry, and that this should accompany him in his labour* (Eccl. VIII, 15). Do, then, food and

[1] Cf. I, 3. [2] Described as a generation of vanity; cf. Gen. R. LVII, 4.
[3] Which resulted from their wickedness.
[4] As though casting the blame on God.
[5] Because all the ten tribes provoked God, but there were some pious men in the tribes of Judah and Benjamin.

drink accompany a man to the grave? What does accompany him? Torah and good deeds.[1]

1. EVERY MAN ALSO TO WHOM GOD HATH GIVEN RICHES AND WEALTH, AND HATH GIVEN HIM POWER TO EAT THEREOF (V, 18). R. Phinehas said: This attribute does not apply to all human beings, but only to such as the Holy One, blessed be He, delights in.

1. FOR LET HIM REMEMBER THE DAYS OF HIS LIFE THAT THEY ARE NOT MANY (V, 19): this applies to the generation of Eli.[2] FOR GOD ANSWERETH HIM IN THE JOY OF HIS HEART: this alludes to Elkanah who used to lead Israel and bring them up to Jerusalem[3] every year by a different route.[4] For that reason Scripture praises him,[5] *And this man went up out of his city from year to year to worship and to sacrifice unto the Lord of hosts in Shiloh* (I Sam. I, 3).

[1] Cf. II, 14. [2] This means Eli's sons and descendants (I Sam. II, 32).
[3] M.K. remarks that this is an error for 'Shiloh'.
[4] Each year he took a different route to Shiloh to induce other Israelites to follow him. [5] For the good example he set others.

Chapter VI

1. THERE IS AN EVIL WHICH I HAVE SEEN UNDER THE SUN (VI, 1). R. Samuel b. Ammi said: This refers to the devices of cheats; e.g. one who adulterates wine with water, oil with the juice of glaucion,[1] honey with the juice of the wild strawberry, balsam with ass's milk, myrrh with gum, aromatic leaves with vine-leaves, brine with red colouring matter, pepper with vetch, or uses a weight-beam which is longer on one side than the other [to give false measure]. Concerning all these R. Joḥanan b. Zakkai remarked, 'Woe is me if I say it,[2] and woe is me if I do not say it. If I say it there is the danger that cheats will learn what to do; and if I do not say it, the cheats may assert, "The Sages are unacquainted with our actions."' Finally he did say it,[3] *For the ways of the Lord are right* (Hosea XIV, 10).

1. A MAN TO WHOM GOD GIVETH RICHES, WEALTH, AND HONOUR (VI, 2). R. Abba b. Kahana entered an assembly and heard the voice of R. Levi who was sitting and expounding this verse, A MAN TO WHOM GOD GIVETH, as follows: RICHES denotes the master of Scripture; WEALTH the master of Mishnah, AND HONOUR the master of Ṭosefta[4]; SO THAT HE WANTETH NOTHING FOR HIS SOUL OF ALL THAT HE DESIRETH alludes to the great collections of Mishnah, as, e.g., the Mishnah of R. Akiba, of R. Ḥiyya, of R. Hoshaya, and of Bar Ḳappara[5]; YET GOD GIVETH HIM NOT POWER TO EAT THEREOF means that it is forbidden to decide questions of law from them[6]; BUT A STRANGER EATETH IT, i.e. the master

[1] A species of poppy. He sells the mixture as pure oil.
[2] I.e. quote these ways of adulterating commodities.
[3] The necessity to expose the frauds overcame the fear that others might learn to practise them. The teacher's duty is to advocate what is right irrespective of the consequences. [4] V. p. 59, n. 1. [5] V. p. 58, n. 2.
[6] They lacked the acknowledged authority of the Mishnah of R. Judah ha-Nasi.

of Talmud[1] who declares what is unclean and clean, prohibited and permitted. R. Abba b. Kahana stood up and kissed him on his head, saying, 'If I had only come up to hear this explanation from your mouth, it would be enough for me.' R. Ishmael says: *The rich man is wise in his own eyes* (Prov. XXVIII, 11) refers to the master of Talmud, *But the poor that hath understanding searcheth him through* (*ib.*) to the master of *Haggadah*.[2]

1. IF A MAN BEGET A HUNDRED CHILDREN (VI, 3): this alludes to Cain who begat a hundred children, AND LIVE MANY YEARS: he lived many years, SO THAT THE DAYS OF HIS YEARS ARE MANY, BUT HIS SOUL BE NOT SATISFIED with his money and he was not satisfied with [what he possessed of] the world's good things. AND MOREOVER HE HAVE NO BURIAL: because he was kept in suspense [as to his fate] until the Flood came and swept him away, as it is written, *He blotted out every living substance*—yeḳum (Gen. VII, 23). (What means '*yeḳum*'? Living beings; R. Bun said: The inhabited earth[3]; R. Eliezer says: '*Yeḳum*' means the money which gives standing[4] to its owner's feet; R. Samuel said: '*Yeḳum*' is an allusion to Cain who was swept away by the Flood.) AN UNTIMELY BIRTH IS BETTER THAN HE: this is his brother Abel.[5]

Another interpretation of IF A MAN BEGET A HUNDRED CHILDREN: this is Ahab who begat a hundred children. R. Aḥa said: But it is written, *Now Ahab had* seventy *sons in Samaria* (II Kings X, 1)! (R. Hoshaya said: As he had seventy sons in Samaria so he

[1] Though he be a 'stranger' to, i.e. not proficient in, Scripture and Mishnah. Only through a proficiency in the Talmud, i.e. the dialectic and full discussion of the laws stated in the Mishnah collections, might one be competent to give actual rulings.
[2] His subject being less abstruse than Talmud, even the less intelligent can follow him. [3] M.K. explains: the builders, i.e. human beings.
[4] '*Yeḳum*' is connected with *ḳum*, 'to stand.'
[5] The Heb. for UNTIMELY BIRTH is *nefel*, from the root *nafal*, 'to fall,' and Abel fell by his brother's violence.

also had seventy in Jezreel, each of whom possessed two mansions, one for summer and one for winter, as it is written, *I will smite the winter-house with the summer-house* (Amos III, 15). R. Judah b. R. Simon said: They each had two for summer and another two for winter, as it is stated, *And the houses of ivory*[1] *shall perish* (*ib.*). The Rabbis said: They each possessed six, as it is stated, *And the great houses shall have an end* (*ib.*).)[2] AND LIVE MANY YEARS: he lived many years, BUT HIS SOUL HAVE NOT ENOUGH OF GOOD: of money, AND MOREOVER HE HAVE NO BURIAL: for it is written, *In the place where dogs licked the blood of Naboth shall dogs lick thy blood* (I Kings XXI, 19); AN UNTIMELY BIRTH IS BETTER THAN HE: viz. a harlot's abortion.[3]

1. FOR IT COMETH IN VANITY, AND DEPARTETH IN DARKNESS (VI, 4): [Was Ahab, then,] without light or bath? It means, without Torah and good deeds.[4]

1. MOREOVER IT HATH NOT SEEN THE SUN NOR KNOWN IT (VI, 5). The matter may be likened to two men who were sailing on a ship. When it reached the harbour, one of them disembarked and went into the country and saw there much food and drink and luxury. On returning to the ship he asked the other, 'Why did you not go into the country?' He said to him, 'What did you, who landed and entered, see there?' He replied, 'I saw much food and drink and luxury.' The other inquired, 'Did you enjoy any of it?' 'No,' was the answer; whereupon the man retorted, 'I who did not enter am much better off than you for not having landed and seen it!'[5]

[1] These are additional to the aforementioned.
[2] These too are additional: hence six in all.
[3] This would have burial whereas Ahab did not.
[4] 'E.J. emends and explains: for he (the untimely birth) COMETH IN VANITY—without light or bath; AND DEPARTETH IN DARKNESS without Torah or good deeds (the Torah being likened to light).
[5] Because he has less regret at not having partaken of the good things on land.

That is what is written, THIS HATH GRATIFICATION RATHER THAN THE OTHER.

1. YEA, THOUGH HE LIVE A THOUSAND YEARS TWICE TOLD . . . ALL THE LABOUR OF MAN IS FOR HIS MOUTH, AND YET THE APPETITE IS NOT FILLED (VI, 6 f.). R. Samuel said: However man toils and accumulates [merit for the performance of] the precepts and good deeds in this world, it is insufficient [to requite the boon granted him by God of] the breath which comes from his mouth. AND YET THE SOUL[1] IS NOT FILLED: even when it departs it does not fill the cavity.[2] How does the soul depart? R. Joḥanan said: Like rushing waters from a channel[3]; R. Ḥanina said: Like swirling waters from a channel; R. Samuel b. Rabbi said: Like a moist and inverted thorn [tearing its way] out of the throat.

R. Ḥanina B. Isaac said: All that a man toils for precepts and good deeds is FOR HIS MOUTH, and not for the mouth of his son or daughter. AND YET THE SOUL IS NOT FILLED: because the soul is aware that whatever it toils for is for itself and therefore never has enough of Torah and good deeds. To what may the matter be likened? To a villager who married a woman of royal lineage. Though he bring her everything in the world, it is not esteemed by her at all. Why? Because she is a king's daughter [and is used to comforts]. So is it with the soul; though you bring it all the luxuries in the world, they are nothing to it. Why? Because it is of heavenly origin.

Three creatures are not grateful [for the benefits which they receive from] their owners: the soul, the earth, and a woman. 'The soul,' as it is said, YET THE SOUL IS NOT FILLED. 'The earth,' as it is said, *The earth that is not satisfied with water* (Prov. XXX, 16). 'And a woman,'

[1] So lit. [2] At the time of death the soul does not pass out of the body smoothly but with violence (Mah.).

[3] When the sluice-bars are raised (so Jast.). Rashi (on Ber. 8*a*) explains: Like ropes pulled through loopholes in the boards of a ship. Levy renders: like a cord drawn out of the gullet.

as it is said, *She eateth and wipeth her mouth*, etc. (*ib.* 20).[1] Three give abundantly and receive abundantly, viz., the sea, the earth, and the Government. R. Joshua of Siknin said: Six times the word *nefesh* (soul) occurs [in Leviticus I][2] corresponding to the six days of Creation. The Holy One, blessed be He, said to the soul, 'All that I have made during the six days of Creation I made for your sake, but you rob and sin and act with violence.'[3]

1. FOR WHAT ADVANTAGE HATH THE WISE MORE THAN THE FOOL? OR THE POOR MAN THAT HATH UNDERSTANDING, IN WALKING BEFORE THE LIVING? (VI, 8).[4] So what can [the poor man] do? Let him go to one greater than himself in Torah who will explain his learning to him.

Another interpretation of OR THE POOR MAN THAT HATH UNDERSTANDING: How can a man who is poor in property go to a rich man?[5] So what can he do? Let him engage in commerce [himself]. Another interpretation of OR THE POOR MAN THAT HATH UNDERSTANDING: What can such a man [lacking the means] do with business transactions! What can he do? Is he to sit idle? Let him learn a handicraft, and the Holy One, blessed be He, will support him so that he can live.

1. BETTER IS THE SEEING OF THE EYES THAN THE WANDERING OF THE DESIRE (VI, 9). Better is he

[1] Since they are not satisfied, it may be assumed that they are not grateful (Y.T.) 'Owners' here refer to those who supply (e.g. the food for appetite, the water for the earth). The last verse refers to an adulteress: since she is unfaithful to her husband, she is obviously not grateful to him for his protection and sustenance. Or perhaps *And wipeth her mouth* is understood to mean that she has not had enough and is ready for more. [2] *If a soul sin.* [3] This and the preceding are given as examples of things receiving yet not being satisfied.

[4] Understood to mean: how can a person who is deficient in learning attain to eternal life?

[5] A poor man is said to be like a dead man; consequently LIVING is here defined as a rich man. A wealthy man will not engage in partnership or co-operate with a poor man. Therefore the latter must trade on his own account.

who can explain his teaching clearly than he who mechanically goes on with his studies.[1]

1. WHATSOEVER COMETH INTO BEING, THE NAME THEREOF WAS GIVEN LONG AGO (VI, 10). This refers to Adam, as it is said, *And the Lord God took the man* (Gen. II, 15), so it was known that he was designated *man*.[2] It may be likened to a king and a governor who were seated in a chariot, and the populace wished to greet the king with cries of 'Sire!' but did not know which of the two was he. What did the king do? He pushed the other out of the chariot and everybody knew that that man was the governor. Similarly when the Holy One, blessed be He, created the first man, the ministering angels were mistaken in him and wanted to proclaim before him 'Holy!' What did the Holy One, blessed be He, do? He cast a sleep upon him and all knew that he was man; and He said to him, *Dust thou art and unto dust shalt thou return* (*ib.* III, 19).

Another interpretation of WHATSOEVER COMETH INTO BEING, THE NAME THEREOF WAS GIVEN LONG AGO: This refers to Moses, as it is said, *And the Lord called unto Moses* (Lev. I, 1); and it was known to all that this Moses was a prophet at the time the Holy One, blessed be He, told him, *Come now therefore, and I will send thee unto Pharaoh that thou mayest bring forth* My *people* (Ex. III, 10). When, however, the incident [of the golden calf] occurred, He told him, *Go, get thee down, for* thy *people that thou broughtest up out of the land of Egypt, have dealt corruptly* (*ib.* XXXII, 7). Moses spoke before Him: 'Lord of the universe, when they are good they are Thine, and when bad they are mine! Whether good or bad they are Thine.' It may be likened to a king who had a vineyard which he leased to a tenant[3] to cultivate. When it produces good wine the king says to him, 'How

[1] Lit. 'than he who studies and becomes used to an accustomed phraseology and goes on'. THE WANDERING OF THE DESIRE is understood as a mere proceeding with studies without seeking to understand them. [2] But not God. [3] V. p. 148, n. 1.

excellent is the wine of *my* vineyard!' but when it produces bad wine the king says, 'The wine of my tenant's vineyard is bad.' The tenant weeps and cries, saying, 'My lord king, when it produced good wine it was yours, but when it produces bad wine it is mine! Whether good or bad it is yours.' Similarly said Moses, 'Whether good or bad they are Thine.' Moses, however, was unable to contend with One stronger than himself; for when he said to Him, *Let me go over, I pray thee, and see the good land* (Deut. III, 25), the Holy One, blessed be He, told him, *Let it suffice thee, speak no more unto Me of this matter* (*ib.* 26).

Another interpretation of WHATSOEVER COMETH INTO BEING: This refers to Jeremiah, and it was known to all that he was a prophet, as it is said, *Before I formed thee in the belly I knew thee* (Jer. I, 5).

1. SEEING THERE ARE MANY WORDS THAT INCREASE VANITY, WHAT IS MAN THE BETTER (VI, 11)? For instance, they who rear monkeys, cats, porcupines, chimpanzees, and sea-dogs; of what use are they?[1] It is either a bite or a sting [one gets from them], so of what use are they? [He receives] either a wound or a blow from them. Similarly what benefit has a person who removes stones from his field and places them in the public road? One either stumbles over them or suffers a contusion. (Some read the word [for 'contusion'] as *marẓumi* [instead of *marmuẓi*].) A pious man was once removing stones from his field and placing them in the public road. Another pious man who was there ran after him, saying, 'Why do you remove stones from what does not belong to you and place them in what does belong to you?' The man laughed at him; but after a while that pious man fell into want and had to sell his field. He was walking along that public road and stumbled [over the stones]. He exclaimed, 'Not for nothing did that pious man tell me, "You are placing them in what does belong to you."'[2] WHAT IS MAN THE BETTER?

[1] Since they may not be eaten and are harmful animals. WORDS here means 'things', 'objects'.
[2] Now that he was poor, the public road was his domain.

1. FOR WHO KNOWETH WHAT IS GOOD FOR MAN IN HIS LIFE (VI, 12)? R. Huna said in the name of R. Aḥa: David used a phrase without explaining it and its exposition was given by his son Solomon; and Solomon used a phrase without explaining it and its exposition was given by his father David. Solomon said, FOR WHO KNOWETH WHAT IS GOOD FOR MAN IN HIS LIFE, ALL THE DAYS OF HIS VAIN LIFE WHICH HE SPENDETH AS A SHADOW? How is this to be understood? If life is like a shadow cast by a wall, there is substance in it; if like the shadow cast by a date-palm, there is substance in it! David came and explained, *His days are as a shadow that passeth away* (Ps. CXLIV, 4). 'David used a phrase without explaining it and its exposition was given by his son Solomon.' David said, *Man is like unto a breath* (*ib.*). To what breath? If he were like the steam from an oven, there is substance in it; if like the steam of a stove, there is substance in it! Solomon came and explained it, *Vanity of vanities* (Eccl. I, I).[1]

Another interpretation of FOR WHO KNOWETH WHAT IS GOOD FOR MAN IN HIS LIFE? R. Phinehas said: Since the days of man's life are vain, few in number and like a shadow, what benefit has he from his existence? Let him, then, occupy himself with words of Torah which are all of them life.

FOR WHO CAN TELL A MAN WHAT SHALL BE AFTER HIM UNDER THE SUN? Solomon said: I will tell you what is best of all, viz. *A good name is better than precious oil* (*ib.* VII, I).

[1] Repeated from I, 2.

SECOND SECTION[1]

CHAPTER VII

1. A GOOD NAME IS BETTER THAN GOOD[2] OIL (VII, 1). Good oil flows downwards while a good name ascends. Good oil is transient while a good name endures for ever. Good oil is spent while a good name is not spent. Good oil is bought with money while a good name is free of cost. Good oil is applicable only to the living while a good name is applicable to the living and the dead. Good oil can only be acquired by the rich while a good name can be acquired by poor and rich. [The scent of] good oil is diffused from the bed-chamber[3] to the dining-hall while a good name is diffused from one end of the world to the other. Good oil falls upon a dead body and becomes rancid—as it is said, *Dead flies make the ointment of the perfumer fetid and putrid* (Eccl. X, 1)—while a good name falls upon a dead person and does not become putrid, as it is said, *And he went up and lay upon the child . . . and he stretched himself upon him* (II Kings IV, 34).[4] Good oil falls upon water and is washed away[5] while a good name falls upon water and is not washed away, as it is said, *And the Lord spoke unto the fish and it vomited out Jonah upon the dry land* (Jonah II, 11).[6] Good oil is burnt when it falls upon fire but a good name falls upon fire without being burnt, as it is written, *Then Shadrach, Meshach and Abed-nego came forth out of the midst of the fire* (Dan. III, 26).

R. Judah b. R. Simon said: We find that men who had been anointed with good oil entered the place of life and came out burnt, while men of good name entered the

[1] V. the Introduction. [2] So lit. E.V. '*precious*'.
[3] Where it was used in a person's toilet.
[4] The effect of Elisha, the possessor of a good name, when he came in contact with the lifeless body of the child, was to revive it.
[5] The two do not mix. [6] Jonah, who possessed a good name, was not destroyed by being cast into the sea.

place of the dead and came out alive. Nadab and Abihu entered the place of life [the Sanctuary] and died,[1] whereas Hananiah, Mishael, and Azariah entered the furnace and came out alive. Therefore it is said, A GOOD NAME IS BETTER THAN GOOD OIL.

2. The Rabbis say: The Holy One, blessed be He, told Moses, 'Go and appoint a High Priest for Me.' He spoke before Him, 'Lord of the universe, from which tribe?' He answered, 'From the tribe of Levi.' 'With what am I to anoint him?' He answered, 'With the anointing oil.' Thereupon Moses rejoiced, saying, 'How is my tribe beloved by the Holy One, blessed be He!' The Holy One, blessed be He, said to him, 'By thy life, it is not thy tribe, but thy brother [that is beloved by Me].' That is what is written, *And bring thou near unto thee Aaron thy brother* (Ex. XXVIII, 1). Whence is it known that his consecration was to be with the anointing oil? As it is said, *Then shalt thou take the anointing oil* (*ib.* XXIX, 7). His service was, however, invalid and he rendered himself liable to punishment unless the names of the tribes were engraven [upon the breastplate] over his heart, as it is written, *And Aaron shall bear the names of the children of Israel in the breastplate of judgment upon his heart* (*ib.* XXVIII, 29). The Holy One, blessed be He, said, 'Dearer to me are the names of the tribes than the anointing oil with which priests and kings are anointed.'[2]

R. Nehemiah said: The Holy One, blessed be He, told Moses, 'Go and anoint a High Priest for Me.' He spoke before Him, 'Lord of the universe, from which tribe?' He answered, 'From the tribe of Levi.' 'With what am I to anoint him?' He answered, 'With the anointing oil.' At that time Moses rejoiced, saying, 'How is my tribe beloved by the Holy One, blessed be He!' The Holy One, blessed be He, said to him, 'By thy life, it is not thy tribe, but thy brother [that is beloved by Me].'

[1] V. Lev. x, 1 f.
[2] This illustrates how the good name (of the tribes) is better than good oil.

That is what is written, '*And bring thou near unto thee Aaron thy brother.*' Whence is it known that his consecration was to be with the anointing oil? As it is said, '*Then shalt thou take the anointing oil.*' His service was, however, invalid and he rendered himself liable unless the names of the tribes were engraven over his two shoulders, as it is written, *And Aaron shall bear their names before the Lord upon his two shoulders for a memorial* (*ib.* 12). It is written, *Six of their names on the one stone* (*ib.* 10): R. Bibi said: Should they lack even one letter [of the names], they could not be used. R. Oshaya learnt: This applies even if a single point is missing.

R. Simeon b. Yoḥai learnt: There are three crowns: the crown of Torah, the crown of priesthood, and the crown of royalty.[1] Aaron merited the crown of priesthood and received it; David merited the crown of royalty and received it. As for the crown of Torah, it lies unappropriated for the generations.[2] If one attains [the crown of] Torah, it is as though he attained all three; if one does not attain [the crown of] Torah, it is as though he has attained none of them.

R. Bun said in the name of R. Samuel b. Naḥmani: We find that the Holy One, blessed be He, went a five hundred years' journey to acquire a name for Himself, as it is written, *Whom God went to redeem unto Himself for a people, and to make Him a name* (II Sam. VII, 23).[3] R. Jose of Galilee said: [He went to redeem] the people and its God.[4] (R. Akiba remarked to him, 'You have made the Holy profane!')[5] The Israelites spoke before the Holy One, blessed be He: 'If it is possible to say so, Thou hast redeemed Thyself'; as it is said, *Whom thou didst*

[1] Ab. IV, 13 (Sonc. ed., p. 51).
[2] So that all who merit it may receive it.
[3] He went from heaven to earth, which according to the Rabbis was a five hundred years' journey.
[4] Because when Israel is in servitude God is declared to be in a like state.
[5] By suggesting that God had to redeem Himself. R. Akiba's remark has been bracketed, as according to this rendering what follows ('The Israelites spoke, etc.) would be a continuation of R. Jose's teaching. 'E.J. explains it quite differently.

redeem to Thee out of Egypt, the nation and his God (*ib.*).[1] It is written, *Whom God went* (halak) *to redeem* (I Chron. XVII, 21), and here it states, '*Whom God went* (haleku)[2] *to redeem!*' '*Halak*' refers to the Holy One, blessed be He, '*haleku*' to Moses and Aaron.[3]

3. R. Simeon b. Yoḥai said: More beloved [by God] is a good name than the ark of the covenant, because this went before the Israelites only a distance of three days, as it is said, *And the ark of the covenant of the Lord went before them three days' journey* (Num. X, 33), while a good name goes from one end of the world to the other. Whence do we know this? From David, as it is said, *And the fame of David went out into all lands, and the Lord brought the fear of him upon all nations* (I Chron. XIV, 17). More beloved is a good name than the priesthood and royalty, because these ceased[4] while a good name never ceases. The disciples of R. Abba and Abba of Zidon said in the name of R. Samuel b. Naḥman: Dearer were [the progenitors of the] tribes in their death than in their lifetime; because while they were alive it was not said, '*Six of their names on the one stone*,' but this was said when they were dead.

R. Judah said: Miriam and Jochebed acted as midwives for the Israelites, as it is written, *The Hebrew midwives, of whom the name of one was Shiphrah, and the name of the other Puah* (Ex. I, 15). Shiphrah is Jochebed [and she is so called] because she straightened (*meshappereth*) the limbs of the babes. Another explanation is: because she was fruitful (*she-parah*) and multiplied. Another explanation is: because the Israelites were fruitful (*she-paru*) and multiplied through her. Another explanation is: because she embellished (*shipperah*) them with precepts and good

[1] E.V.: '[*In driving out*] *from before Thy people, whom Thou didst redeem to Thee out of Egypt, the nations and their gods.*'
[2] Here the verb is plural.
[3] The words are therefore understood as, 'they went to redeem God.' 'E.J., however, explains that 'God' in this verse refers to Moses and Aaron, as we find the word actually applied to the former in Ex. VII, 1: *See, I have made thee a God* (A.V., which is lit. translation) *to Pharaoh.*
[4] The High Priesthood ceased.

deeds. Another explanation is: she embellished [herself so as to gain] a name of praise, as the word is used in *By His breath the heavens are serene*—shiphrah (Job XXVI, 13). Puah is Miriam [and she was so called] because she used to cry out (*po'ah*) to the woman and the child came forth. Another explanation is: she used to cry out and weep for her brother Moses who had been cast into the river, as it is said, *And his sister stood afar off* (Ex. II, 4). Another explanation of Puah is: she revealed (*hofi'ah*)[1] the career of her brother. Another explanation is: she cried out in the presence of Pharaoh and told him, 'Woe to you because of the day of judgment!'

It has been taught: A man is called by three names: one which his father and mother call him, a second which other persons call him, and a third by which he is designated in the book of the generations of his creation.[2]

4. R. Phinehas said: Man is beloved by his name, but I do not know by which of them.[3] Solomon came and explained, A GOOD NAME IS BETTER THAN PRECIOUS OIL, AND THE DAY OF DEATH THAN THE DAY OF ONE'S BIRTH.[4] When a person is born he is designated for death; when he dies he is designated for life [in the Hereafter]. When a person is born all rejoice; when he dies all weep. It should not be so; but when a person is born there should be no rejoicing over him, because it is not known in what class he will stand by reason of his actions, whether righteous or wicked, good or bad. When he dies, however, there is cause for rejoicing if he departs with a good name and leaves the world in peace. It is as if there were two ocean-going ships, one leaving the harbour and the other entering it. As the one sailed out of the harbour all rejoiced, but none displayed any joy over the

[1] Lit. 'caused it to shine forth'.—She prophesied before his birth that he would redeem Israel.

[2] An obscure phrase. Probably the meaning is: the name which he gains for himself as the result of his conduct in life.

[3] Radal changes the order of the words and reads: I do not know by which name a man is beloved.

[4] I.e. a man is to be estimated by the reputation he leaves behind him when he dies.

one which was entering the harbour. A shrewd man was there and he said to the people, 'I take the opposite view to you. There is no cause to rejoice over the ship which is leaving the harbour because nobody knows what will be its plight, what seas and storms it may encounter; but when it enters the harbour all have occasion to rejoice since it has come in safely.' Similarly, when a person dies all should rejoice and offer thanks that he departed from the world with a good name and in peace. That is what Solomon said, AND THE DAY OF DEATH [IS BETTER] THAN THE DAY OF ONE'S BIRTH.

You find that when the righteous are born nobody feels any difference, but when they die everybody feels it. When Miriam was born nobody felt it, but when she died the well[1] ceased to exist and all felt [her loss]. The well made her death known. When Aaron, the High Priest, was born nobody felt it, but when he died and the clouds of glory departed all felt [his loss]. The cloud thus made his death known. When Moses our teacher was born nobody felt it, but when he died all felt it, because the manna made his death known by ceasing to fall. When Joshua was born nobody felt it, but when he died all felt it, as it is said, *And they buried him in the border of his inheritance . . . on the north of the mountain of Gaash* (Josh. XXIV, 30). The Rabbis said: We have searched the whole of Scripture, but have not found a place named '*mountain of Gaash*'. What, then, do the words mean? Because the Israelites were completely engrossed (*nithga'ashu*)[2] and failed to show proper respect to Joshua [at his death] the Holy One, blessed be He, made as though to shake the mountain and even cause it to reel (*hag'ish*) over them in order to hurl them to destruction. [The reason was that] the land of Israel was being apportioned and they were heart and soul in the allotment [and so they forgot their duty to their dead leader]. One was occupied with his

[1] On the basis of Num. XX, 1 f, the legend arose that a well was created by God in honour of Miriam which accompanied the Israelites in their journeying, but disappeared at her death (Ta'an. 9*a*).
[2] In settling in Canaan.

field, another with his vineyard, another with his olive-yard, another with the charcoal he was burning. All were engaged in their work; therefore the Holy One, blessed be He, made as though to shake the world over them, and for that reason they all felt [Joshua's death] and it was made known to them.

When David was born nobody felt it, but when he died all felt it, as it is said, *And when Hadad heard in Egypt that David slept with his fathers, and that Joab the captain of the host was dead* (I Kings XI, 21). R. Phinehas said: Is not 'sleeping with one's fathers' the same as 'dying'?[1] The fact is that since David was a king, '*slept*' is written in connection with him; Joab being only captain of the host, '*was dead*' is written in connection with him. Another explanation: is not 'sleeping with one's fathers' the same as 'dying'? Since David had been anointed with the anointing oil, '*slept*' is written in connection with him; and since Joab had not been so anointed, '*was dead*' is written in connection with him. Another explanation: is not 'sleeping with one's fathers' the same as 'dying'? Since David died in his bed, '*slept*' is written in connection with him; and since Joab was slain, '*was dead*' is written in connection with him. Another explanation: is not 'sleeping with one's fathers' the same as 'dying'? Since David had sons who succeeded him, '*slept*' is said of him; and since Joab was not succeeded by his sons, '*was dead*' is said of him. Therefore all felt it when David died inasmuch as [the succession of] Solomon made his death known.[2]

When Samuel was born nobody felt it, but when he died all felt it, as it is said, *And Samuel died, and all Israel gathered themselves together and lamented him, and buried him* (I Sam. XXV, 1). R. Joshua b. Levi said: The proverb declares, 'When a person has been bitten by a snake a

[1] Why does the text use different terms?
[2] M.K.: Solomon made known David's death when he prayed at the dedication of the Temple, *Remember the good deeds of David Thy servant* (II Chron. VI, 42); *supra*, IV, 3.

piece of rope terrifies him.'[1] R. Samuel b. Naḥman said: They gave him what was due to him, as it is stated, *And he went from year to year in circuit to Bethel, and Gilgal, and Mizpah; and he judged Israel in all those places* (*ib.* VII, 16).[2] One text states, *And Samuel died* (*ib.* XXV, 1), and another states, *Now Samuel was dead* (*ib.* XXVIII, 3)! R. Assi said: The latter expression indicates the actual occurrence of his death; the former is only mentioned in connection with the incident of Nabal, as it is stated, '*And Samuel died*' . . . *and there was a man in Maon.* R. Samuel b. Naḥman said: All Israel lamented and clapped hands [in mourning] over the death of the righteous man, but this wicked [Nabal] held carousal.[3] R. Judah said: It teaches you that if one repudiates an obligation of benevolence,[4] it is as though he repudiates the cardinal doctrine [of God's existence].[5] As for king David (peace be upon him), he was benevolent to all, saying, 'Even to a murderer as well as to the slain, to a pursuer as well as to the pursued, I show kindness as to a righteous man.' That is what is written, *But as for me, in Thy mercy do I trust; my heart shall rejoice in Thy salvation. I will sing unto the Lord because the doing of benevolence is with me* (Ps. XIII, 6).[6]

1. IT IS BETTER TO GO TO THE HOUSE OF MOURNING, THAN TO GO TO THE HOUSE OF FEASTING (VII, 2). Why? BECAUSE THE HEART OF THE WISE IS IN THE HOUSE OF MOURNING (*ib.* 4); for if one mourns[7] the Holy One, blessed be He,

[1] They remembered the terrifying experience when they neglected their duty to Joshua, so they did not forget their duty when Samuel died.
[2] The Israelites did not perform their duty to Samuel from fear, but in recognition of his services to them. [3] I Sam. XXV, 16.
[4] Here the term refers to the showing of proper respect to the dead.
[5] To lament the death of a righteous man and concern oneself with his burial is such an obligation. Nabal repudiated it and also denied God, as it is stated *The fool* (nabal) *hath said in his heart: There is no God* (Ps. XIV, 1).
[6] E.V.: '*Because He hath dealt bountifully with me.*'
[7] I.e. takes to heart the lessons to be learnt in the time of bereavement, the vanity of worldly things and the virtue of humility

causes him to rejoice, as it is said, *The humble also shall increase their joy in the Lord* (Isa. XXIX, 19). Another interpretation of IT IS BETTER TO GO TO THE HOUSE OF MOURNING, THAN TO GO TO THE HOUSE OF FEASTING: it is better to follow a line of conduct wherein there is recompense than one in which there may be no recompense.[1] It is better to follow a line of conduct which serves both the living and the dead[2] than one which serves only the living. It is better to follow a line of conduct which serves both rich and poor[3] than one which serves only the rich. It is better to follow a line of conduct in which there is consolation [to be offered to the bereaved] than one in which there is no consolation to offer.

2. R. Berekiah said: [Examples of] benevolence occur in the Torah, at its beginning, middle, and end. At its beginning, as it is written, *And the rib, which the Lord God had taken from the man, made He* (wayiben) *a woman, and brought her unto the man* (Gen. II, 22)—this teaches that the Holy One, blessed be He, plaited Eve's hair and brought her to Adam, acting as groomsman to them, because in the sea-towns[4] they call plaits *binyata*. In the middle, as it is written, *And the Lord appeared unto him by the terebinths of Mamre* (*ib.* XVIII, 1), which teaches that He visited him[5]; *And it came to pass after the death of Abraham, that God blessed Isaac his son* (*ib.* XXV, 11), i.e. the benediction pronounced upon mourners.[6] At its end, as it is said, *And He buried him*[7] *in the valley* (Deut. XXXIV, 6).

R. Ḥanin said: What is 'a line of conduct wherein there

[1] Since all have to die, to do an act of benevolence will lead to a similar consideration being paid to the doer when he dies, but there can be no such certainty of a similar consideration in the case of going to a house of feasting. [2] Visiting mourners is not only a comfort to them but an honouring of the dead. [3] Death visits rich families as well as poor, but the latter cannot make feasts.

[4] I.e. in foreign countries where a dialect of Aramaic was spoken

[5] In Abraham's weakness which followed on his circumcision.

[6] Cf. Keth. 8*b* (Sonc. ed., p. 37). [7] So lit. E.V. '*And he was buried*'.

is recompense'? Jacob died in the land of Egypt; so for whom was it proper to attend to his burial? Was it not the Holy One, blessed be He, who had told him, *I will go down with thee into Egypt, and I will also surely bring thee up again* (Gen. XLVI, 4)? But Joseph came and appropriated the pious act to himself, as it is written, *And Joseph went up to bury his father* (*ib.* L, 7). Joseph died in Egypt; so for whom was it proper to attend to his burial? Was it not the tribes whom he had made to swear, as it is said, *And Joseph took an oath of the children of Israel* (*ib.* 25). Moses came and appropriated the pious act to himself, as it is said, *And Moses took the bones of Joseph with him* (Ex. XIII, 19). When Moses died, the Holy One, blessed be He, repaid him with His own glory, as it is said, '*And He buried him in the valley.*'

3. It is written, *And the Lord God made for Adam and for his wife garments of skin, and clothed them* (Gen. III, 21). We find that the Holy One, blessed be He, performs acts of benevolence: He adorns brides, blesses bridegrooms, visits the sick, buries the dead, and comforts mourners. 'He adorns brides,' as it is written, '*And the rib which the Lord God had taken*' (*ib.* II, 22).[1] R. Joḥanan said: He made her, adorned her, and displayed her to Adam. R. Abbahu said: Perhaps you may think that He displayed her to him from between a carob-tree or a sycamore; not so, but after decking her with twenty-four articles of adornment[2] He displayed her to him, as it is said, '*And brought her unto the man*' (*ib.*). 'Blesses bridegrooms,' as it is said, *And God blessed him* (*ib.* I, 28). 'Visits the sick,' as it is said, '*And God appeared unto him by the terebinths of Mamre*' (*ib.* XVIII, 1). 'Buries the dead,' as it is said, '*And He buried him in the valley*' (Deut. XXXIV, 6). 'Comforts mourners,' as it is said, *And the name of it was called*[3] *Allon-bacuth* (Gen. XXXV, 8). R. Samuel b. Naḥman said: What is '*Allon-bacuth*' (oak of weeping)? While [Jacob]

[1] As explained above. [2] Enumerated in Isa. III, 18 ff.
[3] Lit. 'he called its name'.

was observing the mourning for Deborah, his nurse, the news reached him of [the death of] his mother Rebekah, and therefore he wept two weepings.[1] Therefore it is said, '*Allon-bacuth.*' Of Jacob it states, *And He blessed him* (*ib.* 9), i.e. He blessed him with the benediction for mourners.

4. R. Simon said: We find that certain persons went to the house of feasting but their names are not recorded, whereas they who went to the house of mourning had their names recorded. Og went to Abraham's feast but his name was not recorded.[2] The three friends of Job, on the other hand, went to the house of mourning and their names are recorded. We find that certain persons went to the house of feasting but were not excluded from Gehinnom, whereas they who went to the house of mourning were excluded from Gehinnom. Og attended Abraham's feast and was not excluded from Gehinnom, whereas they who went to the house of mourning were excluded from Gehinnom.[3] R. Issachar of Kefar-Mandi[4] said: It is the fate of the wicked to be placed in the lowest stratum of Gehinnom, as it is stated, *As for the wicked, He distributes them below* (Job XXXIV, 26).[5] The three friends of Job went to the house of mourning and were excluded from Gehinnom, as it is written, *They came every one from his own place* (*ib.* II, 11)—it is not written here, 'Every one from his house, or his city, or his land,' but '*From his own place*', i.e. from the place reserved for them in Gehinnom they were excluded and delivered. We find that persons went to the house of feasting and the Holy Spirit did not attend upon them, as, e.g., Og; whereas the three friends of Job went to the house of mourning and the Holy Spirit did attend upon them, as it is written, *Then answered Eliphaz* (*ib.* IV, 1), *Then answered Bildad* (*ib.* VIII, 1). For it has been taught in the name of R. Meir: Wherever it is mentioned that So-and-so

[1] V. Gen. R. LXXXI, 5. [2] V. Gen. R. LIII, 10. [3] Cf. Job. XLII, 8 ff.
[4] Or 'Mandu', N. of Sepphoris.
[5] E.V.: '*He striketh them as wicked men.*'

'answered and said', he spoke in the holy tongue [Hebrew] and by the Holy Spirit.

5. AND THE LIVING WILL LAY IT TO HIS HEART. What has this to teach? Do a kindness that one may be done to you. Attend a funeral that people should attend your funeral; mourn for others so that others should mourn for you; bury so that others should concern themselves with your burial; act benevolently so that benevolence should be done to you.

R. Mana said: AND THE LIVING WILL LAY IT TO HIS HEART: these are the righteous who set their death over against their heart[1]; and why do they beat upon their heart? As though to say, 'All is there.'[2]

Another interpretation of AND THE LIVING WILL LAY IT TO HIS HEART: it alludes to Him who lives eternally and rewards a man for every step he takes to perform benevolence. For R. Jonah said: We may not discuss *halachoth* in front of the bed upon which a corpse lies.[3] But there is the case of R. Joḥanan who asked R. Jannai in front of the bier of R. Simeon b. Jehoẓadaḳ, 'If a man dedicated his offering to the repair of the Sanctuary, does the law of trespass apply to it?' and he answered him, 'Since the priests insist on slaughtering it themselves, the law of trespass applies to it.'[4] It is, however, mentioned that R. Jannai gave his answer when he was some distance away from the bier.

It has been taught: The bearers are forbidden to put on sandals, lest the sandal of one of them break, with the consequence that he is delayed in the carrying out of his pious duty.

R. Ze'ira slipped in a field. When they went to raise

[1] I.e. their thoughts.

[2] Death being the consequence of sin (v. p. 131), the righteous beat their heart as the source of evil longing.

[3] So as not to divert the mind from mourning. Radal omits 'for' at the beginning of the sentence, because the statement has no connection with what precedes.

[4] By insisting that none but they shall slaughter it, they treat it as a proper sacrifice, and therefore the law of trespass applies to it.

him they found that he was suffering pain (in the field).[1] They asked him, 'Why has this happened?' He said to them, '[To remind us] that this is the world from which we came and to which [we are going].'[2] That is what is stated, AND THE LIVING WILL LAY IT TO HIS HEART.[3]

1. VEXATION IS BETTER THAN LAUGHTER (VII, 3). Solomon said: If my father had been a little vexed with Adonijah, it would have been better for him than the laughter with which the Attribute of Justice gloated over him.[4] Why? FOR BY THE SADNESS OF THE COUNTENANCE THE HEART MAY BE GLADDENED. If David had shown him a sad [i.e. a displeased] countenance, he might have led him to mend his ways, but [it is written], *And his father had not grieved him all his life* (I Kings I, 6). It was the same with Amnon; if his father David had been a little vexed with him, it would have been better for him than the laughter with which the Attribute of Justice gloated over him. Why? FOR BY THE SADNESS OF THE COUNTENANCE THE HEART MAY BE GLADDENED. But [it is written], *For Amnon only is dead* (II Sam. XIII, 33).

Another interpretation of VEXATION IS BETTER THAN LAUGHTER: If the Holy One, blessed be He, had been vexed with the generation of the Flood, it would have been better for them than the laughter with which the Attribute of Justice gloated over them, as it is said, *Their seed is established in their sight with them* (Job XXI, 8).[5]

Another interpretation of VEXATION IS BETTER

[1] The words in brackets should be deleted.

[2] 'E.J. renders the passage thus: R. Ze'ira suddenly became silent whilst speaking. When they (his listeners) went to render him assistance (thinking that something untoward had occurred) they found him exhausted (weakened). 'What is the reason of this?' asked they, and he answered, 'It is the world from which we have come.' (He had been engaged in a funeral eulogy and the thought of the Hereafter had rushed upon him and rendered him dumb.)

[3] The last three paragraphs are quoted from J. Ber. 6*b*.

[4] I.e., had David been stricter with Adonijah, the latter would have been spared his ultimate fate, for which v. I Kings II, 23 ff.

[5] Cf. Gen. R. XXXVI, 1.

THAN LAUGHTER: If the Holy One, blessed be He, had been vexed with the men of Sodom it would have been better for them than the laughter with which the Attribute of Justice laughed over them, as it is said, *There houses are safe, without fear* (*ib.* 9).[1]

1. THE HEART OF THE WISE IS IN THE HOUSE OF MOURNING (VII, 4). R. Isaac said: It may be likened to one who said to his servant, 'Go and bring me a desirable object.' He asked, 'Where can I find a desirable object?' and the master replied, 'If you find many persons going to a place, a desirable object is likely to be there.'[2]

1. IT IS BETTER TO HEAR THE REBUKE OF THE WISE (VII, 5): viz. the expositors of Scripture, THAN FOR A MAN TO HEAR THE SONG OF FOOLS: these are the interpreters who raise their voices in sing-song style to make the people hear.[3]

Another interpretation of IT IS BETTER TO HEAR THE REBUKE OF THE WISE: this is the reproof with which our master Moses rebuked the people; THAN FOR A MAN TO HEAR THE SONG OF FOOLS: this refers to the blessings of the wicked Balaam through which their heart became haughty and they fell at Shittim.[4]

1. FOR AS THE CRACKLING OF THORNS UNDER A POT, SO IS THE LAUGHTER OF A FOOL (VII, 6). R. Levi b. R. Zeira made this the text of his address on obtaining permission [to preach][5] and said: When all other woods

[1] But their fate was to be destroyed (Gen. XIX, 24).

[2] Death being common, men are constantly going to a house of mourning, and precious spiritual truths are to be learnt there.

[3] The teacher did not impart instruction direct. He gave an interpreter the gist of his subject and the latter conveyed it in an amplified form to the congregation. These interpreters did not always reproduce the teaching faithfully but embellished it to obtain praise for themselves.

[4] V. Num. XXV, 1 ff.

[5] This seems to refer to an inaugural address or one in celebration of some promotion. Perhaps it means when he received permission to give religious rulings (i.e. when he became a Rabbi), which may have been marked by a discourse.

are kindled their sound does not travel far; but when thorns are kindled, their sound travels far, as though to say, 'We too are wood.'[1]

1. SURELY OPPRESSION TURNETH A WISE MAN INTO A FOOL (VII, 7). [OPPRESSION ('OSHEḲ):] i.e. the controversy (*'eseḳ*) in which the disciples of the Sages engage one with another; TURNETH A WISE MAN INTO A FOOL: it confuses his wisdom.[2] AND A GIFT DESTROYETH THE UNDERSTANDING: R. Joshua b. Levi said: Eighty *halachoth* I learnt from Judah b. Pedayah concerning a grave which had been ploughed over, but through being occupied with the needs of the community I forgot them.

Who is a disciple of the Sages? R. Abbahu said in the name of R. Joḥanan: Whoever neglects his personal affairs for his study. It has been learnt: [He is a disciple of the Sages] who when questioned about any *halachah* from his repertory is able to answer.

2. R. Joḥanan b. Zakkai had five disciples, and as long as he lived they sat before him. When he died, they went to Jabneh.[3] R. Eleazar b. Arach, however, joined his wife at Emmaus,[4] a place of good water and beautiful aspect. He waited for them to come to him, but they did not come. As they failed to do so, he wanted to go to them, but his wife did not let him. She said, 'Who needs whom?' He answered, 'They need me.' She said to him, 'In the case of a vessel [containing food] and mice, which goes to which? Do the mice go to the vessel or does the vessel come to the mice?' He listened to her and remained there until he forgot his learning. After a while, they came to him and asked, 'Which is better to eat along with a relish, wheaten-bread or barley-bread?' but he was unable

[1] In like manner, the fool cackles to make his presence felt.
[2] For a different version, cf. Ex. R. VI, 2.
[3] Where their master had established an Academy after the destruction of Jerusalem.
[4] A town on the road between Jerusalem and Jaffa.

to answer.[1] (R. Eliezer and R. Jose say: [By 'relish' is to be understood] two articles of food combined together.)

Rabbi [Judah ha-Nasi] used to make two appointments[2] every year; if they proved worthy they continued in office, and if not they died. When Rabbi was about to die, he said to his son, 'You should not act so, but appoint them all together[3] and appoint R. Ḥanina first.' But why did he not do so himself? R. Jose b. Zebid said: Because the men of Sepphoris[4] protested against it. Because they made a protest [Rabbi refused to appoint R. Ḥanina]! Surely, they protest against many things and if we listened to them in this matter we should have to listen to them in the others too![5] [But the true reason why Rabbi did not appoint R. Ḥanina is as] R. Eleazar b. R. Jose said: Because R. Ḥanina corrected Rabbi publicly. Rabbi was sitting and expounding the verse, *But they that shall at all escape from them, shall be on the mountains like doves of the valley, all of them moaning* (Ezek. VII, 16). [Rabbi read the word for '*moaning*' as *homiyoth*] and R. Ḥanina said to him, 'The word is *homoth.*' Rabbi asked him, 'Where did you learn Scripture?' He replied, 'Before R. Hamnuna of Babylon.' He said, 'When you go back there tell *him* to appoint you a Sage,' from which R. Ḥanina knew that he would never be appointed by Rabbi. When Rabbi died, his son wished to appoint him, but he declined the office, saying, 'I will not accept the appointment until you have first appointed R. Aphes of Daroma.'[6] There was an old man present who said, 'If R. Ḥanina

[1] The anecdote demonstrates that the dispute between R. Eleazar and his wife turned a wise man into a fool. 'E.J. gives an involved but nevertheless plausible explanation showing that they asked him a question of law, not of mere taste.

[2] The Principal of the Academy and the President of the *Beth Din* (M.K.).

[3] I.e. nominate a succession of teachers, one to follow on the other, in the event of death (M.K.).

[4] The town to which Rabbi moved shortly before he died. Since R. Ḥanina belonged to that town, the other scholars there were opposed to his appointment as Principal of the Academy

[5] In what follows the reading in J. Ta'an. 68*a* has been adopted. The text has: R. Bun said to him, 'Before whom did you learn Scripture?' and the intervening sentences have fallen out.

[6] A town in S. Palestine.

is appointed first I am second, and if R. Aphes of Daroma is first I am second.' R. Ḥanina agreed to be appointed third and was privileged to live many years. He said, 'I do not know why I have been worthy to live many years, whether it is because of this incident, or whether it is because when coming up from Tiberias to Sepphoris I took a roundabout route in order to greet R. Simeon b. Ḥalafta. I do not know through which of these two actions [I have reached such an advanced age].'

Another interpretation of SURELY OPPRESSION TURNETH A WISE MAN INTO A FOOL: The oppression wherewith Dathan and Abiram oppressed Moses[1] caused his wisdom to depart from him. AND A GIFT (MATTANAH) DESTROYETH THE UNDERSTANDING: this is written *methunah* (patience)[2]—if Moses had been patient, he would have been saved [from speaking against God], but they provoked him and made him lose his temper, saying to him, *The Lord look upon you and judge, because ye have made our savour to be abhorred in the eyes of Pharaoh* (Ex. v, 21). He could not endure their words, and he also lost his temper and said in his anger, *Since I came to Pharaoh in Thy name, he hath dealt ill with this people; neither hast Thou delivered Thy people at all* (*ib.* 23). The Holy One, blessed be He, said to him, 'I wrote concerning thee that thou art a wise man, but thou art hasty and speakest thus of Me! By thy life, it is for thee to know and make known that BETTER IS THE END OF A THING, i.e. of My children, THAN THE BEGINNING THEREOF (VII, 8), which I have given them in Egypt, as it is stated, *Now shalt thou see what I will do to Pharaoh* (Ex. VI, 1).' At that time the Holy One, blessed be He, exclaimed, 'Alas for them that are lost and no longer to be found. I have lost Abraham, Isaac, and Jacob who never criticised Me, and I have not found any others like them. At that time the Attribute of Justice wished to attack Moses, as it is written, *And God* (Elohim) *spake unto Moses* (*ib.* 2), and '*Elohim*' denotes the Attribute

[1] Cf. Ex. R. V, 20. [2] I.e. it can be read so.

of Justice; but it continues, *He said unto him: I am the Lord* (*ib.*).[1] He said to him, 'Thou art a human being and cannot tolerate them; I, the Lord, am merciful and compassionate; with My attributes I will show mercy'; as it is stated, *I have made, and I will bear* (Isa. XLVI, 4).

1. BETTER IS THE END OF A THING THAN THE BEGINNING THEREOF (VII, 8). R. Meir was sitting and expounding in the House of Study of Tiberias, when his teacher, Elisha,[2] passed in the street, riding a horse on the Sabbath. It was told R. Meir, 'Behold, Elisha, your teacher, is passing [riding a horse] on the Sabbath.' He went out to him, and Elisha asked, 'With what were you engaged?' He answered him, 'With the verse, *So the Lord blessed the latter end of Job more than his beginning* (Job XLII, 12).' ['How did you explain it?' he asked,] and he told him, '"*Blessed*" means that He doubled his wealth.' Elisha said to him, 'Not so did your teacher Akiba explain it; but "*So the Lord blessed the latter end of Job more than his beginning*" means that He blessed him for the merit of the repentance and good deeds which were his from his beginning.' R. Meir asked, 'And how do you explain, BETTER IS THE END OF A THING THAN THE BEGINNING THEREOF?' He inquired, 'What have you to say on it?' He replied, 'You have, e.g., the man who acquires a stock of goods in his youth and loses money on it, but in his old age he makes a profit out of it. Another illustration of BETTER IS THE END OF A THING THAN THE BEGINNING THEREOF: You have a man who begets children in his youth and they die; he begets children in his old age and they survive. Another illustration of BETTER IS THE END, etc.: You have a man who commits evil deeds in his youth but in his old age performs good deeds. Another illustration of BETTER IS THE END, etc.: You have the man who learns Torah in his youth and forgets it, but

[1] *Lord* is God in His Attribute of Mercy; cf. Gen. R. XII, 15.
[2] Elisha b. Abuyah, who abandoned Judaism.

in his old age he returns to it; that is an instance of BETTER IS THE END OF A THING THAN THE BEGINNING THEREOF.' Elisha said to him, 'Not so did your teacher Akiba explain it; but his interpretation was: Good is the end of a thing when it is good from its beginning. So it happened with my father, Abuyah, who was one of the great men of his generation. When he came to arrange for my circumcision, he invited all the eminent men of Jerusalem, and all the eminent men of the generation, among them being R. Eliezer and R. Joshua. After they had eaten and drunk, some recited songs and others alphabetical acrostics. R. Eliezer said to R. Joshua, "They are occupied with what interests them, so shall we not occupy ourselves with what interests us?" They began with subjects connected with the Pentateuch, then with the Prophets, and after that with the Hagiographa. The words were as joyful as when they were given from Sinai and fire surrounded them; for were they not originally delivered from Sinai with fire, as it is said, *The mountain burned with fire unto the heart of heaven* (Deut. IV, 11)? My father thereupon remarked, "Since the might of the Torah is so great, should this child survive to me I will dedicate him to the Torah." Because his intention was not for the name of Heaven,[1] my study of the Torah did not endure with me. What do you say is the meaning of the verse, *Gold and glass cannot equal it* (Job XXVIII, 17)—what have you to say on it?' R. Meir answered, 'These are the words of the Torah which are as difficult to acquire as vessels of gold and glass.' He said to him, 'Not so did your teacher Akiba explain it; but his interpretation was: as vessels of gold and glass can be repaired if broken, so can a disciple of the Sages recover his learning if he has lost it.'

Elisha then remarked, 'Turn back.' 'Why?' R. Meir asked. 'Because this is the Sabbath limit.'[2] 'How do you know?' 'By the hoofs of my horse [which tell me

[1] He wanted to glory in the fame of his son as a student of Torah.
[2] On the Sabbath one is not allowed to walk beyond two thousand cubits from the last house of a town.

that he] has already gone two thousand cubits.' R. Meir exclaimed, 'You possess all this wisdom and yet you do not repent.' He replied, 'I am unable.' 'Why?' He said to him, 'I was once on my horse riding behind the Temple on the Day of Atonement which occurred on the Sabbath, and I heard a *Bath Ḳol* crying out, "*Return, ye backsliding children* (Jer. III, 22), *Return unto Me, and I will return unto you* (Mal. III, 7), with the exception of Elisha b. Abuyah who knows My might and yet rebelled against Me!"'

How did this happen to him?[1] He once saw a man climb to the top of a palm-tree on the Sabbath, take the mother-bird with the young, and descend in safety. At the termination of the Sabbath he saw a man climb to the top of a palm-tree and take the young but let the mother-bird go free, and as he descended a snake bit him and he died. Elisha exclaimed, 'It is written, *Thou shalt in any wise let the dam go, but the young thou mayest take unto thyself; that it may be well with thee, and that thou mayest prolong thy days* (Deut. XXII, 7). Where is the well-being of this man, and where is the prolonging of his days!' He was unaware how R. Akiba explained it, viz. '*That it may be well with thee*' in the World [to Come] which is wholly good, '*And that thou mayest prolong thy days*' for the world which is unending. Some say that it was because he saw the tongue of R. Judah the baker[2] in the mouth of a dog and exclaimed, 'If it happened so with a tongue which laboured in the Torah all its days, how much more so will it be with a tongue which does not know nor labour in the Torah!' He went on to say, 'If this is so, there is no reward for the righteous nor is there a resurrection of the dead.' Still others say that it happened because when his mother was pregnant with him, she passed by idolatrous temples and smelled [the offerings]. They gave her some of that kind [of food] and she ate it, and it burned in her stomach like the venom of a serpent [and affected him].

[1] That Elisha b. Abuyah abandoned Jewish teachings and practice.
[2] A martyr in the Hadrianic persecution

Some time later Elisha b. Abuyah became ill, and it was told R. Meir that he was sick. He went to visit him and said, 'Repent.' He asked, 'Having gone so far will I be accepted?' R. Meir replied, 'Is it not written, *Thou turnest man to contrition* (Ps. XC, 3), i.e. up to the time that life is crushed out [the penitent is accepted]?' Then Elisha b. Abuyah wept and died. R. Meir rejoiced, saying, 'My master seems to have departed in a mood of repentance.' When, however, they buried him, fire came to burn his grave. They went and told R. Meir, 'The grave of your master is ablaze!' He went out, spread his *ṭallith* over it, and said to him, '*Tarry this night* (Ruth III, 13) in this world which is wholly night, *And it shall be in the morning, if he who is good will redeem thee, he will redeem thee* (*ib.*).[1] What means "*And it shall be in the morning*"? In the world which is wholly good. [What means] "*If he who is good will redeem thee*"? It alludes to the Holy One, blessed be He, as it is said, *The Lord is good to all* (Ps. CXLV, 9). *But if He* [i.e. God] *will not redeem thee, then will I* [Meir] *redeem thee, as the Lord liveth; lie down until the morning*' (Ruth *loc. cit.*). The fire was then extinguished.

R. Meir's disciples asked him, 'Rabbi, in the World to Come should you be asked, "Whom do you want, your father or your teacher?" what would you say?' He replied, 'First my father and then my teacher.' They said to him, 'And will they listen to you?'[2] He answered them, 'Is there not a Mishnaic teaching that [in the event of a fire on the Sabbath] the case of a book may be saved with the book and the case of phylacteries together with the phylacteries![3] So may Elisha be saved through the merit of his knowledge of Torah.' Eventually Elisha's daughters came to beg alms from our Master,[4] who quoted, *Let there be none to extend kindness unto him, neither let there be any to be gracious unto his fatherless children*

[1] So rendered here.
[2] If you were to beg for your teacher, Elisha, to be received in view of his evil deeds. [3] Shab. XVI, 1. [4] Rabbi Judah the Prince.

(*ib.* CIX, 12). Said they, 'Rabbi, consider not his actions but his Torah!' Thereupon Rabbi wept and decreed that they were to be supported, and exclaimed, 'If a man [like Elisha] whose study of Torah was not for the name of Heaven has reared such daughters, how much more so will it be with him whose study of Torah is for the name of Heaven!'

AND THE PATIENT IN SPIRIT IS BETTER THAN THE PROUD IN SPIRIT. A Persian came to Rab and said to him, 'Teach me the Torah.' He [consented, and, pointing to the first letter of the alphabet], told him, 'Say *aleph*.' The man remarked, 'Who says that this is *aleph*? There may be others who say that it is not!' 'Say *beth*,' to which he remarked, 'Who says that this is *beth*?' Rab rebuked him and drove him out in anger. He went to Samuel and said to him, 'Teach me the Torah.' He told him, 'Say *aleph*.' The man remarked, 'Who says that this is *aleph*?' 'Say *beth*,' to which he remarked, 'Who said this is *beth*?' The teacher took hold of his ear and the man exclaimed, 'My ear! my ear!' Samuel asked him, 'Who said that this is your ear?' He answered, 'Everybody knows that this is my ear,' and the teacher retorted, 'In the same way everybody knows that this is *aleph* and that is *beth*.'[1] Immediately the Persian was silenced and accepted the instruction. Hence, AND THE PATIENT IN SPIRIT IS BETTER THAN THE PROUD IN SPIRIT—better is the forbearance which Samuel displayed with the Persian than the impatience which Rab showed towards him, for otherwise the Persian might have returned to his heathenism. The text was accordingly applied to him, THE PATIENT IN SPIRIT IS BETTER THAN THE PROUD IN SPIRIT.

Furthermore, Aquila the proselyte[2] asked R. Eliezer, 'Is the love which the Holy One, blessed be He, feels towards the proselyte (*ger*) manifested only in the grant of food and clothing, as it is said, *Loveth the stranger* (ger)

[1] A somewhat similar story is told of Shammai and Hillel in Shab. 31*a*.
[2] V. p. 37, n. 1.

in giving him food and raiment (Deut. x, 18)? So numerous are the peacocks and pheasants I possess that even my slaves do not take notice of them!' He replied to him, 'Is, then, a thing trifling in your eyes which our father Jacob begged from the first, as it is said, *And will give me bread to eat and raiment to put on* (Gen. XXVIII, 20)? Is that something insignificant?' He went to R. Joshua and put the same question to him. He replied, '[The meaning is that] a proselyte who has become converted for the name of Heaven[1] is worthy that his daughters should marry into the priesthood. "*Bread*" signifies the shew-bread,[2] and "*raiment*" indicates the priestly vestments.' His disciples criticised his statement and said to him, 'Is, then, the thing insignificant in your eyes for which the patriarch begged, as it is said, "*And will give me bread to eat*"? So why do you put him off with a trifle?'[3] [R. Joshua] therefore began to speak more persuasively to him, saying, '"*Bread*" means the Torah, as it is stated, *Come, eat of My bread* (Prov. IX, 5), and "*raiment*" signifies glory, as it is stated, *By Me kings reign* (*ib.* VIII, 15).' Hence THE PATIENT IN SPIRIT IS BETTER—better is the forbearance which R. Joshua displayed with Aquila the proselyte than the impatience which R. Eliezer showed towards him, for otherwise he might have returned to his heathenism. The text was accordingly applied to him, THE PATIENT IN SPIRIT IS BETTER THAN THE PROUD IN SPIRIT.

1. BE NOT HASTY IN THY SPIRIT TO BE ANGRY (VII, 9). R. Judan said: According as the spinner winds [the yard] on his distaff so he will manage to take it off from his distaff.[4] When the kettle boils over it pours [the boiling water] on its own side. If a man spits into the air, it will fall on his face.

[1] From pure motives. [2] Cf Lev. XXIV, 5 ff.
[3] Lit. 'with a reed'. The assurance of food and clothing, which is the literal interpretation is a more substantial promise than the fanciful explanation which R. Joshua had given. Cf. Gen. R. LXX, 5.
[4] This and what follows are proverbs which teach that the hasty man injures himself.

1. WISDOM IS GOOD WITH AN INHERITANCE (VII, 11): i.e. wisdom is good when it is an inheritance.[1] Another interpretation is: Wisdom is good when there is an inheritance together with it, as we have learnt in *The Ethics of the Fathers:* R. Gamaliel, the son of R. Judah the patriarch, said: Excellent is the study of the Torah together with a worldly occupation, etc.[2]

Another interpretation of WISDOM IS GOOD: Good was the wisdom of Moses, as it is said, *A wise man scaleth the city of the mighty* (Prov. XXI, 22),[3] WITH AN INHERITANCE: since he gave the Torah to Israel as an inheritance. Another interpretation of WISDOM IS GOOD: this is the wisdom of Bezalel who gave the Ark to Israel as an inheritance. When Moses said to him, 'Make an Ark and the vessels and a Tabernacle,'[4] he retorted, 'Our teacher Moses, are we to bring the vessels and suspend them in the air! First let the Tabernacle be constructed and then the Ark.' Moses said to him, 'Perhaps you were sitting in the shadow of God (*beẓel'el*)[5] and so you know [the order in which they are to be made]! First [He commanded], *They shall make an ark* (Ex. XXV, 10), and after that, *Thou shalt make the tabernacle'* (*ib.* XXVI, 1).[6] Hence WISDOM IS GOOD WITH AN INHERITANCE: good was the wisdom of Bezalel, WITH AN INHERITANCE: viz. the Ark which he caused Israel to inherit.

Another interpretation of WISDOM IS GOOD: viz. of Joshua, WITH AN INHERITANCE: since he gave Israel possession of the land. YEA, A PROFIT TO THEM THAT

[1] I.e. wisdom acquired through successive generations of teachers. Or, transmitted from father to son for several generations. It will then be free from error. [2] Ab. II, 2 (Sonc. ed., p. 12).

[3] Perhaps the Midrash applies the verse to Moses' ascent to heaven and receiving the Torah in despite of the angels, who wished to withhold it from him; cf. Ex. R. XXVIII, 1. [4] That is the order in Ex. XXV, 10, 23; XXVI, 1. [5] A play on the name Bezalel.

[6] But in the sequel Bezalel was proved right, because in Ex. XXXI, 7 ff., describing the making of them, the order is reversed. Actually, however, the erection of the Tabernacle was commanded *first* (Ex. XXV, 8) and then the construction of the Ark (in XXV, 10). Commentators accordingly emend: Moses replied, 'By thy life! It was indeed told to me in that order, but it was I who forgot.' Cf. Ber. 55*a*.

SEE THE SUN.[1] Another interpretation of WISDOM IS GOOD: when it is accompanied by ancestral merit. Happy is he when the merit of his ancestors abides with and illumines him!

1. [FOR WISDOM IS A DEFENCE, EVEN AS MONEY IS A DEFENCE (VII, 12)]. R. Aḥa said in the name of R. Tanḥum: If a man studied Torah and taught it, observed and performed its precepts, but had the means to support [needy scholars] and failed to do so, behold he comes within the category of *Cursed be he that confirmeth not the words of this law* (Deut. XXVII, 26). If he studied and did not teach or observe or perform the precepts, and had not the means to support [needy scholars] and yet did so [by self-denial], behold he comes within the category of 'Blessed be he that confirmeth the words of this law', since every 'cursed' implies a 'blessed'.[2] R. Huna said: The Holy One, blessed be He, will make a shade and a canopy for those who perform the precepts[3] by the side of those who have acquired a knowledge of Torah. What was the reason for his dictum? FOR WISDOM IS A DEFENCE, EVEN AS MONEY IS A DEFENCE.[4]

Three hundred nazirites went up to offer nine hundred sacrifices[5] in the days of Simeon b. Sheṭaḥ. In the case of one hundred and fifty he found a way out[6] but not with the rest. Simeon b. Sheṭaḥ went to King Jannaeus[7] and

[1] M.K. remarks that a commentator adds here the note: As he said, *Sun, stand thou still upon Gibeon* (Josh. X, 12). Radal suggests as the correct reading: WISDOM IS GOOD: i.e. ancestral merit, YEA, A PROFIT TO THEM THAT SEE THE SUN: happy, etc.

[2] For the reverse. *Yaḳim* (E.V. '*confirmeth*') is understood to mean to uphold, whence to support. Hence if one *does* support the Torah (through supporting its students) he is blessed.

[3] Here, those who support needy students.

[4] Lit. 'in the shadow of wisdom, in the shadow of money'. The money mentioned here was utilised in benevolence, particularly in maintaining poor scholars.

[5] On the fulfilment of his vow, the nazirite had to bring three offerings (Num. VI, 14).

[6] He discovered a flaw in their vow which rendered it null, and so absolved them from the necessity of bringing the sacrifices.

[7] His brother-in-law. Alexander Jannaeus was king of Judea 105–79 B.C.E.

said to him, 'There are three hundred nazirites who wish to offer nine hundred sacrifices, but they have not the means. You give a half from your resources and I will give half from mine, so that they may go and sacrifice.' Jannaeus gave half and [the hundred and fifty] went and brought their offerings. People came and slandered Simeon b. Sheṭaḥ to King Jannaeus, telling him, 'All that the nazirites offered was provided by you, and Simeon b. Sheṭaḥ has contributed nothing.' When he heard this he was enraged against Simeon b. Sheṭaḥ, and when the latter heard it he fled. Some time later certain men from the kingdom of Persia were there, sitting at the table of King Jannaeus. While at the meal they said to Jannaeus, 'Your Majesty, we remember that there was an old man here who expounded to us the words of the Torah.' He said to Salome, [Simeon's] sister, the wife of Jannaeus, 'Send and fetch him.' She replied, 'Give me your word [that you will not harm him] and send him your ring [as a sign of goodwill]; then he will come.' He gave her his word and Simeon came. On his arrival he sat between the king and queen. Jannaeus asked him, 'Why did you flee?' He answered, 'I heard that you were angry with me, and I was afraid of you lest you should kill me; so I fled and fulfilled this verse, *Hide thyself for a little moment, until the indignation be overpast* (Isa. XXVI, 20).' 'Why did you deceive me?' the king asked. 'Heaven forfend!' he replied, 'I did not deceive you; but [you paid] with your money and I with my learning,[1] as it is written, FOR WISDOM IS A DEFENCE, EVEN AS MONEY IS A DEFENCE.' 'Why did you seat yourself between the king and queen?' He replied, 'It is thus written in the Book of Ben Sira, *Extol her* [Torah], *and she shall exalt thee and make thee to sit between princes*.'[2] The king said to him, 'Do you see how I pay you respect?' He replied, 'Not you, but my learning gains me respect, as it is written, "*Extol her, and she shall exalt thee.*"'

[1] Through which he was able to absolve 150.

[2] The first half of the quotation is from Prov. IV, 8, and the second half from the Apocryphal book, Ecclesiasticus XI, 1.

The king told his attendants, 'Mix a cup of wine for him that he may say Grace.' He asked, 'What formula shall I use in the Grace?[1] Shall I say, "Blessed be He of whose bounty Jannaeus has eaten"?' The king exclaimed, 'You still remain obstinate! Never have I heard Jannaeus mentioned in the Grace!' He retorted, 'Am I to say, "Blessed be He of whose bounty *we* have eaten" when I have not eaten?' He ordered, 'Bring him something to eat'; and after his meal he said, 'Blessed be He of whose bounty we have eaten.'

R. Joḥanan said: Simeon b. Sheṭaḥ's colleagues were at variance with him [over this incident]. R. Abin said: [They differed] over the second part,[2] but R. Jeremiah said: Over the first part.[3] This statement of R. Jeremiah must be reversed,[4] because there it was plain to him but here he was in doubt.[5] There it was plain to him in accordance with the view of R. Simeon b. Gamaliel, but here he was in doubt in accordance with the view of the Rabbis. For it has been learnt: If a man went up, sat down with others at table and ate the relish with them, although he did not partake with them a quantity of corn-food equal to the size of an olive, he is to be included for *zimmun*. This is the statement of the Rabbis; but R. Jacob b. Aḥa said in the name of R. Issi: He may never be included for *zimmun* until he has eaten a quantity of corn-food equal to the size of an olive. It has further been learnt: If two have eaten corn-food and one has eaten other than corn-food, he may be included with them [for *zimmun*]. In accordance with whom do we rule thus? In accordance with R. Simeon b. Gamaliel.

[1] For the introductory formula, v. A.P.B., p. 279.
[2] His ruling that he could not recite Grace for them until he had eaten.
[3] That he said, 'Blessed be He of whose bounty Jannaeus has eaten,' although he had not joined in their meal.
[4] And R. Jeremiah's opinion must be contrary to Simeon's with regard to his ruling that he had to eat before reciting Grace for others.
[5] 'There' (in the case of Simeon) he was sure that Simeon could recite Grace in the circumstances, but 'here' (the case mentioned in J. Ber. 11*b*) he was doubtful whether a person who had only partaken of vegetables could recite Grace; v. Gen. R. XCI, 3.

Three councillors were in Jerusalem, viz. Ben Ẓiẓith Hakeseth,[1] Naḳdimon b. Gorion and Ben Kalba-Shebua, each of whom was capable of supplying food for the city[2] for ten years. There was also there Ben Baṭṭiaḥ,[3] the nephew of R. Joḥanan b. Zakkai, who was appointed in charge of the stores, as chief of the zealots[4] in Jerusalem, and he arose and burnt the storehouses.[5] When R. Joḥanan b. Zakkai heard of this he exclaimed, 'Woe!' It was reported to Ben Baṭṭiaḥ, 'Your uncle exclaimed "Woe!"' He sent and had him brought, and asked, 'Why did you exclaim "Woe!"?' He replied, 'I did not exclaim "Woe!" but "Weh!"[6] because so long as the precious stores were intact the people would not jeopardise their lives in battle.' Through the difference between 'woe' and 'weh' R. Joḥanan escaped death[7]; and the verse was applied to him, THE EXCELLENCY OF KNOWLEDGE IS, THAT WISDOM PRESERVETH THE LIFE OF HIM THAT HATH IT.

It is related of R. Joḥanan that he was once seized with faintness through hunger. He went to Emmaus and sat down to the east of a fig-tree[8] and was cured. He was asked, 'Whence have you [that the fig is a remedy]?' He replied, 'From David, as it is written, *And they gave him a piece of a cake of figs . . . and when he had eaten, his spirit came back to him* (I Sam. XXX, 12)'; and they applied to him the text, THE EXCELLENCY OF KNOWLEDGE IS, THAT WISDOM PRESERVETH THE LIFE OF HIM THAT HATH IT.

R. Jose b. Jasin was journeying in a boat, coming from Tarshish, when his attendant said to him, 'I require to go down [into the water to immerse myself because of my ritual impurity].' He answered, 'You should not go

[1] In Giṭ. 56*a* it is said that he was given this name because his fringes (*ẓiẓith*) used to trail on cushions (*keseth*). [2] Jerusalem.

[3] He was a leader of the zealot party. [4] Reading סיקרין for קסרין.

[5] To induce the men to go out to fight and obtain food.

[6] An exclamation denoting approval.

[7] The zealot would have had his uncle put to death if he had expressed disapproval. This anecdote is related in Lam. R. I, 5.

[8] M.K. remarks that there is a reading which inserts here 'and ate of its figs'.

down into the sea because it is dangerous.' The attendant said, 'But I wish to recite the *shema*'.'[1] 'Recite it,' he replied.[2] 'I want to eat,' he said. 'Then eat,' was the answer. When they reached the harbour, R. Jose said to him, 'You are now forbidden to do these things until you have bathed'; and the text was applied to him, THE EXCELLENCY OF KNOWLEDGE IS, THAT WISDOM PRESERVETH THE LIFE OF HIM THAT HATH IT.[3]

R. Meir was being sought by the [Roman] Government.[4] He fled and passed by the store of some Romans. He found them sitting and eating swine's flesh. When they saw him they said, 'Is it he or not? Since it may be he, let us call him over to us; if he comes and eats with us [it cannot be he].' He dipped one of his fingers in the swine's blood and placed another finger in his mouth, dipping one finger and sucking the other. They said one to the other, 'If he were R. Meir, he would not have done so.'[5] They let him go and he fled. The text was therefore applied to him, THE EXCELLENCY OF KNOWLEDGE IS, THAT WISDOM PRESERVETH THE LIFE OF HIM THAT HATH IT.

Rabbi [Judah ha-Nasi] was dying in Sepphoris and the men of that town declared, 'Whoever comes and announces that Rabbi has died will be put to death by us.' Bar Ḳappara went, looked through a window,[6] and squeezed himself in, his head being wrapped up and his garments rent[7] and exclaimed, 'My brethren, sons of Jedayah,[8] hear me, hear me! Angels and mortals have taken hold of the tablets of the covenant.[9] The angels were victorious and have snatched the tablets.' They cried, 'Rabbi is dead!' He said to them, 'It is you who have said it; I have not said

[1] According to the law this might not be done when a person was ritually unclean. [2] Although he had not bathed.
[3] The Rabbi's knowledge of the law may have saved the attendant from drowning. [4] For abducting his sister-in-law from a brothel; v. 'A.Z. 18*b* (Sonc. ed., p. 93 f.). [5] They did not notice the deception.
[6] Where the people were assembled.
[7] Signs of mourning.—He knew by now that Rabbi was dead.
[8] A name given to Sepphoris because the levitical family of Jedayah had been exiled there. [9] I.e. Rabbi, the eminent teacher of the Torah.

it.' Why did he not say it? Because it is written, *He that uttereth a bad report*[1] *is a fool* (Prov. x, 18). They rent their garments [so violently] that the sound of the tearing reached Gufta three miles away; and the text was applied to him, THE EXCELLENCY OF KNOWLEDGE IS, THAT WISDOM PRESERVETH THE LIFE OF HIM THAT HATH IT.

R. Nehemiah said in the name of R. Mana: Miracles took place on that day. It was the eve of the Sabbath, and the inhabitants of all the cities assembled for the mourning over Rabbi. They set his body down in eighteen Synagogues and then conveyed him to Beth Shearim,[2] and the day was extended for them until each Israelite was able to reach home, kindle his Sabbath light, roast his fish, and fill his cask with water. When the last of them had done this, the sun set and the cock crowed.[3] The people began to cry out, 'Woe, we have desecrated the Sabbath!' A *Bath Ḳol* went forth and declared, 'Whoever was not remiss in mourning for Rabbi is destined for the life of the World to Come, with the exception of Ḳaẓra[4] who was there but did not accompany the funeral procession.' On hearing this, the man went up and threw himself from the roof, killing himself with the fall. A *Bath Ḳol* went forth and said, 'Also Ḳaẓra for [what he did on] the roof[5] is destined for the life of the World to Come.'

1. CONSIDER THE WORK OF GOD; FOR WHO CAN MAKE THAT STRAIGHT WHICH HE HATH MADE CROOKED (VII, 13)? When the Holy One, blessed be He, created the first man, He took him and led him round all the trees of the Garden of Eden, and said to him, 'Behold My works, how beautiful and commendable they are! All that I have created, for your sake I created it. Pay heed that you do not corrupt and destroy My universe;

[1] E.V. '*slander*'. [2] Near Sepphoris.
[3] It was actually the dawn of the next day.
[4] Either a proper name or 'a fuller'. [5] Radal suggests the reading: 'and announced from the roof, "Also Ḳaẓra," etc.'

for if you corrupt it there is no one to repair it after you. Not only that, but you will cause death to befall that righteous man [Moses].'[1]

To what may our teacher Moses be likened? To a pregnant woman shut up in a prison. She gave birth there to a son, reared him there and died there. After a while the king passed by the entrance of the prison, and as he passed the son began to cry, 'My lord king, here was I born and here I grew up. For what sin I am kept here I do not know.' He answered, 'For your mother's sin.' So was it with Moses, as it is written, *The Lord God said: Behold, the man*[2] *is become as one of us* (Gen. III, 22), and it is written, *Behold, thy days approach that thou must die*[3] (Deut. XXXI, 14).

1. IN THE DAY OF PROSPERITY BE JOYFUL (VII, 14). If a happy day befall you, make use of it at once. AND IN THE DAY OF ADVERSITY CONSIDER: consider how to repent so that you may be delivered from the doom of Gehinnom. R. Judan said in the name of R. Eliezer: Three things annul decrees, viz. prayer, charity, and repentance, and all three are mentioned in one verse, as it is written, *If My people, upon whom My name is called, shall humble themselves, and pray, and seek My face, and turn from their evil ways; then will I hear from heaven, and will forgive their sin, and will heal their land* (II Chron. VII, 14). '*And pray,*' i.e. prayer; '*And seek My face,*' i.e. charity, as it is stated, *I shall behold Thy face in righteousness* (Ps. XVII, 15); '*And turn from their evil ways,*' i.e. repentance. Following on these '*Then will I hear from heaven*', etc. R. Mana said: Fasting also [annuls evil decrees], as it is stated, *The Lord answer thee in the day of trouble* (*ib.* XX, 2).[4] Why? GOD HATH MADE EVEN THE ONE AS WELL AS THE OTHER.[5]

[1] By bringing death into the world as a punishment.
[2] I.e. Moses. He was godlike and should have been immortal.—*Man* is identified with Moses probably because '*behold*' occurs in both verses.
[3] He had to die because of Adam's sin which resulted in all men becoming mortal. [4] Repeated from v, 6. [5] Lit. 'one to correspond to the other' i.e. prayer, etc., to counteract the penalty of sin.

2. R. Tanhum b. Ḥiyya interpreted the verse of the poor and rich. [IN THE DAY OF PROSPERITY:] i.e. in the day when your fellowman is fortunate rejoice with him. AND IN THE DAY OF ADVERSITY CONSIDER: consider how to support the poor so that you may receive a reward on account of them. The following was the practice of R. Tanḥum: if he was accustomed to buy a pound of meat, he would buy two pounds, one for his own portion and one for the poor; or two bundles of vegetables, one for himself and the other for the poor. EVEN THE ONE AS WELL AS THE OTHER: i.e. the poor and rich, that the latter may earn merit through the former.

3. R. Aḥa interpreted the verse as applying to Torah. [IN THE DAY OF PROSPERITY BE JOYFUL:] by rejoicing in the Torah you will rejoice [in the Hereafter]. AND IN THE DAY OF ADVERSITY CONSIDER[1]: be of the onlookers of whom it is written, *And they shall go forth, and look upon the carcasses of the men* (Isa. LXVI, 24), and be not of those who are looked upon of whom it is written, *For their worm shall not die* (*ib.*). EVEN THE ONE AS WELL AS THE OTHER: i.e. Gehinnom and Paradise. What is the distance between them? A handbreadth. R. Johanan said: [They are divided by] a wall. The Rabbis say: They are parallel,[2] so that one should be visible to the other.

R. Levi interpreted the verse as applying to the festivals which I [God] gave you so that you may be joyful and gladden the Holy One, blessed be He, with the sacrifices. Should a year without drought[3] occur, go out to your vineyard, look and be joyful, look at your oliveyard and be joyful. The Holy One, blessed be He, said, 'I have made no interceder for rain so good as the eighth day of the festival of Tabernacles,'[4] as it is written, *On the eighth day ye shall have a solemn assembly* (Num. XXIX, 35).

[1] Lit. 'see'. [2] Lit. 'equal'.
[3] A euphemism for 'a year of drought', i.e. even a bad year.
[4] When prayers for rain are included in the Service.

1. ALL THINGS HAVE I SEEN IN THE DAYS OF MY VANITY (VII, 15). Samuel the lesser was asked, 'What means that which is written, THERE IS A RIGHTEOUS MAN THAT PERISHETH IN HIS RIGHTEOUSNESS?' He replied, 'It is revealed and known before Him at whose word the world came into being that the righteous man will inevitably at some time come to a decline [from his high standard of conduct]. So the Holy One, blessed be He, said, "While he is still in his righteousness I will remove him [from the world]," as it is stated, THERE IS A RIGHTEOUS MAN THAT PERISHETH IN HIS RIGHTEOUSNESS.'

AND THERE IS A WICKED MAN THAT PROLONGETH HIS LIFE IN HIS EVIL-DOING: So long as a man lives the Holy One, blessed be He, looks to him to repent; but when he is dead the hope of his doing so is gone, as it is said, *When a wicked man dieth, his hope*[1] *shall perish* (Prov. XI, 7). It may be likened to a band of robbers shut up in a prison. One of them made an opening and they all escaped, except one who did not escape. When the governor arrived he began to strike him with a stick, saying, 'Ill-starred and hapless wretch! There was an opening before you and you did not escape!' In like manner the Holy One, blessed be He, in the Hereafter says to the wicked, 'Repentance was before you but you did not repent,' therefore *The eyes of the wicked shall fail and they shall have no way to flee, and their hope shall be the drooping of the soul* (Job XI, 20). For three reasons, said R. Josiah, the Holy One, blessed be He, shows forbearance with the wicked in this world: perhaps they will repent, perhaps they will perform some precepts for which the Holy One, blessed be He, can reward them in this world, and perhaps righteous children will issue from them. Thus we find that He showed forbearance with Ahaz[2] from whom issued Hezekiah, and from Shimei issued Mordecai.[3]

[1] So lit. I.e. the hope that he will repent. E.V. '*expectation*'.
[2] God allowed him to reign for 16 years (II Kings XVI, 2).
[3] Est. II, 5. The Talmud (Meg. 13*a*) identifies him with the Shimei of I Kings II, 8.

1. BE NOT RIGHTEOUS OVERMUCH; NEITHER MAKE THYSELF OVERWISE (VII, 16). Be not more righteous than your Creator, as in the case of Saul of whom it is written, *And Saul came to the city of Amalek*, etc. (I Sam. XV, 5). R. Huna and R. Benaiah say: He began to cavil at his Creator, arguing, 'Thus has the Holy One, blessed be He, ordered you, *Now go, and smite Amalek . . . slay both man and woman, infant and suckling, ox and sheep, camel and ass* (*ib.* 3). If the men sinned, how have the women and children, the cattle, ox and ass, sinned!' A *Bath Ḳol* went forth and said, 'BE NOT RIGHTEOUS OVERMUCH, more than thy Creator!' The Rabbis say: Saul began to cavil at the precept of the heifer whose neck was to be broken, saying, 'Scripture declares, *They shall break the heifer's neck there in the valley* (Deut. XXI, 4). A man commits a murder and the neck of a heifer is broken! If a man has sinned, how has the animal sinned!' A *Bath Ḳol* went forth and said, 'BE NOT RIGHTEOUS OVERMUCH.'

R. Simeon b. Laḳish said: Whoever shows himself merciful in circumstances where he should be pitiless, in the end becomes pitiless when he should be merciful. Whence have we that Saul was pitiless when he should have been merciful? As it is said, *And Nob, the city of the priests, smote he with the edge of the sword, both men and women, children and sucklings, and oxen, and asses, and sheep* (I Sam. XXII, 19), and Nob should not have been treated like the seed of Amalek.[1] The Rabbis say: Whoever makes himself merciful in circumstances where he should be pitiless will eventually be overtaken by the Attribute of Justice, as it is said, *So Saul died and his three sons* (*ib.* XXXI, 6).

1. BE NOT OVERMUCH WICKED (VII, 17). R. Berekiah said: Is it, then, allowed to be a little wicked! The meaning, however, is: You should not say that since one

[1] There was no Divine decree that they should be destroyed. Or perhaps: and should not Nob have been treated, etc.?—I.e. Saul should have shown at least as much compassion for Nob as he did for the seed of Amalek.

act has incurred the [Divine] displeasure everything else too [done by the same person] will incur the Divine displeasure.[1]

1. IT IS GOOD THAT THOU SHOULDEST TAKE HOLD OF THE ONE (VII, 18): i.e. Scripture; YEA, ALSO FROM THE OTHER WITHDRAW NOT THY HAND: i.e. Mishnah; FOR HE THAT FEARETH GOD SHALL DISCHARGE HIMSELF OF THEM ALL: as, e.g., R. Abbahu of Cæsarea.[2]

1. WISDOM IS A STRONGHOLD TO THE WISE MAN (VII, 19): i.e. to the Holy One, blessed be He, as it is said, *He is wise in heart, and mighty in strength* (Job IX, 4). THAN TEN RULERS THAT ARE IN A CITY: than the ten 'sayings' with which the world was created.[3]

Another interpretation of WISDOM IS A STRONGHOLD TO THE WISE MAN: i.e. to Adam, as it is written, *Thou seal most accurate, full of wisdom, and perfect in beauty, thou wast in Eden the garden of God* (Ezek. XXVIII, 12 f.). THAN TEN RULERS THAT ARE IN A CITY: i.e. the ten organs that minister to the soul,[4] viz. the gullet for [the passage of] food, the windpipe for voice, the liver for anger, the gall for jealousy, the lungs to absorb liquids, the stomach to grind [food], the milt for laughter, the kidneys to advise, the heart to give understanding, and the tongue to decide.

2. Another interpretation of WISDOM IS A STRONGHOLD TO THE WISE MAN: i.e. Noah, THAN TEN RULERS THAT ARE IN A CITY: than the ten

[1] I.e. do not think that there is no hope in repentance.
[2] In 'A.Z. 4*a* he claimed to be expert in Scripture as well as Mishnah.
[3] Cf. Ab. V, 1. The meaning seems to be that God's wisdom and might are to be learnt from the Torah even more than from the universe, His creation (Mah.). M.K. and 'E.J. render and explain: That God possesses wisdom and strength may be learned from the ten words with which He created the world.
[4] The wisdom of the Torah is a stronghold against the desires of man's physical nature.

generations from Adam to Noah, because out of them all He had converse only with him.[1]

Another interpretation of WISDOM IS A STRONGHOLD TO THE WISE MAN: i.e. to Abraham, THAN TEN RULERS THAT ARE IN A CITY: of the ten generations from Noah to Abraham. The Holy One, blessed be He, did not choose any of them or make a covenant with them but only with him, as it is said, *In that day the Lord made a covenant with Abram* (Gen. xv, 18).

Another interpretation of WISDOM IS A STRONGHOLD TO THE WISE MAN: i.e. to Jacob, THAN TEN RULERS THAT ARE IN A CITY: than the ten [progenitors of the] tribes who went down to Egypt and came up again without knowing that Joseph was alive; but Jacob knew it, as it is said, *Now Jacob saw that there was corn* (sheber) *in Egypt* (*ib.* XLII, 1), i.e. he knew that his hope (*sibro*) was in Egypt.

3. Another interpretation of WISDOM IS A STRONGHOLD TO THE WISE MAN: i.e. to Moses, THAN TEN RULERS THAT ARE IN A CITY: than the ten organs which minister to the body and were subdued by Moses, viz. from the mouth to the gullet, from the gullet to the digestive organ, from the digestive organ to the maw, from the maw to the first stomach,[2] from the first stomach to the duodenum, from the duodenum to the second stomach, from the second stomach to the intestines, from the intestines to the jejunum, from the jejunum to the ileum, from the ileum to the rectum, from the rectum to the anus, and from the anus to outside the body; and Moses had no need of them to let food either in or out, as it is said, *And he was there with the Lord forty days and forty nights; he did neither eat bread, nor drink water* (Ex. XXXIV, 28).

Another interpretation of WISDOM IS A STRONGHOLD TO THE WISE MAN, i.e. to Israel, as it is

[1] Reckoning from after the fall of Adam, since God spoke with him in the Garden. [2] In Lev. R. III, 4, the order is different.

said, *Surely this great nation is a wise and understanding people* (Deut. IV, 6), THAN TEN RULERS THAT ARE IN A CITY: which minister to the soul, viz. the gullet for food, the windpipe for voice, the liver for anger, the gall for jealousy, the lungs to absorb liquids, the stomach to grind [food], the milt for laughter, the kidneys to advise, the heart to give understanding, and the tongue to decide.

4. Another interpretation of WISDOM IS A STRONGHOLD TO THE WISE MAN; i.e. to David, THAN TEN RULERS THAT ARE IN A CITY: than the ten elders who are mentioned in the Book of Psalms, viz. Adam, Abraham, Moses, David, and Solomon. On these five there is no difference of opinion; but who are the other five? Rab and R. Joḥanan give answers. Rab said: Asaph, Heman, Jeduthun, the three sons of Korah who are counted as one, and Ezra.[1] R. Joḥanan said: This Asaph is the same as the Asaph included among the sons of Korah, but because he possessed [a knowledge of] Torah he became worthy to compose a Psalm together with his brothers and also by himself. According to the opinion of Rab, Asaph was distinct from the sons of Korah, as it is said, *Under the hand of Asaph, who prophesied according to the direction of the king* (I Chron. XXV, 2). Rab and R. Joḥanan differ on another point. Rab said: *For Jeduthun* (Ps. XXXIX, 1) refers to an actual person. R. Joḥanan said: '*For Jeduthun*' means: [Asaph] prophesied concerning the laws (*dathin*) and ordinances which passed over him and Israel. R. Huna said in the name of R. Aḥa: Although ten men composed the Book of Psalms,[2] it is named after none of them but after David, king of Israel. They illustrate this by a parable. To what is the matter like? To a band of men who wished to sing a pæan to the king. He said to them, 'You are all pleasant, all pious, all worthy to sing a pæan to me; but let So-and-so sing it for you

[1] Ezra is apparently an error. 'E.J. substitutes Melchizedek who is mentioned in Ps. CX, *q.v.* [2] V. B.B. 14*b*

all because his voice is sweet.' Similarly when the ten righteous men wished to compose the Book of Psalms, the Holy One, blessed be He, said to them, 'You are all pleasant, pious and worthy to utter hymns before Me, but let David utter them for all of you because his voice is sweet.' That is what is written, *The sweet singer of Israel* (II Sam. XXIII, 1).[1]

1. FOR THERE IS NOT A RIGHTEOUS MAN UPON EARTH, THAT DOETH GOOD, AND SINNETH NOT (VII, 20). R. Judan said: Can there be a righteous man who sins? It refers in fact to managers and dispensers of charity who give to the deserving what should be given to the undeserving and *vice versa*. AND SINNETH NOT: the word (*ḥaṭa'*) is here used in the same sense as in, *Every one could sling stones at a hair-breadth, and not miss*—yaḥaṭi' (Judg. XX, 16).[2]

1. ALL THIS HAVE I TRIED BY WISDOM (VII, 23). It is written, *And God gave Solomon wisdom . . . even as the sand that is on the sea-shore* (I Kings V, 9). The Rabbis and R. Levi discuss this statement. The Rabbis say: It is written, '*As the sand.*' What means '*As the sand*'? He was given wisdom equal to that of all Israel.[3] R. Levi said: As the sand is a fence to the sea [that it should not overflow], so was wisdom a fence to Solomon. A proverb declares, 'If thou lackest knowledge, what hast thou acquired? If thou hast acquired knowledge, what lackest thou?' It is written, *And Solomon's wisdom excelled the wisdom of all the children of the east, and all the wisdom in Egypt* (*ib.* 10). What, then, was the wisdom of '*The children of the east*'? They were skilled in astrology and divination with birds and expert in augury. R. Simeon b. Gamaliel said: For three things I praise the men of

[1] Cf. with this paragraph S.S. R. IV, 4, § 1.
[2] The meaning is accordingly: it is impossible for an almoner not to miss his aim in the dispensing of charity, since he cannot always distinguish between the deserving and undeserving. [3] Israel is also compared to the sand which is upon the seashore (Gen. XXII, 17).

the East: they do not kiss on the mouth but on the hand, they do not tear their food with the mouth but cut it with a knife, and they do not take counsel except in an open space, because they do not deliberate except in a field.[1]

What was '*The wisdom of Egypt*'? You find that when Solomon wished to build the Temple he sent to Pharaoh-Neco, saying, 'Send me workmen for hire because I wish to build the Temple.' What did he do? He assembled all his astrologers who forecast the men who were destined to die in the course of the year, and these he sent. When they came to Solomon, he foresaw by the Holy Spirit that they were to die during that year; so he presented them with shrouds and sent them back with the message, 'If you are short of shrouds for the needs of your dead, behold here they are with their shrouds; arise and bury them.'

For he was wiser than all men (*ib.* 11): than Adam. What, then, was Adam's wisdom? You find that when the Holy One, blessed be He, wished to create Adam, He took counsel with the ministering angels and said to them, '*Let us make man*' (Gen. I, 26). They spoke before Him, '*Lord of the universe, what is man, that Thou art mindful of him?* (Ps. VIII, 5).' He replied to them, 'The man whom I desire to create will have wisdom exceeding yours.' What did He do? He gathered all the cattle, beasts, and birds, set them before them, and said, 'Give names to these.' They were nonplussed[2] and knew not [what to call them]. He went to Adam and asked him, 'What are the names of these?' He answered, 'Lord of the universe, it would be proper to call this "ox", and this "lion", and this "horse", and this "camel", and this "eagle",' and so with them all. Then He asked him, 'What is thy name?' He answered, '"Adam," because I was created from the ground (*adamah*).' 'And what is My name?' He answered, '"Lord," because Thou art Lord over all Thy creatures.' That is what is written, *I am the Lord*,

[1] To prevent eavesdropping. [2] Lit. 'stood'.

that is My name (Isa. XLII, 8)—that is the name by which Adam called Me, that is My name which I agreed upon with Myself, that is My name which I agreed upon between Myself, My creatures, and the ministering angels.

Than Ethan the Ezrahite (I Kings V, 11)[1]: than Abraham,[2] as it is written, *Maschil of Ethan the Ezrahite* (Ps. LXXXIX, 1). *And Heman* (I Kings *loc. cit.*): i.e. Moses, as it is written, *He is trusted* (ne'eman) *in all My house* (Num. XII, 7). *And Calcol:* i.e. Joseph, as it is written, *And Joseph sustained*—kilkel (Gen. XLVII, 12). The Egyptians exclaimed, 'Would this slave have been king over us but for his wisdom?' They took seventy[3] tablets and placed them before him and he read each one in its language. Not only that, but he used to speak in the holy tongue[4] with which they were unfamiliar and so they could not understand him, as it is said, *He appointed it in Joseph for a testimony . . . the speech of one that I knew not did I hear* (Ps. LXXXI, 6). *And Darda:* i.e. the generation (*dor*) of the wilderness which was altogether imbued with knowledge (*de'ah*). *The sons of Mahol:* i.e. Israel whom the Holy One, blessed be He, forgave (*maḥal*) for the incident of the golden calf.

2. *And he spoke three thousand proverbs* (I Kings V, 12). R. Samuel b. Naḥmani said: We have searched the whole of Scripture and we cannot find that Solomon composed[5] more than some eight hundred verses, and you say, '*three thousand*'! It teaches, however, that every verse which Solomon composed contains two or three meanings. The Rabbis say: It means that in connection with every verse he composed three thousand proverbs, and to every proverb there are a thousand and five meanings; as it is written, *And his songs* (shiro)—i.e. the remainder of (*shiyyuro*) the proverbs—*Were a thousand and five* (*ib.*).[6]

[1] Returning to the text: *He* (Solomon) *was wiser than all men.*
[2] Cf. Lev. R. IX, 1.
[3] Seventy was the traditional number of the languages of the world. Each tablet was inscribed with a different language.
[4] Hebrew.
[5] Lit. 'prophesied'.
[6] Cf. I, 13, and the different rendering given there of this last phrase, which should possibly be repeated here.

3. *And he spoke of trees* (*ib.* 13): is it, then, possible for a man to speak of trees? Solomon in fact asked, 'Why is the leper purified by means of the tallest and lowliest of trees, viz. with the cedar and hyssop?[1] Because through making himself lofty like the cedar a man is smitten with leprosy; but when he makes himself small and humbles himself like the hyssop, which is a lowly plant, he will eventually be healed.' Similarly, why is an animal rendered permissible as food through [the cutting of] two organs[2] and a bird through one organ? Because the animal is created from dry land and the bird from the sea[3]; as Bar Ḳappara said: Birds were created from alluvial mud. R. Abin said in the name of R. Samuel of Cappadocia: The feet of the fowl resemble [in their covering] the scale-covered skin of fish.[4]

And of creeping things (I Kings V, 13): Solomon asked, 'Why in the case of eight creeping things mentioned in the Torah is one liable if he catches or wounds any of them on the Sabbath,[5] but he is not culpable in the case of the other creeping things, forbidden animals, and reptiles? Because they have skins.' *And of fishes* (*ib.*): He asked, 'Why do all cattle, beasts, and birds require the ritual act of slaughter (*sheḥiṭah*) but fish do not? It is deduced from the following verse, *If flocks and herds be slain* (Num. XI, 22),[6] but in connection with fish it is not written ["*slain*"] but *If all the fish of the sea be gathered together for them*' (*ib.*).[7]

Jacob of Kefar-Nibbuyara[8] gave a ruling in Tyre that fish required *sheḥiṭah*. R. Haggai heard of it and sent and had him brought. He asked him, 'From where did you get your decision?' He answered, 'From the text, *Let*

[1] Lev. XIV, 49. [2] I.e. both the gullet and the windpipe have to be cut to constitute a proper act of *sheḥiṭah*.
[3] Cf. Gen. I, 20, 24. Now animals require the cutting of both organs, while fish require no *sheḥiṭah* at all. Therefore in the case of birds a compromise is made, and one organ must be severed.
[4] This is evidence of the origin of birds from the element of water.
[5] V. Shab. XIV, I. [6] The technical term *shaḥaṭ* is used here.
[7] I.e. they can be taken home and eaten without *sheḥiṭah*.
[8] Near Tiberias.

the waters swarm with swarms of living creatures, and let fowl fly above the earth (Gen. I, 20)—as birds require *sheḥiṭah* so do fish.' He exclaimed, 'Lay him down that he may receive lashes.' Jacob answered, 'Shall a man who expounds something from the Torah receive lashes!' He answered, 'You have not decided correctly.' He asked, 'From where, then, [should the law be deduced]?' He replied, 'From the following: *If flocks and herds, etc.*, i.e. the former by *sheḥiṭah* and the latter [fish] by gathering.' He said, 'Go on with your beating, because there is benefit in receiving punishment.'[1]

4. Jacob of Kefar-Nibbuyara gave a ruling in Tyre that the son of a heathen woman may be circumcised on the Sabbath. R. Haggai heard of it and sent and had him brought. He asked him, 'From where did you get your decision?' He answered, 'From the text, *And they declared their pedigrees* (yithyalledu) *after their families* (Num. I, 18), and it is also written [in connection with circumcision], *He that is born* (yelid) *in the house or bought with money* (Gen. XVII, 12).'[2] He exclaimed, 'Lay him down that he may receive lashes.' Jacob said, 'Shall a man who expounds something from the Torah receive lashes!' He answered, 'You have not decided correctly.' He asked, 'From where, then, [should the law be deduced]?' He replied, 'Lie down [to be punished] and listen. If a son of gentile parents comes to you, saying, "I wish to be made a Jew on condition that you circumcise me on the Sabbath or the Day of Atonement," may the holy day be desecrated for him or not? Of course it may not, because the Sabbath and the Day of Atonement may only be desecrated for the son of an Israelite father and mother.' 'On what grounds [do you say thus]?' he asked; and R. Haggai answered, 'Lie down [and listen]: *To put away all the wives and such as are born of them* (Ezra X, 3).' He exclaimed, 'Would you punish me because of something which is derived from

[1] He admitted his error, and the thrashing would teach him to be more careful in deciding questions of law. [2] Cf. Gen. R. VII, 2.

a non-Pentateuchal book!' He answered, 'But it is written there, *And let it be done according to the Torah* (*ib.*).' He asked, 'From which [verse of the] Torah?' 'It is stated, *Neither shalt thou make marriages with them* (Deut. VII, 3). Why? *For he will turn away thy son* (*ib.* 4)—"*thy son,*" one who comes from an Israelite mother is called "*thy son*", but thy son who issues from a Gentile woman or a handmaid is not called [technically] "*thy son*" but "her son"!' He said, 'Go on with your beating, because there is benefit in receiving punishment.'

Solomon said: Concerning all these [ordinances of the Torah] I have stood and investigated [their meaning], but the chapter of the Red Heifer[1] I have been unable to fathom. When I laboured therein and searched deeply into it, I SAID: I WILL GET WISDOM; BUT IT WAS FAR FROM ME.

1. AND I FIND MORE BITTER THAN DEATH THE WOMAN (VII, 26). The Rabbis say: Because she demands of man things which are beyond his power she ultimately kills him with a bitter death. A man once had a neighbour who was a bandit and used to go out to commit robbery at night, while by day he supported his sons and daughters [in comfort]. That man's wife exclaimed, 'How unlucky I am to be attached to you! Do you not see how [luxuriously] our neighbour's children eat and drink?' The husband said to her, 'Do you want me to act like him?' She replied, 'What of it!' He said to her, 'Come and persuade him to let me go with him.' They went and persuaded him, so that he agreed to take him with him. The bandit went out [with his men to rob] that night, but the guard had planned to go after them. Since he was familiar with the roads he fled and was saved; but this man, being ignorant of the roads, was captured and hanged, and they quoted the proverb over him, 'The last of the robbers is the first of the hanged.'

[1] Num. XIX.

2. Three complaints are serious to the body: heart disease is serious to the body, disease of the bowels is more serious to the body than heart disease, but an empty purse is most serious of all.

R. Judah said: There are fourteen things which are stronger one than the other, and each one is dominated by the next. The ocean-deep is strong, but the earth dominates it because the deep is subservient to it. The earth is strong, but the mountains are stronger and dominate it. The mountain is strong, but iron dominates it and breaks it. Iron is strong, but fire makes it melt away. Fire is strong, but water dominates it and extinguishes it. Water is strong, but the clouds carry it. The clouds are strong, but wind disperses them. The wind is strong, but a wall dominates and withstands it. A wall is strong, but a man dominates and demolishes it. Man is strong, but trouble creeps over [and weakens] him. Trouble is strong, but wine dominates it and causes it to be forgotten. Wine is strong, but sleep overcomes its effects. Sleep is strong, but illness dominates it and prevents it. Illness is strong, but the Angel of Death dominates it and takes life away. Stronger [i.e. worse] than them all, however, is a bad woman.

3. WHOSE HEART IS SNARES AND NETS: because she catches [her victims] both on the sea and the dry land.[1] HER HANDS ARE BOUND: R. Eleazar said: Were it not for the fact that it is written HER HANDS AS BANDS,[2] she would take hold of a man in the street and say to him, 'Come and be intimate with me.' She may be likened to a biting bitch which its owner holds by a chain, and although it is tied up it seizes a man by his garments in the street. Similarly were it not for the fact that it is written HER HANDS ARE BOUND, a woman would snatch at a man in the street. See what is written,

[1] SNARES are used to trap animals and NETS to catch fish.

[2] So lit.; i.e. she is under the law, *He shall rule over thee* (Gen. III, 16), i.e. it is usual for a man to solicit the woman and not *vice versa*. E.V. '*And her hands as bands*'.

She caught him by his garment, saying: Lie with me (Gen. XXXIX, 12). WHOSO PLEASETH GOD SHALL ESCAPE FROM HER: i.e. Joseph, BUT THE SINNER SHALL BE TAKEN BY HER: i.e. Potiphar. Another interpretation of WHOSO PLEASETH: i.e. Phinehas, BUT THE SINNER: i.e. Zimri.[1] Another interpretation of WHOSO PLEASETH: i.e. Palti,[2] BUT THE SINNER: i.e. Amnon.[3]

R. Issi of Cæsarea interpreted the verse as applying to heresy. WHOSO PLEASETH: i.e. R. Eleazar, BUT THE SINNER: i.e. Jacob of Kefar-Nibbuyara. Another illustration of WHOSO PLEASETH: i.e. Eleazar b. Dama, BUT THE SINNER: i.e. Jacob of Kefar-Sama. Another illustration of WHOSO PLEASETH: i.e. Ḥananiah the nephew of R. Joshua, BUT THE SINNER: i.e. the inhabitants of Capernaum. Another illustration of WHOSO PLEASETH: i.e. Judah b. Naḳosa, BUT THE SINNER: i.e. the *minim*. Another illustration of WHOSO PLEASETH: i.e. R. Nathan, BUT THE SINNER: i.e. his disciple. Another illustration of WHOSO PLEASETH: i.e. R. Eliezer and R. Joshua, BUT THE SINNER: i.e. Elisha.[4]

1. BEHOLD, THIS HAVE I FOUND, SAITH ḲOHELETH (VII, 27). [The verb SAITH is feminine] whereas in another passage[5] it is masculine! R. Jeremiah said: It alludes to the Holy Spirit which is sometimes used as masculine and sometimes as feminine.

ADDING ONE THING TO ANOTHER, TO FIND OUT THE ACCOUNT. R. Isaac said: Usually when a man comes to grief through sin and incurs the penalty of death at the hand of Heaven, how is atonement made for him? His ox dies, or his poultry is lost, or his flask

[1] Num. XXV, 14.
[2] Saul's son-in-law, who since his marriage with Michal was invalid, refused to consummate it (v. Sanh. 19*b*, Sonc. ed., p. 103).
[3] V. II Sam. XIII, 14.
[4] Most of the names occur in the reference to the *minim* in I, 8. Elisha may be Elisha b. Abuyah the apostate. [5] Sc. in I, 2.

is broken, or he stumbles [and injures] his little finger and a drop of blood flows from it,[1] and a part of life is as the whole of life[2]; as it is said, ADDING ONE THING TO ANOTHER, TO FIND OUT THE ACCOUNT—one [sin] is added to another and the account [of the transgression] is exacted. To what point is the account exacted?[3] R. Phinehas said: Even for a single [transgression].

1. WHICH YET MY SOUL SOUGHT, BUT I FOUND NOT; ONE MAN AMONG A THOUSAND HAVE I FOUND (VII, 28). Usually if a thousand men take up the study of Scripture, a hundred of them proceed to the study of Mishnah, ten to Talmud, and one of them becomes qualified to decide questions of law. That is what is written, ONE MAN AMONG A THOUSAND HAVE I FOUND. Another interpretation of MAN: i.e. Abraham, BUT A WOMAN AMONG ALL THOSE HAVE I NOT FOUND: i.e. Sarah.[4] Another interpretation of MAN: i.e. Amram, BUT A WOMAN: i.e. Jochebed. Another interpretation of MAN: i.e. Moses, BUT A WOMAN: i.e. the wives of the men in the wilderness.[5] Another interpretation of MAN: i.e. Moses who came in the thousandth generation, BUT A WOMAN: i.e. the Torah[6] which was given to the thousandth generation, as it is written, *The word which He commanded to a thousand generations* (Ps. CV, 8). This teaches that the Holy One, blessed be He, examined all the vessels but found none so well pitched as that of Moses[7] who stretched forth his hand and received the Torah.

[1] This is the substituted punishment.
[2] The blood being the life (Gen. IX, 4), God accepts the drop as though it were the life of the sinner.
[3] This is the apparent meaning here, and it is so explained by 'E.J. V. Gen. R. XLIX, 13; the rendering there, however, would be irrelevant here. [4] She seems to be mentioned as the exception who is worthy of distinction. [5] V. Lev. R. II, 1. [6] The word is feminine.
[7] Hence watertight—i.e. who would prove a worthy receptacle for the Torah. Moses was the 26th generation from the Creation of the world, and the Rabbis hold that 974 generations which God contemplated creating were left uncreated. Thus the Torah was given to the thousandth (intended) generation.

1. BEHOLD, THIS ONLY HAVE I FOUND, THAT GOD MADE MAN UPRIGHT (VII, 29). [Adam] was upright, as it is said, THAT GOD MADE MAN (ADAM) UPRIGHT, and it is written, *Behold, the man was*[1] *as one of us* (Gen. III, 22)—as one of the ministering angels. When, however, he became two,[2] then THEY SOUGHT OUT MANY INVENTIONS.[3]

[1] This is the Midrashic interpretation. E.V. '*is become*'.
[2] By the creation of Eve.
[3] Adam then lost his uprightness and sinned.

CHAPTER VIII

1. WHO IS AS THE WISE MAN (VIII, 1)? This alludes to the Holy One, blessed be He, of whom it is written, *He is wise in heart, and mighty in strength* (Job IX, 4.) AND WHO KNOWETH THE INTERPRETATION OF A THING? [That is God] who expounded the Torah to Moses. A MAN'S WISDOM MAKETH HIS FACE TO SHINE: R. Simeon said: Great is the power of the prophets in that they liken the creature to his Creator, for it is written, *And I heard the voice of a Man* [i.e. God] *between the banks of Ulai* (Dan. VIII, 16). R. Judan said: There is a clearer text than that, as it is written, *And upon the likeness of the throne was a likeness as the appearance of a man upon it above* (Ezek. I, 26).[1] AND THE BOLDNESS OF HIS FACE IS CHANGED: because He changes from the Attribute of Judgment to the Attribute of Mercy towards Israel.

2. Another interpretation of WHO IS AS THE WISE MAN? This alludes to Adam of whom it is written, *Thou seal most accurate, full of wisdom . . . thou wast in Eden the garden of God* (*ib.* XXVIII, 12 f.). AND WHO KNOWETH THE INTERPRETATION OF A THING? Because he gave distinguishing names to all things.[2] A MAN'S WISDOM MAKETH HIS FACE TO SHINE: his beauty[3] made his face to shine. R. Levi said: The ball of Adam's heel outshone the sun. Do not be surprised at this, because usually when a man makes two complete[4] salvers, one for himself and another for a member of his household, whose does he make more beautiful? Is it not his own? Similarly, Adam was created for the service of the Holy One, blessed be He, and the sun for the service of Adam; so was it not right that the ball of his heel

[1] V. *supra* on II, 21. [2] V. VII, 23.
[3] Which reflected the wisdom with which God had endowed him.
[4] In Lev. R. XX, 2, 'complete' is omitted.

should outshine the sun, and how much more so the beauty of his face!

R. Levi said in the name of R. Ḥama b. Ḥanina: The Holy One, blessed be He, set up thirteen canopies for them in the Garden of Eden, as it is written, '*Thou wast in Eden the garden of God.*'[1] R. Simeon b. Laḳish said that he made eleven canopies, while the Rabbis declare that the number was ten. They do not differ [in the source of their statements]; but he who said there were thirteen counted *Every precious stone was thy covering* (*ib.*) as indicating three canopies, he who said there were eleven counted this as one, and they who said there were ten did not make even one of it. And after all this glory [sentence was passed upon Adam], *Dust thou art, and unto dust shalt thou return* (Gen. III, 19). AND THE BOLDNESS OF HIS FACE IS CHANGED: When the Holy One, blessed be He, said to him, *Hast thou eaten of the tree?* (*ib.* 11), the anger of the Holy One, blessed be He, caused the boldness of his face to change and He expelled him from the Garden of Eden.

3. Another interpretation of WHO IS AS THE WISE MAN? This alludes to Israel of whom it is written, *Surely this great nation is a wise and understanding people* (Deut. IV, 6). AND WHO KNOWETH THE INTERPRETATION OF A THING? Because they knew how to explain the Torah with forty-nine reasons for the ritual cleanness [of an object] and a corresponding number for its uncleanness. You find that when Israel stood at Mount Sinai and said, *All that the Lord hath spoken will we do, and hear* (Ex. XXIV, 7), there was granted them something of the lustre of the *Shechinah* of the Most High. When they sinned, however, they were made haters of[2] the Holy One, blessed be He, as it is written, AND THE BOLDNESS OF HIS FACE CHANGED,[3] and the anger of the

(Sonc. ed., p. 302), Gen. R. XVIII, 1.
,uld be emended to 'they became hated by'.
b., by the change in the verb, can mean, 'but he who is bold : hated.'

Holy One, blessed be He, changed the words applied to them into what is written, *Nevertheless ye shall die like men* (Ps. LXXXII, 7).

4. Another interpretation of WHO IS AS THE WISE MAN? This alludes to a Rabbinical scholar. AND WHO KNOWETH THE INTERPRETATION OF A THING? Because he knows how to expound his learning. A MAN'S WISDOM MAKETH HIS FACE TO SHINE: when he is asked a question and is able to answer. AND THE BOLDNESS OF HIS FACE IS CHANGED: when he is asked a question and does not know how to answer. R. Ḥiyya was sitting and teaching, 'Whence do we learn that the law of substitution does not apply to a firstling?'[1] when the face of Bar Pedaiah brightened, and he [R. Ḥiyya] said, 'This man knows what I sit and teach.'

An idolater saw R. Judah b. R. Ilai, and, noticing that his face shone, exclaimed, 'This man is one of three things: he is either intoxicated, or a usurer, or a breeder of pigs.' R. Judah b. R. Ilai heard the remark and said, 'A curse upon you! I am none of these three things. I am not a usurer, for it is written, *Thou shalt not lend upon interest to thy brother* (Deut. XXIII, 20); nor am I a breeder of pigs because this is forbidden to a son of Israel, as we have learnt in the Mishnah: It is not right to breed pigs in any place whatever.[2] Nor am I intoxicated, for even the four cups of wine which I drink on the night of Passover[3] give me a headache from Passover to Pentecost.'[4] 'Why, then, is your face so bright?' he asked; and the Rabbi answered, 'My study of Torah brightens my face, as it is written, A MAN'S WISDOM MAKETH HIS FACE TO SHINE.'

R. Abbahu went to Cæsarea, and when he returned from there his face was shining. On seeing him the disciples went and said to R. Joḥanan: 'This R. Abbahu must have

[1] V. Lev. XXVII, 33, and Naz. 7*b* Mishnah. [2] B.Ḳ. VII, 7.
[3] The ritual in the home on this occasion includes the drinking of four cups of wine. [4] Which occurs seven weeks later.

found a treasure.' 'Why [do you say so]?' he asked; and they replied, 'His face is shining.' He said to them, 'Perhaps he heard a new point of Torah.' They went to him and asked, 'What new point of Torah did you hear?' He replied, 'An ancient *Tosefta*[1] was quoted [in Cæsarea]'; and they applied to him the text, A MAN'S WISDOM MAKETH HIS FACE TO SHINE.

5. Another interpretation of WHO IS AS THE WISE MAN? This alludes to Moses of whom it is written, *A wise man scaleth the city of the mighty* (Prov. XXI, 22). AND WHO KNOWETH THE INTERPRETATION OF A THING? Because he expounded the Torah to Israel. R. Mana of Shaab[2] said in the name of R. Joshua b. Levi: In connection with every law which the Holy One, blessed be He, communicated to Moses, He expounded to him its uncleanness and purification[3]; but when He reached the chapter, *Speak unto the priests* (Lev. XXI),[4] he spoke before Him, 'Lord of the universe, if these [the priests] are defiled wherewith do they regain their state of purity?' He gave no answer, and at that time the face of Moses changed.[5] When, however, He reached the chapter of the Red Heifer,[6] the Holy One, blessed be He, said to Moses, 'Moses, when I made to you the statement, "*Speak unto the priests,*" and you asked Me, "If they are defiled wherewith do they regain their state of purity?" I gave you no answer. This is their method of purification, *And for the unclean they shall take of the ashes of the burning of the purification from sin* (Num. XIX, 17).' He spoke before Him, 'Lord of the universe, is this purification?'[7] The Holy One, blessed be He, replied, 'Moses, it is a statute, and I have made a decree, and nobody

[1] Lit. 'addendum', i.e. a traditional teaching which was not included in the Mishnah. [2] In Galilee.
[3] What renders unclean and how the state of uncleanness is removed.
[4] The circumstances which defile a priest are specified in this chapter.
[5] He was crestfallen because he thought that he was unworthy to receive the instruction. [6] Num. XIX.
[7] How can ashes remove the defilement caused by contact with the dead?

can fathom[1] my decree,' as it is written, *This is the statute of the law* (*ib.* 1).

1. I [COUNSEL THEE]: KEEP THE KING'S COMMAND (VIII, 2).[2] R. Levi said: This means, I will keep the command of the Supreme King of kings, the Holy One, blessed be He, the mouth which uttered, *I am the Lord thy God* (Ex. XX, 2). AND THAT IN REGARD OF: [this refers to,] *Thou shalt have no other gods before Me* (*ib.* 3). THE OATH OF GOD: i.e. *Thou shalt not take the name of the Lord thy God in vain* (*ib.* 7).

1. BE NOT HASTY TO GO OUT OF HIS PRESENCE (VIII, 3): R. Ḥiyya b. Gamda opened his discourse with the text, *My son, despise not the chastening of the Lord* (Prov. III, 11). It has been learnt: [In dividing up a Scriptural reading in the Synagogue] one should begin and conclude with a verse which is auspicious[3]; as the Mishnah declares: In the reading of the section of blessing a break may be made; but in the passage of curses there may be no break, but the same person reads it all.[4] '*My son, despise not the chastening of the Lord,*'[5] because *I will be with him in trouble* (Ps. XCI, 15). The Holy One, blessed be He, said, 'My children are being cursed, and shall I be blessed!'[6] *Neither spurn thou* (taḳoẓ) *His correction* (Prov. *loc. cit.*), i.e. make not the correction[7] of the Holy One, blessed be He, into fragments (*ḳuẓẓin*). R. Levi b. Panṭi once read

[1] Lit. 'stand upon'. 'Decree' is a term for a law to which no rational explanation can be assigned. [2] Lit. 'mouth'. [3] J. Meg. 74*b*.

[4] Meg. III, 6. The reference is to Lev. XXVI, 3 ff., and Deut. XXVIII. In former times each person 'called up' to the Reading of the Law (Pentateuch) actually read a portion himself.

[5] This is understood to mean: do not break off in the middle of the 'chastening', i.e. the passage of the curses—as though you despised it, but read the whole.

[6] After a portion of Scripture is recited it is followed by a benediction. Such a blessing of God is inappropriate after a passage containing curses, since God is Himself involved in the plight of Israel.

[7] The word for *correction* (tokeḥah) is the term for the Scriptural passages containing the curses. They may not be divided when read in the Synagogue.

the 'curses' in the presence of R. Huna and muttered them.[1] He said to him, 'Raise your voice; they are not curses but reproofs. "*My son, despise not the chastening of the Lord, neither spurn thou His correction.*"'

1. FORASMUCH AS THE KING'S WORD HATH POWER (VIII, 4). R. Bun said: It is written, *Ye shall not try the Lord your God* (Deut. VI, 16), yet *God did try Abraham* (Gen. XXII, 1)! It is written, *Thou shalt not take vengeance, nor bear any grudge* (Lev. XIX, 18), yet, *The Lord is a jealous and avenging God* (Nahum I, 2)! R. Levi said: It is like the case of a teacher who exhorted his pupil and told him, 'Do not pervert justice,' while he himself perverted justice; 'Show no partiality,' while he himself showed partiality.[2] His pupil said to him, 'Rabbi, to you it is permitted but forbidden to me!' He replied to him, 'I only tell you not to lend an Israelite money on interest, but one may do so to a Gentile; as it is stated, *Unto a foreigner thou mayest lend upon interest* (Deut. XXIII, 21).' In like manner the Israelites spoke before the Holy One, blessed be He: 'Lord of the universe, behold Thou hast written in Thy Torah, "*Thou shalt not take vengeance, nor bear any grudge*," whereas Thou takest vengeance and bearest a grudge!' He replied to them, 'Against Israel I do not bear a grudge, as it is written, *He will not always contend, neither will He keep His anger for ever* (Ps. CIII, 9); but with regard to idolaters, *The Lord taketh vengeance on His adversaries, and He reserveth wrath for His enemies* (Nahum *loc. cit.*). I caused to be written in My Torah, "*Thou shalt not take vengeance, nor bear any grudge*" against the children of thy people, but thou mayest take vengeance of idolaters, as it is said, *Avenge the children of Israel of the Midianites* (Num. XXXI, 2),' to fulfil that which

[1] He did not read them in a loud and distinct voice, because he thought that curses should be recited in a modified tone.

[2] Gen. R. LV, 3 (*q.v.* for the whole passage) inserts here: 'Do not lend money on interest,' but he lent money on interest. His pupil said to him, 'You tell me not to lend on interest whereas you do: to you it is permitted but forbidden to me!'

is said, FORASMUCH AS THE KING'S WORD HATH POWER.

1. WHOSO KEEPETH THE COMMANDMENT SHALL KNOW NO EVIL THING (VIII, 5): this alludes to Esther who was occupied with the commandment to remove the leaven.[1] AND A WISE MAN'S HEART DISCERNETH TIME AND JUDGMENT: this alludes to Mordecai, as it is written, *Now Mordecai knew all that was done* (Est. IV, 1).

1. FOR TO EVERY MATTER THERE IS A TIME (VIII, 6): and to every time there is a matter. As man wishes so can he act in this world; but there [in the Hereafter] will be a judgment and reckoning.[2]

1. THERE IS NO MAN THAT HATH POWER OVER THE WIND (VIII, 8).[3] The Rabbis say: A man has no power over the wind of the Angel of Death to make him withhold it from him. Whence do we know that the angels are called 'winds'? As it is said, *Who maketh winds Thy messengers* (Ps. CIV, 4). NEITHER HATH HE POWER OVER THE DAY OF DEATH: A man cannot say to the Angel of Death, 'Wait for me until I make up my accounts and then I will come.' AND THERE IS NO DISCHARGE IN WAR: A man cannot say [when summoned to war], 'Here is my son, or my slave, or a member of my household in place of me.' NEITHER SHALL WICKEDNESS DELIVER HIM THAT IS GIVEN TO IT: Nobody can question His decision, nor can a man say, 'I appeal against His verdict.'

R. Nehemiah said: THERE IS NO MAN THAT HATH POWER OVER THE WIND: No prophet of Israel

[1] In Est. III, 12, it is related, *Then were the king's scribes called in the first month, on the thirteenth day thereof*. On the evening of that day the Jew is expected to remove all leaven from the house in preparation of the Passover. Esther was occupied with doing this, and so was unaware of what had been taking place and had to be informed by Mordecai.

[2] As the verse continues: AND JUDGMENT. V. *supra* on III, 17.

[3] Or, spirit, and similarly in the whole passage.

has power over the Spirit of the Holy One, blessed be He, to make Him withhold it from him, as it is stated, *And if I say: I will not make mention of Him, nor speak any more in His name, then there is in my heart as it were a burning fire shut up in my bones* (Jer. XX, 9). NEITHER HATH HE POWER OVER THE DAY OF DEATH: as it is written, *Such as are for death to death* (*ib.* XV, 2). AND THERE IS NO DISCHARGE IN WAR: as it is written, *Cast them out of My sight, and let them go forth* (*ib.* 1). NEITHER SHALL WICKEDNESS DELIVER HIM THAT IS GIVEN OVER TO IT: R. Haggai said in the name of R. Isaac: Because there were scoffers in that generation who sneered with their mouth and pointed with their fingers, saying, *The vision that he seeth is for many days to come* (Ezek. XII, 27). Therefore the prophet said to Israel: By your lives, *It shall be no more delayed, for in your days, O rebellious house, will I speak the word and will perform it* (*ib.* 25).

R. Eliezer b. Jacob says: THERE IS NO MAN THAT HATH POWER: over the spirit of the kingdoms[1] to make them withhold it from him. NEITHER HATH HE POWER OVER THE DAY OF DEATH: as it is said, *The snares of death confronted me* (Ps. XVIII, 6). AND THERE IS NO DISCHARGE (MISHLAḤATH) IN WAR: as it is written, *A sending* (mishlaḥath) *of messengers of evil* (*ib.* LXXVIII, 49). NEITHER SHALL WICKEDNESS DELIVER HIM THAT IS GIVEN OVER TO IT: but if they repent, they cool [the anger of the '*messengers of evil*'].

The Rabbis say: THERE IS NO MAN THAT HATH POWER: over his own spirit to withhold it from himself.[2] R. Ḥanina said: It is written, *And formed* (yoẓer) *the spirit of man within him* (Zech. XII, 1)—He bound up (*ẓar*) the spirit of man within his body; for were it not so, when trouble comes upon him, he would take and cast it out from within him.[3]

[1] Which oppressed Israel. Warsaw ed. reads: over the spirit of exiles.
[2] Man cannot rid himself of his spirit (perhaps his emotions, or his life) by merely wishing it. [3] Cf. Gen. R. XIV, 4.

R. Levi said: Some fifty-two times it is written, '*king* David,' but when he was near his death it is written, *Now the days of David drew nigh that he should die* (I Kings II, 1), because NEITHER HATH HE POWER OVER THE DAY OF DEATH.[1]

R. Joshua of Siknin said in the name of R. Levi: The two trumpets which were in the days of Moses were hidden away. One verse states, *When they shall blow with them, all the congregation shall gather themselves unto thee* (Num. X, 3), and another verse states, *Assemble unto me all the elders of your tribes* (Deut. XXXI, 28)![2] Where, then, were the trumpets? It is said that they were already hidden away during the lifetime of Moses. The Holy One, blessed be He, said, 'Why shall he die and his sons blow the trumpets before him? No!'[3] because NEITHER HATH HE POWER OVER THE DAY OF DEATH. R. Eleazar said in the name of R. Simon: The Holy One, blessed be He, conferred a great honour upon Moses by telling him, *Make thee two trumpets of silver* (Num. X, 2), and not giving the command to Joshua.[4]

1. ALL THIS HAVE I SEEN, EVEN APPLIED MY HEART THERETO, WHATEVER THE WORK THAT IS DONE UNDER THE SUN; WHAT TIME ONE MAN HAD POWER OVER ANOTHER TO HIS HURT (VIII, 9). There is a time which is bad for him who exercises the power, and there is a time which is bad for him upon whom it is exercised. R. Eleazar said: You never find anyone incurring guilt through another unless the latter is similarly guilty,[5] as it is stated, WHAT TIME ONE MAN HAD POWER OVER ANOTHER TO HIS HURT.

[1] Rendered: neither hath he power *in* the day of death—his kingship is of no avail then.
[2] This order was addressed to the Levites (Deut. XXXI, 25).
[3] Therefore God hid them. For a clearer version, cf. Gen. R. XCVI, 3.
[4] Cf. Num. R. XV, 15.
[5] Nobody is the cause of a man sinning in connection with him unless he himself had committed the same wrong. Cf. the saying of Hillel, 'Because thou drownedst others, they have drowned thee, and at last they that drowned thee shall themselves be drowned' (Ab. II, 7).

R. Jonathan said: Even[1] with a stick or a strap they incur guilt through this man, as it is stated, *For the yoke of his burden, and the staff of his shoulder, the rod of his oppressor, Thou hast broken as in the day of Midian* (Isa. IX, 3)—this means, on the day of judgment (*din*). R. Ḥama b. Gorion said: (Even a wolf),[2] even barren trees will have to give judgment and reckoning, and the Rabbis deduce the proof from this verse, *For the trees of the field is man* (Deut. XX, 19)[3]; as man will have to give judgment and reckoning, so will barren trees have to give judgment and reckoning.

1. AND SO I SAW THE WICKED BURIED, AND THEY ENTERED INTO THEIR REST (VIII, 10). R. Judah b. Simon said: If this speaks of the dead mentioned by Ezekiel [XXXVII] does it not say here that they were WICKED, whereas those [referred to by Ezekiel] were righteous? If the text speaks of the son of the woman of Zarephath,[4] does it not say here BURIED, whereas he had not been buried! If the text speaks of Zedekiah the son of Chenaanah,[5] does it not say here THEY ENTERED INTO THEIR REST, whereas he had not so entered, but *As they were burying a man, that, behold, they spied a band; and they cast the man into the sepulchre of Elisha, and as soon as the man touched the bones of Elisha, he revived, and stood up on his feet* (II Kings XIII, 21).[6] [It is written here], '*he revived,*' which might be taken to mean for ever; therefore it is stated '*And stood up on his feet*', which teaches that his standing up was merely temporary, only that he might be separated from that righteous man.[7] So what means AND THEY ENTERED (BA'U)? R. Samuel said: Their sun set and they became

[1] Gen. R. XXVI, 6 (*q.v.*) inserts 'a wolf or a dog': i.e., even if death is caused by an animal or an inanimate object, these too incur retribution.
[2] These words are bracketed in the text and should be deleted.
[3] E.V.: '*For is the tree of the field man?*' [4] V. I Kings XVII, 9.
[5] *Ib.* XXII, 24. [6] Nowhere else in Rabbinic literature is the man identified with this Zedekiah.
[7] Since it is improper to bury a wicked person by a righteous man, such as Elisha had been. V. Sanh. 47*a* (Sonc. ed., p. 311).

clean,[1] as the word is used in *And when the sun is down* (ba'), *he shall be clean* (Lev. XXII, 7). R. Levi said: [BURIED refers to the wicked who are accounted dead even when they are alive, as it is written], *The wicked man travaileth with pain* (mithḥolel) *all his days* (Job XV, 20), i.e. he is dead and slain (*meth weḥalal*), as in the verse, *And thou, O wicked one, art slain* (Ezek. XXI, 30).[2]

Another interpretation is that it speaks of proselytes who come and repent. WENT AWAY FROM THE HOLY PLACE: because they went into a holy place, viz. the Synagogue and Houses of Study. AND WERE FORGOTTEN IN THE CITY: their evil deeds were forgotten. BUT THEY THAT HAD DONE RIGHT: But the good deeds which they performed in the city were discovered.[3] THIS ALSO IS VANITY: R. Isaac said: This is not VANITY![4] But what is vanity is that they did not enter [the Israelite fold] of their own accord. R. Bun said: The righteous went to them, and so they entered [the fold] as Joseph to Asenath,[5] Joshua to Rahab, Boaz to Ruth, and Moses to Hobab. R. Aḥa said: This is not VANITY, but [what is vanity is] that human beings[6] do not enter and become hallowed beneath the wings of the *Shechinah*.

1. BECAUSE SENTENCE AGAINST AN EVIL WORK IS NOT EXECUTED SPEEDILY (VIII, 11): because a man sins and the Attribute of Justice does not overtake him, THEREFORE THE HEART OF THE SONS OF MEN IS FULLY SET IN THEM TO DO EVIL. What

[1] This might mean that the death of the wicked is an atonement for their sins, and they thus become clean. M.K. and 'E.J., however, understand 'clean' literally, and render: The unclean (figuratively the wicked) were hidden (figuratively buried) because of their uncleanness, and then the sun set, and they became clean.
[2] Addressed to a living person. E.V.: '*Thou art to be slain.*'
[3] The Heb. for FORGOTTEN can also mean in Rabbinics 'discovered' (lit. 'found out'). [4] That proselytes had repented of their evil deeds.
[5] She only became a convert because she happened to marry Joseph (Gen. XLI, 45). It is similar with the others who are mentioned. Their conversion did not originate with themselves but was the effect of contact with a righteous person. [6] Despite the example of the righteous.

do they say? 'Behold, the haughty go in and come out without stumbling.'[1] BUT IT SHALL NOT BE WELL WITH THE WICKED (VIII, 13).

1. THERE IS A VANITY WHICH IS DONE UPON EARTH (VIII, 14): Happy are THE RIGHTEOUS MEN UNTO WHOM IT HAPPENETH ACCORDING TO THE WORK OF THE WICKED in this world: woe to the WICKED MEN TO WHOM IT HAPPENETH ACCORDING TO THE WORK OF THE RIGHTEOUS.[2]

1. SO I COMMENDED MIRTH (VIII, 15). R. Tanḥuma in the name of R. Naḥman, the son of R. Samuel b. Naḥman, and R. Menaḥma said (another version: R. Jeremiah and R. Meyasha said in the name of R. Samuel b. R. Isaac): All the eating and drinking mentioned in this Book signify Torah and good deeds. R. Jonah said: The most clear proof of them all is, AND THAT THIS SHOULD ACCOMPANY HIM IN HIS LABOUR ('AMALO). The last word should be read as *'olamo* (his world)—in this world: *ALL* THE DAYS OF HIS LIFE alludes to the grave. Are there, then, food and drink in the grave which accompany a man to the grave! It means in fact Torah and good deeds which a man performs.[3]

1. WHEN I APPLIED MY HEART TO KNOW WISDOM, AND TO SEE THE BUSINESS THAT IS DONE UPON THE EARTH—FOR NEITHER DAY NOR NIGHT DO MEN SEE SLEEP WITH THEIR EYES (VIII, 16). [The meaning of the last phrase is,] he neither sees repentance[4]

[1] Because punishment does not befall them immediately after their sin, they think they will escape altogether.

[2] The meaning becomes clear on referring to Hor. 10*b* (Sonc. ed., p. 72) from which this is quoted: Happy are THE RIGHTEOUS MEN UNTO WHOM IT HAPPENETH in this world ACCORDING TO THE WORK OF THE WICKED in the World to Come (i.e. they suffer in this world to expiate their sins). Woe to the WICKED MEN . . . RIGHTEOUS in the World to Come (i.e. they prosper in this world for any good they may have done and receive punishment in the Hereafter).

[3] Repeated from II, 24.

[4] Since SLEEP (SHENAH) obviously cannot be seen with the eyes, the Midrash identifies the word with *shinui*, 'change,' from evil to good, i.e. by means of penitence.

nor performs it. Two good things are near you and far from you, as well as far from you and near you. Repentance is near you and far from you, as well as far from you and near you. Death is near you and far from you, as well as far from you and near you.[1]

1. THEN I BEHELD ALL THE WORK OF GOD (VIII, 17).[2] R. Phinehas and R. Jeremiah said in the name of R. Ḥiyya b. Abba: Many have begged [for ability] to perform and to fathom the Torah but have been unable to do so. Why? BECAUSE THOUGH A MAN LABOUR TO SEEK IT OUT, YET HE SHALL NOT FIND IT. YEA FURTHER, THOUGH A WISE MAN THINK TO KNOW IT: it alludes to Solomon on the day when he said that he would multiply [wives] without their turning [his heart away].[3]

R. Joshua of Siknin said in the name of R. Levi: It is written, *That bringeth princes to nought; He maketh the judges of the earth as a thing of nought* (Isa. XL, 23): this alludes to Moses when he said, *The cause that is too hard for you ye shall bring unto me, and I will hear it* (Deut. I, 17). The Holy One, blessed be He, said to him, 'Moses, you are to judge the hard causes![4] I will have a case brought to you which your pupil's pupil and even women are able to decide, but you will be unable to elucidate.' Which was it? The case of the daughters of Zelophehad.[5] The Rabbis say: Heaven forfend! Moses was not boasting, but this is what he intended: the cause that is too hard for you, if I have a clear opinion of it, then I will announce its decision, otherwise I will refer it to God.

[1] M.K. explains each statement separately. Repentance is near because God is always ready to receive the penitent, but it is far because the sinner hesitates to abandon his evil ways; and although it is far for this reason, he can always bring it near if he so desires. Death is near when it is decreed by God, but it can be averted by good deeds; and when it is to take place in the distant future, wickedness can bring it near. Mah. makes the two statements interdependent: if repentance is near, death is far, and *vice versa*. Death is regarded as a good thing, v. Gen. R. IX, 5, 10.
[2] Understood here as the Torah. [3] He ignored the warning of Deut. XVII, 17, and married many wives. Cf. 1 Kings XI, 1 ff.
[4] God resented his apparent boastfulness. [5] Num. XXVII, 1 ff.

CHAPTER IX

1. Simeon b. Abba opened his discourse thus: ALL THINGS COME ALIKE TO ALL; THERE IS ONE EVENT TO THE RIGHTEOUS (IX, 2): this alludes to Noah, as it is said, *In his generations a man righteous and whole-hearted* (Gen. VI, 9). It is reported that when he came out of the ark, a lion attacked and injured him so that he limped. AND TO THE WICKED: this alludes to Pharaoh [Neco].[1] It is reported that when Pharaoh came to sit upon Solomon's throne, which he had taken with his daughter's *kethubah*,[2] he did not understand its mechanism, and a lion attacked and injured him so that he limped. They both died with a limp, hence THERE IS ONE EVENT TO THE RIGHTEOUS AND TO THE WICKED.

TO THE GOOD: this alludes to Moses, as it is said, *When she saw that he was a goodly child* (Ex. II, 2). R. Meir said: '*Goodly*' indicates that he was [born] circumcised.[3] AND TO THE CLEAN: this alludes to Aaron who was concerned with the purity of Israel. AND TO THE UNCLEAN: these are the spies, who delivered an evil report about the Land and did not enter it, while the others [Moses and Aaron] spoke of the goodness and praiseworthiness of the land of Israel and did not enter it.

TO HIM THAT SACRIFICETH: this alludes to Josiah, as it is written, *And Josiah gave to the children of Israel, of the flock, lambs and kids, all of them for the passover-offerings* (II Chron. XXXV, 7). AND TO HIM THAT SACRIFICETH NOT: this alludes to Ahab who abolished offerings from the altar. They were both killed by arrows.[4]

[1] 'Neco' is added from Lev. R. XX, 1. For Solomon's marriage with Pharaoh's daughter, v. I Kings III, 1.
[2] The phrase, 'to which he . . . *kethubah*,' does not occur in Lev. R. Its meaning is doubtful, and it should perhaps be deleted.
[3] V. Soṭ. 12*a* (Sonc. ed., p. 61).
[4] V. I Kings XXII, 34; II Chron. XXXV, 23. Ahab fostered Baal-worship to such an extent that he may be said to have abolished offerings from the altar (of God).

AS IS THE GOOD: this alludes to David of whom it is written, *And goodly to look upon* (I Sam. XVI, 12). (R. Isaac said: He was '*goodly to look*' in the *halachah* and whoever looked at him remembered his learning.) SO IS THE SINNER: this alludes to Nebuchadnezzar, as it is written, *Break off thy sins by almsgiving* (Dan. IV, 24). The former built the Temple[1] and reigned forty years, while the latter destroyed it and reigned forty years; hence THERE IS ONE EVENT TO THE RIGHTEOUS AND TO THE WICKED.

AND HE THAT SWEARETH: this alludes to Zedekiah, as it is written, *And he also rebelled against king Nebuchadnezzar, who made him swear by God* (II Chron. XXXVI, 13). (By what did he make him swear? R. Jose said: He made him swear by the covenant [of his circumcision]. Rabbi [Judah ha-Nasi] said: He made him swear by the altar.) AS HE THAT FEARETH AN OATH: this alludes to Samson, as it is stated, *And Samson said unto them: Swear unto me that ye will not fall upon me yourselves* (Judg. XV, 12).[2] They both died after having their eyes plucked out.[3]

Another interpretation is: TO THE RIGHTEOUS: i.e. Aaron's sons, AND TO THE WICKED: i.e. Korah and his company. The latter entered [the Tabernacle] to offer incense with intent to quarrel and came out burnt,[4] and the sons of Aaron, who did not enter it with intent to quarrel, likewise came out burnt, as it is written, *And the Lord spoke unto Moses, after the death of the two sons of Aaron, when they drew near before the Lord, and died* (Lev. XVI, 1).

1. FOR TO HIM THAT IS JOINED—YEḤUBBAR (IX, 4). R. Aḥa said: The word is written *yibḥar* (will choose),

[1] V. on II, 15.
[2] Zedekiah did not fear an oath, and so broke it, but had Samson not feared an oath, he would never have relied upon their oath so as to surrender to them (Y.T.). [3] Judg. XVI, 21; II Kings XXV, 7.
[4] Num. XVI, 35.

i.e. he who chooses the Good Inclination in preference to the Evil Inclination, viz. the righteous; and he who chooses the Evil Inclination in preference to the Good Inclination, viz. the wicked: [both are included in] TO ALL THE LIVING THERE IS HOPE: even they who stretched forth their hand against the Temple [and destroyed it] have hope. That they should be restored to life [in the Hereafter] is impossible because they stretched forth their hand against the Temple; and that they should be utterly destroyed is impossible because they repented; so concerning them it is written, *And sleep the perpetual sleep* (Jer. LI, 39).[1] The Rabbis say: The children of the wicked among the heathen and the soldiers of Nebuchadnezzar will not live [in the Hereafter] nor will they be punished [in Gehinnom], but concerning them it declares, '*And sleep a perpetual sleep.*' R. Joḥanan said: Every drop which the Holy One, blessed be He, rained down upon the generation of the flood He made to boil[2] before letting it fall upon them; as it is stated, *What time they wax warm, they vanish* (Job VI, 17), i.e. their [destruction by] scalding was absolute.

FOR A LIVING DOG IS BETTER THAN A DEAD LION. The accursed Hadrian asked R. Joshua b. Ḥananiah, saying, 'Am I [not] better than your teacher Moses?' 'Why?' he asked. 'Because I am alive and he is dead, as it is written, FOR A LIVING DOG IS BETTER THAN A DEAD LION.' The Rabbi said to him, 'Can you order that nobody should kindle a fire for three days?' 'Certainly I can,' he replied [and issued the command]. In the evening of that day, they both went up to the roof of the palace and saw smoke ascending in the distance. The Rabbi asked, 'What is that?' He replied, 'One of my officers is ill and a physician went in to visit him and told him, "Unless you have hot drinks you cannot be cured." ' The Rabbi said to him, 'May this breath be your last! While you are alive your order is

[1] Cf. Ruth R. III, 1.
[2] In Gen. R. XXVIII, 9, 'in Gehinnom, brought it forth' is added here.

neglected; whereas when our teacher Moses decreed for us, *Ye shall kindle no fire throughout your habitations upon the Sabbath day* (Ex. XXXV, 3), no Jew has ever kindled a fire on the Sabbath from his days and his decree has not been annulled throughout all these years until now, and yet you say, "I am better than he!" '

1. FOR THE LIVING KNOW THAT THEY SHALL DIE (IX, 5). R. Ḥiyya Rabbah and R. Jonathan were walking in front of the bier of R. Simeon, the son of Jose b. Leḳunia, and the *ṭallith* of R. Jonathan dragged upon his coffin.¹ R. Ḥiyya Rabbah said to him: 'My son, lift up your *ṭallith*, so that [the dead] shall not say, "To-morrow they will come to us, and yet they revile us." '² He said to him, 'My master, is it not written, BUT THE DEAD KNOW NOT ANYTHING?' He answered, 'My son, you know Scripture but not *Midrash*. FOR THE LIVING KNOW refers to the righteous who are called LIVING even in their death; BUT THE DEAD KNOW NOT refers to the wicked who, even in their lifetime, are called DEAD. Whence do we know that the righteous are called living even in their death? As it is said, *Unto the land of which I swore unto Abraham, to Isaac, and to Jacob,*³ *saying* (Ex. XXXIII, 1). It is not stated here "to the patriarchs", but *"unto Abraham, to Isaac, and to Jacob"*; He said to Moses, "Go and tell them that the oath which I swore to them I have fulfilled," as it is stated, *To thee will I give it, and to thy seed for ever* (Gen. XV, 15). The wicked are called dead, as it is written, *I have no pleasure in the death of the dead* (Ezek. XVIII, 32).⁴ Can *"the dead"* die! In fact it alludes to the wicked who, even in their

---

¹ The reading should probably be 'upon the graves'.
² The *ṭallith* was provided with fringes (v. Num. XV, 38), from which the dead are exempt. R. Ḥiyya meant that by allowing his fringes to trail over their coffins (or graves) R. Jonathan seemed to be reproaching the dead that they lacked a precept which he possessed.
³ They are spoken of as though still living, although they had long been dead. Hence the comment, 'Go and tell them, etc.'
⁴ So lit., with which is to be compared *ib.* XXXIII, 11, *I have no pleasure in the death of the* wicked (E.V. '*of him that dieth*').

lifetime, are called dead.' [R. Jonathan] said to him, 'Blessed be he who has taught me *Midrash*,' and kissed him on his head.

1. AS WELL THEIR LOVE (IX, 6), which they had for idolatry more than for the Holy One, blessed be He; AS THEIR HATRED in showing hatred of the Holy One, blessed be He, by the work of their hands; AND THEIR PROVOCATION[1] wherewith they provoked Him with their idolatry, as it is said, *They roused Him to jealousy with strange gods* (Deut. XXXII, 16); NEITHER HAVE THEY A PORTION FOR THE WORLD[2] [to Come], whereas Israel has a portion and a good reward, as it is said, GO THY WAY, EAT THY BREAD WITH JOY (IX, 7).

[1] E.V. '*envy*'. [2] E.V. '*for ever*'.

(Ended is the Second Section.)

THE THIRD SECTION[1]

1. GO THY WAY, EAT THY BREAD WITH JOY. R. Huna b. R. Aḥa said: When the children leave their school,[2] a *Bath Ḳol* goes forth and says to them, 'GO THY WAY, EAT THY BREAD WITH JOY, the breath of your mouth has been accepted by Me like the sweet savour [of incense].' Likewise when the Israelites leave the Synagogues and Houses of Study, a *Bath Ḳol* goes forth and says to them, 'GO THY WAY, EAT THY BREAD WITH JOY, your prayer has been heard before Me [and was] as the sweet savour.'

Another interpretation of GO THY WAY, EAT THY BREAD WITH JOY: this refers to the section of the *ḥallah*[3]; AND DRINK THY WINE WITH A MERRY HEART: this refers to the section of the drink-offerings[4]; FOR GOD HATH ALREADY ACCEPTED THY WORKS: this refers to the entrance of Israel into the Land, as it is said, *When ye are come into the land of your habitations* (Num. XV, 2).

R. 'Azariah in the name of R. Judah b. R. Simon interpreted the verse as referring to our father Abraham. When the Holy One, blessed be He, said to him, *Take now thy son, thine only son* (Gen. XXII, 2) [and he went on the journey], on the first day he saw nothing and on the second day he saw nothing. What is written of the third day? *He saw the place afar off* (*ib.* 4). What did he see? He beheld a cloud lying on the mountain, and said, 'I think this is the mountain upon which the Holy One, blessed be He, has told me to offer my son Isaac.' He said to him, 'Isaac, my son, do you see what I see?' He answered, 'Yes.' 'What do you see?' he asked him, and he replied, 'A cloud lying on the mountain.' He asked Eliezer and Ishmael, his young men,[5] 'Do you see anything?' They answered, 'No.' He said, 'Since you see

[1] V. Introduction. [2] To go home for their meal.
[3] Num. XV, 17–21. [4] *Ib.* 5 ff. [5] V. Gen. XXII, 3.

nothing and the ass sees nothing, *Abide ye here with* ('im) *the ass* (*ib.* 5), because you are people ('*am*) like an ass.'

Then he took Isaac, led him up mountains and down valleys, and took him up a high and lofty mountain. He built an altar, arranged the wood, bound him upon it, and took hold of the knife to slay him; and had not an angel come and told him, *Lay not thy hand upon the lad* (*ib.* 12), he would have slain him. When Isaac returned to his mother, she asked him, 'Where have you been, my son?' He answered her, 'Father took me, led me up mountains and down valleys, took me up a certain mountain, built an altar, arranged the wood, bound me upon it, and took hold of a knife to slay me. If an angel had not come from heaven and said to him, "*Abraham, Abraham, lay not thy hand upon the lad,*" I should have been slain.' On his mother, Sarah, hearing this, she cried out, and before she had time to finish her cry her soul departed, as it is written, *And Abraham came to mourn for Sarah and to weep for her* (*ib.* XXIII, 2). From where did he come? He came from Mount Moriah.

R. Judah b. R. Simon said: Abraham felt some uneasiness in his heart and thought, 'Perhaps there was some disqualification in my son, and for that reason he was not accepted [as an offering].' A *Bath Ḳol* issued forth and said to him, 'Abraham, Abraham, GO THY WAY, EAT THY BREAD WITH JOY . . . FOR GOD HATH ALREADY ACCEPTED THY WORKS, God hath accepted thy sacrifice.'

R. Mana of Shaab and R. Joshua of Siknin in the name of R. Levi interpreted the verse as referring to the New Year and Day of Atonement. It may be likened to a province which owed arrears of taxes to the king who sent a tax collector to collect it.[1] When he was ten miles away, the eminent men of the province went out and greeted him with praises; so he remitted a third to them. When he was five miles away, those of the middle class went out and

[1] In Lev. R. XXX, 7, it is the king himself who goes to collect it. This is preferable since he, and not his agent, had the power to remit taxes.

greeted him with praises; so he remitted a third to them. When he came near, the men, women, and children went out and greeted him; so he forgave them the whole amount, saying to them, 'What has gone has gone; from now onwards will be the reckoning.' Similarly on the eve of the New Year, the eminent men of the generation fast, and the Holy One, blessed be He, remits them a third of their sins, as it is said, *For with Thee there is forgiveness, that Thou mayest be feared* (Ps. cxxx, 4). (R. Aḥa said: [The meaning is,] From the New Year forgiveness is arranged by Thee, '*That Thou mayest be feared*'; that the fear of Thee may be upon Thy creatures.) On the days between the New Year and the Day of Atonement individuals fast, and the Holy One, blessed be He, remits to them another third of their sins. On the Day of Atonement all fast, and the Holy One, blessed be He, remits to them another third of their sins; thus by the time the men, women, and children fast the Holy One, blessed be He, forgives them all their sins and says, 'What has gone has gone; from now onwards will be the reckoning.' A *Bath Ḳol* goes forth and says to them, 'GO THY WAY, EAT THY BREAD WITH JOY, your prayer has been heard.'

Abba Taḥnah the pious was entering his city on the Sabbath-eve at dusk with his bundle slung over his shoulder, when he met a man afflicted with boils lying at the cross-roads. The latter said to him, 'Rabbi, do me an act of charity and carry me into the city.' He remarked, 'If I abandon my bundle, from where shall I and my household support ourselves? But if I abandon this afflicted man I will forfeit my life!'[1] What did he do? He allowed the Good Inclination to master the Evil Inclination, and carried the afflicted man into the city. He then returned for his bundle and entered at sunset. Everybody was astonished[2] and exclaimed, 'Is this Abba Taḥnah the pious!' He too felt uneasy in his heart and said, 'Do you think that I perhaps desecrated the Sabbath?'

[1] God would punish him for refusing the request.
[2] At seeing this pious man carrying his bundle when the Sabbath was about to begin.

At that time the Holy One, blessed be He, caused the sun to shine, as it is written, *But unto you that fear My name shall the sun of righteousness arise* (Mal. III, 20). He again felt uneasy and said, 'Do you think that my reward has not been received?'[1] A *Bath Ḳol* went forth and said to him, 'GO THY WAY, EAT THY BREAD WITH JOY, AND DRINK THY WINE WITH A MERRY HEART, FOR GOD HATH ALREADY ACCEPTED THY WORKS, thy reward has been received.'

Another interpretation of GO THY WAY, EAT THY BREAD WITH JOY: It speaks of Daniel, *The man greatly beloved* (Dan. X, 11), as it is said, *Yea, while I was speaking in prayer, the man Gabriel, whom I had seen in the vision at the beginning, being caused to fly swiftly* [i.e. flying and again flying][2] *approached close to me about the time of the evening offering. And he made me to understand, and talked with me* (*ib.* IX, 21 f.). R. Haggai said in the name of R. Isaac: Daniel, '*The man greatly beloved*,' said: 'The Holy One, blessed be He, knew that I had finished my prayer[3] so He, sent the angel who spoke with me—as it is stated, "*And He understood, and he talked with me*"—and what did he talk with me? He told me, *At the beginning of thy supplications a word went forth* (*ib.* 23)—he told me, "It has been decreed that the Temple shall be rebuilt; and to fulfil thy request I said, '*At the beginning of thy supplications that thou art greatly beloved*,' since He longs for thy prayer."' R. Samuel b. Onia said in the name of R. Aḥa: Three times in this passage it is written *beloved* [for this reason: Gabriel] said to him, 'Enough for thee that thy Creator holds thee in love, His [angelic] retinue holds thee in love, and His Torah holds thee in

[1] That because God performed this miracle to vindicate me, I will receive no further reward for my benevolent act. M.K. mentions a reading which omits 'not', and this seems preferable.

[2] The Heb. is lit. 'being caused to fly in a flight', the word for 'flying' occurring twice. This is interpreted to mean that he covered the distance in two flights, resting in between. Cf. Ber. 4*b*.

[3] The Heb. for evening offering (*minḥah*) also denotes the early evening (i.e. afternoon) prayer. *And he made me to understand* is interpreted as 'He (God) understood'.

love.' For it is written, *From the first day that thou didst set thy heart to understand, and to humble thyself before thy God, thy words were heard* (*ib.* x, 12), thy prayer was heard. A *Bath Ḳol* went forth and said to him, 'GO THY WAY, EAT THY BREAD WITH JOY . . . FOR GOD HATH ALREADY ACCEPTED THY WORKS, thy prayer has been heard.'

1. LET THY GARMENTS BE ALWAYS WHITE; AND LET THY HEAD LACK NO OIL (IX, 8). R. Joḥanan b. Zakkai said: If the text speaks of white garments, how many of these have the peoples of the world; and if it speaks of good oil, how much of it do the peoples of the world possess! Behold, it speaks only of precepts, good deeds, and Torah. R. Judah ha-Nasi said: To what may this be likened? To a king who made a banquet to which he invited guests. He said to them, 'Go, wash yourselves, brush up your clothes, anoint yourselves with oil, wash your garments, and prepare yourselves for the banquet,' but he fixed no time when they were to come to it. The wise among them walked about by the entrance of the king's palace, saying, 'Does the king's palace lack anything?'[1] The foolish among them paid no regard or attention to the king's command. They said, 'We will in due course notice when the king's banquet is to take place, because can there be a banquet without labour [to prepare it] and company?' So the plasterer went to his plaster, the potter to his clay, the smith to his charcoal, the washer to his laundry. Suddenly the king ordered, 'Let them all come to the banquet.' They hurried the guests, so that some came in their splendid attire and others came in their dirty garments. The king was pleased with the wise ones who had obeyed his command, and also because they had shown honour to the king's palace.[2] He was angry with the fools who had neglected his command and disgraced his palace. The king said, 'Let those who

[1] That the king must make long preparations for the banquet; consequently we must be ready at any moment to be called in.

[2] By preparing adequately for the banquet.

have prepared themselves for the banquet come and eat of the king's meal, but those who have not prepared themselves shall not partake of it.' You might suppose that the latter were simply to depart; but the king continued, 'No, [they are not to depart]; but the former shall recline and eat and drink, while these shall remain standing, be punished, and look on and be grieved.' Similarly in the Hereafter, as Isaiah declares, *Behold, My servants shall eat, but ye shall be hugry* (Isa. LXV, 13). Ziwatai said in the name of R. Meir: These will recline and eat and drink, while the others will recline without eating and drinking; because the vexation of him who stands [at a banquet without participating in it] is not the same as of him who reclines [without participating in it]. He who stands without eating and drinking is like an attendant, but he who reclines and does not eat suffers very much more vexation and his face turns green.[1] That is what the prophet says, *Then ye shall sit*[2] *and discern between the righteous and the wicked* (Mal. III, 18).

Bar Ḳappara and R. Isaac b. Ḳappara said: It may be likened to the wife of a royal courier[3] who adorned herself in the presence of her neighbours. They said to her, 'Your husband is away, so for whom do you adorn yourself?' She answered them, 'My husband is a sailor; and if he should chance to have a little spell of [favourable] wind, he will come quickly and be here standing above my head. So is it not better that he should see me in my glory and not in my ugliness?' Similarly, LET THY GARMENTS BE ALWAYS WHITE [and unstained] by transgressions; AND LET THY HEAD LACK NO OIL: [let it not lack] precepts and good deeds.

It has been taught: Repent one day before your death. R. Eliezer was asked by his disciples, 'Rabbi, does any man know when he will die so that he can repent?' He answered them, 'Should he not all the more repent to-day

[1] With longing.
[2] *Weshabtem* (ye shall return) is read as *wiyshabtem* (ye shall sit). E.V.: '*Then shall ye again discern.*'
[3] Who went on missions for his master which took him to foreign lands.

lest he die the day after, and then all his days will be lived in repentance. For that reason it is said, LET THY GARMENTS BE ALWAYS WHITE.'[1]

1. ENJOY LIFE WITH THE WIFE WHOM THOU LOVEST (IX, 9). Rabbi [Judah ha-Nasi] said in the name of the holy brotherhood: Acquire a handicraft for yourself together with Torah.[2] What is the reason [for this teaching]? ENJOY LIFE WITH THE WIFE WHOM THOU LOVEST. Why does he call them 'the holy brotherhood'? Because it included R. Jose b. Meshullam and R. Simeon b. Menasia who used to divide the day into three parts—a third for Torah, a third for prayer, and a third for work. Others declare that they laboured in the Torah throughout the winter and in their work throughout the summer. R. Isaac b. Eleazar used to call R. Joshua b. R. Ṭimi and R. Borḳai 'a holy brotherhood', because they divided the day into three parts—a third for Torah, a third for prayer, and a third for work.

It has been learnt: One who mourns [the death of his wife] is forbidden to remarry until thirty days have elapsed.[3] R. Judah says: Until three Festivals[4] have passed, one after another, corresponding to the three occurrences of the word LIFE in this verse. When does this rule apply? If he has children; but if he is childless or if his children are young, he is permitted [to remarry without this interval] so as not to diminish procreation [in the first case] or so that they may be looked after [in the second]. When the wife of R. Ṭarfon died, after the grave had been filled in, he said to her sister during [the seven days of] mourning, 'Marry me and rear your sister's children.' But although he married her, he did not consummate the marriage until after thirty days.

It has been learnt: A mourner is forbidden to go to a

[1] Shab. 153*a*.
[2] Ḳid. 30*b* (Sonc. ed., p. 148). The thought is the same as in the aphorism: 'Excellent is the study of Torah together with a worldly occupation' (Ab. II, 2). For the Torah symbolised as a woman, v. p. 211.
[3] Cf. M.Ḳ. 23*a*. [4] Passover, Pentecost, and Tabernacles.

house of feasting until thirty days have elapsed. It has been learnt: It is incumbent on a father to circumcise his son, redeem him,[1] teach him Torah, teach him a handicraft, and take a wife for him. Some add, also to teach him to swim. 'To circumcise him'—how do we know it? As it is said, *And he that is eight days old shall be circumcised among you, every male throughout your generations* (Gen. XVII, 12). 'To redeem him'—how do we know it? As it is said, *And all the firstborn of man among thy sons shalt thou redeem* (Ex. XIII, 13). 'To teach him Torah'—how do we know it? As it is written, *And ye shall teach them your sons* (Deut. XI, 19). 'To teach him a handicraft'—how do we know it? As it is written, *Therefore choose life* (*ib.* XXX, 19).[2] 'Take a wife for him'—how do we know it? As it is written, *Take ye wives, and beget sons and daughters; and take wives for your sons, and give your daughters to husbands* (Jer. XXIX, 6). 'Also to teach him to swim'—how do we know it? As it is said, '*Therefore choose life.*'[3]

A man who has no wife lives without good, help, joy, blessing, and atonement.[4] 'Without good'—how do we know it? *It is not good that the man should be alone* (Gen. II, 18). 'Help'—how do we know it? *I will make a help meet for him* (*ib.*). 'Joy'—how do we know it? *And thou shalt rejoice, thou and thy house* (Deut. XIV, 26).[5] 'Blessing'—how do we know it? *To cause a blessing to rest on thy house* (Ezek. XLIV, 30). 'Atonement'—how do we know it? *And make atonement for himself and for his house* (Lev. XVI, 6). R. Joshua b. Levi says: He also lives without life, as it is stated, ENJOY LIFE WITH THE WIFE WHOM THOU LOVEST. He lives without peace, as it is stated, *Peace be both unto thee and peace be to thy house* (I Sam. XXV, 6). R. Ḥiyya b. Gamda said: He is also an incomplete man, as it is stated, *And blessed* them *and called* their *name*

[1] If the son is a firstborn. [2] *Life* is interpreted here as 'handicraft' as in the beginning of the Midrash to this verse.
[3] The Talmud gives as the reason: his life may depend on it. This passage is quoted from Ḳid. 29*a et seq.* (Sonc. ed., pp. 137 ff.).
[4] Cf. Yeb. 62*b* (Sonc. ed., p. 418).
[5] *House* means 'wife'. Cf. Yoma 2*a*.

Adam (Gen. v, 2), i.e. when they were both as one [as the effect of marriage] they were called 'Adam', but when they are not both as one they are not called 'Adam'. Some say that [when unmarried] a man diminishes the Divine Image,[1] as it is stated, *For in the image of God made He man* (*ib.* IX, 6).

1. WHATSOEVER THY HAND ATTAINETH TO DO BY THY STRENGTH, THAT DO (IX, 10). R. Menaḥma said in the name of R. Bun: This verse must be revised [for its exposition]: If thou knowest that THERE IS NO WORK, NOR DEVICE, NOR KNOWLEDGE, NOR WISDOM IN THE GRAVE WHITHER THOU GOEST, then WHATSOEVER THY HAND ATTAINETH TO DO BY THY STRENGTH, THAT DO [while in this world].

R. Aḥa was longing to behold the face of R. Alexandri.[2] He appeared to him in his dream and showed him two things; one was that nobody had a place nearer to the centre[3] than the slain of Lydda[4] (blessed be He who removed the reproach of Julianus and Pappus),[5] and the other was that happy was he who came here [to the next world] with his learning in his possession.

Zabdi b. Levi was longing to behold the face of R. Joshua b. Levi. He appeared to him in his dream and showed him men whose heads[6] were erect and others whose heads were bent. He asked him, 'Why is it so?' He answered, 'Those whose heads are erect have their learning in their possession, while those whose heads are bent have not their learning in their possession.'

R. Simeon b. Laḳish (another version: R. Joshua b. Levi) was longing to see R. Ḥiyya Rabbah [in a dream]. People told him, 'You are not worthy of this.' 'Why?' he asked, 'did I not study Torah as he did?' They answered, 'You did not teach Torah as he did; and not only that,

[1] By not begetting children. [2] In a dream, since the latter was dead.
[3] In heaven. Lit. 'there is no division more internal than theirs'.
[4] Nobody occupied a higher place than they in Paradise. For their martyrdom, cf. III, 17. [5] God has avenged them, v. *supra* on III, 17.
[6] Lit. 'faces'.

he had to go into exile.'[1] He said to them, 'And have I not been in exile!' They answered, 'You went into exile to learn, but he to teach.' He kept three hundred fasts, and then R. Ḥiyya appeared to him in his dream and told him, 'If one is a nobody [in knowledge of Torah] but conducts himself as though he were somebody,[2] better for him if he had never been created.'

R. Assi fasted thirty days to behold R. Ḥiyya Rabbah [in a dream] but did not see him. It was told him,[3] 'You are not worthy of this.' He said to them, 'Show him to me and let be what will be.' He then saw the steps [of R. Ḥiyya's heavenly throne], and his eyesight grew dim. Should you say that R. Assi was not an eminent man, [the following anecdote proves the contrary]. A weaver came before R. Joḥanan and said, 'I saw in my dream that the heavens fell and one of your disciples supported it with his hand.' He asked, 'Do you know him?' He replied, 'If you make them pass in front of me, I would recognise him.' They passed in front of him, and when he came to R. Assi he exclaimed, 'This is he!'

R. Huna the exilarch said to the Sages, 'When I die, carry me to [the tomb of] R. Ḥiyya Rabbah.' When he died, they conveyed him to the land of Israel, saying, 'R. Huna is worthy of being brought here by the side of R. Ḥiyya Rabbah. Who will enter [the tomb] and place his body there?' R. Haggai said, 'I will carry him in.' It was related [of R. Haggai] that he was eighteen years of age,[4] constant in his study, and never experienced seminal emission. They said to him, 'You want a pretext [for entering the tomb] because you are an old man, and if you die there you have no interest in life.' He said

[1] I.e. leave his home for the sake of the Torah, and the hardships he endured earned him merit.

[2] So M.K. 'E.J. renders: He who is somebody (i.e. learned) but keeps his learning to himself (does not teach).

[3] A message came to him from Heaven. He endangered himself if he beheld R. Ḥiyya.

[4] The text is corrupt, since he is described later as an old man. In M.K. 25*a* the reading is: I will carry him in because I completed my study when I was eighteen and never experienced, etc.

to them, 'Do this thing for me. Fetch a cord and bind my legs together. If I come out, well and good; and if not, drag me out by my legs.' This was done to him; and he went in and found [on the tomb] three inscriptions,[1] 'Judah, my son, after thee there is none other.[2] Hezekiah, my son, after thee there is none other. Joseph, son of [the patriarch] Israel, after thee there is none other.' [R. Haggai] raised his eyes to look around, but he was told, 'Lower your face.' He then heard the voice of R. Ḥiyya Rabbah saying to his son Judah, 'My son, permit R. Huna the exilarch to occupy [your grave space].' But [R. Huna] declined to occupy [R. Judah's] place. [R. Haggai heard heavenly voices exclaim, 'Since he declined to occupy R. Judah's place], therefore his seed shall never cease.'[3] [R. Haggai] came out from there aged eighty years, and his years were doubled for him.[4]

2. R. Ze'ira was longing to behold R. Jose b. R. Ḥanina. He appeared to him [in a dream] and R. Ze'ira asked him, 'Next to whom are you seated [in the heavenly Academy]?' He answered, 'Next to R. Joḥanan.' 'And R. Joḥanan next to whom?' 'Next to R. Jonathan b. Amram.' 'And R. Jonathan b. Amram next to whom?' 'Next to R. Ḥiyya Rabbah.' ('And R. Ḥiyya Rabbah next to whom?' 'Next to R. Joḥanan.')[5] 'And is not R. Joḥanan [worthy to sit] next to R. Ḥiyya Rabbah?' He replied, 'In the region of fiery sparks and flaming tongues, who will let the smith's son[6] enter?'

When R. Naḥum, the man who was holy of holies, died, the people covered the faces of the statues with mats, saying, 'Let him not see them in his death as he did not look upon them in his lifetime.' But could he look

[1] The word in the original is of uncertain meaning and the text is doubtful.
[2] None to equal him for piety. Judah and Hezekiah were the sons of R. Ḥiyya.
[3] The words in brackets are mainly added from the version in J. Kil. 32*a*.
[4] As a reward for occupying himself with the burial of R. Huna.
[5] M.K. and 'E.J. think that the bracketed passage should be deleted.
[6] R. Joḥanan's cognomen was Bar Nappaḥa, lit. 'the smith's son'. The paragraph is quoted from B.M. 85*b* (Sonc. ed., p. 491).

upon them [being dead]? R. Ashian said: There is no difference between the righteous and the wicked except the power of speech.[1] R. Simeon b. Laḳish said: There is no difference between the righteous [when dead] and ourselves [while we are living] except the power of speech. R. Ze'ira said: The dead person hears the praise spoken of him in his coffin as though in a dream. Why was he called, 'Naḥum, the man who was holy of holies'? Because he never looked upon the image on a coin. R. Ḥiyya said: [It is written,] *Turn ye not unto the idols* (Lev. XIX, 4), i.e. do not turn to them for the purpose of worshipping them; but Rabbi [Judah ha-Nasi] said: Do not turn to them even to look at them.

Why was Rabbi called 'our holy Rabbi'? Because he never looked upon his circumcision. Antoninus had himself circumcised, and he once said to Rabbi, 'Examine my circumcision.' He replied, 'I have never looked upon my own, so shall I look upon yours!'

3. When Rabbi was dying in Sepphoris, the men of that town declared, 'Whosoever comes and announces that Rabbi is dead will be put to death by us.' Bar Ḳappara went, looked through a window, and squeezed himself in, his head being wrapped up and his garments rent, and exclaimed, 'My brethren, sons of Jedayah, hear me, hear me! Angels and mortals have taken hold of the tablets of the covenant. The angels were victorious and have snatched the tablets.' They cried, 'Rabbi is dead!' He said to them, 'It is you who have said it; I have not said it.' Why did he not say it? Because it is written, *He that uttereth a bad report is a fool* (Prov. x, 18). They rent their garments [so violently] that the sound of the tearing reached Gufta three miles away; and the text was applied to him, *The excellency of knowledge is, that wisdom preserveth the life of him that hath it* (Eccl. VII, 12).

R. Nehemiah said in the name of R. Mana: Miracles

[1] After death the faculties survive, except that in the case of the wicked they are deprived of speech. Accordingly R. Naḥum would have been able to see the statues.—M.K. and 'E.J. delete R. Ashian's statement.

occurred on that day. It was the eve of the Sabbath, and the inhabitants of all the cities assembled for the mourning over Rabbi. They set his body down in eighteen Synagogues and then conveyed him to Beth Shearim, and the day was extended for them so that each Israelite had time to arrive home, kindle his Sabbath light, roast his fish, and fill his cask with water [before Sabbath]. When the last of them had done this, the sun set and the cock crowed. The people began to cry out, 'Woe, we have desecrated the Sabbath!' A *Bath Ḳol* issued forth and declared, 'Whoever did not stint himself in mourning for Rabbi is destined for the life of the World to Come, with the exception of Ḳaẓra who was there but did not accompany the funeral procession.' On hearing this, the man went up and threw himself from the roof, killing himself by the fall. A *Bath Ḳol* went forth and said, 'Also Ḳaẓra for [what he did on] the roof is destined for the life of the World to Come.'[1]

1. I RETURNED, AND SAW UNDER THE SUN, THAT THE RACE IS NOT TO THE SWIFT, etc. (IX, 11). THAT THE RACE IS NOT TO THE SWIFT: this alludes to the patriarch Jacob. Yesterday, *Jacob lifted up his feet* (Gen. XXIX, 1)[2]; to-day it is written, *He gathered up his feet into the bed and expired* (*ib.* XLIX, 33). NOR THE BATTLE TO THE STRONG: this alludes to Jacob. Yesterday, *Jacob went near and rolled the stone from the well's mouth* (*ib.* XXIX, 10). (R. Joḥanan said: He did it like a man who removes a stopper from the mouth of a flask.) To-day it is written, *And the sons of Israel carried Jacob their father* (*ib.* XLVI, 5), i.e. [they conveyed him to Egypt] bodily, and he could not be carried even in a litter. NEITHER YET BREAD TO THE WISE: this alludes to Jacob. Yesterday, *Jacob offered a sacrifice in the mountain, and called his brethren to eat bread, and they did eat bread* (*ib.* XXXI, 54). (Were they, then, his brothers? He had only one brother [Esau] and

[1] Repeated from VII, 12, *q.v.* for notes.
[2] Lit. E.V.: '*Jacob went on his journey.*'

would that he had buried him! Were they not his sons? But when they reached his shoulder,[1] he likened them to himself and called them his 'brethren'.) To-day [he has to tell his sons], *Go again, buy us a little food* (*ib.* XLIII, 2). NOR YET RICHES TO MEN OF UNDERSTANDING: this alludes to Jacob [of whom it is written], *And the man increased* (wayyifroẓ) *exceedingly* (*ib.* XXX, 43). (R. Simon said in the name of R. Simeon: This teaches that he had a reflection of the World to Come, as the word is used in, *The breaker* (poreẓ) *is gone up before them* (Micah II, 13).)[2] To-day it is written, *Joseph sustained his father* (Gen. XLVII, 12). NOR YET FAVOUR TO THOSE WHO KNOW[3]: this alludes to Jacob. Yesterday [he was able to say], *I know it, my son, I know it* (*ib.* XLVIII, 19)—i.e. I know the incident of Judah and Tamar and the incident of Reuben and Bilhah[4]; so if things not revealed to you have been revealed to me, how much more so things which have been revealed to you! But to-day he tells him, *If now I have favour in thy sight . . . bury me not, I pray thee, in Egypt* (*ib.* XLVII, 29).

Another interpretation of THE RACE IS NOT TO THE SWIFT: this alludes to Asahel, as it is said, *And Asahel was as light of foot as one of the roes that are in the field* (II Sam. II, 18). (In what did his lightness consist? He ran over the ears of the standing corn and left them unbroken.) Yesterday, '*Asahel was light of foot,*' but to-day *Abner with the hinder end of the spear smote him* (*ib.* 23). NOR THE BATTLE TO THE STRONG: this alludes to Abner, as it is written of him, *Art not thou a valiant man? and who is like thee in Israel?* (I Sam. XXVI, 15). (For R. Assi said in the name of R. Johanan: It was easier for a man to move a wall built to a thickness of six cubits than one foot of Abner.) But to-day it is written, *Should Abner die as a churl dieth?* (II Sam. III, 33). NEITHER YET BREAD TO THE WISE: this alludes to Solomon. Yesterday, *Solomon's provision for one day was thirty measures*

[1] I.e. grew up to be righteous and strong like their father.
[2] V. Gen. R. LXXIII, 11. [3] Lit. E.V.: '*men of skill.*'
[4] Gen. XXXVIII; XXXV, 22.

of fine flour, and threescore measures of meal; ten fat oxen, etc. (I Kings v, 2 f.). (R. Joḥanan said: So it was every day, and so each of his wives prepared a meal for him hoping that he would dine with her.) But to-day it is written, *This was my portion from all my labour* (Eccl. II, 10).[1] Some say that this refers to his pitcher, others to his stick, and still others to his girdle. NOR YET RICHES TO MEN OF UNDERSTANDING: this alludes to Job. Yesterday, *His possessions also were seven thousand sheep*, etc. (Job I, 3), *And his possessions are increased in the land* (*ib.* 10). (R. Jose b. R. Ḥanina said: He broke the general rule[2]; because everywhere it is customary for wolves to kill goats, but in the case of Job the goats killed the wolves.) But to-day [he cries], *Have pity upon me, have pity upon me, O ye my friends* (*ib.* XIX, 21). NOR YET FAVOUR TO THOSE WHO KNOW: this alludes to Joshua. R. Aḥwa b. R. Zera said: Joshua made two remarks in the presence of Moses which failed to find favour in his sight—one in connection with the appointment of the elders and the other in connection with the golden calf. 'In connection with the appointment of the elders,' as it is written, *My lord Moses, shut them in*—kela'em (Num. XI, 28), by which he meant, 'Destroy them (*kallem*) and remove them from the world.' Moses replied to him, *Art thou jealous for my sake?* (*ib.* 29), by which he really meant, 'Joshua, am I jealous of you?[3] Would that my sons were like you. Would that all Israel were like you! *Would that all the Lord's people were prophets* (*ib.*)!' 'The other in connection with the golden calf,' as it is said, *And when Joshua heard the noise of the people as they shouted* (Ex. XXXII, 17). Moses said to him, 'A man who is destined to exercise authority over sixty myriads is unable to distinguish between one sound and

[1] Said by him when he was reduced to poverty. V. Midrash *ad loc.*
[2] Lit. 'fence of the world'.
[3] According to the Rabbis (Sanh. 17*a*) the elders who roused Joshua's ire (Num. XI, 26–28) did so because they prophesied that Moses would die and Joshua would lead the Israelites into Eretz Israel. This explains the present comment.

another! *It is not the voice of them that shout for mastery* —geburah (*ib.* 18)—as the word is used in *Israel prevailed* —gabar (*ib.* XVII, 11)—*Neither is it the voice of them that cry for being overcome* (ḥalushah)—as the word is used in *Joshua discomfited* (wayyaḥalosh) *Amalek* (*ib.* 13)—*But the noise of them that sing do I hear.*' R. Assi said: [He meant by this,] 'The noise of idolatrous praise do I hear.' R. Judan said in the name of R. Assi: There is no generation which has not received a small particle of the calf.[1]

2. Another interpretation of THE RACE IS NOT TO THE SWIFT: this alludes to Moses who yesterday flew up to the heavens and ascended like a bird, as it says, *And Moses went up to God* (*ib.* XIX, 3). To-day [it is said to him], *Thou shalt not go over this Jordan* (Deut. III, 27) —not even a measured distance of fifty cubits[2] was he able to pass over. NOR THE BATTLE TO THE STRONG: this alludes to Moses. Yesterday [it was told of him], *Kings of armies flee, they flee* (Ps. LXVIII, 13). What means '*Flee, they flee*'? They flee in their going and they flee in their return.[3] R. Judan said in the name of R. Aibu: It is not written here 'angels (*mal'ake*) of armies' but '*Kings* (malke) *of armies*', i.e. even the kings of the angels,[4] Michael and Gabriel, were afraid of Moses. But to-day he was unable to look upon the common soldiers among them, as it is written, *For I was in dread of Af* (*Anger*) *and* Ḥemah—*hot displeasure* (Deut. IX, 19).[5] NEITHER YET BREAD TO THE WISE: this alludes to Moses. Yesterday he was appointed the officer to arrange the receptions in Pharaoh's palace, as it is said, *When Moses was grown up, that he went out unto his brethren*

[1] Later generations also feel the effect of that great sin.
[2] The width of the Jordan at that spot.
[3] This is not clear. Mah. explains that it refers to the statement in Mek. on Jethro that at every word of God which the Israelites heard at Revelation they recoiled twelve miles and the angels gently led them back as one leads a child (*yidodun*—E.V. '*they flee*' may be rendered: they take little steps—like a child).
[4] *Ẓeba'oth* (E.V. '*armies*') is understood to mean the hosts (of heaven), i.e. angels. [5] Explained to mean angels. V. p. 112.

(Ex. II, 11). What means '*was grown up*'?[1] His greatness was to arrange for [the food of the palace] to be brought in and taken out. But to-day [when he fled to Midian it was said of him], *Call him, that he may eat bread* (*ib.* 20). NOR YET RICHES TO MEN OF UNDERSTANDING: this alludes to Moses. Whence did riches come to him that he was wealthy? R. Ḥanin said: The Holy One, blessed be He, disclosed to him the existence of a sapphire mine in his tent, and he found it, and from it Moses grew rich, as it is said, *Hew thee* (*ib.* XXXIV, 1), i.e. the chippings[2] are for yourself. But to-day [when he is to die], all this wealth availed him nothing. NOR YET FAVOUR TO THOSE WHO KNOW: this alludes to Moses. Yesterday [it was said to him], *For thou hast found grace in My sight* (*ib.* XXXIII, 17); but to-day, *Speak no more unto Me of this matter* (Deut. III, 26). BUT TIME AND CHANCE (PEGA') HAPPENETH TO THEM ALL: Time strikes (*poga'ath*) a man and causes all these vicissitudes to happen to him, and then he prays (*mafgia'*). What is he to do? Let him go and engage in prayer and supplication; then he will be delivered from them. R. Huna asked Samuel, 'What means that which is written, BUT TIME AND PEGA' (PRAYER)?' He replied, 'Sometimes a man engages in prayer and is answered, while sometimes he engages in prayer and is not answered. You have nobody who composed more prayers and supplications than Moses our teacher; yet in the end it was said to him, "*Behold, thy days approach that thou must die*"' (*ib.* XXXI, 14).

1. FOR MAN ALSO KNOWETH NOT HIS TIME; AS THE FISHES THAT ARE TAKEN IN AN EVIL NET (IX, 12). R. Berekiah asked, 'Is there, then, an evil net and a good net? R. Simeon b. Lakish said: [The former] denotes a fish-hook.[3] That is what is written, *Even those men that did bring up an evil report of the land died by the plague* (Num. XIV, 37). How did they die? The Rabbis

[1] The Heb. can also mean 'became great'.
[2] The tablets were of sapphire. Cf. Num. R. IX, 48.
[3] This is a painful way of being caught.

and R. Simeon b. Yoḥai give answers. The Rabbis say: Croup ascended into their throat so that they choked and died; R. Simeon b. Yoḥai said: They died by their limbs dropping off. R. Judah b. R. Simon said: The reason for the answer given by the Rabbis is that here is mentioned *EVIL* NET, and in the other place '*evil* [*report*]' is mentioned; and as the '*evil*' mentioned here refers to a hook which descends the fish's throat and chokes it, so in the other passage '*evil*' means that croup ascended into their throat and they died. R. Berekiah explains the reason of R. Simeon b. Yoḥai: '*Plague*' is mentioned here, and 'plague' is mentioned elsewhere, viz. *This shall be the plague* (Zech. XIV, 12); as in the latter passage it means the dropping off of the limbs,[1] so here also it has that meaning. R. Berekiah said: There is a net which catches in the sea but not on land and likewise a net which catches on land but not in the sea; a hook, however, is used for catching both in the sea and on land, because it descends into the fish's throat and chokes it.

R. 'Azariah and R. Jonathan b. R. Haggai said in the name of R. Isaac b. Marion who reported it in the name of R. Ḥanina: There is a man who sins against earth[2] but not against Heaven, [and another who sins] against Heaven but not against earth. He, however, who utters slanders sins against both, as it is said, *They have set their mouth against the heavens, and their tongue walketh through the earth* (Ps. LXXIII, 9). R. Eleazar said: We find that they walk against Heaven[3] while their tongue slavers (*shotet*) on earth. What is the reason [for this statement]? '*They have set* (shattu) *their mouth against the heavens, and their tongue walketh through the earth.*'

R. Joḥanan said: A man does not utter slander until he denies the cardinal principle [of God's existence], as it is stated, *Who have said: Our tongue will we make*

[1] The text continues, *Their flesh shall consume away.*
[2] I.e. against his fellowmen.
[3] As v. 11 states, *They say: How doth God know?* The consequence of their denial of God is to cause wickedness on earth.

mighty; our lips are with us; who is lord over us? (*ib.* XII, 5). R. Isaac said: *Now consider this, ye that forget God* (*ib.* L, 22)—this alludes to those who utter slander, as it is stated, '*Who have said: Our tongue will we make mighty; our lips are with us; who is lord over us?*'

1. THIS ALSO HAVE I SEEN AS WISDOM UNDER THE SUN (IX, 13). R. Samuel b. Ammi said: This refers to the devices of cheats in their guile; e.g. one who adulterates wine with water, oil with the juice of glaucion, honey with the juice of the wild strawberry, balsam with ass's milk, myrrh with gum, pepper with vine-leaves. One should not use a weight-beam which is longer on one side than the other [to give false measure],[1] nor a stick for levelling grain which is thick on one side and narrow on the other. A weight-beam or an instrument for levelling grain that contains a [secret] receptacle in which metal [can be inserted], or a carrying-yoke[2] in which is a [secret] receptacle for money, or a beggar's cane which has a receptacle for water, or a stick which has a receptacle for a *mezuzah* and for pearls[3]—behold, these contract ritual defilement. Concerning all of them R. Johanan said: Woe is me if I say it, and woe is me if I do not say it.[4] If I say it there is the danger that I may teach cheats what to do; and if I do not say it I may hamper a disciple [by not imparting to him the knowledge] and he will declare what is clean to be unclean. Another reason [why one should say it] is: Cheats should not think, 'The Sages are unacquainted with our actions.' R. Samuel said: For all that, *The ways of the Lord are right, and the just do walk in them; but transgressors do stumble therein* (Hosea XIV, 10).[5]

1. THERE WAS A LITTLE CITY (IX, 14): i.e. the world, AND FEW MEN WITHIN IT: i.e. the

[1] Cf. VI, 1. [2] A pole or sort of yoke carried on one or two shoulders, from which merchandise, etc., is suspended.
[3] The *mezuzah* is used as a fraudulent means of smuggling precious stones. [4] Quoted from Kel. XVII, 16. [5] The truth must be revealed.

generation of Enosh and the generation of the Flood. AND THERE CAME A GREAT KING AGAINST IT, AND BESIEGED IT: i.e. the supreme King of kings, the Holy One, blessed be He, AND BUILT GREAT BULWARKS AGAINST IT: i.e. craft and guile.[1]

1. NOW THERE WAS FOUND IN IT A MAN POOR AND WISE (IX, 15): i.e. Noah, as it is stated, *For thee have I seen righteous before Me in this generation* (Gen. VII, 1). AND HE BY HIS WISDOM DELIVERED THE CITY: for he said to the people, 'Woe, ye foolish ones! To-morrow a flood will come, so repent.' They answered him, 'If punishments begin, they will begin with your house.' When Methuselah died, they said to Noah, 'Have punishments not begun with your house!' YET NO MAN REMEMBERED THAT SAME POOR MAN: the Holy One, blessed be He, said to them, 'You have not remembered him, but I will remember him,' as it is stated, *And God remembered Noah* (*ib.* VIII, 1).

2. Another interpretation of NOW THERE WAS A LITTLE CITY: i.e. Egypt. AND FEW MEN WITHIN IT: i.e. the Egyptians.[2] AND THERE CAME A GREAT KING AGAINST IT, AND BESIEGED IT: i.e. the wicked Pharaoh, AND BUILT GREAT BULWARKS AGAINST IT: i.e. craft and trickery.[3] NOW THERE WAS FOUND IN IT A MAN POOR AND WISE: i.e. the righteous Joseph, AND HE BY HIS WISDOM DELIVERED THE CITY: for he said to Pharaoh, *Let Pharaoh do this, and let him appoint overseers over the land . . . and let them gather all the food of these good years that come* (*ib.* XLI, 34 f.). YET NO MAN REMEMBERED THAT SAME POOR MAN: the Holy One, blessed be He, said to them, 'You have not remembered him, but I will remember him,' as it is stated, *Joseph was the governor over the land* (*ib.* XLII, 6).

[1] Cf. Gen. R. XXXIII, 2.
[2] Who were reduced in numbers by the seven years' famine.
[3] He refused to sell them corn. Cf. Gen. R. XCI, 5.

3. Another interpretation of NOW THERE WAS A LITTLE CITY: i.e. Egypt, AND FEW MEN WITHIN IT: i.e. Joseph's brothers, as it is said, *And Joseph's ten brethren went down to buy corn* (*ib.* 3). AND THERE CAME A GREAT KING AGAINST IT, AND BESIEGED IT: i.e. Joseph, AND BUILT GREAT BULWARKS AGAINST IT: this refers to the three decrees which he enacted, viz. that no slave might enter Egypt,[1] that nobody could enter with two asses [to carry away corn], and nobody might enter without writing [in a book] his name, and the name of his father, grandfather and grandmother.[2] NOW THERE WAS FOUND IN IT A MAN POOR AND WISE: i.e. Judah, AND HE BY HIS WISDOM DELIVERED THE CITY: because he said [to his father concerning Benjamin], *I will be surety for him* (*ib.* XLIII, 9), and further because he said to Joseph, *Now, therefore, let thy servant, I pray thee, abide instead of the lad a bondman to my lord* (*ib.* XLIV, 33). YET NO MAN REMEMBERED THAT SAME POOR MAN: the Holy One, blessed be He, said, 'You have not remembered him, but I will remember him,' as it is stated, *And he sent Judah before him unto Joseph* (*ib.* XLVI, 28).

4. Another interpretation of NOW THERE WAS A LITTLE CITY: i.e. Egypt, AND FEW MEN WITHIN IT: i.e. Israel, as it is stated, *Thy fathers went down into Egypt with threescore and ten persons* (Deut. X, 22). AND THERE CAME A GREAT KING AGAINST IT: i.e. Pharaoh, AND BESIEGED IT, AND BUILT GREAT BULWARKS AGAINST IT: in that he decreed against them enactments one severer than the other, viz. he withheld the Israelites from connubial intercourse, prevented them from practising circumcision, and made them grow their hair plaited [after the heathen fashion]. NOW THERE WAS FOUND IN IT A MAN POOR AND WISE: i.e. Moses, as it is stated, *And Moses said: Thus*

[1] To buy corn, but the master must come in person.
[2] This book was brought for Joseph's inspection every night, and in this way he discovered when his brothers arrived.

saith the Lord: About midnight will I go out into the midst of Egypt (Ex. XI, 4), AND HE BY HIS WISDOM DELIVERED THE CITY: as it is said, *And they shall take the blood*, etc. (*ib.* XII, 7).[1] YET NO MAN REMEMBERED THAT SAME POOR MAN[2]: the Holy One, blessed be He, said, 'You have not remembered him, but I will remember him,' [as it is stated,] *Then He remembered the days of old, the days of Moses* (Isa. LXIII, 11).

5. Another interpretation of NOW THERE WAS A LITTLE CITY: i.e. Sinai,[3] AND FEW MEN WITHIN IT: i.e. Israel. AND THERE CAME A GREAT KING AGAINST IT: i.e. the Supreme King of kings, the Holy One, blessed be He, AND BESIEGED IT, AND BUILT GREAT BULWARKS AGAINST IT: i.e. the two hundred and forty-eight positive commandments and three hundred and sixty-five prohibitions. NOW THERE WAS FOUND IN IT A MAN POOR AND WISE: i.e. Moses, as it is said, *No hand shall touch it* (Ex. XIX, 13),[4] AND HE BY HIS WISDOM DELIVERED THE CITY: as it is said, *Whosoever toucheth the mount shall be surely put to death* (*ib.* 12).[5] YET NO MAN REMEMBERED THAT SAME POOR MAN: the Holy One, blessed be He, said, 'You have not remembered him, but I will cause him to be remembered,' as it is said, *Remember ye the law of Moses My servant* (Mal. III, 22).

6. Another interpretation of NOW THERE WAS A LITTLE CITY: i.e. Sinai, AND FEW MEN WITHIN IT: i.e. Israel. AND THERE CAME A GREAT KING AGAINST IT: i.e. the Evil Inclination, AND BUILT GREAT BULWARKS AGAINST IT: as it is said [of the

[1] By sprinkling the blood on the doorposts the Israelites escaped death.
[2] The Israelites forgot what he had done for them and murmured against him.
[3] The Rabbis declared that Sinai was one of the lowliest of mountains.
[4] The Midrash apparently applies this to the Mountain. E.V. '*him*'.
[5] The point of these two quotations is not clear. ענף יוסף explains that Moses was poor in that he understood the prohibition to apply to himself too. Perhaps the 'saving' of the city means that he preserved the awe in which Sinai was held by his strict warning of death.

golden calf], *This is thy god, O Israel* (Ex. XXXII, 4). NOW THERE WAS FOUND IN IT A MAN POOR AND WISE: i.e. Moses, as it is stated, *And Moses besought the Lord his God, and said: Lord, why doth Thy wrath wax hot against Thy people?* (*ib.* 11). YET NO MAN REMEMBERED THAT SAME POOR MAN: the Holy One, blessed be He, said: 'You have not remembered him, but I will cause him to be remembered,' as it is stated, *Therefore He said that He would destroy them, had not Moses His chosen stood before Him in the breach, to turn back His wrath, lest He should destroy them* (Ps. CVI, 23).

7. Another interpretation of NOW THERE WAS A LITTLE CITY: i.e. the Synagogue, AND FEW MEN WITHIN IT: i.e. the congregation. AND THERE CAME A GREAT KING AGAINST IT: i.e. the Supreme King of kings, the Holy One, blessed be He, AND BESIEGED IT, AND BUILT GREAT BULWARKS AGAINST IT: i.e. tortuous paths and concealed spots.[1] NOW THERE WAS FOUND IN IT A MAN POOR AND WISE: i.e. the scholarly elder or the Reader. For when the elder sits and expounds Torah, and the congregation respond after him, 'Amen, may His great name be blessed,'[2] should there be outstanding against them for a hundred years a document of [severe] decrees, the Holy One, blessed be He, forgives all their sins. YET NO MAN REMEMBERED THAT SAME POOR MAN: the Holy One, blessed be He, said: 'You have not remembered him but I will cause him to be remembered,' as it is stated, *Thou shalt rise up before the hoary head, and honour the face of the old man* (Lev. XIX, 32).[3]

8. Another interpretation of NOW THERE WAS A LITTLE CITY: i.e. the body, AND FEW MEN WITHIN

[1] The rendering follows Levy: It apparently means that there are pitfalls of ignorance in the way of the proper observance of the Torah, and it is for the elder to illumine them.
[2] The discourse was followed by a doxology to which these words were the response. [3] *Old man* is defined by the Rabbis as the scholar.

IT: i.e. the limbs. AND THERE CAME A GREAT KING AGAINST IT: i.e. the Evil Inclination. (Why is it called GREAT? Because it is thirteen years older than the Good Inclination.)[1] AND BESIEGED IT, AND BUILT GREAT BULWARKS AGAINST IT: i.e. tortuous paths and concealed spots.[2] NOW THERE WAS FOUND IN IT A MAN POOR AND WISE: i.e. the Good Inclination. (Why is it called POOR? Because it is not found in all persons, nor do most of them obey it.) AND HE BY HIS WISDOM DELIVERED THE CITY: for whoever obeys the Good Inclination escapes [punishment]. David said: Happy is he who obeys it, as it is written, *Happy is he that considereth the poor* (Ps. XLI, 2). YET NO MAN REMEMBERED THAT SAME POOR MAN: the Holy One, blessed be He, said: 'You have not remembered it, but I will remember it,' as it is written, *I will take away the stony heart out of your flesh, and I will give you a heart of flesh* (Ezek. XXXVI, 26).

1. THEN SAID I: WISDOM IS BETTER THAN STRENGTH; NEVERTHELESS THE POOR MAN'S WISDOM IS DESPISED, AND HIS WORKS ARE NOT HEARD (IX, 16). R. Joḥanan said: Was the wisdom of R. Akiba,[3] who was poor, despised! It alludes, however, to an elder who sits [and expounds Torah] but makes his words poor [by not practising them]; as, e.g., an elder who sits and expounds, *Thou shalt not respect persons* (Deut. XVI, 19) while he does respect persons, *Neither shalt thou take a gift* (*ib.*) while he accepts bribes, 'Thou shalt not lend on usury,' while he does lend. Samson followed [the lust of] his eyes, yet *He judged Israel in the days of the Philistines twenty years* (Judg. XV, 20). In connection with Gideon it is said, *Gideon made an ephod thereof, and put it in his city, even in Ophrah; and all*

[1] Cf. IV, 13.
[2] Cf. n. 1 on p. 253. Here it means that the Tempter lays pitfalls in the way of the unwary and seeks to inveigle them into the tortuous paths of wrongdoing.
[3] He is quoted as an instance of a poor man whose wisdom was anything but despised.

Israel went astray after it there (*ib.* VIII, 27), and yet he judged Israel![1] Hence POOR MAN means nothing else than one who makes his words poor.

1. THE WORDS OF THE WISE SPOKEN IN QUIET ARE [MORE] ACCEPTABLE (IX, 17): these are the expositors; THAN THE CRY OF A RULER AMONG FOOLS: these are the interpreters[2] who stand in front of the congregation.

Another interpretation of THE WORDS OF THE WISE SPOKEN IN QUIET ARE [MORE] ACCEPTABLE: i.e. Amram and his *Beth Din*.[3] R. Bun said: They assembled behind a stone wall or a fence, and argued, 'What use is there for us to marry wives and beget children whom the Egyptians cast into the river? Let the world have been continued up to now!'[4] THAN THE CRY OF A RULER AMONG FOOLS: this refers to Pharaoh who decreed, *Every son that is born ye shall cast into the river* (Ex. I, 22); but it was not the judgment [of God] that attention should be paid to his decree.[5]

1. WISDOM IS BETTER THAN WEAPONS OF WAR (IX, 18): this refers to the wisdom of the patriarch Jacob; THAN WEAPONS OF WAR: of the wicked Esau. R. Levi said: Jacob equipped them[6] with weapons underneath and clothed them in white garments on top. He then prepared himself for three things, viz. prayer, a gift, and battle. Whence do we learn that he prepared himself for prayer? As it is said, *Deliver me, I pray thee, from the hand of my brother* (Gen. XXXII, 12). Whence that he prepared himself for a gift? As it is said, *Then thou shalt*

[1] These are examples of men who 'made their words poor' by not practising what they taught. [2] V. p. 179, n. 3.

[3] On account of Egyptian oppression, they had to function in secret.

[4] I.e. since it is useless for us to have children, the world must come to an end so far as we are concerned. Or the words can be construed as a question, 'Is the world to be continued only up to now?' They decided that it was their duty to carry out their marital obligations.

[5] The text is doubtful. Radal emends: But nobody paid attention to his decree. [6] His sons and herdsmen, when he heard that Esau was approaching with a band of four hundred men.

say: They are thy servant Jacob's, it is a present sent unto my lord (*ib.* 19). Whence that he prepared himself for battle? As it is said, *He put the handmaids and their children foremost . . . and he himself passed over before them and bowed himself to the ground* (*ib.* XXXIII, 2 f.). He said, 'It is better that he should attack me and not my children.' *So Esau returned that day on his way unto Seir* (*ib.* 16)—why to Seir? R. Eleazar and R. Samuel b. Naḥmani give answers. R. Eleazar said: Because of the bond of indebtedness.[1] R. Samuel b. Naḥmani said: Out of shame.[2] BUT ONE SINNER DESTROYETH MUCH GOOD: this alludes to the wicked Esau who destroyed all the good things and gifts of the World to Come.

2. Another interpretation of WISDOM IS BETTER: this refers to the wisdom of Serah the daughter of Asher[3]; THAN WEAPONS OF WAR: than the weapons of Joab, as it is said, *Then cried a wise woman out of the city* (II Sam. XX, 16), which indicates that he was some distance away. *And he came near unto her; and the woman said: Art thou Joab* (*ib.* 17)? [She meant,] 'You are a destroyer, and you do not act up to your name.[4] You are not a son of Torah nor is David; for is it not written in the Torah, *When thou drawest nigh unto a city to fight against it, then proclaim peace unto it* (Deut. XX, 10)? Perhaps [you have come here] for war'? As it is written, *Then she spoke, saying: They were wont to speak in old time, saying: They shall surely ask counsel at Abel; and so they ended the matter* (II Sam. XX, 18). She said to him, 'Up to here the words of Torah are ended without being fulfilled.'[5] He asked her, 'Who

[1] Involved in the decree imposed upon Isaac's descendants, *And they shall afflict them* (Gen. XV, 13). Esau departed to Seir to avoid coming within the scope of this decree; Gen. R. LXXXII, 13.
[2] At having sold his birthright.
[3] Gen. XLVI, 17. Cf. Gen. R. XCIV, 9, where there is a clearer version of what follows. [4] Joab is explained as 'a father' (*ab*) to Israel.
[5] Meaning that Joab had not proclaimed peace to the city but intended to attack it. Or perhaps it should be rendered: Have the words of the Torah ended by now, so that they need not be fulfilled?

are you?' She replied to him, 'Who am I? I am *Of them that are peaceable* (shelume) *and faithful in Israel* (*ib.* 19). I am she who completed (*hishlamti*) the number of Israelites in Egypt[1]; I am she who delivered up (*hishlamti*) the faithful Joseph to the faithful Moses.'[2] *Seekest thou to destroy a city and a mother in Israel?* (*ib.*)—'*a city,*' i.e. *Abel of Beth-Maacah* (*ib.* 15), and me who am *A mother in Israel.* Forthwith, *And Joab answered and said: Far be it, far be it from me, that I should swallow up or destroy* (*ib.* 20), i.e. far be it from Joab, far be it from David, far be it from his government.[3] *The matter is not so; but a man of the hill-country of Ephraim, Sheba the son of Bichri by name, hath lifted up his hand against the king, even against David* (*ib.* 21). If it mentions '*against the king*', why add '*even against David*', and if it mentions '*against David*' why add '*against the king*'? R. 'Azariah and R. Jonathan b. R. Haggai said in the name of R. Isaac b. Marion: It is to teach you that whoever hardens his face against the disciples of the Sages and the great [teacher] of the generation is as though he hardens his face against the king; so how much more so in the case of David who was king, sage, and a great [teacher] in his generation! R. Judan said: Whoever hardens his face against the king is as though he hardens his face against the *Shechinah*, as it is written, '*Hath lifted up his hand against the King, even against David*'—'*Against the King,*' i.e. the Supreme King of kings, the Holy One, blessed be He, and then '*against David*', i.e. David, king of Israel.

Deliver him only, and I will depart from the city (*ib.*). She asked him, 'How do you know [that he is guilty of death]?' He answered, 'Whoever acts brazenly against the house of David is condemned from Above.' Immediately, *Then the woman went unto the people in her wisdom* (*ib.* 22), and said to them, 'Will you not obey Joab and will you not obey David? Which nation or king-

[1] She made up the number 70 who descended into Egypt.

[2] It is related that Moses inquired of her where Joseph was buried when he wished to take his bones to Canaan; Soṭ. 13*a* (Sonc. ed., p. 67).

[3] This comment explains the repetition of *far be it.*

dom has stood against them!' They asked her, 'What does he want?' She replied, 'A thousand men.' They said to her, 'Let every man give according to his means.'[1] She then said to them, 'I will go and try to persuade him to take less.' She pretended to go [to interview Joab] and return; and she told them, 'He wants five hundred.' They replied, 'Let every man give according to his means.' She said to them, 'I will go and appeal to him, perhaps he will reduce the number.' She pretended to go and return; and she told them, 'He wants only one man, and he is a stranger in our midst.' They replied, 'Even if he were the best man in the city we would surrender him.' She said to them, 'His name is Sheba the son of Bichri.' Forthwith, 'They took the head of Sheba the son of Bichri and threw it over the wall.'[2] BUT ONE SINNER DESTROYETH MUCH GOOD: i.e. Sheba the son of Bichri.

3. Another interpretation of WISDOM IS BETTER: i.e. the wisdom of Hezekiah, king of Judah, THAN WEAPONS OF WAR: of Sennacherib. R. Levi said: Three captivities did Sennacherib carry away: in the first he carried the tribes of Reuben and Gad into captivity, in the second the ten tribes, and in the third he came against Judah. Immediately Hezekiah arose and armed the men with weapons beneath and clothed them in white garments on top, and prepared himself for three things, viz. for prayer, for a gift, and for battle. 'For prayer,' as it is written, *And Hezekiah prayed unto the Lord*, etc. (Isa. XXXVII, 15 ff.). 'For a gift,' as it is written, *At that time did Hezekiah cut off the gold from the doors of the temple of the Lord, and from* ha'omnoth—*the doorposts* (II Kings XVIII, 16). (What are '*ha'omnoth*'? R. Levi said: Wreaths [on the doors], while the Rabbis say: Hinges.) 'For battle,' as it is said, *And he made weapons and shields in abundance* (II Chron. XXXII, 5). He also stuck a sword

[1] E.J.: every family will have to surrender men in proportion to its size.
[2] This is an inexact quotation from II Sam. XX, 22.

by the entrance of the House of Study and said, 'Whoever does not occupy himself with Torah, may this sword pass over his neck.'[1] *Then came Eliakim the son of Hilkiah, who was over the household* (II Kings XVIII, 37), i.e. the chief of the guard, *and Shebna the scribe*, i.e. the secretary, *And Joah the son of Asaph the recorder*, i.e. the superintendent. BUT ONE SINNER DESTROYETH MUCH GOOD: i.e. Sennacherib, as it is said, *So he returned with shame of face to his own land*, etc. (II Chron. XXXII, 21), *And Esarhaddon his son reigned in his stead* (II Kings XIX, 37).

[1] If this is not a digression, it apparently means that he hoped to be saved by the merit of promoting the study of the Torah, and thus this too is regarded figuratively as part of his warlike preparations.

Chapter X

1. DEAD FLIES MAKE THE OINTMENT OF THE PERFUMER FETID AND PUTRID (X, 1). Ben 'Azzai and R. Akiba commented. Ben 'Azzai said: One dead fly[1] does not make the ointment of the perfumer fetid and putrid; but the meaning is, by a single sin which a man commits he causes the loss of much good to himself. R. Akiba expounded: *Therefore the netherworld hath enlarged her desire, and opened her mouth without measure* (Isa. V, 14)—it is not written here '*ḥuḳḳim*', but '*without* ḥoḳ',[2] i.e. a person who has not [the performance of] one precept [to his credit] which can make the scale of merit incline in his favour. The *Doreshe Reshumot*[3] say: A person is judged by his majority,[4] and he should always estimate himself as half meritorious and half guilty. If he performs one precept, happy is he for making the scale of merit incline in his favour; and if he commits one transgression, woe to him for making the scale of guilt incline against him. R. Simeon b. Eleazar[5] said: Because an individual is judged by his majority and the world is judged by its majority, on account of the single sin which he commits he deprives himself and the world of much good.

2. Another interpretation of DEAD FLIES MAKE THE OINTMENT OF THE PERFUMER FETID AND PUTRID: it speaks of Korah's company. Yesterday they used vile

[1] Since the subject is plural, DEAD FLIES, but the verbs MAKE FETID AND PUTRID are singular, he understands the text in a metaphorical sense.

[2] The word means 'measure' and 'statute'. R. Akiba adopts the second meaning, and dwells on the fact that the word is singular, understanding the Heb. to indicate 'opened her mouth for him who is without one statute (of the Torah to his credit)'.

[3] The name of a School of allegorical interpreters of the Bible.

[4] The majority of his deeds, whether the good or bad predominate.

[5] In Ḳid. 40*b* (Sonc. ed., p. 200), from which this passage is quoted, the author is R. Eleazar b. R. Simeon.

language[1] against Moses, saying, 'Moses is not a prophet of truth, Aaron is not High Priest, nor is the Torah from Heaven'; but to-day they make declaration[2] before Moses, saying, 'Moses is a prophet of truth, Aaron is High Priest, and the Torah is from Heaven.' MORE PRECIOUS THAN WISDOM AND HONOUR[3] is [Moses'] prophecy; A LITTLE FOLLY: i.e. Moses' decree[4] which he spoke, viz. *But if the Lord make a new thing, and the ground open her mouth* (Num. XVI, 30).

Another interpretation of DEAD FLIES MAKE THE OINTMENT OF THE PERFUMER FETID AND PUTRID: it speaks of Doeg and Ahitophel. Yesterday they used vile language against David, saying, 'He comes from a disqualified family [and should not be king], for is he not descended from Ruth the Moabitess!' but to-day they utter words which reflect their sense of shame. MORE PRECIOUS THAN WISDOM AND HONOUR is David's prophecy; A LITTLE FOLLY [on their part caused him to exclaim], *But Thou, O God, wilt bring them down into the nethermost pit* (Ps. LV, 24).

Another interpretation of DEAD FLIES MAKE THE OINTMENT OF THE PERFUMER FETID AND PUTRID: it speaks of the generation of Elijah. Yesterday they used vile language against Him, saying, *O Baal, answer us* (I Kings XVIII, 26), but to-day they make declaration, saying, *The Lord He is God, the Lord He is God* (*ib.* 39). MORE PRECIOUS THAN WISDOM AND HONOUR—THAN WISDOM, i.e. the Torah, AND HONOUR, i.e. Elijah's prophecy; A LITTLE FOLLY [of the priests of Baal brought it about that] *Elijah brought them down to the brook Kishon, and slew them there* (*ib.* 40).

1. A WISE MAN'S UNDERSTANDING IS AT HIS RIGHT HAND (X, 2). R. Ḥanina b. Papa said: It may

[1] The Heb. for this is the same as that for MAKE . . . FETID.
[2] From Gehinnom; v. B.B. 74*a* (Sonc. ed., p. 294).
[3] E.V.: '*So doth a little folly outweigh wisdom and honour.*'
[4] The folly of Korah's company led Moses to issue the decree which resulted in their being swallowed up in the earth and their admission that he was right and they were wrong.

be likened to two men who possessed two measures, one of wheat and the other of barley. One of them said to the other, 'If you are [the owner] of the barley, I am [the owner] of the wheat; and if I am [the owner] of the wheat, you are [the owner] of the barley. In any event I take [my portion] from the wheat.' Similarly Abraham said to Lot, *If thou wilt take the left hand, then I will go to the right; or if thou take the right hand, then I will go to the left* (Gen. XIII, 9).[1] R. Ḥanina b. R. Isaac said: It is not written here *esme'olah* (I will go to the left), but '*asme'ilah*' (I will cause to go to the left), i.e. even if you act disrespectfully towards me, I shall cause you to be on the left.[2]

When a person came before Rabbi [Judah ha-Nasi] for judgment, if he accepted his verdict, well and good; but if not, he would say to a member of his household, 'Show him the left side,'[3] and he displayed to him a cutting off from that direction.[4]

Another interpretation of A WISE MAN'S UNDERSTANDING IS AT HIS RIGHT HAND: this alludes to Jacob, as it is said, *Then Jacob rose up, and set his sons and his wives upon the camels* (Gen. XXXI, 17). BUT A FOOL'S UNDERSTANDING AT HIS LEFT: this alludes to the wicked Esau, as it is said, *And Esau took his wives and sons* (*ib.* XXXVI, 6).[5]

[1] The translation given in the E.V. of this last phrase is not accepted in the comment that follows, because the verb is in the causative mood. Cf. Gen. R. XLI, 6.

[2] I.e. I will force you to go left, even if you brazenly demand the right to choose. This is given as an illustration of the present text, that a wise man's understanding is to go to the right Possibly, too, the point of the Midrash is that RIGHT HAND and LEFT are not to be understood literally, but indicate right and wrong respectively.

[3] An indication that he was in the wrong and that he was to be forced to accept Rabbi's ruling. This is quoted to illustrate the use of the term LEFT.

[4] So lit. M.K. comments: Some explain that he showed him a sickle to indicate that if he did not accept the verdict against him, he would be punished. He adds an alternative explanation: he struck him a cutting blow on the left side.

[5] Jacob thought of the males before the females, whereas Esau, who thought only of women, reversed the order. Cf. Gen. R. LXXIV, 5.

1. YEA ALSO, WHEN A FOOL WALKETH BY THE WAY, HIS UNDERSTANDING FAILETH HIM, AND HE SAITH TO EVERY ONE THAT HE IS A FOOL (X, 3). The fool thinks that all people are fools like himself, and does not know that he is a fool and all the people are wise.

1. IF THE SPIRIT OF THE RULER RISE UP AGAINST THEE,[1] LEAVE NOT THY PLACE (X, 4). This means that should ruling power come to you, do not cast away your humility, to teach you that whoever casts away his humility causes death to befall his world[2] and sin to befall his generation. From whom do you learn this? From Zechariah, as it is said, *And the spirit of God clothed Zechariah the priest, and he stood above the people* (II Chron. XXIV, 20). Did he, then, walk over the heads of the people! It means that he imagined himself greater than all the people. He was son-in-law of the king, a priest, a prophet, and a judge; so he began to speak arrogantly and say to them, *Why transgress ye the commandments of the Lord that ye cannot prosper* (*ib.*)? At once *They conspired against him, and stoned him with stones at the commandment of the king* (*ib.* 21).[3]

R. Judan asked R. Aḥa, 'Where did Israel slay Zechariah, in the Court of Israel or in the Court of the Women?' He replied, 'In neither of these but it was in the Court of the Priests. Nor did they treat his blood as was done with the blood of the hind or ram. It is written of the blood of the ram or hind when it is shed, *He shall pour out the blood thereof, and cover it with dust* (Lev. XVII, 13). But in the case of this righteous man they did not treat his blood like the blood of the hind or ram. For what purpose was all this? *That it might cause fury to come up, that vengeance might be taken* (Ezek. XXIV, 8). You find that when Nebuzaradan came up to destroy Jerusalem, the

[1] Heb. עליך. In the passages that follow it is rendered, 'upon' or 'to thee', rather than 'against thee'. [2] Radal emends to 'himself'.
[3] Thus he caused his own death and *ipso facto* the people to sin by murdering him.

Holy One, blessed be He, hinted to the blood and it began to seethe. He said to it, "The time has come for you to collect your debt." [Nebuzaradan] asked them, "Tell me, what kind of blood is this?" They answered, "The blood of bulls, rams, and lambs which we sacrifice to the Holy One, blessed be He." Immediately he had bulls, rams, and lambs brought, which he slew over it in large numbers, but it did not stop [seething]. He said to them, "If you tell me, well and good; otherwise I will comb your flesh with iron combs." At first they said nothing; but when he spoke to them in this manner, they said to him, "What can we hide from you? We had a priest-prophet and he reproved us in the name of Heaven, saying, 'Accept [what I tell you].' We did not accept it from him, but rose against him and killed him." He said to them, "I will appease the blood." He took the Great Sanhedrin and slew them over it, but it did not become still. He slew the Minor Sanhedrin over it, but it did not become still. He took the priestly novitiates and slew them over it, but it did not become still. He slew school-children by it, but it did not become still. He exclaimed, "Zechariah, the choicest of your people have I destroyed; is it your wish that they all perish?" It immediately became still. That wicked man contemplated repenting in his heart, saying, "If it is written of one who destroys a single life from Israel, *Whoso sheddeth man's blood, by man shall his blood be shed* (Gen. IX, 6), how much truer is it of me who destroyed many lives!" Forthwith the Holy One, blessed be He, was filled with compassion, and hinted to the blood, and it was absorbed in that same place.' R. Judan said: They committed seven transgressions on that day: they killed a priest, a prophet, and a judge, they shed innocent blood, they defiled the Temple Court, and it was done on the Sabbath which was also the Day of Atonement.[1]

Jahaziel, on the other hand, did not act so[2]; but *Upon*

[1] Cf. III, 16, and Lam. R. Proem XXIII.
[2] He did not behave haughtily like Zechariah.

Jahaziel, the son of Zechariah, the son of Benaiah, the son of Jeiel, the son of Mattaniah, the Levite, of the sons of Asaph, came the spirit of the Lord in the midst of the congregation (II Chron. XX, 14). What means '*In the midst of the congregation*'? He placed himself on the same level as the congregation.

Another interpretation of IF THE SPIRIT OF THE RULER RISE UP AGAINST THEE: it speaks of Noah. He entered the ark with the permission [of God] and came out with His permission. Whence do we know that he entered it with permission? *And the Lord said unto Noah: Come thou and all thy house into the ark* (Gen. VII, 1). And whence do we know that he came out with permission? *And God spoke unto Noah, saying: Go forth from the ark* (*ib.* VIII, 15).[1]

Another interpretation of IF THE SPIRIT OF THE RULER RISE UP AGAINST THEE: it speaks of Joshua. In the same manner that Israel crossed the Jordan with the permission [of God], so they did not go up [out of the Jordan] without His permission. Whence do we know that they crossed with permission? As it is stated, *Pass through the midst of the camp . . . for within three days ye are to pass over this Jordan* (Josh. I, 11). They went up with permission, as it is said, *Joshua therefore commanded the priests, saying: Come ye up out of the Jordan* (*ib.* IV, 17).

Another interpretation of IF THE SPIRIT OF THE RULER RISE UP AGAINST THEE: it speaks of David. Before he became king [it is said of him], *David was the youngest* (I Sam. XVII, 14)[2]: but when he had become king [it is stated], *Then David the king stood upon his feet, and said: Hear me, my brethren, and my people* (I Chron. XXVIII, 2).[3]

[1] The favour which God had shown him did not make him proud, and he did not presume to leave the ark until he was commanded to do so. Thus he fulfilled, LEAVE NOT THY PLACE. Similarly in the interpretations that follow those to whom the verse is applied did not leave their place, either literally or metaphorically in the sense that they did not lose their humility. [2] The Heb. could also mean 'smallest', 'most insignificant'. [3] By these words he placed himself on a level with the common people and displayed humility.

Another interpretation of IF THE SPIRIT OF THE RULER RISE UP AGAINST THEE: it speaks of Mordecai. Before greatness came to him it is written, *While Mordecai sat in the king's gate* (Est. II, 21), and when greatness came to him [it is written], *And Mordecai returned to the king's gate* (*ib.* VI, 12).

1. THERE IS AN EVIL WHICH I HAVE SEEN UNDER THE SUN, LIKE AN ERROR WHICH PROCEEDETH FROM A RULER (X, 5). Thus spoke Jacob to Laban: *With whomsoever thou findest thy gods, he shall not live* (Gen. XXXI, 32); and so it was LIKE AN ERROR WHICH PROCEEDETH FROM A RULER, since the death of Rachel ensued.[1]

The son of R. Joshua b. Levi had a choking fit. He went and brought one of [the followers of Bar Pandira][2] to relieve his choking. [R. Joshua] asked him, 'What did you pronounce over [my son]?' He replied, '[I quoted] one text after another.'[3] He exclaimed, 'Better that he had been buried and you had not quoted these texts over him.' And so it was to him LIKE AN ERROR WHICH PROCEEDETH FROM A RULER, [for his son died].

R. Jeremiah of the branch[4] used to take a crown formed of olive branches and bind it round his head [at a wedding]. Samuel heard about it and said, 'It were better that his head should be cut off and he did not act thus'[5]; and so it happened to him.

Antoninus the younger, grandson of Antoninus the elder, asked our holy Rabbi,[6] 'Who will die first, I or

[1] In the erroneous belief that Rachel was innocent of the theft, he uttered the words which caused her early death. [2] The words in brackets are omitted from the text from fear of the censor, Bar Pandira being Jesus.
[3] Scriptural verses used to be cited as incantations. R. Joshua disapproved of the practice.
[4] He was given that name because of the way he danced before bridal couples with a crown of olive branches. The paragraph is repeated from Lam. R. v, 16. [5] Cf. Soṭ. 49*a* (Sonc. ed., p. 265), 'During the war with Vespasian the Rabbis decreed against the use of crowns worn by bridegrooms.' [6] V. p. 242.

you?' He answered, 'I will.' His disciples said to him, 'Our master, all the world prays for your good life and you speak in this manner!' He replied to them, 'If my time to die comes, what of it? And if the Angel of Death comes to take me, what can one say to him? "Do not come to me," or "I will not come"? Not only that, but if it happens so [and I die first], people will say, "Blessed be the God of the Jews who even know the time of their death."' So it was to him LIKE AN ERROR WHICH PROCEEDETH FROM A RULER [and he died first].

Another interpretation of THERE IS AN EVIL WHICH I HAVE SEEN, etc., LIKE AN ERROR FROM A RULER: this refers to Eli the priest who told Samuel, 'My sons will not inherit my place, nor will your sons inherit your place.' And so it was to him LIKE AN ERROR WHICH PROCEEDETH FROM A RULER.[1]

1. FOLLY IS SET ON GREAT HEIGHTS (X, 6): these are the Chaldeans, as it is written, *All the princes of the king of Babylon came in, and sat in the middle gate* (Jer. XXXIX, 3). What means '*the middle* (hatawek) *gate*'? The place where they decide (*meḥattekin*) *halachot*.[2] AND THE RICH SIT IN LOW PLACE: i.e. the Sanhedrin, as it is said, *They sit upon the ground, and keep silence* (Lam. II, 10).[3]

1. I HAVE SEEN SERVANTS UPON HORSES (X, 7): i.e. the Ishmaelites,[4] AND PRINCES WALKING AS SERVANTS: i.e. Joseph. R. Levi said: A servant[5] bought him and the sons of a handmaid[6] sold him, and the son of free men[7] was sold to both of them.

R. Akiba went up to Rome where a eunuch of the court met him and said to him, 'You are the Rabbi of the Jews?' He replied, 'Yes.' He said to him, 'Infer three

[1] V. 1 Sam. IV, 11; VIII, 1 ff. [2] Cf. on III, 16. [3] V. Lam. R. *ad loc.*
[4] Who bought Joseph from his brothers. Actually they had camels and not horses (Gen. XXXVII, 25). [5] Potiphar, who was Pharaoh's servant.
[6] The Ishmaelites were descended from Hagar, Sarah's handmaid.
[7] The patriarchs.

things from me, viz. he who has ridden upon a king's horse, or upon the ass of a son of free men, or has sandals on his feet,[1] is a human being[2]; but he who has none of these things, a man buried in his grave is better than he.' He answered, 'You have mentioned three things; hear from me three things in their stead. The beauty of the face is the beard, the joy of the heart is a wife, *Children are a heritage of the Lord* (Ps. CXXVIII, 3)—woe to the man[3] who lacks these three things.' Not only that, but he quoted against him the verse, I HAVE SEEN SERVANTS UPON HORSES. When the eunuch heard this, he dashed his head against the wall and killed himself.

Another interpretation of I HAVE SEEN SERVANTS UPON HORSES: i.e. Ahab, AND PRINCES WALKING AS SERVANTS: i.e. Elijah, as it is said, *And the hand of the Lord was on Elijah; and he girded up his loins, and ran before Ahab to the entrance of Jezreel* (I Kings XVIII, 46).

1. HE THAT DIGGETH A PIT SHALL FALL INTO IT (X, 8). This alludes to the wicked Pharaoh, as it is said, *And Pharaoh charged all his people, saying: Every son that is born ye shall cast into the river* (Ex. I, 22); SHALL FALL INTO IT: as it is said, *But overthrew Pharaoh and his host in the Red Sea* (Ps. CXXXVI, 15).

Another interpretation of HE THAT DIGGETH A PIT: i.e. Haman, as it is said, *To destroy, to slay, and to cause to perish all Jews* (Est. III, 13); SHALL FALL INTO IT: as it is said, *That his wicked device, which he had devised against the Jews, should return upon his own head* (*ib.* IX, 25).

AND WHOSO BREAKETH THROUGH A FENCE, A SERPENT SHALL BITE HIM: i.e. Dinah. While her father and brothers were sitting in the House of Study, *She went out to see the daughters of the land* (Gen.

[1] This passage occurs in Shab. 152*a* where it is related that the eunuch conversed with R. Joshua b. Ḳorḥah who had no sandals on his feet. The remark was intended as an insult to Jews in general who had been reduced in circumstances by their defeat at the hands of the Romans.
[2] Is worthy of being called a man. [3] As a eunuch he lacked all these.

XXXIV, 1). She brought upon herself her violation by Shechem the son of Hamor the Hivite, who is called A SERPENT,[1] and he bit her; as it is written, *And Shechem the son of Hamor the Hivite, the prince of the land, saw her, and he took her*, etc. (*ib.* 2). *'He took her'*—he spoke seductively to her, as the word is used in *Take with you words* (Hosea XIV, 3); *And lay with her*—in natural intercourse; *And humbled her*—in unnatural intercourse.

R. Simeon b. Yoḥai and his son R. Eleazar were in hiding in the cave of Peḳa for thirteen years during [the Hadrianic] persecution, and subsisted on locusts and dates. At the end of thirteen years R. Simeon b. Yoḥai went out and sat at the entrance of the cave. He saw a fowler spreading his net to catch birds, and heard a *Bath Ḳol* proclaim, 'An amnesty!' and [a bird] was caught. He heard a *Bath Ḳol* a second time proclaim, 'A sentence [of death]!' and [a bird] was saved.[2] He remarked, 'Even a bird cannot escape without [the decree of] Heaven, so how much less a human being! Let us go down and cure ourselves[3] in the waters of the hot spring of Tiberias.' They went down and were cured in the waters of the hot spring of Tiberias. Then they exclaimed, 'We ought to do some good and bestow benefit upon the inhabitants of this town, as did the patriarch Jacob, as it is written, *And he encamped* (wayyiḥan) *before the city* (Gen. XXXIII, 18),[4] which means that he made a store and sold them goods cheaply.' [R. Simeon] set up a store [in Tiberias] and sold goods cheaply. He then said, 'We ought to cleanse Tiberias [of the dead buried there].' What did he do? He took lupins and scattered them in the street, and whoever had died [and been buried there] rose to the surface.[5]

[1] 'Hivite' is connected with *ḥiwya*, the Aramaic word for 'serpent'.
[2] In Gen. R. LXXIX, 6, the wording is reversed. When the cry was 'amnesty' the bird escaped. This version is preferable.
[3] The sand in which they lived so long had affected their skin.
[4] The Heb. *wayyiḥan* is now derived from *ḥen*, 'grace': he was gracious to, i.e. conferred benefit upon the city. [5] The corpses were then buried outside the town which became cleansed of defilement.

A Cuthean saw him doing this and said, 'Shall I not make sport of this elder of the Jews?' What did he do? He took a corpse and hid it in the street which R. Simeon had cleansed. (Some say [that he hid it in the street called] 'Geribah', and others in the street of Bar Ḳardima.) He went and said to him, 'Did you cleanse such-and-such a street?' 'Yes,' he replied. He said to him, 'Supposing I produce for you one corpse from there!' He answered, 'Bring it out and show me.' R. Simeon b. Yoḥai at once perceived by the Holy Spirit that the man had himself hidden it there; so he declared, 'I decree that he who is lying down shall stand up and he who is standing up shall lie down.'[1] Another version is: 'I decree that he who is above shall descend and he who is below shall ascend'; and so it happened to him.

When R. Simeon departed he passed by the Synagogue of Magdala and heard the voice of Naḳai the scribe saying, 'Ben Yoḥai cleansed Tiberias!'[2] R. Simeon said, 'May such-and-such come upon me if there are not in my possession traditions [from my teachers] as numerous as the hairs of my head that Tiberias will in the future be cleansed, and will become [a place of residence] for those who eat *terumah*[3] save only in this spot and this'[4]; but he did not believe him.[5] R. Simeon said to Naḳai, 'You have broken down the fence of the disciples of the Sages,'[6] and he applied to him WHOSO BREAKETH THROUGH A FENCE, A SERPENT SHALL BITE HIM; and so it happened to him.[7]

R. Simeon b. Yoḥai passed through [Beth Neṭufa][8] in

[1] The corpse will revive and the Cuthean die.
[2] It was spoken in scorn, asserting that Tiberias was really unclean.
[3] His meaning is that Tiberias will be so cleansed that even priests will reside in it.
[4] He specified places which would be unclean.
[5] In Gen. R. the reading is 'but you will not be included in the number with us (to see this fulfilled) when it is purified'.
[6] In Gen. R. *ad loc.* it is stated that R. Simeon had acted in full collaboration with the Sages, and that even this scoffer had been among them. By his present action therefore he was undermining their authority.
[7] In Gen. R. his fate was to be reduced to a heap of bones.
[8] The name of the place is added from Gen. R. *loc. cit.*

the Sabbatical year, and saw a man gathering aftergrowths of the seventh year. He said to him, 'Is it not the seventh year!'[1] The man retorted, 'But was it not you who permitted it! For have we not learnt: [R. Simeon says:] All aftergrowths are permitted with the exception of the aftergrowths of cabbage, because the like of these come not under the heading of wild vegetables?'[2] He replied to him, 'But do not my colleagues differ from me [and declare all aftergrowths forbidden]!'[3] He applied to him WHOSO BREAKETH THROUGH A FENCE, A SERPENT SHALL BITE HIM; and so it happened to him.

1. WHOSO QUARRIETH (MASSIA') STONES SHALL BE HURT THEREWITH (X, 9). Whoever removes (*massia'*) himself from his study [of Torah][4] will in the end be troubled. He will require a subject without finding it. AND HE THAT CLEAVETH WOOD IS BENEFITED[5] (YISSAKEN) THEREBY. So long as he labours therein he will derive benefit from it, as the word is used in, *She became a companion* (sokeneth) *to him* (I Kings I, 4).

Another interpretation of WHOSO QUARRIETH STONES: [Whoever removes stones] from place to place,[6] SHALL BE HURT THEREWITH. AND HE THAT CLEAVETH WOOD IS BENEFITED THEREBY: R. Meyashah said: By virtue of two cleavings wherewith the patriarch Abraham cleft the wood on Mount Moriah, he merited that the Red Sea should be divided for his descendants into twelve strips.[7]

1. IF THE IRON BE BLUNT (X, 10): if the teacher shows himself blunt to his pupil like iron,[8] AND HE

[1] When this act is prohibited; v. Lev. XXV, 5. [2] Sheb. IX, I.
[3] And since they are in the majority their view is binding.
[4] For STONES compared to Torah, v. Lam. R. IV, I.
[5] This is the Midrashic rendering. E.V.: '*endangered.*' [6] From a private domain to a public one, causing somebody to stumble over them.
[7] Cf. Gen. R. LV, 8. [8] Has no patience to impart instruction.

NOT FACES[1]: and the teacher does not make the aspects [of the subject] clear to the pupil, SPOILT: deterioration of conduct will result in the pupil. THEN MUST HE PUT TO MORE STRENGTH: What should [the pupil] do? Let him bring ten men who should persuade the teacher [to instruct him], so that finally he will cause the rightness of wisdom to excel.[2]

Another interpretation of IF THE IRON BE BLUNT: if the pupil has been blunt [i.e. annoying] to his teacher [by his obtuseness]—as it is said, *Iron sharpeneth iron; so a man sharpeneth the countenance of his friend* (Prov. XXVII, 17)[3]—and the teacher does not make the instruction clear to the pupil, SPOILT: deterioration of conduct will result in the pupil. THEN MUST HE PUT TO MORE STRENGTH: Let [the pupil] go and bring ten men and they will pacify his teacher. BUT WISDOM IS PROFITABLE TO DIRECT: In the end he will abandon his anger towards him and direct his study.

Another interpretation of IF THE IRON BE BLUNT: if your study has been hard to you like iron, AND HE NOT FACES, SPOIL[4]: And [your teacher] does not come to you to make it clear to your face, then denounce him with all your might. One of the disciples of R. Simeon b. Yoḥai forgot his learning; so he went weeping to the cemetery. After he had wept much [his teacher] appeared to him in his dream and said to him, 'When you throw three pebbles at me I will come.' The disciple went to an interpreter of dreams and related to him what had occurred. He told him, 'Repeat your lesson three times and it will come to you [so that you will not forget it].' He did this, and so it happened to him.

R. Berekiah said: If the nation [of Israel] has grown blunt [i.e. powerless][5] whose might was like iron—as it is written, *You hath the Lord taken and brought forth out of the iron furnace, out of Egypt* (Deut. IV, 20)—AND

[1] E.V. '*And one do not whet the edge*' is lit. 'and he not faces spoilt'.
[2] Based on the text BUT WISDOM IS PROFITABLE TO DIRECT.
[3] Quoted to illustrate the use of IRON as a simile for learning.
[4] Read the verb here as imperative. [5] Through famine.

HE NOT FACES: and the Holy One, blessed be He, does not brighten the faces of the generation [with relief], SPOILT: there are evil deeds in that generation. What should they do? THEN MUST HE PUT TO MORE STRENGTH: let them decree fasts [to repent], and the Holy One, blessed be He, will grant them eternal forgiveness.

R. Ḥama b. Papa said in the name of R. Judah b. R. Simon: If the heavens become blunt [i.e. hard] above your heads like iron—as it is stated, *I will make your heavens as iron* (Lev. XXVI, 19)—and the Holy One, blessed be He, does not brighten the faces [with relief], there is deterioration of conduct in that generation. What should they do? Let them decree a fast and the Holy One, blessed be He, will send relief to His world.

1. IF THE SERPENT BITE BEFORE IT IS CHARMED (X, 11)[1]: R. Abba b. Kahana said: Never does a serpent bite unless it has been incited from Above, nor does a lion rend [its prey] unless it has been incited from Above, nor does a government interfere with men unless it has been incited from Above.

R. Samuel b. Naḥmani said: The serpent was asked, 'Why when your tongue bites only one limb do they all feel it and tremble?' It replied, 'You ask me that? Put the question to the possessor of a tongue![2] [You ask,] "Why does your tongue slaver?" It caused me [to have my poisonous sting].[3] [You ask,] "Why is your body speckled?" My tongue caused it to be so.[4] [You ask,] "Why does your tongue bite one limb and yet they all feel it and tremble?"' It answered, 'You ask me that? Put the question to the possessor of a tongue who speaks here but [by his slander] kills somebody in Rome, or [speaks] in Rome and kills somebody here at the other

[1] Lit. 'without a charm', the latter word meaning 'whisper', which can also indicate 'incitement'. [2] The human being who has the power of speech and can do great harm by slanderous talk.
[3] My tongue made Eve sin, and this is my punishment.
[4] Through my tongue it was decreed that I should always be recognised as the cause of sin, and my speckled body makes me conspicuous.

end of the world. [You ask,] "Why do you lurk among the hedges?" Because I broke through a fence of the world.'[1] R. Simeon b. Yoḥai taught: The serpent broke through a fence of the world and was therefore made the executioner of all who break through fences.

R. Simeon b. Laḳish stated: When the Holy One, blessed be He, said to the serpent, *Upon thy belly shalt thou go* (Gen. III, 14), the ministering angels descended and cut off its hands and legs, and its cry went from one end of the world to the other. The serpent came and indicated the downfall of Edom [Rome], as it is said, *The sound thereof shall go like the serpent's* (Jer. XLVI, 22). The Rabbis apply this to the following verse, *The name of the third river is Tigris* (Gen. II, 14). The Tigris was asked, 'Why is your sound [of flowing water] audible?' It answered, 'Would that it were audible among the rivers.' The Euphrates was asked, 'Why have you not a sound [of flowing] which is heard as the sounds of other [rivers] are heard?' It answered, 'My actions prove [my merits]; for if a man sows herbage in me it comes up in thirty days, and if he plants a tree in me it comes up in thirty days.'[2]

1. THE WORDS OF A WISE MAN'S MOUTH ARE GRACIOUS (X, 12): this alludes to Cyrus, king of Persia, who said, *Whosoever there is among you of all His people, his God be with him, let him go up to Jerusalem* (Ezra I, 3). BUT THE LIPS OF A FOOL WILL SWALLOW UP HIMSELF: [this also alludes to Cyrus] because he swallowed his words and went back on them.[3]

1. THE BEGINNING OF THE WORDS OF HIS MOUTH IS FOOLISHNESS (X, 13): [i.e. Cyrus] who said, *He is the God Who is in Jerusalem* (*ib.*)[4] AND THE END OF HIS TALK IS GRIEVOUS MADNESS:

[1] The Divine command. [2] On this passage v. Gen. R. XVI, 3.
[3] Cyrus is identified with Artaxerxes who ordered the work on the rebuilding of the Temple to stop (Ezra IV, 17 ff.).
[4] Thus confining him to Jerusalem, as it were ('E.J.).

because he retracted and annulled his decrees, saying, 'Whoever [of the Jews] has crossed over [into Judea] has crossed, but whoever has not crossed shall not do so.'

Another explanation of THE BEGINNING OF THE WORDS OF HIS MOUTH IS FOOLISHNESS: i.e. Ahasuerus, as it is said, *And in the reign of Ahasuerus, in the beginning of his reign, wrote they an accusation against the inhabitants of Judah and Jerusalem* (*ib.* IV, 6).[1] AND THE END OF HIS TALK IS GRIEVOUS MADNESS: because he went up and put a stop to the work of [rebuilding] the Temple.

1. A FOOL ALSO MULTIPLIETH WORDS (X, 14): R. Berekiah in the name of R. Simon interpreted the verse as applying to Moses. The Holy One, blessed be He, said to Moses, 'I wrote of you that you are wise, and you stand multiplying words! You are not wise; *Speak no more unto Me of this matter* (Deut. III, 26).'

1. THE LABOUR OF FOOLS WEARIETH EVERY ONE OF THEM (X, 15): i.e. a disciple who stands [without making progress] in his study. FOR HE KNOWETH NOT HOW TO GO TO THE CITY: should he not go to his teacher[2] who will restore his learning to him?

Another interpretation of THE LABOUR OF FOOLS WEARIETH EVERY ONE OF THEM: i.e. Jephthah, FOR HE KNOWETH NOT HOW TO GO TO THE CITY: should he not have gone to Phinehas to annul his vow for him? But Jephthah remarked, 'Shall I, a chieftain and ruler in Israel, go to Phinehas!' and Phinehas remarked, 'Shall I, the High Priest and the son of a High Priest, go to an ignorant person!' Between the two of them the poor girl perished and they were both condemned for her blood. Jephthah's punishment was that limb after limb fell away from his body and was buried;

[1] The accusation is stigmatised as FOOLISHNESS. He was apparently impressed by it, though he did not act upon it until later. Artaxerxes is identified with Ahasuerus.

[2] *'Ir* (city) is read as *'ar* (watcher) [in study], i.e. a teacher.

as it is written, *He was buried in the cities*[1] *of Gilead* (Judg. XII, 7). In how many places, then, was he buried that it is stated, '*He was buried in the* cities *of Gilead*'? It teaches that each limb fell away from his body separately and was buried in its place [where it dropped off]. What loss did Phinehas sustain [as a punishment]? The Holy Spirit departed from him for two hundred years[2]; for it is not written here 'And Phinehas the son of Eleazar was ruler over them,' but *And Phinehas the son of Eleazar was ruler over them in time past, the Lord being with him* (I Chron. IX, 20).[3]

1. WOE TO THEE, O LAND, WHEN THY KING IS A BOY (X, 16). It is written, *Then came there two women, that were harlots* (I Kings III, 16). Who were they? R. Meir says: They were female spirits; the Rabbis say: They were *yebamoth*; R. Simon says in the name of R. Joshua: They were really harlots, and Solomon gave his verdict without hearing witnesses and without giving a warning.[4] *And the one woman said: Oh, my lord . . . and it came to pass on the third day after I was delivered . . . and this woman's child died in the night* (*ib.* 17 ff.) because she slipped and fell on him. *And she arose at midnight . . . and when I rose in the morning to give my child suck . . . and the other woman said: Nay, but the living is my son . . . Then said the king: The one saith*, etc. (*ib.* 20 ff.). R. Phinehas and R. Jeremiah said in the name of R. Ḥiyya b. Abba and R. Bibi, and the tradition goes back to the name of R. Pedath: The procedure of judging a case is as follows: The judge sits and those to be judged stand, (and the mediator decides between them)[5]; the plaintiff states his claim, the defendant replies, and the judge

[1] So lit. E.V. '*One of the cities of*'.
[2] The phrase 'two hundred years' does not occur in the parallel passages, Gen. R. LX, 3, Lev. R. XXXVII, 4. The text unnecessarily inserts here 'as it is written'. [3] I.e. when the Lord was with him, which implies that at some time the Holy Spirit left him.
[4] To the litigants, against the seriousness of perjury.
[5] In J. Sanh. 21*b* the words in brackets do not occur, and they should be deleted.

decides between them. R. Simon said: From where[1] do we learn that it is necessary for the judge to repeat their pleas? From these verses: *Then said the king: The one saith: This is my son that liveth and thy son is the dead; and the other saith: Nay, but thy son is the dead, and my son is the living. And the king said: Fetch me a sword . . . and the king said: Divide the living child in two . . . Then spoke the woman whose the living child was*, etc. (*ib.* 24 ff.). R. Judah said in the name of R. Ilai: If I had been there I would have wound a rope of wool around [Solomon's] neck, and when he said, '*Fetch me a sword*,' had she [the child's mother] not been filled with compassion for the babe, he would already have been strangled; and concerning that time it states, WOE TO THEE, O LAND, WHEN THY KING IS A BOY.[2] Then [Solomon] in his wisdom began a concluding argument[3] and said, 'Was it for nothing that the Holy One, blessed be He, created for man two eyes, two ears, two legs, and two hands? The Holy One, blessed be He, foresaw that this case was to happen.'[4] So he did not tarry,[5] but [immediately] said, *Give her the living child, and in no wise slay it* (*ib.* 27). Concerning that time it states, HAPPY ART THOU, O LAND, WHEN THY KING IS A FREE MAN, AND THY PRINCES EAT IN DUE SEASON (X, 17)[6]: viz. [they have their enjoyment] in the time of the World to Come, AND NOT IN DRUNKENNESS: in his strength, and not in his weakness.[7] *Then the king answered and said: 'Give her the living child, and in no wise slay it'*; and the

[1] The text has 'from here'.
[2] The Rabbi disapproved of the ordeal to which the mother had been put, and considers Solomon's method of judging fit for a boy and not a wise judge.
[3] Levy renders: he (Solomon), in an argumentative fashion, began (arguing) in his wisdom.
[4] That the child might be cut in two and a half given to each woman.
[5] He did not keep the real mother in suspense.
[6] The application of this verse, HAPPY, etc., to the present instance does not agree with the view just expressed by R. Judah.
[7] SHETI (DRUNKENNESS) is changed to *teshishu* (weakness). 'E.J.: who serves God in his strength, i.e. in his prime, and does not wait until he is weak with age before serving Him.

Holy Spirit cried out, saying, '*She is the mother thereof*, certainly.'

R. Samuel b. Naḥmani said: In three places did the Attribute of Justice cry out: in the *Beth Din* of Shem, the *Beth Din* of Samuel, and the *Beth Din* of Solomon. Whence do we know that it did so in the *Beth Din* of Shem? As it is stated, *And Judah acknowledged them, and said: She is right; it is from Me* (Gen. XXXVIII, 26).[1] the Holy Spirit crying out and saying, 'It is from Me that all these things happened.' Whence do we know that it did so in the *Beth Din* of Samuel? As it is said, *Here I am; witness against me before the Lord . . . And he said unto them: The Lord is witness against you, and His anointed is witness this day, that ye have not found aught in my hand* (I Sam. XII, 3 ff.). This is not followed by 'And *they* said: He is witness,'[2] but '*And* he *said: He is witness*'. Who said: '*He is witness*'? The Holy Spirit declared, 'You testify concerning what is disclosed, whereas I testify concerning the matters that are hidden.' Whence do we know that it did so in the *Beth Din* of Solomon? As it is stated, '*Then the king answered and said: Give her the living child*,' etc., and the Holy Spirit cried out, saying, '*She is the mother thereof*, certainly.'[3]

Another interpretation of WOE TO THEE, O LAND, WHEN THY KING IS A BOY: this refers to the kings of Israel[4]; HAPPY ART THOU, O LAND, WHEN THY KING IS A FREE MAN: this refers to the kings of Judah. AND THY PRINCES FEAST IN THE MORNING: this refers to the kings of Israel; AND THY PRINCES EAT IN DUE SEASON: this refers to the kings of Judah.

1. BY SLOTHFULNESS ('AẒALTAYIM) THE RAFTERS SINK IN (X, 18): Because the Israelites shrank (*nith'aẓlu*) from encamping in disharmony at

[1] E.V.: '*She is more righteous than I*,' lit. 'she is righteous from me'.
[2] Although E.V. renders '*And they said*', in the Heb. the verb is singular.
[3] Cf. Mak. 23*b* (Sonc. ed., pp. 168 f.).
[4] In general the kings of Israel were evil and the kings of Judah good.

Mount Sinai,[1] THE RAFTERS[2] SINK IN, as it is written, *He bowed down the heavens also, and came down* (Ps. XVIII, 10). AND THROUGH IDLENESS (SHIFLUTH) OF THE HANDS THE HOUSE LEAKETH: Because the Israelites humbled themselves (*nishtaplu*)[3] so as not to encamp in discord at Mount Sinai, THE HOUSE LEAKETH, as it is written, *Yea, the clouds dropped water* (Judg. V, 4).

Another interpretation of BY SLOTHFULNESS THE RAFTERS SINK IN: Because the Israelites were too slothful to repent in the days of Jeremiah, THE RAFTERS[4] SINK IN, as it is written, *And the covering of Judah was laid bare* (Isa. XXII, 8), i.e. what should have been covered He disclosed.[5] AND THROUGH IDLENESS OF THE HANDS THE HOUSE LEAKETH: Because the Israelites were too debased to repent in the days of Jeremiah, it is written, *For, behold, the Lord commandeth, and the great house shall be smitten into splinters, and the little house into chips* (Amos VI, 11). R. Huna said: '*Splinter*' is not the same as '*chip*'; from the latter there are no fragments [which can be utilised], but from the former there are fragments [which can be used].

Another interpretation of BY SLOTHFULNESS THE RAFTERS SINK IN: R. Kohen interprets the verse of a woman. Because a woman is too slothful to examine herself in the time of her impurity she becomes ill, as it is said, *Of her that is sick with her impurity* (Lev. XV, 33). AND THROUGH IDLENESS OF THE HANDS: and because she is too debased to examine herself [at that time] she is afflicted with a blood-issue, as it is said, *And if a woman have an issue of her blood many days not in the time of her impurity* (*ib.* 25).

[1] Ex. XIX, 2 reads *They encamped in the wilderness, and there Israel encamped before the mount.* The second verb is singular, from which the Rabbis deduced that at Sinai the Israelites were all of one mind.
[2] Here a symbol of heaven. [3] Same root as SHIFLUTH, both being derived from *shafel*, 'low,' 'meek,' 'humble.' [4] Here a symbol of the Temple. [5] Or, He uncovered (i.e. disgraced) its (the Temple's) chiefs. Cf. Lam. R., Proem XXI.

1. A FEAST IS MADE FOR LAUGHTER (X, 19). For the revelries connected with idolatry they prepare food. AND WINE MAKETH GLAD THE LIFE: i.e. the Torah, as it is said, *The precepts of the Lord are right, rejoicing the heart* (Ps. XIX, 9). AND MONEY ANSWERETH ALL THINGS: R. Joshua of Siknin said in the name of R. Levi: Sometimes [a man's prayer] is answered, and at other times he is not answered. At those times when he uses his money for charity he is answered, as it is said, *So shall my righteousness answer for me* (Gen. XXX, 33); but at those times when he does not use it for charity, it accuses him, as it is stated, *To have perverted witness against him* (Deut. XIX, 16).[1]

R. Simeon b. Lakish received an invitation from a neighbour, [and on going to him] saw men stand up and dance and clap their hands, and receive food and drink. He exclaimed, 'This is good; I too will stand up and dance and sing.' He stood up, danced and sang, and they gave him a cask of old wine. So he applied to himself the text, A FEAST IS MADE FOR LAUGHTER.

1. CURSE NOT THE KING, NO, NOT IN THY THOUGHT—MADDA' (X, 20). R. Judah b. R. Simon said: The Holy One, blessed be He, says to man: 'Because I endowed you with intellect (*madda'*) above cattle, beasts and birds, you revile and blaspheme before Me. I made eyes for you and for the animal, ears for you and for it, hands for you and for it, legs for you and for it, a mouth for you and for it. (Man is like the beast that perisheth[2] —the word *nidmu* (perisheth) means nothing else than silence,[3] i.e. Thou hast silenced them before Thee)[4]. Behold the honour I have bestowed upon you, but you do not appreciate all this benefit,' as it is written, *Man understandeth not honour* (Ps. XLIX, 21).[5]

[1] Cf. on I, 13. [2] Cf. Ps. XLIX, 13.
[3] *Nidmu* is here connected with the root *damam*, 'to be silent'.
[4] 'E.J.: although animals have organs of speech, like man, God has silenced them and made them dumb.
[5] E.V.: '*Man that is in honour understandeth not*'.

Another interpretation is: CURSE NOT THE KING who is of your own generation, NO, NOT IN THY THOUGHT. AND CURSE NOT THE RICH IN THY BEDCHAMBER: a rich man of your own generation do not curse.[1] FOR A BIRD OF THE AIR SHALL CARRY THE VOICE: R. Jeremiah b. Eleazar says: This means the raven, which by the art of divination [hears what is said and communicates it to others].[2] AND THAT WHICH HATH WINGS SHALL TELL THE MATTER: because walls have ears.

Another interpretation is: CURSE NOT THE KING, i.e. the King of the universe, NO, NOT IN THY THOUGHT. AND CURSE NOT THE RICH IN THY BEDCHAMBER: i.e. Him who is the rich One of the universe. FOR A BIRD OF THE AIR SHALL CARRY THE VOICE: R. Joshua of Siknin said in the name of R. Levi: There are reports for good and reports for evil. 'There are reports for good,' as it is said, *And the Lord heard the voice of your words . . . they have well said all that they have spoken* (Deut. v, 25). (Ḥiyya b. Adda and Bar Ḳappara [discuss the phrase '*They have well said,*' lit. 'They have done well all that they have spoken']. Ḥiyya b. Adda said: Well-spoken words are like well-prepared incense; Bar Ḳappara said: They are like well-trimmed lamps.)[3] 'There are reports for evil,' as it is said, *And the Lord heard the voice of your words, and was wroth, saying: Surely there shall not one of these men, even this evil generation, see the good land* (*ib.* I, 34 f.).

R. Abbahu said in the name of R. Taḥlifa his father-in-law: It is written, *Therefore I swore in My wrath* (Ps. xcv, 11)—the Holy One, blessed be He, said: '"*I swore* in My wrath," but retracted, *That they should not enter into My rest* (*ib.*)—into this resting-place they will not

[1] He can do you harm and you may need his help.

[2] This probably means that the raven can be employed to reveal secrets through the art of bird divination.

[3] The verb is used in connection with the lamp in the Tabernacle (Ex. xxx, 7), and in Ker. 6*b* it is mentioned that when the ingredients were ground for the incense a formula was uttered which included this verb. Cf. SS. R. II, 14, § 4.

enter, but they will enter into another resting-place.'[1] R. Bibi said in the name of R. Joshua b. Levi: It may be likened to a king who was angry with his son and drove him away from the palace, swearing that nobody should let him enter there. What did the king do? Since [the palace] was already built, he demolished and rebuilt it, and brought his son in. Consequently he permitted him to enter and yet fulfilled his oath. Similarly spake the Holy One, blessed be He: ' "*I swore in My wrath,*" but retracted, "*That they should not enter into My rest*"—into this resting-place they will not enter, but they will enter into another resting-place.'

AND THAT WHICH HATH WINGS SHALL TELL THE MATTER. R. Bun said: When a man sleeps, the body tells [what has been done] to the spirit, the spirit to the soul, the soul to the angel, the angel to a cherub, and the cherub to THAT WHICH HATH WINGS. Who is that? The seraph, and the seraph carries and relates it before Him at whose word the universe came into being.

Another interpretation is: CURSE NOT THE KING, a king who is in your presence,[2] NO, NOT IN THY THOUGHT, AND CURSE NOT THE RICH IN THY BEDCHAMBER: viz. the great man in your place of residence. FOR A BIRD OF THE AIR SHALL CARRY THE VOICE: The Holy One, blessed be He, said to David: 'Did you not exclaim, *All mine enemies shall be ashamed and sore affrighted* (Ps. VI, 11)? Who were your enemies? Was it not Saul? And did you not declare, *In the day that the Lord delivered him from the hand of all his enemies, and from the hand of Saul* (*ib.* XVIII, 1)?' David answered, 'Lord of the universe, sins of presumption Thou bringest up against me; consider them to me as sins of error.' That is what is stated, *Shiggaion of*

[1] Driven from the first Temple they will be allowed to enter the second Temple.

[2] 'E.J. renders: the king who is before thee, i.e. your predecessor, whose place you are waiting to take. There seems more point in this rendering, and it is similarly explained by Mah. in Lev. R. XXXII, 2.

David, which he sang unto the Lord, concerning Cush a Benjamite (*ib.* VII, 1).[1]

Another interpretation is: CURSE NOT THE KING: i.e. Moses, as it is said, *And there was a king in Jeshurun* (Deut. XXXIII, 5). AND CURSE NOT THE RICH IN THY BEDCHAMBER: i.e. Moses. From where did Moses derive his riches? From the chippings of the tablets. R. Ḥanin said: The Holy One, blessed be He, disclosed to him a sapphire mine in his tent, and from it Moses grew rich, as it is said, *Hew* thee *two tables of stone* (Ex. XXXIV, 1), i.e. the chippings are for yourself.[2]

[1] *Shiggaion* is connected with *shegagah* 'a sin committed in error', and Cush the Benjamite is identified with Saul.
[2] Repeated from IX, 11.

CHAPTER XI

1. CAST THY BREAD UPON THE WATERS (XI, 1). R. Bibi said: If it is your desire to practise charity, bestow it upon those who labour in the Torah, because THE WATERS means nothing else than words of Torah, as it is said, *Ho, every one that thirsteth, come ye for water* (Isa. LV, 1).

R. Akiba said: When I was travelling at sea, I saw a ship which had been wrecked, and I was greatly concerned about a Rabbinical scholar who had been on board and went down with the ship. On arriving at the province of Cappadocia, however, I noticed him sitting before me and asking questions. I said to him, 'My son, how did you come up out of the sea?' He replied, 'Rabbi, through your prayer on my behalf one wave tossed me to another, and so on until they brought me ashore.' I asked him, 'My son, what good deeds do you possess [which rescued you from drowning]?' He answered, 'When I went aboard the ship, a poor man accosted me and cried, "Help me," and I gave him a loaf. He then said to me, " As you have restored my life to me by your gift, so will your life be restored to you." ' [R. Akiba added :] I applied to him the text, CAST THY BREAD UPON THE WATERS.[1]

A large ship was once sailing on the ocean, when a gale caught it and drove it to a place where there was no flowing water. When [the passengers] saw that they were in dire straits,[2] they said, 'Come, let us share our provisions, so that if we die we all die, and if we live we all live.' [As a reward for this] the Omnipresent enlightened their eyes [with a plan]. They took a kid, roasted it, and hung it up on the west side of the ship. A large animal, attracted by the odour, came and began to drag [the ship] until it drew it to where the water was flowing, and they continued their voyage. When they reached their destination and entered Rome, they narrated the incident to

[1] A different version occurs in Yeb. 121*a* (Sonc. ed., p. 857).
[2] Of dying from thirst and hunger, because they were stranded.

R. Eliezer and R. Joshua, who applied to them the text, CAST THY BREAD UPON THE WATERS.

Bar Ḳappara was walking up and down the cliffs by the sea at Caesarea, when he saw a ship which had been wrecked in the ocean and a proconsul emerging from it naked. On seeing him, [Bar Ḳappara] went to him, greeted him, and gave him two *sela's*. What [else] did he do? He brought him to his house, gave him to eat and drink, handed him three more *sela's*, and said, 'On a great man like you one should expend three more *sela's*.' Some time later Jews were arrested in a riot.[1] They asked, 'Who will go and intercede for us?' and they said one to the other, 'Bar Ḳappara [is the man to go] because he is highly esteemed by the government.' He told them, 'You know that this government does nothing without being paid.' They said to him, 'Here are five hundred *dinars*; take them and go to intercede for us.' He took the five hundred *dinars* and went to the government. When the proconsul saw him, he stood up, greeted him, and asked, 'Why has the Rabbi troubled to come here?' He answered, 'I beg of you to have mercy upon these Jews.' He said to him, 'You know that this government does nothing without being paid.' He told him, 'I have with me five hundred *dinars*; take them and intercede for us.' He replied, 'These *dinars* are pledged to you in exchange for the five *sela's* which you gave me; your people are spared in return for the food and drink which you provided for me in your house; and as for you, go in peace and great honour.' They applied to him the text, CAST THY BREAD UPON THE WATERS.

R. Eleazar b. Shammua was walking on the rocks by the sea, when he saw a ship which was tossed about in the water suddenly[2] sink with all on board. He noticed a man sitting on a plank of the ship [carried] from wave to wave until he stepped ashore. Being naked he hid himself among the rocks by the sea. It happened to be the time for

[1] So Jast. Radal explains: caught dealing in prohibited merchandise.
[2] Lit. 'in the twinkling of an eye'.

the Israelites to go up to Jerusalem for the Festival. He said to them, 'I belong to the descendants of Esau, your brother; give me a little clothing wherewith to cover my nakedness because the sea stripped me bare and nothing was saved with me.' They retorted, 'So may all your people be stripped bare!' He raised his eyes and saw R. Eleazar who was walking among them; he exclaimed, 'I observe that you are an old and respected man of your people, and you know the respect due to your fellow-creatures. So help me, and give me a garment wherewith to cover my nakedness because the sea stripped me bare.' R. Eleazar b. Shammua was wearing seven robes; he took one off and gave it to him. He also led him to his house, provided him with food and drink, gave him two hundred *dinars*, drove him fourteen Persian miles, and treated him with great honour until he brought him to his home. Some time later the wicked emperor died, and they elected this man king in his stead, and he decreed[1] concerning that province that all the men were to be killed and all the women taken as spoil. They said to R. Eleazar b. Shammua, 'Go and intercede for us.' He told them 'You know that this government does nothing without being paid.' They said to him, 'Here are four thousand *dinars*; take them and go and intercede for us.' He took them and went and stood by the gate of the royal palace. He said to [the guards], 'Go, tell the king that a Jew is standing at the gate, and wishes to greet the king.' The king ordered him to be brought in. On beholding him the king descended[2] from his throne and prostrated himself before him. He asked him, 'What is my master's business here, and why has my master troubled to come here?' He replied, 'That you should have mercy upon this province and annul this decree.' The king asked him, 'Is there any falsehood written in the Torah?' 'No,' was the reply; and he said to him, 'Is it not written in your Torah, *An Ammonite or a Moabite shall not enter into the assembly of the Lord* (Deut.

[1] In revenge for what the inhabitants had said to him.
[2] Lit. 'threw himself'.

XXIII, 4)? What is the reason? *Because they met you not with bread and with water in the way* (*ib.* 5). It is also written, *Thou shalt not abhor an Edomite, for he is thy brother* (*ib.* 8); and am I not a descendant of Esau, your brother, but they did not treat me with kindness! And whoever transgresses the Torah incurs the penalty of death.' R. Eleazar b. Shammua replied to him, 'Although they are guilty towards you, forgive them and have mercy upon them.' He said to him, 'You know that this government does nothing without being paid.' He told him, 'I have with me four thousand *dinars*; take them and have mercy upon the people.' He said to him, 'These four thousand *dinars* are presented to you in exchange for the two hundred which you gave me, and the whole province will be spared for your sake in return for the food and drink with which you provided me. Go also into my treasury and take seventy robes of honour in return for the robe you gave me, and go in peace to your people whom I forgive for your sake.' They applied to him the text, CAST THY BREAD UPON THE WATERS.

It is related of a certain man that every day he took a loaf and threw it into the great sea. One day he went and bought a fish; on cutting it open he found a valuable object in it. People said of him, 'This is the man whose loaf stood him in good stead,' and they applied to him the text, CAST THY BREAD UPON THE WATERS.

R. Isaac said: It is related that a merchant was travelling with an officer, who in the course of the journey conceived a strong liking for him. When they entered the city, [the merchant] took him to his house and provided him with food and drink. Some time later the merchant was arrested for selling garments which were stained with blood. The officer, hearing of it, went to him [in prison] and asked, 'What are you doing here?' He narrated to him what had happened, and [the officer] said to him, 'When you appear for judgment, tell them, "So-and-so knows evidence in my favour."' When he appeared for judgment, he said, 'So-and-so knows evidence in my favour.' They asked [the officer], 'What evidence do you know in his favour?'

He replied, 'The brother of the murdered man was in my debt and had nothing to pay; so I took his garments and gave them to this man to sell for me.' [The judges] declared, 'A trustworthy man received [the garments] from a trustworthy man, so he goes free.' They applied to him the text, CAST THY BREAD UPON THE WATERS.

R. Eleazar b. R. Simai interpreted the verse in connection with the patriarch Abraham. The Holy One, blessed be He, spake to him: 'You said, *And I will fetch a morsel of bread* (Gen. XVIII, 5); I swear by your life that I will repay it to your descendants in the wilderness, in their settlement [in the holy land], and in the Hereafter. In the wilderness, as it is said, *Behold, I will cause to rain bread from heaven for you* (Ex. XVI, 4); in their settlement, as it is said, *A land of wheat and barley* (Deut. VIII, 8); in the Hereafter, as it is said, *May he be as a rich cornfield in the land* (Ps. LXXII, 16). You said, *And wash your feet* (Gen. XVIII, 4); I swear by your life that I will repay it to your descendants in the wilderness, in their settlement, and in the Hereafter. In the wilderness, as it is said, *Then washed I thee with water* (Ezek. XVI, 9); in their settlement, as it is said, *Wash you, make you clean* (Isa. I, 16); in the Hereafter, as it is said, *When the Lord shall have washed away the filth of the daughters of Zion* (*ib.* IV, 4). You said, *Let now a little water be fetched* (Gen. *loc. cit.*); I swear by your life that I will repay it to your descendants in the wilderness, in their settlement, and in the Hereafter. In the wilderness, as it is said, *Spring up, O well* (Num. XXI, 17); in their settlement, as it is said, *A land of brooks of water* (Deut. VIII, 7); in the Hereafter, as it is said, *And it shall come to pass in that day, that the mountains shall drop sweet wine, and the hills shall flow with milk, and all the brooks of Judah shall flow with waters*, etc. (Joel IV, 18). You said, *And recline yourselves under the tree* (Gen. *loc. cit.*); I swear by your life that I will repay it to your descendants in the wilderness, in their settlement, and in the Hereafter. In the wilderness, as it is said, *He spread a cloud for a screen* (Ps. CV, 39), in their settlement, as it is said, *Ye shall dwell in booths seven days; all that are home-born in Israel shall dwell in booths* (Lev. XXIII, 42); in the Hereafter, as it is said, *And there shall be a pavilion for a shadow in the day-time from the heat'* (Isa. IV, 6).[1]

1. DIVIDE A PORTION INTO SEVEN, YEA, EVEN INTO EIGHT (XI, 2). R. Eliezer and R. Joshua comment. R. Eliezer says: DIVIDE A PORTION INTO SEVEN alludes to the seven days of the week, as the word is used in *And it came to pass on the seventh* [day] (I Kings XVIII, 44),[2] i.e. the Sabbath day. YEA, EVEN INTO EIGHT alludes to the eight days of circumcision, for it is written, *And put his face between his knees* (*ib.* 42). Why '*between his knees*'?[3] He spoke before the Holy One, blessed be He, 'Lord of the universe, even if there be in the possession of Thy children only these two commandments, Sabbath and circumcision, it is right that Thou shouldest have mercy upon them.' R. Joshua says: DIVIDE A PORTION INTO SEVEN alludes to the seven days of Passover; YEA, EVEN INTO EIGHT alludes to the eight days of the Festival [of Tabernacles]. And whence do we know that Pentecost, the New Year, and the Day of Atonement are to be included?[4] The text states EVEN and this word denotes inclusion.

R. 'Azariah says: DIVIDE A PORTION INTO SEVEN alludes to the seventh generation[5] which Moses circumcised; YEA, EVEN INTO EIGHT alludes to the eighth generation which Joshua circumcised,[6] for it is written, *At that time the Lord said unto Joshua: Make thee knives of flint, and circumcise again the children of Israel the second*

[1] Cf. Gen. R. XLVIII, 10.

[2] E.V.: '*At the seventh time.*' Since the previous verse mentions that the lad went seven times, the text should have stated 'at the last time'. Therefore '*seventh*' is interpreted to mean the Sabbath, i.e. Elijah appealed to God to send rain through the merit of the Sabbath.

[3] He appealed for rain through the merit of circumcision.

[4] As occasions when the benediction is pronounced: 'Who hast kept us in life, and hast preserved us, and hast enabled us to reach this season.'

[5] There were seven generations between Abraham and Moses.

[6] 'E.J. inserts: and some maintain that in Egypt too it was Joshua who circumcised them. This explains the comment that follows. v. Ex. R. XIX, 5.

time (Josh. v, 2). From this it is to be deduced that he had already circumcised them a first time. *And Joshua made him knives of flint, and circumcised the children of Israel at Gibeah-ha-araloth* (*ib.* 3), [the name meaning], he made 'a hill of foreskins'.

R. Nehemiah interpreted the verse in connection with the princes. DIVIDE A PORTION INTO SEVEN: for it is written, *On the seventh day Elishama the son of Ammihud, prince of the children of Ephraim* (Num. VII, 48); YEA, EVEN INTO EIGHT: for it is written, *On the eighth day Gamaliel the son of Pedahzur, prince of the children of Manasseh* (*ib.* 54).

R. Judah interpreted the verse in connection with the consecration. DIVIDE A PORTION INTO SEVEN: as it is said, *These are the days of consecration; for He shall consecrate you seven days* (Lev. VIII, 33); YEA, EVEN INTO EIGHT: for it is written, *And it came to pass on the eighth day* (*ib.* IX, 1).

R. Huna said: DIVIDE A PORTION INTO SEVEN: i.e. the seven days of a woman's impurity; YEA, EVEN INTO EIGHT: i.e. the eight days of circumcision, as it is said, *And in the eighth day the flesh of his foreskin shall be circumcised* (*ib.* XII, 3).

R. Levi said: DIVIDE A PORTION INTO SEVEN: i.e. the seven days [of dwelling in] the booth; YEA, EVEN INTO EIGHT: for it is written, *On the eighth day ye shall have a solemn assembly* (Num. XXIX, 35).

R. Eleazar b. R. Simeon had wasted away [with illness]. Once when his arm was bare his wife saw it and both laughed and wept. She exclaimed, 'Happy am I for what my portion has been in this world![1] Happy am I to have been attached to this righteous body!' Then she wept and exclaimed, 'Woe that this righteous body is for the earth!' When he was about to die, he said to her, 'I am dying, but the worm will have no power over me. A maggot, however, is destined to pierce behind my ear, because I once entered a place and heard the voice of a

[1]In being the wife of this pious man. That is why she laughed happily.

man insulting [a scholar],[1] and it was within my power to punish him but I did not.' On his death he was taken to Gush Ḥeleb[2] [for burial]. R. Simeon [his father] appeared [in a dream] to the inhabitants of Meron[3] and said to them: 'One right eye[4] I had, and you have not placed him by me!' The men of Meron went with the intention of bringing R. Eleazar's body, but the inhabitants of Gush Ḥeleb came out after them with sticks and lances. One year when the great fast [of the Day of Atonement] approached they said, 'Now is the time to bring him here, while they [the men of Gush Ḥeleb] are occupied [with their religious observances].' They went with the intention of bringing the body, when two fiery serpents appeared and began to proceed in front of them. [Regarding this as a favourable omen], the people said, 'This is the time for us to bring him.' On arriving at the cave [in which the Rabbi was buried] the two serpents stood aside. The people asked, 'Who will go in and bring him out?' His widow said, 'I will enter and bring him out, because I have a sign in connection with him.' She entered to bring him out, and found a maggot piercing behind his ear. She wanted to remove it, but heard a *Bath Ḳol* proclaim, 'Leave the creditor to collect his debt!' They brought him and placed him by his father, and from that time R. Simeon no longer appeared to the men of Meron.

Whenever R. Eleazar b. R. Simeon entered the house of meeting, the face of Rabbi [Judah ha-Nasi] darkened [with displeasure].[5] His father said to him, 'My son, it is proper [that you should bear with him] for he is a lion the son of a lion while you are a lion the son of a fox.'[6] When [R. Eleazar] died, [Rabbi] sent an offer of marriage to his widow. She returned the reply, 'Shall a vessel which has been used for a sacred purpose be used for a profane purpose!'[7] He asked, 'What did he do which I

[1] This is added from B.M. 84*b* (Sonc. ed., p. 483).
[2] Giscala in Galilee. [3] In Galilee, S. of Giscala, where R. Simeon was buried. [4] I.e. his son Eleazar.
[5] R. Eleazar used to criticise his opinions; v. B.M. 84*b* (Sonc. ed., p. 485).
[6] Rabbi's father considered R. Simeon a greater scholar than himself.
[7] She held her late husband to have been far superior to Rabbi.

have not done similarly?' She answered, 'When he sat studying the Torah, he did so with all his might, and he used to say, "May all the pains of Israel come upon me!" and they did befall him. When his time for studying came, he used to say, "Let everybody return home."'[1] He answered, 'I likewise will act so.' He called out [for the pains of Israel] to come [upon him] and they befell him. [Subsequently] he wished them to depart from him, but they did not. Some declare that for thirteen full years[2] he suffered from toothache. He sent and informed her of this [renewing his proposal], but she answered, 'I have heard that we raise [things] to a higher degree of sanctity but do not debase to a lower degree.'

YEA, EVEN INTO EIGHT: for it is written, *On the eighth day ye shall have a solemn assembly* (Num. XXIX, 35).[3]

1. IF THE CLOUDS BE FULL OF RAIN, THEY EMPTY THEMSELVES UPON THE EARTH (XI, 3). If the disciples of the Sages are full of Torah, they empty it upon Israel who are called EARTH, as it is said, *For ye shall be a delightsome land* (Mal. III, 12). AND IF A TREE FALL IN THE SOUTH, OR IN THE NORTH: if the proper time for a Rabbinical scholar arrives for him to teach, whether in the south or the north, THERE SHALL IT BE: there shall all Israel gather and preserve his wisdom, listening to him and learning from him.

Another interpretation of IF THE CLOUDS BE FULL OF RAIN: if the prophets are full of prophecy, THEY EMPTY THEMSELVES UPON THE EARTH: they prophesy concerning Israel who are called EARTH, as it is said, '*For ye shall be a delightsome land.*' (Aquila the proselyte[4] renders *I will also command the clouds that they rain no rain upon it* (Isa. V, 6) by 'I will also command the prophets not to prophesy prophecies for them'.) AND IF A TREE FALL IN THE SOUTH, OR IN THE

[1] Presumably this means that he wanted no disturbance whatever.
[2] Lit. 'thirteen years from day (to day)'.
[3] Inserted in error from above. [4] V. p. 37, n. 1.

NORTH: if the proper time for prophets arrives to prophesy, whether in the south or the north, THERE SHALL IT BE: there shall all Israel gather and hear their prophecy and learn from them.

R. Isaac said: If you see troubles approaching, [know that] they come UPON THE EARTH, meaning, on account of Israel who are called EARTH, as it is said, '*For ye shall be a delightsome land.*'[1] If the time has come for a Rabbinical scholar to depart from the world—as, e.g., R. Mona in Sepphoris and R. Bun in Tiberias[2]—IN THE SOUTH, OR IN THE NORTH, IN THE PLACE WHERE THE TREE FALLETH, THERE SHALL IT BE: there will all Israel [gather] and bestow loving kindness upon him.[3]

1. HE THAT OBSERVETH THE WIND SHALL NOT SOW (XI, 4): He who observes the [evil] spirit[4] of [heathen] kingdoms, will not sow precepts and good deeds. AND HE WHO REGARDETH THE CLOUDS[5] of [heathen] kingdoms, SHALL NOT REAP precepts and good deeds.

1. AS THOU KNOWEST NOT WHAT IS THE WAY OF THE WIND (XI, 5). Seven things are concealed from man, viz. the day of death, the day of consolation [from his troubles],[6] the profundity of divine judgment,[7] the source from which one will profit,[8] what is in the heart of his fellow, what is in a woman's conception, and when the kingdom of Edom [Rome] will fall. Whence do we know this of the day of death? As it is said, *For man also knoweth*

[1] The idea is that God is more exacting with Israel than with other peoples, so that a lapse by the former is punished where it might be overlooked in the case of the latter.
[2] Sepphoris and Tiberias are respectively in the S. and N. of Galilee.
[3] Pay him honour at his funeral. [4] The same word as WIND.
[5] As the clouds obscure the sun, so these kingdoms obscure the Torah.
[6] So Rashi to Pes. 54*b*. Or, perhaps, the advent of the Messiah.
[7] It is extremely difficult to judge correctly. That is the purpose of the quotation that is given, to show that only God can probe a matter to its full depths ('E.J.). Perhaps too it refers to the profundity of Divine judgment in the Hereafter, meting out reward and punishment.
[8] In business, etc.

not his time (Eccl. IX, 12). Whence is it of the day of consolation? As it says, *I the Lord will hasten it in its due time* (Isa. LX, 22). Whence of the profundity of divine judgment? As it is said, *For the judgment is God's* (Deut. I, 17). Whence of the source from which one will profit? As it is said, *This is the gift of God* (Eccl. V, 18).[1] Whence of what is in the heart of his fellow? As it is said, *I the Lord search the heart* (Jer. XVII, 10). Whence of what is in a woman's conception? As it is said, NOR HOW THE BONES DO GROW IN THE WOMB OF HER THAT IS WITH CHILD. Whence of the date when the kingdom of Edom will fall? As it is said, *For the day of vengeance that is in My heart* (Isa. LXIII, 4).

1. IN THE MORNING SOW THY SEED (XI, 6). R. Eliezer and R. Joshua comment. R. Eliezer says: If you have sown in the early season, sow also in the late season, because you do not know which will succeed for you, whether the early or late sowing, FOR THOU KNOWEST NOT WHICH SHALL PROSPER, WHETHER THIS OR THAT.[2] R. Joshua says: If you are married in your youth and your wife died, marry again in your old age. If you had children in your youth, have them also in your old age, as it is said, IN THE MORNING SOW THY SEED, AND IN THE EVENING WITHHOLD NOT THY HAND; FOR THOU KNOWEST NOT WHICH SHALL PROSPER, WHETHER THIS OR THAT.

R. Ishmael and R. Akiba comment. R. Ishmael says: If you have studied Torah in your youth, study also in your old age, because you do not know which [knowledge of] Torah will endure, whether that of your youth or old age, OR WHETHER THEY BOTH SHALL BE ALIKE GOOD. R. Akiba says: I had twelve thousand disciples from Gabbatha[3] to Antipatris,[4] and they all died during my lifetime between Passover and Pentecost, so that finally

[1] Not being sure what will bring one profit, he must regard all profit as a gift of God. [2] R. Eliezer interprets the text literally, whereas the other Rabbis give it a metaphorical interpretation.
[3] Gibbethon in the territory of Dan. [4] N.N.W. of Jerusalem.

there remained to me only seven, viz. R. Judah, R. Nehemiah, R. Meir, R. Jose, R. Simeon b. Yoḥai, R. Eliezer the son of R. Jose of Galilee, and R. Joḥanan the sandal-maker. He said to them, 'The former only died because they were envious of one another in knowledge of Torah. Do not follow their example.' At once they arose and filled all the land of Israel with knowledge of Torah.

R. Nathan (another reading: R. Kohen) interpreted the verse of a wife. If you married in your youth, marry also in your old age. Why? Because you do not know which children will survive for you, whether those of your youth or old age, OR WHETHER THEY BOTH SHALL BE ALIKE GOOD.

1. AND THE LIGHT IS SWEET, AND A PLEASANT THING IT IS FOR THE EYES TO BEHOLD THE SUN (XI, 7). Sweet is the light of the Torah; AND A PLEASANT THING IT IS FOR THE EYES: happy is he whose study enlightens him like the sun.[1] R. Aḥa says: Sweet is the light of the World to Come; happy is he who is worthy to behold that light, as it is stated, *Moreover the light of the moon shall be as the light of the sun* (Isa. XXX, 26).

1. FOR IF A MAN LIVE MANY YEARS, LET HIM REJOICE (XI, 8): in the joy of the Torah; AND REMEMBER THE DAYS OF DARKNESS: these are the days of evil,[2] FOR THEY SHALL BE MANY. The Torah which a man learns in this world IS VANITY in comparison with the Torah [which will be learnt in the days] of the Messiah.

1. REJOICE, O YOUNG MAN, IN THY YOUTH (XI, 9). R. Samuel b. R. Isaac said: The Sages sought to suppress the Book of Ḳoheleth because they discovered therein words which tend towards heresy. They declared, 'This is the wisdom of Solomon that he said, REJOICE,

[1] He is free of doubts and perplexities. [2] Mentioned in XII, 1.

O YOUNG MAN, IN THY YOUTH! Now Moses said, *That ye go not about after your own heart* (Num. XV, 39), whereas Solomon said, WALK IN THE WAYS OF THY HEART! Is restraint to be abolished? Is there no judgment and no Judge?' But since he continued, BUT KNOW THOU, THAT FOR ALL THESE THINGS GOD WILL BRING THEE INTO JUDGMENT, they exclaimed, 'Well has Solomon spoken.'[1]

R. Ḥiyya Rabbah and R. Simeon b. Ḥalafta make statements. R. Ḥiyya Rabbah said: It may be likened to a man who fled from the executioner; he ran away and the executioner ran after him. People said to him, 'Run less that you have not to make a longer return.'[2] Similarly it is stated, BUT KNOW THOU, THAT FOR ALL THESE THINGS GOD WILL BRING THEE INTO JUDGMENT. R. Simeon b. Ḥalafta says: It may be likened to a man who swam in the river [to escape his pursuers]; he ran away and they ran after him. People said to him, 'Go not far into the water that you may not have far to come out and weary yourself.' Similarly it is stated, BUT KNOW THOU, THAT FOR ALL THESE THINGS GOD WILL BRING THEE INTO JUDGMENT.

R. Ḥanina b. Papa said: It may be likened to a man who used to steal the taxes. They arrested him and said to him, 'Give up what is in your possession.' He answered them, 'Take whatever I have with me'; but they retorted, 'Do you think that we will only extract what is with you at the present time? We demand from you all that is with you and all that you stole during the years you were a thief!' Similarly it is stated, BUT KNOW THOU, THAT FOR *ALL* THESE THINGS GOD WILL BRING THEE INTO JUDGMENT.

R. Levi said: It may be likened to a bird shut up in a cage. Another bird came, stood by it and said to it, 'Happy are you, for see how your food is provided for you!' It replied, 'May you be unlucky and unfortunate! You

[1] Repeated from I, 3. [2] He cannot escape, so running away is futile.

consider my food but pay no attention to my being shut up; to-morrow they will take me out and slay me!' Similarly it is stated, BUT KNOW THOU, THAT FOR ALL THESE THINGS GOD WILL BRING THEE INTO JUDGMENT.[1]

R. Tanḥum said: It may be likened to a worthless person who came to a shopkeeper and said, 'Give me fat meat, old wine, and various kinds of dainties.' He ate and drank and felt exhilarated; but as he was about to depart, the shopkeeper said to him, 'Pay the cost of what you have eaten!' He replied, 'My stomach is in front of you, cut it open [and remove your goods]!' The shopkeeper was a clever man; so what did he do? He took some matting, wrapped the man in it, and set him by the entrance of the shop. When anybody passed, he said to him, 'Give charity for this dead man that we may buy shrouds for him.' A contemptible and ill-natured person passed and said to him, 'How long is this ill-fated wretch to rot here?' He replied, 'By your life, until the money is provided.' When the money had been provided, he said to the man, 'Go to destruction!' Similarly it is stated, BUT KNOW THOU, THAT FOR ALL THESE THINGS GOD WILL BRING THEE INTO JUDGMENT.

Another interpretation of REJOICE, O YOUNG MAN, IN THY YOUTH: R. Judan and R. Phinehas comment. R. Judan said: IN THY YOUTH, i.e. in the Torah which you studied in your youth; AND LET THY HEART CHEER THEE IN THE DAYS OF THY YOUTH,[2] i.e. the Mishnah, AND WALK IN THE WAYS OF THY HEART, AND IN THE SIGHT OF THINE EYES, i.e. the Talmud[3]; BUT KNOW THOU, THAT FOR ALL THESE THINGS GOD WILL BRING THEE

[1] The comparison is with the wicked person who is allowed to indulge in the good things of this world. Fools look only to his temporary prosperity and not to what awaits him afterwards.

[2] Not the same Heb. word as that translated YOUTH in the first clause. It rather denotes 'adolescence', and so indicates the higher branch of study, viz. Mishnah.

[3] The study of Talmud demands the application of the heart.

INTO JUDGMENT, i.e. precepts and good deeds.[1] R. Phinehas says: REJOICE, O YOUNG MAN (BAḤUR), IN THY YOUTH: What caused you to be chosen (*hibbaḥer*) [for an eminent position] in your old age? The Torah which you studied in your youth; and if you have been chosen [for an eminent position] in your old age, do not go your own way in matters of Torah, but WALK IN THE WAYS OF THY HEART, i.e. the learning which you derived from your teacher.[2] BUT KNOW THOU, THAT FOR ALL THESE THINGS GOD WILL BRING THEE INTO JUDGMENT: it is for Him to pay you the reward of the precepts and good deeds.

R. Simeon b. Yoḥai says: It may be likened to a man who used to speak contemptuously of women[3] and indulged in lewdness. He used to say, 'Which woman do I desire [as my wife]?' When he grew old he wanted to marry; but people said to him, 'You ill-fated wretch, which woman wants you now that your nose is nipped,[4] your ears heavy of hearing, and your eyes dim!' Similarly it is stated, FOR ALL THESE THINGS GOD WILL BRING THEE INTO JUDGMENT. It may be likened to a man who possessed fields and vineyards but did not separate *terumah* and the tithes. He grew old and lost all his property. He then exclaimed, 'If I now had fields and vineyards, would I not separate *terumah* and tithes?' But they tell him, 'What has already been has been.' Similarly it is stated, BUT KNOW THOU, THAT FOR ALL THESE THINGS GOD WILL BRING THEE INTO JUDGMENT.[5]

[1] Because one who studies Torah without carrying out the precepts and allowing them to control his conduct will be punished.
[2] He should follow tradition and established custom.
[3] And thought no one good enough to be his wife.
[4] Hanging down like a faded plant (Jast.).
[5] Verse 10 is attached to the first verse of the next chapter for exposition

CHAPTER XII

1. THEREFORE REMOVE VEXATION FROM THY HEART (XI, 10). R. Levi said: All rags are 'ill-smells'[1] and all 'ill-smells' are foolish. Solomon said: Since CHILDHOOD AND YOUTH ARE VANITY, therefore REMEMBER THY CREATOR (XII, 1). We have learnt: Akabiah b. Mehaleel said: Ponder well three things [and thou wilt not come into the power of sin: know] whence thou camest—from a fetid drop; whither thou art going—to a place of dust, of worm and maggot; and before whom thou art destined to give an account and reckoning—before the Supreme King of kings, the Holy One, blessed be He.[2] R. Joshua b. Levi of Siknin said: All three of them Akabiah derived from one word,[3] viz. *boreka* (thy pit), *be'erka* (thy well), and *bora'aka* (thy Creator)—*boreka*, i.e. a malodorous secretion, *be'erka*, i.e. worm and maggot,[4] and *bora'aka*, i.e. the Supreme King of kings, the Holy One, blessed be He, before whom thou art destined to give an account and reckoning. Therefore it is said, REMEMBER THEN THY CREATOR IN THE DAYS OF THY YOUTH, while in the possession of thy strength. BEFORE THE EVIL DAYS COME, i.e. the days of old age; AND THE YEARS DRAW NIGH, i.e. [the time of] sufferings. R. Ḥiyya b. R. Nehemiah said: It refers to the days of the Messiah in which is neither merit nor guilt.[5]

1. BEFORE THE SUN . . . DARKENED (XII, 2): i.e. the bright countenance; AND THE LIGHT: i.e. the

[1] So Jast. who explains: paltry persons are quarrelsome. Levy renders: All bragging excites resentment, and all hot rage (resentment) betrays the fool. [2] Ab. III, 1 (Sonc. ed., p. 26).
[3] Since the text does not say, 'Remember the Lord' or 'thy God', but THY CREATOR, the word must have been intentionally selected for exposition. [4] In Lev. R. XVIII, 1, the respective interpretations of *boreka* (thy pit) and *be'erka* (thy well) are reversed, so they should be here also. [5] Because all evil will then be abolished.

nose; AND THE MOON: i.e. the forehead[1]; AND THE STARS: i.e. the cheekbones. AND THE CLOUDS RETURN AFTER THE RAIN: R. Levi explains this in two ways, one as referring to scholars [the wise] and the other as referring to fools. According to the first interpretation, when he [the scholar] comes to weep, his eyes run down with tears; according to the second, when he [the fool] comes to ease himself, his motion anticipates him.[2]

1. IN THE DAY WHEN THE KEEPERS OF THE HOUSE SHALL TREMBLE (XII, 3): i.e. the ribs; AND THE STRONG MEN SHALL BOW THEMSELVES: i.e. the arms, but R. Ḥiyya b. R. Nehemiah says that the allusion is to the ribs. AND THE GRINDERS CEASE: i.e. the stomach[3]; BECAUSE THEY ARE FEW: i.e. the teeth; AND THOSE THAT LOOK OUT SHALL BE DARKENED IN THE WINDOWS: i.e. the eyes. R. Ḥiyya b. R. Nehemiah says: It refers to the laps of the lungs from which the sound of the voice issues.

1. AND THE DOORS SHALL BE SHUT IN THE STREET (XII, 4): i.e. the orifices of man; WHEN THE SOUND OF THE GRINDING IS LOW: because the stomach ceases to grind; AND ONE SHALL START UP AT THE VOICE OF A BIRD: when the old man hears birds chirping he imagines that bandits have come to rob him; AND ALL THE DAUGHTERS OF MUSIC SHALL BE BROUGHT LOW: i.e. the lips. R. Ḥiyya b. R. Nehemiah said: It refers to the kidneys which submit plans for the heart to decide.

1. ALSO WHEN THEY SHALL BE AFRAID OF THAT WHICH IS HIGH (XII, 5): when they call an old man

[1] In Lev. R. *loc cit.* the reading is: MOON, i.e. nose. This is preferable because the word for 'moon', *yareaḥ*, is connected with *reaḥ* (smell). There are other variants in the two versions.

[2] Whereas the sensible man does not wait so long. The rendering is that of 'E.J. here and M.K. in Lev. R. *loc. cit.*

[3] Which grinds the food.

to a place [i.e. invite him to a banquet], he says to them, 'Are there ups and downs [in the way to it]?'[1] AND TERRORS SHALL BE IN THE WAY: R. Abba b. Kahana and R. Levi comment. One said: Fear of the journey falls upon him [and he asks], 'Shall I go or not go?' and decides not to go. The other [viz. R. Levi] said: He begins to map out the way there, saying, 'As far as that street and that place I am strong enough to go, but up to the place [where the banquet is to be held] I will not have the strength to go.' AND THE ALMOND-TREE SHALL BLOSSOM: R. Levi said: It refers to the nut of the spinal column. Hadrian (may his bones rot and his name be obliterated!) asked R. Joshua b. Ḥananiah, 'Whence will man sprout in the Hereafter?'[2] He replied, 'From the nut of the spinal column.' He said to him, 'Prove it to me.' He had one brought; he placed it in water but it did not dissolve, in fire but it was not burnt, in a mill but it was not ground. He placed it on an anvil and struck it with a hammer; the anvil split and the hammer was broken but it remained unaffected.[3]

AND THE GRASSHOPPER SHALL DRAG ITSELF ALONG: i.e. the ankles; AND THE CAPERBERRY (ABIYYONAH) SHALL FAIL: i.e. sexual desire, (*ta'awah*)[4] which brings peace between man and wife, ceases [in old age]. R. Simeon b. Ḥalafta was accustomed to visit our teacher [R. Judah ha-Nasi, each month]. When he became old, he was unable to do so. Yet on one occasion he did pay this visit. Said Rabbi to him, 'Why am I worthy to behold the master's face to-day?'[5] He replied, 'Distant objects have become near and near objects have become distant, two have become three, and what used to bring peace has ceased.' (The explanation

[1] An old man is not attracted to a banquet if the journey there presents difficulties.
[2] From what part of the body will the dead grow into a living being?
[3] Hence even if the rest of the body disintegrates this will remain intact, and it will provide the starting point for its reintegration.
[4] The Midrash derives ABIYYONAH from *ta'awah*, 'desire.'
[5] The remark was sarcastic and implied disapproval of his omission to visit him before.

is as follows: 'Distant objects have become near,' i.e. the eyes which used to see from afar cannot now [in old age] see even from near. 'Near objects have become distant,' i.e. the ears which used to catch a thing at the first or second hearing now cannot catch it even after a hundred hearings. 'Two have become three,' i.e. a stick in addition to the two legs. 'What used to bring peace in the house has ceased,' i.e. sexual desire which created love between man and wife.)

BECAUSE MAN GOETH TO HIS LONG HOME. It is not written here 'To *the* long home' but TO HIS LONG HOME. R. Simeon b. Laḳish said: It may be likened to a king who entered a province accompanied by generals, commanders, and officers. Although they all entered through the same gate, each went and lodged in a place corresponding to his rank. Similarly, although all human beings experience death, each has a HOME for himself [according to his conduct in life]. AND THE MOURNERS GO ABOUT THE STREETS: i.e. the maggots [which crawl on the corpse].[1]

1. BEFORE THE SILVER CORD IS SNAPPED ASUNDER (XII, 6): i.e. the spinal cord; AND THE GOLDEN BOWL (GULLATH) IS SHATTERED: the skull (*gulgoleth*). R. Ḥiyya b. R. Nehemiah said: It refers to the gullet (*gargereth*) which banishes the gold and makes the silver run.[2] AND THE PITCHER IS BROKEN AT THE FOUNTAIN: i.e. a man's stomach.[3] Three days after [death] a man's stomach bursts and gives back [its contents] to the mouth, saying, 'Take what you stole and robbed with violence and placed in me.' R. Haggai dreived the thought from this verse, *I will spread dung upon your faces, even the dung of your sacrifices* (Mal. II, 3).[4] Bar Ḳappara said:

[1] Y.T. suggests that the meaning may be that the mourners mourn on account of the maggots, i.e. the sorrow of death is increased by the knowledge that the body will be consumed by maggots.
[2] It impoverishes the glutton who spends all his money on food.
[3] Shaped like a pitcher.
[4] I.e. while your face is still recognisable, viz. up to three days after death.

The full intensity of mourning lasts up to the third day because the appearance of the face is still recognisable, for we have learnt: Evidence [of identity][1] may be legally tendered only on [proof afforded by] the full face with the nose, etc. AND THE WHEEL FALLETH SHATTERED INTO THE PIT: Two teachers [comment]. One said: Like the wheels of Sepphoris[2]; while the other said: Like the boulders (*righaya*) of Tiberias,[3] as the word is employed in *The clods* (rigbe) *of the valley are sweet unto him* (Job XXI, 33).

1. AND THE DUST RETURNETH TO THE EARTH AS IT WAS (XII, 7). R. Phinehas and R. Hilkiah said in the name of R. Simon: When is it that THE SPIRIT RETURNETH UNTO GOD WHO GAVE IT? When THE DUST RETURNETH TO THE EARTH[4] *AS IT WAS*[5]; otherwise *The souls of Thine*[6] *enemies, them shall He sling out, as from the hollow of a sling* (I Sam. XXV, 29). R. Samuel b. Naḥmani said in the name of R. Abdimi of Ḥaifa: It may be compared to a *kohen ḥaber* who handed to a *kohen 'am ha'areẓ* a loaf of bread made from *terumah* in a state of ritual purity, and said to him, 'See I am ritually clean, my house is clean, my utensils are clean, and this loaf which I give you is clean; if you return it to me in the same condition that I hand it to you, well and good; otherwise I will burn it in your presence.' Similarly spake the Holy One, blessed be He, to man, 'Behold I am pure, My habitation is pure, My attendants are pure, and the soul which I gave you is pure. If you return it to Me as I give it to you, well and good: otherwise I will burn it in your presence.' All this applies in the days of his old

[1] In respect of a dead man to enable the widow to remarry. This is a quotation from Yeb. 120*a* (Sonc. ed., p. 848) which continues: Evidence of identification may be tendered by those only who saw the corpse within three days of death, because after then the face is not recognisable.
[2] Which are placed over wells, around which the cord runs with the pitcher. [3] Which roll down into the lake.
[4] If the person has lived righteously.
[5] Emended text (Radal). I.e. when the body returns to the earth AS IT WAS when born, pure and free from sin.
[6] Here understood as the enemies of God, the wicked.

age; but as for the days of his youth, if he sins he is punished with a flux of blood and leprosy. Therefore Moses warned Israel, *When any man hath an issue out of his flesh* (Lev. xv, 2).[1]

R. Joshua b. Levi[2] interpreted the text in connection with the Sanctuary. The prophet said to Israel, REMEMBER THEN THY CREATOR: remember who created you while His selection[3] of you still endures, while the covenant of the priesthood still endures, as it is said, *And I did choose him out of all the tribes of Israel to be My priest* (I Sam. II, 28); while the covenant of the Levites still endures, as it is said, *For the Lord thy God hath chosen him out of all thy tribes* (Deut. XVIII, 5); while the covenant with Jerusalem still endures, as it is said, *The city which I have chosen* (I Kings XI, 32); while the covenant with the kingship of the house of David still endures, as it is said, *He chose David also His servant* (Ps. LXXVIII, 70); while the Sanctuary still endures, as it is said, *For now have I chosen and hallowed this house* (II Chron. VII, 16), while you [Israel] still endure, as it is said, *The Lord thy God hath chosen thee to be His own treasure* (Deut. VII, 6).

BEFORE THE EVIL DAYS COME: these are the days of the exile, as it is stated, *Ye that are made to wander for*[4] *the evil day* (Amos VI, 3); AND THE YEARS DRAW NIGH WHEN THOU SHALT SAY that ancestral merit has ceased [to protect Israel]. BEFORE THE SUN ... DARKENED: i.e. [the downfall of] the kingship of the house of David, as it is said, *And his throne as the sun before Me* (Ps. LXXXIX, 37); AND THE LIGHT: i.e. the Torah, as it is said, *For the commandment is a lamp and the Torah is light* (Prov. VI, 23); AND THE MOON: i.e. the Sanhedrin, for it is written, *It shall be established for ever as the moon* (Ps. LXXXIX, 38); AND THE STARS: these are the disciples of the Sages; AND THE CLOUDS

[1] The ending is due to the fact that the passage is quoted from Lev. R. XVIII, 1, which is the Midrash to Lev. XV, 2.

[2] In Lam. R., Proem XXIII, in which this dictum occurs, it is assigned to R. Joshua of Siknin in the name of R. Levi.

[3] In the Heb. this resembles the word for YOUTH.

[4] E.V.: '*Ye that put far away*.'

RETURN AFTER THE RAIN: you find that all the hard blows which Jeremiah prophesied for them befell them only after the destruction of the Temple.[1]

IN THE DAY WHEN THE KEEPERS OF THE HOUSE SHALL TREMBLE: this refers to the watches of the priests and the Levites[2]; AND THE STRONG MEN SHALL BOW THEMSELVES: these are the priests. R. Abba b. Kahana said: Aaron consecrated twenty-two thousand Levites on one day,[3] as it is said, *And Aaron offered them for a sacred gift before the Lord* (Num. VIII, 21). R. Ḥanina said: The bird's crop is a light thing, yet the priest would take hold of it with one hand and, taking aim, throw it backwards behind the [altar] step, a distance of exactly thirty-two cubits. AND THE GRINDERS CEASE: these are the great collections of Mishnah as, e.g., the Mishnah of R. Akiba, the Mishnah of R. Ḥiyya and R. Hoshaya, and the Mishnah of Bar Ḳappara.[4] BECAUSE THEY ARE FEW: this is the Talmud which is mingled with them. AND THOSE THAT LOOK OUT SHALL BE DARKENED IN THE WINDOWS: you find that when Israel was exiled to Babylon, not one of them was able to expound his learning. AND THE DOORS SHALL BE SHUT IN THE STREET: these are the doors of Neḥushta the daughter[5] of Elnathan which were wide open. WHEN THE SOUND OF THE GRINDING IS LOW: because they neglected words of Torah.[6] R. Samuel b. Naḥmani said: Words of Torah

[1] 'The clouds returning after the rain' is understood as meaning that troubles come after troubles. Similarly the disaster of the destruction of the Temple was followed by the disasters prophesied by Jeremiah.
[2] Tradition was undecided whether the night was divided in the Temple into three or four watches: v. Ber. 3*b*.
[3] This and the following are cited to illustrate the extraordinary strength of the priests. The Levites numbered 22,000 (Num. III, 39), and Aaron is said to have presented (the Heb. literally means waved) them all on one day. [4] V. p. 58, n. 2.
[5] V. II Kings XXIV, 8. She was the mother of king Jehoiachin. There was a tradition that the doors of her house were always open to offer hospitality, but in the national disaster they were closed. The text has *beth* (house of) instead of *bath* (daughter of).
[6] GRINDING is explained as Torah-study in the same manner that GRINDERS was defined as Mishnah collections.

are compared to grinding: as grinding does not cease day or night, so in connection with words of Torah it is stated, *Thou shalt meditate therein day and night* (Josh I. 8). AND ONE SHALL START UP AT THE VOICE OF A BIRD[1]: R. Levi said: For eighteen years a *Bath Ḳol* used to cry out to Nebuchadnezzar and summon him, saying, 'Wicked servant, go up and destroy thy Master's house, because His children are rebellious and do not obey Him.' AND ALL THE DAUGHTERS OF MUSIC SHALL BE BROUGHT LOW: because [Nebuchadnezzar] went up and stopped the singing in the Temple, as it is said, *They drink not wine with a song* (Isa. XXIV, 9). ALSO WHEN THEY SHALL BE AFRAID OF THAT WHICH IS HIGH: [Nebuchadnezzar] was afraid of Him who is supreme in the universe, the Supreme King of kings. AND TERRORS SHALL BE IN THE WAY: [R. Abba b. Kahana said:] the terror of the journey fell upon him; but R. Levi said: He began to consult omens[2] on the way, as it is said, *For the king of Babylon standeth at the parting of the way* (Ezek. XXI, 26), i.e. an arm[3] branching off at the top of two roads which divide off into two directions. Two roads were there, one leading to the wilderness and the other leading to an inhabited place [Jerusalem]. *To use divination* (*ib.*): he began to practise divination using the name of Rome but without success, the name of Alexandria but without success, then the name of Jerusalem and it succeeded. *He shaketh arrows to and fro* (*ib.*), in the name of Rome but without success, in the name of Alexandria but without success, then in the name of Jerusalem and it succeeded. He tried to kindle torches and lanterns in the name of Rome but they would not light, in the name of Alexandria but they would not light, then in the name of Jerusalem and they lit up. He floated ships on the river Euphrates in the name of Rome but they would not go, in the name of Alexandria but they would not go, then in the name of Jerusalem and they

[1] Warsaw ed. inserts: this refers to Nebuchadnezzar. [2] The meaning of the original is uncertain. [3] Sign-post at the cross-roads.

went. *He inquireth of the teraphim* (*ib.*), i.e. of his idols. *He looketh at the liver* (*ib.*): R. Levi said: Like an Arab who slays a lamb and inspects its liver [for omens]. *In his right hand is the lot of Jerusalem* (*ib.* 27): the lot concerning Jerusalem appeared in his right hand.[1] *To set battering-rams*: [this is understood to mean that he appointed] generals. *To open the mouth for the slaughter*: this refers to executioners. *To lift up the voice with shouting*: this alludes to trumpets. *To set battering-rams against the gates*: he arranged camps of besiegers. *To cast up mounds*: i.e. stones for the catapults. *And to build forts*: i.e. scaling-ladders. As for all these things, *It shall be unto them*[2] *as a false divination in their sight who have weeks upon weeks* (*ib.* 28): the prophet said to Israel, 'If you had been worthy you would have read in the Torah which is capable of exposition in seven times seven ways,[3] but now that you are unworthy, behold Nebuchadnezzar comes and practises divinations against you seven times seven.' And what was the purpose of all this? *But it bringeth iniquity to remembrance, that they may be taken* (*ib.*): this alludes to the blood of Zechariah.[4]

AND THE ALMOND-TREE SHALL BLOSSOM: i.e. the prophecy of Jeremiah, as it is stated, *I see a rod of an almond-tree* (Jer. I, 11). R. Eleazar said: As an almond-tree takes twenty-one days from the time it blossoms to the time when its fruit is ripe, similarly the whole decree [concerning the destruction of the Temple] only lasted [the twenty-one days] from the seventeenth of Tammuz to the ninth of Ab.[5]

AND THE GRASSHOPPER SHALL DRAG ITSELF ALONG: this alludes to the image made by Nebuchadnezzar,[6] as it is said, *Nebuchadnezzar the king made an*

[1] The lot which came up in the right hand was the decisive one.
[2] Perhaps (as 'E.J.) the Midrash renders, *And it* was *unto them*, etc., i.e. the Israelites regarded the results of all this divination, which pointed to their own destruction, as false and worthless.
[3] The expert in Torah, it was said, is able to adduce 49 reasons for and against in any disputed point of law. [4] V. p. 263.
[5] On the first date the walls of Jerusalem were pierced and on the second the Temple was destroyed. [6] The image, despite its height, is contemptuously called GRASSHOPPER.

image of gold whose height was threescore cubits, and the breadth thereof six cubits (Dan. III, 1). R. Johanan said: According to this it is stated that an object with the height of sixty cubits and a breadth of six cubits requires a circumference of one in three [to stand erect]![1] R. Bani said: It was like a reed[2]: he set it up but it fell, set it up again and it fell. R. Haggai said in the name of R. Isaac: It did not stand erect until he brought all the silver and gold in Jerusalem and poured it out as a layer and supported the image upon its feet, as it is stated, *They shall cast their silver in the streets, and their gold shall be as an unclean thing* (Ezek. VII, 19).

AND THE CAPERBERRY (ABIYYONAH) SHALL FAIL: this refers to ancestral (*aboth*)[3] merit; BECAUSE MAN GOETH TO HIS LONG HOME: from Babylon they came[4] and there shall they return. AND THE MOURNERS GO ABOUT THE STREETS: this refers to the exile of Jeconiah.[5] You find that when the exile of Zedekiah occurred, the exiles of Jeconiah came out to meet them, clothed in sackcloth beneath but wearing white garments outside, and asked them, 'How is my father? How is my mother? How is my brother?' They told them, 'They are killed'; whereupon they mourned with one hand[6] and praised [Nebuchadnezzar] with the other; to fulfil that which was said, *Your tires shall be upon your heads, and your shoes upon your feet; ye shall not make lamentation nor weep* (Ezek. XXIV, 23).

BEFORE THE SILVER CORD IS SNAPPED ASUNDER: this alludes to the genealogical chain.[7] AND THE GOLDEN BOWL IS SHATTERED: these are the words

[1] The version in Lam. R. is clearer: Can anything whose height is 60 cubits and breadth 6 cubits stand upright? Unless its breadth is a third of its height it cannot stand upright!

[2] This is the reading in Lam. R. and in the Warsaw ed. here. The reading is the Vilna ed. בקנה (with a prop) is probably a misprint for כקנה (like a reed or cane).

[3] Deriving ABIYYONAH from *ab* (father).

[4] Abraham was born in that part of the world.

[5] Jer. XXVII, 20. He is identical with Jehoiachin, and his captivity occurred 11 years earlier.

[6] Beating their breasts.

[7] Gaps were caused in family trees by the slaughter.

of the Torah, as it is said, *More to be desired than gold* (Ps. XIX, 11). AND THE PITCHER IS BROKEN AT THE FOUNTAIN: two teachers comment. One says that it means the pitcher of Baruch was broken upon the fountain of Jeremiah, while the other says that the pitcher of Jeremiah was broken upon the fountain of Baruch[1]; and that is what is stated, *He pronounced all these words unto me with his mouth, and I wrote them with ink in the book* (Jer. XXXVI, 18). AND THE WHEEL FALLETH SHATTERED INTO THE PIT: from Babylon they came and to Babylon they returned. 'From Babylon they came,' as it is stated, *Now the Lord said unto Abraham: Get thee out of thy country* (Gen. XII, 1); 'and to Babylon they returned,' since [Nebuchadnezzar] took the people captive to Babylon.

R. Joḥanan said: *That saith to the deep* (ẓullah): *Be dry* (Isa. XLIV, 27): '*Ẓullah*' alludes to Babylon; and why is it called '*Ẓullah*'? Because they who died in the Flood sank (*ẓalelu*) there; for it is written, *As Babylon hath caused the slain of Israel to fall, so at Babylon shall fall the slain of all the land* (Jer. LI, 49). R. Simeon b. Lakish said: It is written, *They found a plain in the land of Shinar* (Gen. XI, 2). Why is it called '*Shinar*'? Because those who died in the Flood were emptied out (*she-nin'eru*) there. Another explanation of '*Shinar*' is that [the inhabitants] died by suffocation[2] without a lamp burning and without [the body] being washed. Another explanation of '*Shinar*' is that [the Israelites] are emptied (*shehem menu'arim*) there of all the commandments,[3] being without *terumah* and tithes. [Other explanations are:] '*Shinar*' because her princes (*sar*) die young (*ne'arim*). '*Shinar*,' because they

[1] FOUNTAIN is the teacher, PITCHER the pupil. According to the first view, Baruch was deprived of Jeremiah's teaching; according to the second, Jeremiah had been dependent upon Baruch who acted as his scribe and wrote down his words in a book which was burnt by Jehoiachin.

[2] In Ex. XIV, 27, the verb *wayena'er* (He overthrew) is rendered in the Aramaic version by 'He suffocated' and that meaning is read into '*Shinar*'.

[3] Viz. such commandments as could only be performed in the holy land and in connection with the Temple.

raised up a hater (*sone'*) and enemy (*'ar*), and who is he? Nebuchadnezzar.

AND THE DUST RETURNETH TO THE EARTH AS IT WAS: from Babylon they came and to Babylon they returned. AND THE SPIRIT RETURNETH UNTO GOD: this refers to the Holy Spirit. You find that when Jeremiah saw Jerusalem destroyed, the Temple burnt, Israel driven into exile, and the Holy Spirit departed, he began to say over them VANITY OF VANITIES.[1]

1. VANITY OF VANITIES (XII, 8). It has been taught: When a rich man has come into the possession of something good, at first he hungers for it; but on becoming accustomed to it he regards it as contemptible. Similarly with the poor man, when his lot is straitened, his eyes are higher than his station[2]; so the portion which the rich man despises[3] has been desired by one and is desired by the other. Therefore the desire of both of them is equally for the grave; hence ALL IS VANITY.

1. AND BESIDES THAT ḲOHELETH WAS WISE (XII, 9). Towards the end of the Book of Ecclesiastes it is written, ḲOHELETH SOUGHT TO FIND OUT WORDS OF DELIGHT (*ib.* 10), i.e. Ḳoheleth sought to discern clearly the reward bestowed for the performance of the commandments, as it is written, *For in these things I delight, saith the Lord* (Jer. IX, 23). The Holy One, blessed be He, said to him: 'Solomon, it WAS WRITTEN UPRIGHTLY, EVEN WORDS OF TRUTH, i.e. I have recorded it in "The book of uprightness" [the Bible], viz. *Oh, how abundant is Thy goodness, which Thou hast laid up for them that fear Thee* (Ps. XXXI, 20).' It is also written, *For ye shall be a delightsome land* (Mal. III, 12). He likewise sought to discern clearly the reward for

[1] The text was originally *How sitteth solitary*, the opening words of Lamentations. Since the passage from its Midrash was inserted here, this phrase, which is the beginning of the next verse, was substituted.
[2] He envies the status of the rich. The translation follows the emended text as given in M.K. [3] Reading with Radal *mo'es* for *me'iz*.

[the study of] the Torah, as it is said, *All things desirable*[1] *are not to be compared unto her* (Prov. VIII, 11). The Holy One, blessed be He, said to him: 'Solomon, it WAS WRITTEN UPRIGHTLY, EVEN WORDS OF TRUTH, i.e. I have already recorded it in "The book of uprightness," as it is written, *No eye hath seen what God, and nobody but Thee, will work for him that waiteth for Him* (Isa. LXIV, 3).'[2]

Koheleth sought to fathom when the end[3] would be, as it is said, *That ye awaken not, nor stir up love, until it please* (S.S. II, 7).[4] The Holy One, blessed be He, said to him: 'I have already recorded it in "The book of uprightness", viz. *For the day of vengeance that was* in My heart, *and My year of redemption are come*' (Isa. LXIII, 4).[5] R. Saul of Naveh[6] taught in the name of R. Simeon: Should a man tell you when the end of the redemption will occur, reply to him, 'It is written, "*For the day of vengeance that was* in My heart."' R. Judah b. R. Simon said in the name of R. Joshua b. Levi: [The Holy One, blessed be He, spake]: 'Three clues did I indicate and mark for you in connection with the burial of Moses, viz. *In the valley in the land of Moab over against Beth-peor* (Deut. XXXIV, 6), and for all that *No man knoweth of his sepulchre unto this day* (*ib.*); so if the heart has not revealed [the secret] to the mouth, to whom can the mouth reveal it!'

1. THE WORDS OF THE WISE ARE AS GOADS (KADARBONOTH) (XII, 11): i.e. like a girl's ball (*kaddur banoth*). As a ball is thrown from hand to hand without falling to the ground, so *There failed*[7] *not aught of any good thing which the Lord had spoken unto the house of Israel;*

[1] Heb. *hafazim*, of the same root as *delight* (*hefez*) in our text.
[2] E.V.: '*Neither hath the eye seen a God beside Thee, Who worketh for him that waiteth for Him.*' [3] The advent of the Messiah.
[4] Heb. *she-tehpaz*, of the same root as delight (*hefez*) in our text: hence the identification of the two, the verse from S.S. being referred to the advent of the Messiah.
[5] Understood as: the time of the day of vengeance and the year of redemption is a secret with God. [6] In Galilee. [7] Lit. 'fell'.

all came to pass (Josh. XXI, 45). As a ball is flung by hand without falling, so Moses received the Torah at Sinai and delivered it to Joshua, Joshua to the elders, the elders to the prophets, and the prophets delivered it to the Great Synagogue.[1]

Another interpretation of AS GOADS: As the goad directs the heifer so that it ploughs and provides sustenance for its owner, so the words of Torah direct the heart of those who study them from the ways of death to the ways of life. [This implement] is called by three names, viz. '*darban*,' '*malmed*' and '*mardea'*'—'*malmed*' because it directs (*melammed*) the heifer, '*mardea'*' because it teaches knowledge (*moreh dea'*) to the heifer, '*darban*' because it makes intelligence dwell (*dayyer binah*) in the heifer to plough its furrow so as to provide sustenance for its owner. May we not then apply here an argument *a fortiori*? If a man makes a goad for his heifer, how much more should he make one for his [Evil] Inclination which seduces him from this world and the World to Come!

AND AS NAILS FASTENED.[2] The text should have stated nothing else than 'as *trees* planted', but it declares AND AS *NAILS* FASTENED! What it teaches is that they possess the good qualities of both a plant and of iron balls.[3]

Another interpretation of AND AS NAILS FASTENED: As the mark of a nail is recognisable although you extract it from its place, so if a man's sins caused him [to fall] and the Sages stretch out their hand against him,[4] even though he recants, the trace of his [backsliding] is recognisable.

Another interpretation of AND AS NAILS FASTENED: So long as R. Eliezer lived, the people acted according to [the decisions of] R. Joshua; and after R. Eliezer died, the people reverted to their usual practice.[5]

[1] Ab. I, 1. [2] Lit. 'planted'.
[3] The point is not clear. Perhaps it means that learning (the words of the Torah just mentioned) is a living and growing thing, like a plant, and at the same time strong, like iron. [4] Putting him under the ban.
[5] The text is corrupt and should read: So long as R. Eliezer lived, the people used to act according to [the decisions of] R. Eliezer. When he

THOSE THAT ARE COMPOSED IN COLLECTIONS: When are the words of Torah spoken in their most correct form? When they who are versed in them hear them in assemblies.[1] Whence do we know that if one heard [a teaching] from the mouth of an ordinary Israelite, he must regard it as though he heard it from the mouth of a Sage? There is a text, *Which I command thee*[2] *this day* (Deut. VI, 6); and not only as though he heard it from the mouth of [one] Sage but as though from the mouth of [many] Sages, as it is said, THE WORDS OF THE WISE[3] ARE AS GOADS; and not only as though he heard it from the mouth of [many] Sages but as though from the mouth of a Sanhedrin, [as it is said], *Gather unto Me seventy men* (Num. XI, 16)[4]; and not only as though he heard it from the mouth of a Sanhedrin but as though from the mouth of Moses, as it is said, THEY ARE GIVEN FROM ONE SHEPHERD (XII, 11), i.e. Moses[5]; and not only as though he heard it from the shepherd Moses but as though from the mouth of the Holy One, blessed be He, as it is said, FROM ONE SHEPHERD, and SHEPHERD denotes none other than the Holy One, blessed be He, as it is said, *Give ear, O Shepherd of Israel* (Ps. LXXX, 2), and ONE denotes none other than the Holy One, blessed be He, as it is said, *Hear, O Israel, the Lord our God, the Lord is one* (Deut. VI, 4).

We have learnt there [in the Mishnah]: A man may not go out [on the Sabbath] with sandals studded with nails or with a single sandal if he has [no] wound in his

died, they wanted to act according to [the decisions of] R. Joshua; but the Sages told them that since they followed R. Eliezer in his lifetime they must do so after his death. Hence his teachings were like well fixed nails.

[1] The same word as COLLECTIONS. In such circumstances the possibility of error is reduced, because there is likely to be somebody present to correct a mistake.

[2] Addressed to each Israelite.

[3] The word is plural.

[4] In the Heb. the word is singular; hence one man is equal to seventy who constitute a Sanhedrin. Or perhaps this follows from the fact that words of the same root are used for *gather* and COLLECTIONS respectively. [5] V. Ex. III, 1.

foot.[1] How many nails may there be in it? R. Johanan said: Five, corresponding to the five books of the Pentateuch; R. Dosa b. Ḥanina says: Seven, corresponding to the seven days of the week; and R. Ḥanina says: Nine, corresponding to the nine months of gestation. R. Jose b. Ḥanina said: [The shoemaker's] pegging [of the sandal] is not included in the number of the nails. R. Ze'ira asked in the name of R. Abba b. Zabda, 'May they be inserted in a shoe on the Sabbath?'[2] and was told that it was permitted; 'May they be changed [on the Sabbath]?'[3] and he was told that it was permitted; 'May a person place them one on top of the other?'[4] and was told that it was permitted. R. Ḥiyya inserted eleven in one and thirteen in the other,[5] corresponding to the twenty-four books [of the Bible]. As there are twenty-four books [in the Bible], so were there twenty-four watches [of the Levites]; and as there were twenty-four watches [of the Levites] so the number of nails should be twenty-four.[6]

1. AND FURTHERMORE (MEHEMAH), MY SON BE, ADMONISHED (XII, 12): OF MAKING MANY BOOKS THERE IS NO END: [Read the word as] *mehumah*

[1] Because he may be suspected of carrying the other beneath his cloak. 'No' has been omitted in error. The quotation is from Shab. VI, 2. The discussion on the number, as well as on the reason for the prohibition, occurs in the Talmud, *ib.* 60*b*.

[2] 'E.J.: The prohibition was in respect of *sandals*, and R. Ze'ira asked whether shoes or boots studded with nails might be worn on the Sabbath. (This is the meaning of the question, as obviously nails might not be inserted in either shoes or sandals on the Sabbath, this constituting labour.)

[3] The point of the question is obscure. 'E.J. suggests that 'changed' should be emended to 'covered' (the emendation in Heb. is very slight), the question being whether sandals might be *entirely* covered with nails, for in the incident which gave rise to the prohibition the sandals were not so covered.

[4] Either, whether a sandal might be placed over a shoe, then both be sewn together and studded with nails and worn together; or whether the permitted number of nails for *both* sandals (i.e. twice the number already mentioned) may be inserted in *one*, while the other will be without nails altogether ('E.J.).

[5] He did not have 12 in each because even numbers were supposed to be unlucky. Cf. Pes. 110*a*.

[6] V. Num. R. XIV, 4.

(confusion), because whoever brings into his house more than the twenty-four books [of the Bible] introduces confusion into his house, as, e.g., the book of Ben Sira [Ecclesiasticus] and the book of Ben Tagla.[1]

AND MUCH STUDY (LAHAG) IS A WEARINESS OF THE FLESH: [These apocryphal books] are given to talk about (*lahagoth*) but are not given for WEARINESS OF THE FLESH.[2]

1. THE END OF THE MATTER,[3] ALL HAVING BEEN HEARD (XII, 13): The end of man's conduct is that all proclaim his deeds, [saying], 'So-and-so was right-living,' 'So-and-so was God-fearing.' People came and asked Solomon, 'What is the end of all [when a man dies]?' He replied, 'The end is a word.'[4] (R. Levi said: Why is it [a fatal epidemic] called *deber*? Because it leads away (*debir*) both the good and the bad.[5] Why is [the locust] called *gobai*? Because it is [God's means of] exacting (*gabbi*) punishment from man and the other creatures.[6]) For when a man departs from the world,[7] the Holy One, blessed be He, says to the ministering angels: 'See what his fellow-men are saying about him.' [If they say] that he had been right-living and God-fearing, his bier at once flies up into the air.[8] When R. Levi b. Sisi died, Abba the father of Samuel went in and pronounced a funeral oration over him on this text, THE END OF THE MATTER, ALL HAVING BEEN HEARD. To what, [he said], was R. Levi like? To a king who possessed an orchard; in it were a hundred vines from which he made a hundred casks of wine, and this orchard was

[1] This is a warning against reading apocryphal books. The latter work is not extant.

[2] The meaning probably is that much time should not be devoted to this literature so that a man exhausts himself in its study; that must be reserved for the study of the Torah.

[3] Lit. 'word'.

[4] What is said of a person after death.

[5] The relevance lies either in the fact that death has just been mentioned or in the similarity between *dabar* (matter, word) and *deber* (plague, epidemic).

[6] By bringing famine.

[7] This reverts to the discussion on THE END OF THE MATTER.

[8] I.e. his soul ascends to heaven.

dearer to him than all the others he owned. It was reduced to ninety vines, and he made a hundred casks of wine from them. It was reduced to eighty, to seventy, to sixty, to fifty, to forty, to thirty, to twenty, and to ten; and in each case he produced a hundred casks of wine. Finally it was reduced to a single vine,[1] and from it he produced a hundred casks of wine. The king exclaimed, 'This vine is dearer to me than all the orchards which I possess.' Similarly spake the Holy One, blessed be He: 'He [R. Levi] is as dear to Me as the whole world'; and when he died, people remarked, 'THIS IS THE WHOLE MAN.'[2]

1. FOR GOD SHALL BRING EVERY WORK INTO THE JUDGMENT (XII, 14). Rabbi [Judah ha-Nasi] was expounding his portion of Scripture, and when he used to reach one of these six verses, he wept, viz. *For lo, He that formeth the mountains . . . and declareth unto man what is his thought* (Amos IV, 13), which implies that even things which have nothing tangible or any sin in them are inscribed against a man in his record[3]; and who inscribes them? He *That maketh the morning darkness* (*ib.*).[4] Also, *Seek ye the Lord, all ye humble of the earth*, etc. (Zeph. II, 3); *Hate the evil, and love the good*, etc. (Amos V, 15); and the present verse, FOR GOD SHALL BRING, etc.[5]

Also, that the soul be without knowledge is not good (Prov. XIX, 2). R. Bibi said: It may be likened to a man who was accustomed to sexual intercourse at break of dawn and once forgot and practised it before the break of dawn. '*Without knowledge*[6] [it] *is not good*,' how much less if

[1] The vines of the vineyard gradually died until only one was left, yet at each stage the king produced the same quantity of wine. The idea is that as the righteous diminish in number, God spares the world for the sake even of the small numbers left.
[2] Understood as 'he is equal to all men'.
[3] I.e. even things as unsubstantial as thought are declared to man.
[4] The verse ends, *The Lord, the God of hosts, is His name*—i.e. He who is mighty and forgets nothing.
[5] Cf. Lam. R. III, 29 f. for a fuller version. Two verses are omitted here.
[6] I.e. unintentionally.

he did so intentionally![1] Not only that but *He that hasteth with his feet sinneth* (*ib.*). It may be likened to a man before whom are two shops, one selling meat of an animal which had been ritually slaughtered, the other selling the meat of an animal not ritually slaughtered, and he forgot and bought the latter. '*Without knowledge* [it] *is not good*,' how much less if he bought it intentionally! Not only that but '*He that hasteth with his feet sinneth*'.

R. Joḥanan interpreted the verse in connection with the Sabbath. It may be likened to a man before whom were two paths, one smooth and the other full of thorns and pebbles, and he forgot and walked in the latter; so how much worse would it be for him if he walked in it intentionally![2]

R. Joḥanan and R. Simeon b. Laḳish interpreted the verse. R. Joḥanan said: With vows and freewill offerings it is forbidden,[3] but with sin-offerings and trespass-offerings it is permitted. R. Simeon b. Laḳish, on the other hand, said: With vows and freewill offerings it is permitted, but with sin-offerings and trespass-offerings it is prohibited.

R. Judah b. R. Simon said: If one who commits a single transgression '*Without knowledge* [it] *is not good*', how much less so if he committed it intentionally! Therefore GOD SHALL BRING EVERY WORK INTO THE JUDGMENT CONCERNING EVERY HIDDEN THING, WHETHER IT BE GOOD OR WHETHER IT BE EVIL. [When R. Joḥanan came upon this verse he wept][4] and said, 'Has a slave any hope of reparation whose master counts sins of error and sins of presumption as of equal weight!' What is the meaning of CONCERNING EVERY

[1] This illustration is unintelligible, and it must be emended as in Lev. R. IV, 3, *q.v.*

[2] This is according to the view that one must not walk on thorns on the Sabbath. v. discussion in 'Er. 100*b*, where it is finally permitted.

[3] To present oneself in the Temple for the offering of the animal. For the difference of opinion between the two Rabbis, v. Ḥag. 7*a*. Cf. Lev. R. IV, 3, for this and the two preceding paragraphs.

[4] The words in brackets are added from Ḥag. 5*a*.

HIDDEN THING? It refers to a man who kills a louse in the presence of his neighbour, causing him disgust. Samuel said: It refers to a man who spits in the presence of his neighbour, causing him disgust.[1] What means WHETHER IT BE GOOD OR WHETHER IT BE EVIL? The School of R. Jannai said: It refers to a person who gives a poor man a coin publicly; as happened with R. Jannai who saw a person give a poor man a coin publicly, and he said to him, 'It had been better that you did not give it to him than to have given it to him and put him to shame.' The School of R. Shela said: It refers to a man who gives alms to a woman secretly and so brings suspicion upon her. Raba said: It refers to a man who sends to his wife on the Sabbath-eve[2] meat which has not had [the fat and veins] cut out. But it is not so, for, behold, Raba himself sent [such meat to his wife at that time]! It was different with R. Ḥisda's daughter[3] because he was certain about her.[4]

(WHETHER IT BE GOOD OR WHETHER IT BE EVIL.)[5]

[1] Even for that God brings man into judgment.
[2] She is then so busy with her preparations for the Sabbath that she will not have the time to examine the meat to see whether it has been properly treated by the butcher as regards the fat, etc.
[3] Raba's wife.
[4] That she would examine the meat and attend to it herself if necessary.
[5] The text adds these words in brackets, and they may have been followed by a comment which has fallen out to this effect: Why should He bring into judgment something that is good? It teaches that He will subject to judgment even what is good if there be in it an element of evil (Mah.).